Sky-Flowers, On the Day Before

My Life Guided by Zen Buddhism

Kazumitsu Wako Kato

ISBN: 9781695209800 (paperback)

PREFACE

This book is as unusual as its title. The great Japanese Zen master, Dōgen, borrows the phrase "sky-flowers" from the Buddhist philosopher, Nagarjuna, where "flowers growing in the sky" provides a vivid metaphor for things that don't exist—can't exist. But as he so often delighted in doing, Dōgen worked this image over in his mind until it brought him to see all the ways in which "sky-flowers" could be a metaphor for a miraculous depth dimension right there before us within ordinary existing things. That depth dimension in the midst of everyday life radiates out from every page of this wonderful book.

Poised as though giving his "last lecture," Zen priest and Professor Kazumitsu Kato looks back with equanimity and insight over his extraordinary life in Zen, meditating on historically significant events, invaluable lessons, and emotionally moving occasions. Dr. Kato was born into the family of a Zen priest and was raised at the very heart of that tradition in Japan. He describes how he began Zen training at age 6, how his education straddled two separate lines of self-cultivation—the public school system in pre-war Japan and the training offered by the Soto school of Zen. He describes his ordination at age 11 in 1941—precisely the year that the Japanese military would bomb Pearl Harbor, drawing Japan and America fully into the conflict of the Second World War. He describes his childhood memories of the war with vivid detail, from the announcement at school that Japan had attacked Pearl Harbor, achieving a "glorious victory," to a day years later when he and fellow classmates at a factory would be running out of the factory building as it exploded into flames from a sudden bombing. Dr. Kato's memories of the poverty and chaos of post-war Japan—food shortages and living in a cave—are both moving and unnerving.

Although wonderful to read, these reminiscences are not the primary point of the book. Everything explored in his narrative reaches out from the particular to something larger and more comprehensive. Although a memoir, what it gives us is an education in Zen Buddhism. Therefore, when describing his personal experience sitting painfully outside a monastery for several days ritually awaiting admittance to practice Zen there, Dr. Kato treats us to an insightful meditation on time. What is time and how is it experienced when for hours you find yourself in the position of having to stare directly into its abyss? Or in describing his own father's death and funeral in personal detail we get a solid education in Japanese views on death and the cultural practices of memory and memorial that follow it. All along the book illuminates the character of Zen practice and shows us what a life in Zen might entail. The philosophical ruminations scattered through personal memories and histories bring this book to life in extraordinary ways. And throughout the book, the Japanese Zen master Dogen becomes our guide in the same way that he has served as Dr. Kato's guide for almost three quarters of a century.

Just as intriguing as its philosophy, this book places before us a history that is only now coming to light—the history of the introduction of Zen Buddhism to a western audience. Although far too humble a man to even hint at the centrality of his own life in this fascinating history, even a casual reading of this book will demonstrate very clearly how thoroughly Dr. Kato's own life intersects with many of the most important moments in the emergence of

Zen in the United States. His collaborations with Alan Watts, D.T. Suzuki, Shunryu Suzuki, and Taizan Maezumi, among many other founders of American Zen, reveal just how instrumental Kazumitsu Kato was to the unfolding of this significant story.

The author describes his momentous decision to come to America after the war—both the excitement of this possibility and the difficulties and fear that postwar anti-Japanese sentiments would inspire. Accepting a position at the historic Sokoji temple in San Francisco, Dr. Kato boarded a ship in 1952 for a 13 day trip to what would be an entirely new life. Thinking back over the difficulties of those first few years while he learned the English language and American cultural practices, Dr. Kato conjures up images of Dōgen arriving in China without assistance and unable to speak Chinese. Although a high level priest and a man of significant education, Dr. Kato tells stories of the hard and menial labor required to make a living to supplement his meager salary at the temple. Three years later, however, circumstances would forever change not only the fate of this one Zen priest but the destiny of Zen Buddhism in the West. In 1955 Alan Watts, newly arrived in San Francisco as the Dean of the American Academy of Asian Studies, sought Dr. Kato's assistance on two tasks. He was employed to tutor Watts in the study of the Chinese classics and also to teach Zen Buddhism at the Academy.

While completing his own Ph.D. degree at that time, Kazumitsu Kato became a member of Alan Watts' circle of eccentric American followers. He tells stories about the many visitors who spent time at Watts' Mill Valley home, as well as the visits of D.T. Suzuki and others from all over the world. Studying classical Chinese texts with Watts on a weekly basis and teaching with him at the Academy, Kato shares descriptions of this seminal figure that very few are able to provide. True to his Zen form, Dr. Kato expresses deep appreciation for everyone who entered his life. And enter they did, because just at that historical moment and with the significant assistance of Watts and Kato, the "Zen boom" in San Francisco would erupt. We hear about the emergence of the Beat poets, of Gary Snyder, Lawrence Ferlinghetti, and others. And shortly thereafter, we witness the arrival of the monk Shunryu Suzuki who would truly initiate American Zen practice.

Suzuki, the eventual founder of the San Francisco Zen Center, arrived in 1959 to replace Kato who had been serving as interim head of Sokoji. Dr. Kato, by then a professor with a doctoral degree, stepped back to become Suzuki's assistant and worked closely with him during the years that Suzuki was beginning to lead non-Japanese Americans in Zen practice. He tells a wonderful story of Suzuki Roshi's first lecture in America and much more, and throughout these narratives demonstrates an admiration for his friend Suzuki that is profoundly moving.

In addition to his role in the emergence of American Zen in California, Kazumitsu Kato's memoir shows how his life also intersects with an important line in Japanese Zen history. Late in the book, we learn that because his lineage had unfolded as it did, Dr. Kato was the 30th abbot of Fuganji temple in Japan, even though he was at that time living in Los Angeles. Recent historical research has shown that Fuganji was the temple where the celebrated genius of Noh theatre, Zeami, studied and practiced Zen, making that temple one of the most important birthplaces of Zen-inspired Noh theatre in Japan. Dr. Kato narrates how this came to light, both in his life and in the life of contemporary Japan, and of his involvement in the celebration of the importance of Fuganji temple.

The final chapter is a sustained meditation on life, told from the perspective of one who has lived a long life of Zen practice and reflection. He writes, "The way of the Buddha did not lead to renunciation … but rather to a life of full participation." In developing these thoughts, he draws on Dōgen's image of *kattō*, or "entangled vines," a metaphor for vibrant entanglement in all aspects of life. This entanglement, Dr. Kato shows us, is the texture of life itself. "Now looking back on my life," he says, "I can reflect on how wonderful it has been…" "Wonderful" would also be the right word for the account of his life given in this memoir, every page of which exudes a reverence for life that is truly extraordinary.

Dale S. Wright
David B. and Mary H. Gamble Distinguished Professor of Religion
Occidental College
Los Angeles, California
February 12, 2009

ACKNOWLEDGEMENT

I am indebted, first of all, to the inestimable *dharma* forces that have enabled me to write this humble memoir.

In Zen, reality means "I am here, now." There is no past or future. "Now" has no temporal interval. "I" signifies all of *dharma.* Writing this memoir is, according to these terms, contradictory. I am intertwined with those contradictions. My life of conjecture has been guided by Dōgen's Zen Buddhism. Dōgen's Zen can teach all people to live harmoniously with all creatures in any environment—whether amiable or unamiable. Thus, I am impelled to write this memoir.

One summer morning in the early 2000s, my revered friend, the late Dr. Philomène Harrison, over a cup of tea, suggested that I write about my life. I was reluctant to do so at first, but later changed my mind due to her unwavering support and encouragement.

Unfortunately, by the time I finished writing my first draft, Dr. Harrison had passed away. I hired an editor but our sensibilities did not line up in such a way as to facilitate productive improvement. I began looking for a more suitable editor.

In the spring of 2008, I mentioned my work on my memoir to Dr. Dale Wright, a professor of Religious Studies at Occidental College in Los Angeles. We met at a small coffee shop nearby. He came with a young student who was soon to graduate from Occidental. Her name was Alison Reed.

Alison was graduating from the college as an outstanding English student. Right at the coffee shop, upon our very first meeting, we decided that she would edit my memoir. It was the luckiest moment for me. Alison is an excellent editor with a keen sensibility whose depth of knowledge in English is unparalleled. She has helped me greatly during the long course of editing.

Alison improved the entire memoir. Even my fortuitous detours from the main line of events now sit well in a smooth flow of letters.

I would like to mention my wife's niece, Carol Fukuda Hajdu, who looked over, and re-edited three additional drafts of this manuscript. I sincerely thank her for her kindness and help.

My daughter, Kazumi Kato, also helped me. The artwork on the book cover was created by her.

I am thankful indeed to all *dharma*, especially those who came in close contact with me and helped me selflessly. Without their help I never would have finished this work in its present form.

Kazumitsu Kato
Pasadena, California
July 2019

*All Chinese, Japanese, and Sanskrit
verses and quotes appearing in this book
were translated into English
by Kazumitsu Wako Kato*

Chapter 1

HŌSEN-JI, REVISITED

仏道をならふといふは、 自己をならふ也。	To learn Buddhism is to learn yourself.
自己をならふといふは、 自己を忘るる也。	To learn yourself is to forget yourself.
自己を忘るるといふは、 万法に証せらるる也。	To forget yourself is to be one with every existence.
－ 道元	- Dōgen
(『正法眼蔵』「現成公按 」)	(*Shōbōgenzō, (Genjō Kōan)* ("Everything appears as it is")

I was the first male child born at Hōsen-ji in its 400-year history. The year was 1930. Hōsen-ji is a Sōtō Zen temple located in Nagoya, on Japan's central Pacific coast. My older sister, Minako, had been the first child ever born there. My father was among the first generation of priests there to marry, at a time when Zen priests began to leave the Buddhist monastic tradition of celibacy. Hōsen-ji was founded in 1601 by the renowned monk Gentō Sokuchū, the fiftieth Head Priest of Eiheiji Temple, the main temple of Sōtō Zen. He and all his successors up until my father were celibate. This practice established the norm of monk-to-monk succession at the temple. From a modern perspective, my father was my Grand Master's adopted son, but by Zen tradition, my father was a disciple continuing the Grand Master's lineage.

In that historic tradition, I was named as the heir apparent at birth. In the period which included the difficult years of the Second World War as I grew up, our family numbered seven. They were: my Grand Master Genrin, my father Gen'yū and mother, Fusa, my older and younger sisters, Minako and Junko, my younger brother Kengo and I, Kazumitsu (monastic name Wakō given at the ceremony to enter *saṃgha-ārama,* monasticism). At the temple I would spend most of my first twenty-two years engaged in the study and practice of Zen Buddhism, preparing to succeed my father. Even after my father's death in 1944, I continued the same course. In 1952, I was sent to the United States to serve at a temple in San Francisco, Sōkō-ji, returning in 1958 for a brief sojourn at Hōsen-ji to be confirmed as its resident priest, *jūshoku,* in a confirming ceremony called *shinsan,* which literally means ascending the mountain. Buddhist temples were traditionally built on mountains or hills. I was told that this was started in the early Sung Dynasty (960-1280), China. I was overwhelmed by the experience of that ceremony, as well as my visits with our temple members and neighboring temples.

It was 1965 before I returned to Japan again, and at that time I stayed for two months. Memories of growing up there permeated my mind. Upon first glance, Yobitsugi, the town where Hōsen-ji is located in the southern area of Nagoya, seemed unchanged. Up close, however, I saw the myriad of changes that had occurred during my thirteen years in the United States. The people, the wooden buildings, the gardens, trees, shrubs, stones, the steps and the cemetery had changed. It seemed as if even the weather had changed.

Hōsen-ji's post-war temporary housing was gone, and an unfamiliar, beautifully constructed concrete temple now stood in the middle of a well-kept garden. My younger brother and Zen successor, now an abbot there, had directed the new construction. A four-car garage replaced the stone monument on the west side of the grounds. The long, wide stone steps I remembered which had led from the town's thoroughfare, Tōkaidō, had been replaced by a steep, wide concrete driveway. The ancient pine trees I recalled— one shaped like a parasol, and another a stately cone—were gone, and handsome, bright-leafed camphor trees shaded the plaza in front of the new *hondō*, the main hall where all ceremonies take place. After all, change is inevitable—a basic Buddhist tenet is that of impermanence.

What is impermanence? It is the natural opposite of the eternal, continual or perpetual. Things do not endure, but are transitory— like time itself—fleeting, ephemeral, evanescent.

I was happy to see everyone I knew, and they, too, were happy to see me. Nin'yū Yamasaki, my revered Zen teacher, had died in 1958, just four months after I saw him at my *shinsan* ceremony. I felt his absence deeply.

The temple structure of my childhood no longer existed. On May 17, 1945, fewer than three months before the end of World War II, its mid-eighteenth-century buildings had been burned down by incendiary bombs dropped by US Boeing B-29s which flattened large areas of Nagoya, leaving devastating ruin in its wake. Our family of five, now consisting only of my widowed forty-year-old mother, a single parent with the four of us children, ranging from eleven to seventeen years old, immediately took refuge in a cave on the temple hill's west side, which had been used as a bomb shelter. We lived there for several months, as people did in prehistoric times, for there was no other choice. My mother and Nin'yū, then

3

a monk in his mid-fifties, helped run the temple after my father's death. At the end of the war, my mother asked retired carpenters and plasterers to build us a small one-room temporary hut, where we lived for nearly a year.

In 1947 we were grateful when another temporary building, a wooden rental house that survived the bombing, large enough for temple activities, became available for relocation, and was re-assembled at the temple site. In the main section there were four rooms—a small one by the entrance, plus a kitchen and small dining area, and two larger rooms, divided by moveable shoji screens. It was humble compared to the original temple, yet larger than the norm then in Nagoya, when so many were living in makeshift shelters, and the scars of war were visible everywhere. Materials were scarce and rapid inflation reduced the availability of day laborers, making home construction impossible. In those days, food for survival was everyone's highest priority. We ate any edible weeds we could find, and consumed everything, including vegetable peels and fruit cores. The original temple site became our farm after we had cleared shards and rubble, and my mother and I planted wheat, maize, pumpkins, peas, and other vegetables.

The Hōsen-ji of my youth was not a majestic temple, though many in Japan are. Its buildings sat atop a steep hill above the lower region of Yobitsugi, the town whose name dates back to the seventh or eighth century, and means "calling back and forth." The *Manyō-shū,* (Collection of Ten Thousand Leaves, late sixth to late eighth century), contains several poems which refer to the area's topography. Originally, Hōsen-ji was a cliff protruding into the Pacific Ocean. A narrow path skirted its base, washed by the waves, and people on the path would call out to warn each other. A stone monument is inscribed with one of the poems near Hōsen-ji hill. Sakurada (meaning "rich rice paddy"), the present Sakura, is adjacent to Yobitsugi and Ayuchi (possibly a fishing cove, the present Aichi), became the prefecture's name, with Nagoya as its capital. The poem, composed by Takechi-no-muraji Kurohito in the late seventh century, reads:

> Cranes are flying over to Sakurada,
> I hear them crying.
> Ayuchi shore is on the ebb.
> Cranes are crying
> while flying over Ayuchi shore.

> (*Manyō-shū*. Vol. 3, No. 271)

The lower parts of Yobitsugi were the original shore of the Ayuchi, and over time, a natural delta developed as the river carried sand from upstream, and Yobitsugi developed into a seaside hamlet at the mouth of the Yamasaki River. Today the bay's coastline has extended several miles south to the Pacific. The river, which used to be called Salty River, *Shiokawa*—for it rose and fell with the tide, bringing sea water which mingled with the fresh water streaming from its upper reaches—still runs through the west end of town, Yamasaki, the "hilly cape." The townspeople caught freshwater fish and salt water eel in this tidal water.

Most of Japan has four distinct seasons and the Japanese people love nature, which changes with each season. Geographically, Nagoya is located, like most of Japan, in the temperate zone at the northern end of the Pacific Ocean, approximately thirty-five degrees north in latitude, as is Memphis, Tennessee, in the United States. Los Angeles, California, a sister city of Nagoya, is about thirty-four degrees north in latitude. All of Europe falls farther north, even the southernmost portion. Every winter, cold air from Siberia

5

covers most of Japan's main island. When high pressure stalls over the western part of the country and low pressure in the east—a common wintry condition—temperatures drop below freezing. However, coastal Yobitsugi experiences freezing temperatures as few as ten or twelve days annually. When low pressure blankets the area, considerable snow falls, especially in the northern hillsides.

Spring gradually reaches Japan from the southwest to the northeast, and year after year the weather reports describe how the cherry trees blossom in that sequence over a month or so, with an annual variation of only a week to ten days. In late June, warm, moist air reaches Japan from the South Pacific, invariably colliding with the residual Siberian air mass, resulting in month-long rains, which also move from the southwest to the northeast.

In late July, after the rainy season, warm moist air dominates most of Japan and with the strong summer sun, the area becomes sultry and at times is hotter than at the Equator. Thereafter, from the end of August to early October, typhoons reach Japan.

This climate may sound miserable, but the beauty of the seasons prevails. Seasonal flowers or snow embellish the landscape's gentle rise and fall. The moon on clear autumn nights and wintry scenes are traditional subjects of classical Japanese poetry.

***

Japan is not only beautiful but a fertile land for wet rice agriculture. Feudal lords in the seventeenth and eighteenth centuries saw the area's potential productivity, transforming much of the natural landscape into rice paddies by filling the delta area of the Yamasaki River. It was at this time that Yobitsugi, once a dangerous shore of the Ayuchi, became a peaceful farming community. There were many Buddhist temples of various schools in the area, and during the feudal period, under Shogunate government fiat, they acted as census keepers. This system required all villagers to register in temple census books. People were called *danka* or *danna*, donors or supporters of the temple, from the Sanskrit, *dāna* (donors), and supported their temples. Each temple's status was determined by its individual support system. Priests were responsible for funeral and memorial rites, but did not need to preach Buddhism to their *danka*, nor proselytize. Hōsen-ji, founded in 1601, much later than other temples in the area, thus had fewer *danka,* and was consequently a poorer temple.

Below the west side of the temple hill was the town's main street, the old Tōkaidō. Both sides of the street were lined with small unpretentious shops typical of this part of Nagoya before World War II. Hōsen-ji's steep hill rose behind the east side of the shops. There was a broad flat area on top of the hill; I assume from the ancient poems attributed to the area that the hill was situated on a natural plateau. The original temple property occupied approximately 1.4 acres at the southern end of the plateau, its buildings clustered around the flat area in a traditional Zen Buddhist arrangement. The main and largest building at the center of the temple grounds, called the *hondō*, faced south. Behind it was the founder's hall, the *kaisan-dō*. Both buildings were built in 1601. Except for the *kuri*, a two-story building with many rooms, large and small, the living quarters for monks and general activities areas, the *hondō, kaisandō,* and the front gate, *sanmon,* the temple-gate (literally "the mountain gate,") were all built around 1601. The *kuri* was built, I was told, around 1790. South of the *kuri* was the *kōbōdō,* the newest building. When it was built, I was seven, and still remember that rice cakes, *mochi*, were thrown to the crowd of people, in the Japanese tradition. Between the *hondō* and the main gate was a large plaza-like open space, which on festive occasions often drew hundreds of people. I recollect the occasions when townspeople came and danced during the mid-summer Buddhist *obon* observance.

The *kōbōdō* enshrined a wooden statue of Kōbō Daishi, founder of the Shingon School of Buddhism, whose monastic name was Kūkai, known as the Mantra School. Great Master Kōbō was also enshrined there, and was revered and warmly regarded by the inhabitants of neighboring towns, who referred to the Kōbō Daishi (Master Daishi) as "Kōbō-sama," or Kōbō-san." It may seem an odd notion having a Zen temple enshrine a statue the Shingon's School's founding monk, Kūkai, in its temple compound. I did not think anything of this at the time. Hōsen-ji also had an enshrinement of *Skanda*, an Indian Brahman god, a son of *Śiva*, in the temple's kitchen. Every morning we chanted a short mantra before the altar of *Skanda*.

The *hondō* was used for most services and gatherings. At its center was an altar which enshrined the statue of the Medicine Guru, *Yakushi* or *Bhaiśajya Guru* in Sanskrit. In the *kaisandō*, behind the *hondō,* was the old statue of Bodhidharma, the founder of Zen Buddhism in China. On adjacent sides were statues of Dōgen Zenji, Zen Master Dōgen, founder of Sōtō Zen Buddhism in Japan, and of Gentō Zenji, Zen Master Gentō, the founder of this temple. To the right side of the *hondō's* shrine was the *shicchū,* a small room at the corner of the building, used for private teaching. However, this room was generally used to practice *zazen. Zazen* literally means "sitting practice of Zen," and is not a meditative, cognitive, cognizant, remedial or purposeful activity. Simply, it is sitting for the sake of sitting. I was told from my early childhood that the practice of *zazen* was the essential practice of Zen. At Hōsen-ji's *shicchū,* the *zazen* area's north end had a platform approximately six by three feet, and about six inches high, where a pedestal held a statue of Mañjuśrī, a Bodhisattva representing wisdom and detachment from illusion. The hall was large enough to seat fifteen people along its three sides. On a few occasions, I have seen a half dozen people practice *zazen* in this space. During the Second World War, Hōsen-ji had to house thirty or thirty-five soldiers, and they sat in groups to practice *zazen* there.

Behind the *kaisandō* was the cemetery, which extended to the edge of a bamboo grove, and was used mostly for the graves of temple members. Some tomb inscriptions date to the temple's founding. Cemeteries adjacent to Buddhist temples were a long-established tradition until about fifty years ago. Japan adopted cremation with Buddhism but this custom was incorporated with existing grave culture. After this time, commercial graveyards, with euphemistic names like Spiritual Garden and Peace Park, began to replace the traditional cemeteries at temple sites, which had existed since the seventh and eighth centuries.

The *kuri* served for living quarters and general activities. It had twelve rooms, large and small, including four on the second floor, one of which was mine. Eight ground-floor rooms encompassed an entrance hall, guest rooms, rooms for formal activities, such as dining for guests, and the tea ceremony. My father and Grand Master Genrin each had a room on this floor. Those were their bedrooms, as well as the rooms where they sat and relaxed or even entertained guests. Bedding was folded and stored in closets each morning. All these buildings were constructed of *hinoki*, a native cypress wood, and had earthen walls. The *shōji* doors served to separate the rooms. That type of building in Japan basically remained the same for centuries until some years after the Second World War.

***

When I was growing up in Yobitsugi, the old Tōkaidō was the only paved road in the town. I thought of it as a wide street but it was barely two lanes wide, and became a sleepy old road, steeped in history. At that time, horse- and ox-drawn cargo wagons frequented the road, as well as city buses during the day and early evening. In the mid 1950s, a wider, more direct Highway Number One was constructed between Nagoya and Tokyo along the same route. The Japanese National Railway's Tokyo-Osaka Line and also the fastest bullet-train line are called the Tōkaidō Line, for each runs parallel to the original road. My maternal grandparents lived facing the old Tōkaidō, almost perpendicular to it. They had a kimono shop in the front house, with living quarters at the rear. I should note that as a small child I observed my grandmother dyeing her teeth black, as did most married women of her century had done. She was one of the last in her generation to have black teeth. This was a long sustained custom since Emperor Shirakawa's reign, 1071—1086 CE.

The entrance to the temple grounds had a long narrow path ending at a small square, with an open fire pit at its center. Steep stone steps led to a Shinto shrine called *Akiba Gongen,* or the incarnation of a Buddha into a Shinto god. The fire-burning rite was held there once a year. On the right side of the square, wider and shallower steps led to the upper terrace in front of the temple gate, or *sanmon*. To the east, the terrace had a small shrine called *Jizō-dō*, the shrine of *Kṣitigarba-bodhisattva*, who vowed to deliver all sentient beings from suffering. This Bodhisattva was also known as a protector of children, and I sometimes saw young mothers visiting the shrine. Interestingly, a Sōtō Zen temple in Los Angeles has six Jizō statues in front of the main entrance.

Back to Hōsen-ji, along the terrace's north side was a tile-roofed temple gate, *sanmon,* which could be reached by a few stone steps. The Buddhist temple gate, translated as *sanmon* or "mountain-gate" is a synonym for the temple as such. It had large wooden double doors and a small utility entrance door to the right. The main doors were closed to visitors except on special occasions. "From the *sanmon*, a straight granite footpath led to the *hondō*. A path, at about forty-five degrees to the right, traversed the temple square. The *sanmon* terrace, a good lookout point, often drew a crowd when fireworks were scheduled several miles to the south, at Atsuta Grand Shrine, which, like Isé Grand Shrine, is a major Shinto shrine.

On the north and west sides of the main temple a thick bamboo grove covered the steep hillsides, and the bamboo grove's bottom-most edge was where the lower section of Yobitsugi began, which grew slowly over the years. The city of Nagoya became modern-ized at the turn of the century. Heavy industries were built around it, and the city drew workers from other areas. Yobitsugi was sub-sumed into Nagoya in the 1920s. The temple owned several small rental houses to its east, and a narrow path wove through this area, with a small plum grove behind the structures. For six years, as a child, I took this narrow, unpaved path to my primary school. It was very muddy during and after rainfalls. Conversely, the surface of the ground cracked when beaten by the summer sun. For us, the plum grove was a playground where we could run, climb, and pick fruit, which while too sour to eat as fruit, was good for pickling.

When I was six or seven years old, I developed multiple warts on the back of my hands. Due to a commonly held belief at the time, people in town said in unison that I must have urinated over a frog in a roadside ditch. I did not remember doing so, but thought I must have had done so. Though these warts were neither painful nor life threatening, only unsightly, I did not expend any effort to remove them. One day I met an elderly woman who saw the warts. She suggested that I cut an eggplant in half and rub the halves on my hands. Then she said, secretly bury them in the mud in a ditch. She repeated in a soft hissing voice, "Do it so nobody sees you!" I did exactly as she instructed, even though I did not believe what she said. However, good luck followed and my warts disappeared in a few weeks. Ever since this incident, I have looked at frogs in ditches as having a sort of mysterious power. Of course, I never urinated in fields or any open space thereafter lest I have a recurrence of the problem.

There were plenty of open spaces near and around Hōsen-ji while I was growing up and as I recall the scenery was idyllic. Yet, at every stage of my life there were gnawing or afflicting episodes, such as the episode of warts or of some bully boys terrorizing me in that seemingly perfect environment. At times I felt that life was inundated with small, personal sufferings, but had no insight at that time to help me deal with the causes and conditions of those sufferings.

***

When I left this island nation in the early part of the 1950s, quite suddenly, the world had begun changing at a rapid pace. It was at that time that American civilization began to dominate world history. Even this part of the world slowly became Americanized. Long-lasting Japanese traditions and customs were suddenly pushed aside. Two-millennia-old traditional wooden buildings gave way to new structures of concrete and other inorganic materials. Unique forms of clothing, for example, the kimono, cut in the same shape for men and women, though differing in color and motifs, and its traditional accessories, were replaced with western-style clothing, which even included underwear. At the beginning of this change, our people often regarded the kimono-clad style as a residual and primitive custom from feudalistic days.

Was it primitive? What exactly is primitive? Is primitive the opposite of modern or civilized? Primitive may be regarded as an early and original stage of our civilization. Every civilization has a long evolution, some more distant from, others closer still to the ancestral pattern of life. Social zeitgeist dictates change as well as natural evolution. The term "primitive" is relative and arbitrary. My father, mother, and my aunts wore the kimono, sipped green tea in their daily life and in the tea ceremony. I regarded their appearance, each in a stylish kimono, as sophisticated elegance.

Images in one's memory move eventfully but in total silence. When I faced my old *dharma* ancestors' graves behind the *hondō,* I felt that time had moved ever so slowly. It was as if I were pulled back in time to when I was five or six years old. The monks' and priests' tombs were shaped differently from those of lay people. They looked like large cannon balls, round, with pointed tops like pagodas. Grand Master Genrin and my father Gen'yū's tombs were lined up in one section. In my imagination, they were all very much alive, quite animated, and full of laughter and vigor though without making a sound. The bamboo grove on the outskirts of the graves had survived a fire but curiously, about ten years later, for the first time, the bamboo blossomed and the entire grove died. A large oak tree now shaded the area.

Chapter 2

ORDINATION AT AGE ELEVEN

あきらかにしる、剃徐鬚髪して	You must know that if you shave your head
袈裟を著せば	and wear a Buddhist robe,
戒をうけずといふも	even if you have not received the precepts,
これを供養せらん	you can pray and you will
無畏域にいるらん。	enter into state of no fear.
－ 道元	- Dōgen
(『正法眼蔵』「出家功徳」)	(*Shōbōgenzō, (Shukke kudoku)* "Mind is Buddha")

My Grand Master Genrin never married. When he was very young, it was the custom of Zen Buddhist monks and priests to remain celibate. Perhaps the wave of modernism rippled across even the circle of Zen Buddhist priests, leading some to marry. This change happened about the time my father became a priest. To clarify, according to our order's terminology a monk lives in a monastery, adhering to monastic rules, as do those practitioners still in training. A priest, however, lives in the local temple serving the local community. Yet all priests in the Zen School must follow monastic practice before being fully recognized as priests. My Grand Master adopted my father and a younger monk, Gyokusen, during early childhood as apprentices. They hoped to complete the study and training and become monks or priests in Sōtō Zen Buddhism. My father completed his training in due time and became a priest. Gyokusen, instead of becoming a priest, chose to become a teacher. Giving young children to Buddhist temples in those days guaranteed their survival. However, the temple where my father and Gyokusen were adopted was not affluent, and my father had to live at the Shuzen-ji monastery on the Izu Peninsula for over nine years. Gyokusen was sent to a normal school (Teachers' College) where students in those days received monthly stipends. This eased Grand Master Genrin's financial responsibilities. He practiced mendicancy occasionally; that is, he went around the area chanting *sūtras* in front of each house in exchange for a small donation. This practice is called "*takuhatsu*" or "carrying an [alms] bowl," an old Indian tradition, literally meaning "carrying a rice-ball bowl." *Pindapāta* or *pindapātika* translates to rice-ball bowl. Many households would give him a handful of rice, oats, beans, or barley. If they gave money, it was worth a few pennies. I accompanied him a few times, at age six or seven in monastic robes and my Grand Master said that on the days I accompanied him, he received more than when he was alone.

***

At the entrance to Hōsen-ji there were three large mound-shaped bamboo hats the size of small umbrellas hanging on the wall. One was Genrin's, the second, my father's, and the third was mine. All three were the same size. I would put on my hat, secure it with the strap under my chin and disappear under it. The rest of our

15

outfit consisted of white cotton gaiters or leggings wrapped around our shins and calves, white cotton *tabi* socks on our feet and similarly, our arms and hands were guarded with the same white cotton guards. With this outfit we wore white cotton kimonos tucked up to our knees. A black or indigo cotton robe was worn over our white cotton kimono. Both hems came to our knees. Wearing straw sandals tightly fastened over the white socks completed our outfits for mendicant practice, and we carried mendicancy bowls, generally in the left hand, with a bell in the right hand.

Grand Master Genrin chanted the *Heart Sūtra* and a *mantra* after breakfast in front of the kitchen shrine, *idaten* (in Sanskrit, *skanda*) before we left Hōsen-ji around six-thirty. We walked five or six miles and then turned back. We visited each house on the way back to the temple. On a few occasions I could not walk the distance so he put me on his bent back and continued walking. We chanted the "Verse of Homage to Buddha's Relics" in front of each house, which I knew by heart:

> With wholehearted reverence we bow
> to the relics of the true body
> of the Tathāgata Śākyamuni,
> who is fully endowed with myriad virtues;
> to the *dharma* body which is the fundamental ground;
> and to his *stūpa*, which is the whole
> universe.

> With deep respect we venerate the one
> who manifested a body for our sake.
> Through the sustaining power of the Buddha,
> which enters us even as we enter it,
> we verify awakening.

By means of the Buddha's spiritual power,
we benefit living beings,
arouse the thought of awakening,
cultivate *bodhisattva* practice,
and together enter perfect peace,
[and] the knowledge of the equality of all things.
Now let us reverently bow.

Usually, before the verse ended, someone from the house brought a handful of rice or beans and put it into the bowl we carried. Every time this happened Grand Master Genrin bowed and chanted a short verse. I still remember his low unobtrusive chant of that verse he repeated many times. It was as follows:

"*Zaihō-nise, to-mushabetsu...*"
There are two givings;
treasure and the *dharma.*
There are no differences
between the two.
It is *dāna-pāramitā* (the practice of giving),
one of the six bodhisattva practices.
Nothing is absent and
it is fulfilled.

I memorized these verses at an early age and had no difficulty reciting them before each house. Grand Master Genrin told me that mendicancy was a tradition Buddhists had inherited from India, maintained throughout the ages. He usually addressed the Buddha as *Seson*, or *Bhagavat,* the world-honored. The Buddha is addressed in many ways among Buddhists, Tathāgata Śākyamuni or simply the Tathāgata, which in Japanese is "*Nyorai.*" Tathāgata means "one who has come and gone thus," and in Mahāyāna Buddhism Tathāgata is interpreted as "one who has arrived from and gone to *tathatā*, (thusness, absolute reality)." Śākyamuni is a "Serene person of Shakya (tribe)" or a "Sage of Shakya."

Mendicancy was widely practiced even before Gautama Siddhārtha among Indians who retreated to the forests. Siddhārtha was fully engaged in spiritual practices that led to his enlightenment. Then he became the "Enlightened One" or "Buddha." Practitioners who retreated to forests for spiritual pursuits, like Siddhārtha, did not engage in any form of activity for the purpose of gaining sustenance. The sole purpose of mendicancy was to support their lives in order to practice their spiritual pursuit. They spent days and nights steadfastly meditating for many days at a time. Not only that, but often those practitioners fasted for days without going out for alms. According to one legend, Gautama Siddhārtha, after fasting for a long time, was offered a bowl of milk by a merchant's daughter, Sujāta. He received it and drank without hesitation. A moment after he had the bowl of milk, he suddenly became enlightened and thereafter was known as the Buddha. Grand Master Genrin often used the phrase "practice the Buddha's way." His practice of mendicancy, according to his words, was not because he had to survive or to keep the temple afloat, it was his way of "practicing the Buddha's way." It made him realize humbleness and humility and also, it made him realize that whatever he received was enough. His "Buddha's way" seemed to extend to every moment of his life; walking, standing, chanting, sitting, thinking, sleeping and even when experiencing pain. Often, I was reminded that some of my acts weren't in accordance with "the Buddha's way," especially when I desired something strongly. He said, "Desire creates pain when not fulfilled. Even when fulfilled, desire escalates endlessly and will not be quenched until one realizes that desire actually causes pain." Hence monks possessed only the bare necessities—the three essentials: a set of three robes, a sitting mat and a bowl.

In 1927, my father, who was my first teacher, took over the seat as residing priest at Hōsen-ji. Gyokusen, who was the other disciple of Grand Master Genrin, continued his academic study and eventually became a professor. Gyokusen and his family were living in a house in the plum field near the temple. He came to the temple to meditate, chant the sūtras, and weed the property in the early summer when newly sprouted grass became a nuisance. As I remember, he had two outfits: one, a dark blue western suit with a necktie and black shoes, and the other a Buddhist robe. Neither Grand Master Genrin nor my father owned any western clothes. When I was young, I only saw Gyokusen at the temple and I couldn't understand why he wore ordinary lay people's clothing at times.

Any time I asked Gyokusen questions regarding Buddhism or Zen, he always gave me the answer that he would explain later. Then, without fail, he gave me detailed explanations, which were more difficult and covered well more than a reply to my initial questions. Sometimes he drew graphs or charts to explain them. Quite often, after I began studying Buddhism in a more formal way, I recognized that Gyokusen had taught me a lot. In addition, he had shown me the earnest effort of his pursuit of knowledge. Often practitioners take a more direct approach and emphasize practice over the erudite approach. If I asked Grand Master Genrin questions, his answers were quite short and brisk. People either got immediate insight from those brisk answers or did not grasp them at all. Gyokusen's carefully researched and often lengthy answers satisfied me. What he told me stayed within me and often became clear later.

My father had spent a long period of time in monasteries, as I mentioned before. The monastic diet apparently lacked calcium. He had to wear dentures by the time he reached his middle 30s.

Grand Master Genrin was an extremely strong person, yet the same diet took a toll on his bones, especially his spine, bent over by osteoporosis. My father was a perfect candidate for osteoporosis but even before that he suffered from severe diabetes, which later caused kidney failure. In his last years, he suffered from serious illnesses, and became immobilized. I learned good portions of the sūtras at his bedside. He usually sat on the bed in a bright, sunlit room. The room was facing a courtyard with a small pond, and he sat or laid on two soft cotton *futon* mattresses and a layer or two of comforters. He looked very sickly in that big room. Teaching sūtras to his son in a loud chanting voice must have been a difficult task in his condition. I was then eleven or twelve years old. Sometimes I memorized the sūtras but I was lacking in serious effort, which disappointed my father. It must have been very irritating trying to teach his son sūtras written in classic Chinese characters with quasi-Chinese pronunciation and not in modern Japanese. Chinese and Japanese are entirely different languages grammatically except that Japanese adopted the Chinese letters to incorporate into its language. Schools teach only fragments of those forms in the later years of high school. Therefore, for Japanese people, learning sūtras written in classical Chinese was a bilingual pursuit.

I took my vows at Hōsen-ji as a novice monk of Sōtō Zen Buddhism on a bitterly cold winter day in 1941. It was February 1, 1941, to be exact, and I had just reached eleven years of age. In those days, in Japan, my age was counted as twelve years. The Japanese way of counting age starts with conception and birth marking one year, counting the duration in the mother's womb for ten months and ten days. Thereafter, a person's age increased on each New Year's Day. It was different from the western way of counting one's age from the day of birth that measures the time of one's actual appearance on this earth.

It rained briefly on the morning of my ordination, or *tokudo*, and my sister and I worried that the people attending the ceremony would be inconvenienced. We were watching the sky next to the interior garden between the *kaisan-dō*, the founder's hall, and our guestroom. My father noticed us and said, "Oh, you two are looking at the sky. It is felicitous, isn't it? It is truly a well-chosen sky for today. Heaven is sending us five-colored rain today; what a wonderful happening!" My older sister then pushed me and said, "See, your father is wholeheartedly waiting for you to succeed. You must become a monk, all right?"

I knew that "five colors" were significant in Buddhism, since there was a park several miles away called, "*Goshiki-ën*," or "the Park of Five Colors." It was a large park and many Buddha statues and shrines were placed along its brooks and hills. Today, the area has become a commuter suburb of Nagoya, called "*Goshiki-ën*," or "the Park of Five Colors." The colors are blue, yellow, red, white and black. I later learned that the Pure Land, or *Sukhāvatī*, is embroidered with these five colors. According to legend, when the Buddha was born a five-colored rain showered him. This was supposed to be a good omen. I did not know the story then but I felt good hearing my father and my sister viewing the rain as a good omen. At the same time, I felt a heavy responsibility not only to perform the ceremony well, but also to live up to their expectations.

I went through an elaborate ceremony of initiation to commemorate my entrance into Zen monasticism before a dozen priests from the temples nearby. It was called "*tokudo*," which means "becoming a Buddhist monk," or "*tokudo nyusshū*." Here, I have used the term, "initiation," but unlike a Christian ordination, the *tokudo* marks one's entrance into the Buddhist priesthood as a novice monk. In the Sōtō Zen School, to be a monk or a priest one must go through several levels and spend appropriate periods of time of practice to become qualified.

Front row, from left to right: my younger brother Kengo; me; my father
Gen'yu; my maternal grandmother Kyō; my sister Junko. Middle row,
from left to right: My maternal uncle, Ennosuke; maternal grandfather's
brothers Tomiemon and name unknown; maternal aunt, Sada; Aunt Tsuma,
Ennosuke's wife, my cousin Toshiko, my aunt Hidé (my mother's sister,
Sōkichi Oda's wife), cousin Toshiko. Top row, left to right: Muneö Oda
(son of Sōkichi Oda, husband of my cousin Toshiko); my older sister
Minako; cousin Yoshiko; my mother Fusa; my maternal uncle Sōkichi
Oda. Photo taken in 1940, when I was age 10. The photo was partially
burned from a fire caused by an incendiary bomb during the war. My
maternal grandfather died before this event. Since my father was adopted
by the temple where he was raised, I had no paternal relatives.

Let me explain the priest ranks briefly. The first ceremony is
the *tokudo*, which I was going through this time, the initial "ordination", and attaining the rank of *jōza* (this expression came from
thera of "Theravada," the school of *thera* in the Pali language).
Thera in *theravāda* means an accomplished monk or elder monk
but in my case, *jōza* indicates a novice monk.

The next step is going through the *Shuso hōza* ceremony during the "confined ninety-day practice," or *Kessei-ango.* Becoming a *shuso,* or *zagen,* means one can then be seated in the first seat in the Monk's Hall for meditation. In those days, in order to advance to the rank of *shuso,* you had to have several years of practice after reaching the initial level, *jōza.*

After *shuso* is the "inheritance of the Dharma," or *denpō,* from one's life-long master. At this ceremony, the candidate receives three symbolic items, *sanmotsu,* which indicate that one comprehends and will uphold the true Sōtō Zen tradition. Those three items are: a lineage chart, or *shisho,* given by a master to his disciple, a document called *daiji,* stating the essential teachings of Sōtō, and the lineage of the dharma transmission called *kechimyaku.* After this, with permission, one is allowed to change the color of his robes from black to other neutral colors.

Following this, one visits the two Head Temples, Eihei-ji and Sōji-ji, to pay respects, known as *zuisé,* and then reaches the rank of *oshō. Oshō* has an equivalent term in Sanskrit, *upādhyāya,* meaning a teacher who can bestow precepts. In Sōtō Zen, however, an *oshō* is qualified to teach his disciples after he has spent at least ten years or more as a Sōtō Zen practitioner.

The last of the priestly levels is for those who have the *shinsan* (ascension to the mountain) to invite the community of monks to the *kessei ango* (the ninety-day confined practice). After this *shinsan-kessei* at your resident temple you receive the title of *dai-oshō,* which is the title of an official abbotship.

Let me go back to my own "ordination" day (I am using "ordination" for convenience). Before my ordination ceremony my father told me about the procedure and said, "This ceremony is one of the most important ceremonies for you. We are going to follow Zen Master Dōgen's '*A Brief Procedure of Tokudo*' exactly. I am referring to the treatise Dōgen wrote in 1239 at the Kōshō-ji temple in Uji, near Kyoto, for every Sōtō Zen monk to follow. This is no extemporaneous recital. Do it diligently and without mistakes, understand?"

I don't remember exactly how I felt then. I must have been trembling but I don't recall any fear or nervousness. The main part of the ceremony included shaving my head, receiving proper robes and monastic eating bowls, and vowing to uphold all the precepts. Head-shaving symbolizes entry into the Buddhist community, or *saṃgha*, as a monk. The precepts were pillars of Buddhism and Buddhists have observed them from its beginning in India. They have been considered great aids in the practice of Buddhism throughout the ages. Dedicated Buddhists earnestly follow them. These precepts prohibited wrongdoings when the Buddhists lived in groups. All Buddhists vowed to observe them in order to maintain the harmony of *saṃgha*. Consequently, this helped Buddhism's survival.

The ordination ceremony took place before the altar in the *hondō*. Sōtō Zen rituals use the language spoken at the time of Dōgen in the thirteenth century. Many of the terms are in classical Chinese script pronounced in medieval Japanese and I did not know their meanings. Today, most Japanese people cannot comprehend this language.

The ceremony began with the sound of a gong struck in a pattern: first, seven loud strokes in even intervals. They gradually quickened and then subsided into silence. The second pattern began with five loud sounds and grew louder then softer until reaching silence. The third pattern began with three loud sounds, which slowly waned. Then, one loud sound resounded, followed by a softer one, concluding with one last loud sound. Neighboring temple priests entered during the second set of gong sounds. Members of Hōsen-ji were already sitting to watch the ceremony. My father entered the room during the third set of gongs and sat on a chair at the right-hand side of the shrine. Before him was a table on which was an incense burner, a bowl of water, a short branch from a shrub with leaves for sprinkling purification water, two small wooden blocks to strike, and a razor. Beside my father's seat was another table, on which were placed a new robe and monastic eating bowls called *ōryōki,* tightly wrapped in a gray cotton cloth. My father quietly recited, "I take refuge in the buddhas of the ten directions. I take refuge in the dharma of the ten directions..." He recited each and sprinkled the powdered incense in the burner. The chorus of the short verse, "Ten Buddha Names," from Dōgen 's *Pure Rules of Eihei-ji* or the *Eihei Shingi* was then recited. Attending monks followed while my father burned incense:

Vairocana-buddha, pure dharmakāya [Dharma body of the Buddha];
Locana-buddha, complete sambhogakāya [Reward body of the Buddha];
Śākyamuni—buddha, myriad nirmānakāya [Manifested body of the Buddha];
Maitreya-buddha, of future birth;
All buddhas throughout space and time;
Lotus of the wondrous dharma, Mahāyāna sūtra.
Mañjuśrī-bodhisattva, great wisdom;
Samantabhadra-bodhisattva, great activity;
Avalokiteśvara-bodhisattva, great compassion;
All honored ones, bodhisattvas, mahāsattvas;
wisdom beyond wisdom

Mahā Prajñā-Pāramitā Sūtra

After the "Ten Buddha Names," my father recited the dharma phrase that recounts this occasion. He spoke on the familial significance of becoming a monk: all of our patriarchs in the past had been monks. We live, he said, in the three worlds. The three worlds are where people transmigrate. They are the desire-world, or *kāma-dhātu, rūpa-dhātu*, the world of physical existence, and *arūpa-dhātu*, the world of non-physical existence, i.e., spiritual existence. The three worlds make up the whole world where all living beings live. They encapsulate the world of *saṃskāra*, which is entangled in emotions; yet we must rid our attachment to such emotions. I listened to him but much of what he said was too difficult for me to understand.

Following the dharma précis was the ceremony of shaving my head. My father led me to the wooden tablets inscribed with the names of country figureheads and my parents, before which I prostrated once. Then, I returned to my seat and prostrated three times toward the Buddha and again to my father, putting my palms together as I knelt on the floor. My father picked up a razor, chanted a short verse, then poured warm scented water over my head and touched my head with the razor, first on the left side and then on the right side. Then, he gave the razor to Gyokusen, who was acting as *jisha,* or the role of "attending monk." He began shaving the rest, but was a bit shaky. Later, he said my head skin was like rubber and was difficult to shave. While Gyokusen was shaving my head, my father chanted the following verse:

How good to be a Zen student.
He will understand the impermanence of the world.
He will denounce worldly matters and enter into nirvāṇa.
It will be extraordinary and difficult.

Every participant chanted in unison:

We live in the midst of the three worlds [of saṃsāra],
our emotions cannot be severed.
We must reject emotions and enter into the world of detachment.
We must become the person who reflects true compassion.

Then, my father recited the verse:

Shaving and removing hairs and whiskers,
We undisputedly vow together with all sattva [sentient beings],
To sever kleśa [worldly desires, wrath, trouble]
And to attain ultimate nirvāṇa

Everyone chanted together while my head was being shaved. Before the last patch of hair was removed, my father pointed to it and said, "The last of your hair is called *shura* (*cūla*); only the Buddha can cut this off. I am now in the place of the Buddha going to cut it off, if you permit that?" Then I said, "I will permit it." Thus, my head was shaven and this phase of the ceremony ended.

The next part was the bestowing of my new Buddhist name. I was given the monastic name Wakō and another name, Gennō (known as *gō*), so my full Buddhist name would be Gennō Wakō. Kazumitsu Katō was no longer used in my monastic life but at school where I kept this name. Since Buddhist monks are "*shukke*" (those who have left their family or renounced it) and "*nyūdo*" (entered the Way of the Buddha), the family name Katō became less significant. I felt a bit empty because of that. Traditionally this temple, which honors the founder Gentō Sokuchū, ordains everyone with the character "gen" (meaning profound) in his or her name. So, I inherited the name Gennō from my father Gen'yū. He received "gen" from his teacher Genrin. Many years later, I gave my younger brother, who was also my disciple, the name Kigen Kengo, bearing "gen." Kigen thus honored the tradition that had lasted from 1601 to this day.

***

The next phase of the ceremony was the bestowing of a sitting mat or *zagu*, robes, *kesa*, and the eating bowls, or *ōryōki*. They were on a table and my father gave them to me one at the time. Then I sat on the mat, put on the robe and held the bowls. When I received the robe everyone chanted:

How great, the robe of liberation,
a formless field of merit.
Wrapping ourselves in tathāgata's teaching,
we free all living beings.

After receiving the *ōryōki*, everyone chanted the verse. And lastly, my father recited the "Three refuges" and I repeated after him:

I take refuge in Buddha,
I take refuge in dharma,
I take refuge in saṃgha

Following this recital came the bestowing of the three *bodhisattva* ideals: keeping all precepts, practicing all right deeds, and granting compassion to all sentient beings. Thereafter, the ten grave prohibitions were given. My father asked after each precept whether I vowed to uphold it. I replied, "I will vow to uphold," to each of them. Some of these precepts are shared with other Indian faiths such as Yoga and Jainism. They are *ahimsa* or non-violence, *asteya* or no stealing, *aparigraha* or no acceptance of gifts from people, and *brahmacarya,* or abstention from desires. I remember, at eleven years of age, having some anxiety over upholding some of the latter precepts, such as do not slander or criticize others.

The ending of this ceremony was the *ekō*, or transferring of merit, recited by my father, who was now officially my dharma teacher. It finished seamlessly thanks mainly to Gyokusen who scrupulously helped me before and even during the ceremony. Gyokusen, I thought, had a heart of gold even if he seemed overly precise. Temple members at the *kuri* prepared the feast of *"osekihan"*(rice cooked with red beans) for all participants. Everyone congratulated me by exclaiming, "You did well," and "You are a big monk now." Needless to say, I was elated and at the same time relieved that I did not make any mistakes during the ceremony. I had become a Zen monk with the rank of *"jōza."* I could wear a black robe and black *kesa. Kesa (kaśāya* in Sanskrit*)* is a surplice-like garment worn over a kimono-shaped robe and tied at the left shoulder—appropriate attire for a novice monk. I could not pinpoint what it was, but the word *shukke,* meaning to leave family behind, stayed in my mind and a faint notion of pathos stole my jubilation at the height of this excitement. I was beginning to comprehend the idea that my father would no longer be my father but my teacher. And what was I now to be to my mother, brother, and sisters?

***

The formal ceremony, like the one I had just completed, is a heavy task for an eleven-year-old boy. Culture occasionally imposes cruel tasks on people yet that same culture rewards those who conform to the approved pattern. I was now a member of the Buddhist *saṃgha.* I became a monk and was proud and comfortable in that society. But at the same time, I became different from the neighboring children. First of all, my head was shaved every week or so. In my case, my head was shaved every five days: the fourth, ninth, fourteenth, nineteenth, twenty-fourth, and twenty-ninth day of each month. I chanted every night at eight o'clock at the *kōbō-dō* in the temple compound where the neighboring adults, and occasionally children, came to pray. I had to perform rituals during summer vacations, especially during the *obon* season. I visited every member's house and chanted sūtras all day long. It was hot and my knees gave way and became numb after sitting in the formal Japanese position. Often, my classmates and other friends saw me wearing a Buddhist robe and some teased me. My precepts prohibited my fighting against them even when older children slapped my shaved head. Standing out from other children was a bit difficult. This was a constant dilemma during my primary school days. Despite my feelings of isolation from other children, just about every person in the small town of Yobitsugi knew that I was the son of a Buddhist priest and a recently ordained monk. Luckily though, younger children never excluded me as being odd.

When I was initiated into the Zen Buddhist tradition at that primary-school age, my learning was limited to memorizing a few sūtra and understanding simple rituals. My primary Zen teachers were my father and Grand Master Genrin, my father's master. I was born and had grown up in the temple and all the activities were naturally familiar to me. While I knew nothing about Zen or Buddhism, the precepts guided my attitude towards the outside world. When the gong struck I knew to enter the *hondō*. When I sat in the toilet and saw a lizard crawling on the wall I just left it, or when a venomous centipede approached me I just moved away. Not killing any living thing was an essential part of my Buddhist practice.

In the winter mornings, I was awakened at 5 o'clock and after a quick wash up, put on a *kimono* and a black cotton robe. I remained barefoot in all seasons. We were attired in well-worn Buddhist robes. We sat cross-legged in the *zendō,* meaning the meditation room within the *hondō,* for about forty-five minutes. Grand Master Genrin, my father, Gyokusen, and I all sat there. Except in winter, the day broke after our meditation. Following the meditation, we proceeded to the main section of the *hondō* in a formal procession. I led the queue, Gyokusen came next and then my teacher and Grand Master Genrin followed. I lit the candles and incense in a solemn fashion. Gyokusen led the morning chanting. Genrin always stood at the center to officiate the ceremony. My father always stood by the side of the Grand Master, who could not move easily by himself.

The morning service lasted about thirty minutes. When I started this daily routine, it was very difficult to follow because I had not learned all the sūtras yet. But by the time I was eight or nine years old, I had memorized most parts of the ritual including when to bow, when to stand and when to sit. All sūtras were either written in Chinese or were Gyokusen's interpretation of them, transliterated from Sanskrit or Pāli. Gyokusen told me that the Pāli language had been used when Buddhism was flourishing in India. Later many of the sūtras were rewritten in Sanskrit. Then, many of those were translated into Chinese when Buddhism was introduced there. When Buddhism moved to Japan small portions of those sūtras were translated into Japanese but good portions of the Buddhist sūtras remained in the original Chinese form. However, Japanese Buddhists used them in their daily chanting without translating them into Japanese even though many monks did not understand what they were chanting. The typical morning service began with the following order:

Buddha Hall Sūtra chanting,
Sūtra chanting for the *Arhats,*

Sūtra chanting for the Ancestors' Hall and
　Successive Ancestors,
Sūtra chanting for Founding and Former abbots, and
Sūtra chanting for *Dāna* (donors) Hall and
the deceased members of the temple

Sometimes, for unknown reasons, the morning service was
shorter. I loved the shorter service especially during cold and
dark winter mornings. The temple's heating system was a charcoal *hibachi,* or a pot filled with ashes and a small amount of hot
charcoal, which was placed in the center of a room. But the *hondō*
had none of those in place. The early hours of winter mornings
were unbearably frigid. I could not mention this to my father but
I hinted by rubbing my hands together or quivering my shoulders
as if I were patiently enduring the coldness of the *hondō*, all to no
avail. The spacious *hondō* added even more to the sense of coldness, but as a practicing monk I was not allowed to wear socks
during those morning hours in the dead of winter. Stepping on
a tiny grain of sand would cause me to shiver with pain during
those cold winter days.

　We had breakfast after our morning routine. Genrin's breakfast was served in his room by my father, or sometimes, by my
mother. Occasionally he skipped the early hour routine and slept
until breakfast. The rest of us ate together: my father, mother, two
sisters, younger brother, and me. Morning meals in those days
were extremely simple: steamed partially polished rice, homemade
pickles, and *miso* soup, which contained julienned vegetables and
floating cubes of *tofu.* We ate this every morning, 365 days a year.
I learned that Genrin always had a bowl of rice-and-water gruel
with *miso* soup at breakfast throughout his entire life. Gyokusen
returned to his house after the service until the following day unless

some activity called for his presence. At Hōsen-ji, we cleaned the temple after breakfast. In the summer, however, we cleaned before breakfast. We called the cleaning "*samu.*" The only people exempted from this practice were Genrin and Gyokusen. Genrin was then around ninety years of age and his osteoporosis afflicted his torso such that he bowed down almost ninety full degrees; thus his *samu* was limited only to his own room. Genrin sat in his room most of the day except for an occasional stroll. Gyokusen had to leave for school before *samu.*

The kitchen was large enough to cook meals for a couple hundred people at a time. It had an earthen floor and a built-in earthen hearth, approximately three by ten feet. A chimney stood near the center. It had four openings upon which to place large cooking implements. At the center of the kitchen stood a dark brown thick pillar approximately two and a half or three feet in diameter. I was told that it was called "*daikoku-bashira.*" It is the principle post that supports the entire *kuri* building. Half of the kitchen had a floor raised into two levels. On the lower level floor, which was constructed from bamboo sticks—pots, pans, bowls, and even washed vegetables were placed to drain. The upper level floor was made of aged wood, dark in color. The small altar of *Idaten* (the guardian god *Skanda* in Sanskrit) overlooked the room. It was the place where we normally ate meals. It was cool in the summers and cold in the winters due to an open space letting in the draft from below. It may well be my imagination but winters seemed much colder in those days than today.

After completing those morning routines at Hōsen-ji, I went to school until three or three thirty in the afternoon. Genrin and my father performed the Midday Sūtra Chanting of the *Crown of the Victor Dhāraṇi.* I only participated in this during the holidays. The sūtra was relatively short but it was a transliteration of Sanskrit and, to this day, I haven't completely memorized it. Around four thirty in the afternoon we performed the Evening Sūtra Chanting called "*banka*." The *banka* was relatively short:

Great Compassion Dhārani (Ārya Avalokiteśvara verse)
The Gate with Sweet Dew Drops

It took only fifteen to twenty minutes. After the Evening Sūtra Chanting, we had supper in the area adjacent to the kitchen. Our evening meals were at five thirty or six o'clock. We finished quickly for we did not talk during the meals. After the evening meals, my father allowed everyone to talk for awhile. Waiting for the eight o'clock *go-kitō* at the *kōbō-dō* was hard in the winter when the days were shorter. Sometimes I pretended that I was asleep. My father woke me up sometimes but at other times, if I was lucky, he let me sleep. Genrin, after the evening meal, meditated for an hour or so before he retired unless his back pain persisted. This evening meditation was called *yaza*, or "evening sitting." During summertime, the humming and bites from mosquitoes around my face bothered me while practicing *yaza* in the midst of the purple pre-sunset.

My father and I went to the *kōbō-dō* for the evening chanting at exactly eight o'clock. Genrin, as I recall, never participated in the *kōbō-dō* ritual. He died six months after it was built. It was called "*go-kitō*" or the prayer in Shingon Sect style. The *Heart Sūtra* was the sūtra for this occasion, which was recited with the beat of a drum. The longer version of the mantra, *Disaster-Preventing Dhārani,* was also chanted with the rhythmic accompaniment of a drum. In the early years of the *kōbō-dō*, a middle-aged fish vendor named Kinji-san beat the drum every night. Later he taught me to use the drum. I learned quickly and became a regular drummer every night.

***

The *kōbō-dō* has its own unique history. The Hall was dedicated to Great Master Kōbō, or Kūkai, the founder of the Shingon School, or the Mantra School, an esoteric form of Buddhism in Japan. It was the newest building in the old pre-war Hōsen-ji. The *kōbō-dō* was completed in the early spring of 1937, some years before my ordination. A wealthy lumber mill owner, Mr. Gotō, donated the entire building together with the statue of Kōbō Daishi. His company had been harvesting trees at *Kuragari-no-mori*, the "Dark Woods," in Masaki-machi in Nagoya, behind the Atsuta Grand Shrine. When they were cutting down one extremely large camphor tree, the saw suddenly stopped and would not move, so they chopped the tree down from the top and found the trunk base hollow. Inside was a wooden section shaped like a human being who resembled Kōbō Daishi. Mr. Gotō asked an artist to paint a robe, face and other features on it to represent Kōbō Daishi. Since this statue came from, in his words, the womb of a giant tree, he asked my father to name the statue *Oharami Daishi*, or the Impregnating Great Master. This was publicized in the local newspaper and the statue became quite well-known almost overnight. Hōsen-ji had once been a poor temple, but the "Kōbō Daishi" brought, I suppose, a handsome fortune to Hōsen-ji for awhile.

The *kōbō-dō* faced south. The Kōbō Daishi stood against the north side. His body was wrapped in a beautiful palomino colored robe. It was replicated from the legendary color of the Buddha's *kaśāya* (a dull saffron color). Kōbō Daishi was facing west, which was the direction of the land of the Buddha. Japanese Buddhists, irrespective of specific schools, traditionally view the direction of west with special significance because of that fact. Even when someone dies he is laid on the floor, head toward the north and body facing west. West in Buddhism is also the direction of the "Pure Land" or paradise. The Kōbō Daishi figure at Hōsen-ji fit precisely with those Buddhist traditions.

The year 1937, the time *kōbō-dō* was built, was a turbulent year in East Asia. On July seventh of that year Japan sent troops to China and the Sino-Japanese Incident began. This invasion of China ignited international turmoil and consequently escalated into the Second World War. The Japanese government circulated a slogan, "*Umeyo! Fuyaseyo!*" which meant, "Have children! Have many!" I don't know whether Japanese military leaders expected the war to last twenty years or more but Japan definitely needed more soldiers. This state policy helped to enhance the appeal of the *Oharami Daishi* or the Impregnating Great Master. On the monthly anniversaries, hundreds of people, if not a thousand or more, flocked to the temple. Vendors of various types catered to the people. I was amazed but enjoyed the crowd every month. On those evenings, I smelled the fumes of acetylene torches wafting over charcoal-cooked food.

Nothing lasts forever. The verve and ardor around the *kōbō-dō* lasted for five or six years from 1937 until 1942 or 1943 and then began to fade. People continued to visit *kōbō-dō,* but not in large groups anymore due largely to transportation difficulties. Hōsen-ji was not located in a convenient place and the private local trains and city buses ran only once an hour. As the war progressed, buses coming to this section of Nagoya were infrequent, because of the shortage of petroleum fuel. The shortage of necessary materials placed a great strain on everyone's life. With necessity and a bit of ingenuity, buses and automobiles altered their energy sources from petroleum fuel to a wood burning system. Even if they ran, they could not climb up hills with charcoal-fuel. I often saw passengers get out and push the bus on uphill roads. Still, those who wished to have a child or children came to pray at *kōbō-dō* despite the difficulties of the war.

I recorded these events in what my sister termed my "insipid" diary, which was required for all children. It had to be turned in when school began in the autumn. It did not invite my teacher's interest either. Rather, he did not believe my repetitious summer days. In my diary, I wrote on a typical summer day, "I woke up at 4:00 a.m., had morning meditation, *chōka,* morning chanting, and cleaning. Breakfast was at 6:00 a.m. Then I studied new sūtras with my father, and visited two members' houses for chanting. I ate lunch at noon. A group of people came for their ancestral memorial service. I went to Byakugō-ji, a temple next to Hōsen-ji, to see Kitamura-san (a young monk there). I came back for evening chanting around 4:30 p.m. Supper was at 6:00 and then at 8:00 p.m., *kōbō-dō* chanting. I went to bed at 8:45 p.m." My diary had a few words of dissimilarity from day-to-day but otherwise it was identical. A schedule for the entire summer was posted in the kitchen wall about visiting the members' houses, and who was coming to the temple for services at which time, etc. I followed it without fail and included it in my diary. Some of my classmates thought that I had no freedom and that I led an imprisoned life. On the contrary, I had a wonderful library not only of Buddhist texts but of all types of literature from both east and west. My mother bought me books and I, too, had opportunities to buy books pertaining to my own interest. Gyokusen also gave me several books. My schedule, except when people were visiting the temple at certain times for services, was quite flexible. Nin'yū Yamasaki, a colleague of my father, also visited my father fairly often and I enjoyed seeing him.

I don't know what other children wrote in their diaries. Almost every day, they visited me and told me they were bored and had nothing to do. They sat around at the temple gate's vista-point and wondered what to do for the day. They never paid attention to the panoramic view of the vast scenery. After a long procrastination, they decided on such activities as tracing an ant's trail at the gate, catching cicadas in the woods, luring dragonflies with a decoy on rods in the open field, trapping grasshoppers in the wheat field, fishing for carp in the Yamasaki River, or even walking in the rice paddy nearby to catch leeches on their legs. In the late summer evenings, netting fireflies near the river was one of their favorite activities. I did not engage in any of those activities that involved killing, for I had vowed not to engage in the killing of any living beings. Although I did not approve of their proclivity, I did not tell them for fear of spoiling their summer pastimes. I also feared isolation from them. I enjoyed just watching dragonflies, cicadas and fireflies. I began having an innate dislike of hurting or killing any living creature. I do not recall any feeling of envy or jealousy for the other children's activities.

Hōsen-ji returned to being a quiet place again after the flurry of activity at the *kōbō-dō*. Soon the entire temple was burned to the ground by incendiary bombs several months before the end of World War II. *Kuragari-no-mori* in Masaki-machi still stands but it is no longer the "dark woods." It is in the midst of a busy city. Curiously, that small area escaped the fire of 1945. I visited the area in the mid-1980s and read the following sign: "This wood was called *kuragari-no-mori*, 'the dark woods,' before the Second World War."

***

Grand Master Genrin died on October 20, 1937, at ninety-two years of age. Perhaps he did not see the temporary prosperity the *kōbō-dō* brought to Hōsen-ji. He had started and finished his life humbly but his was a richly fulfilled life. When I wanted something, he would whisper to me, "knowing you are satisfied with what you have is the Buddha's Way." I remember that his funeral took place on a beautiful autumn day. His body was placed in a coffin of thick untreated wood. There was a glass window in the front of the casket. Inside, my father had placed him in a perfect sitting position, cross-legged, with his back perfectly upright. It was a lotus position, or *nyasīdat paryaskam ābhujya* in Sanskrit, and was known as a perfect meditation posture. He looked so small in that casket. My grand master Genrin had been an enlightened being and this was the only correct way for him to rest. My father said, "It was so easy to let him sit in this cross-legged-position, since he had meditated this way for ninety years." Genrin had a life of blissful and unreserved humility.

> Atop a thousand-year-old stone,
> traces of the ancients;
> before a hundred-thousand-foot rock,
> a point of emptiness.
> When the bright moon shines
> it always glistens white.
> Don't bother to differentiate
> East from West.

>   – Han-shan

Chapter 3

A MONK IN PUBLIC SCHOOL

仏言	Buddha said,
若無過去世	If there is no past,
応無過去仏	there will be no past buddhas.
無出家受具	If there are no past buddhas, there will be no monks and inherited robes.
あきらかにしるべし、	But you must know that
三世にかならず	in the past, present, and future,
諸仏ましますなり。	there are buddhas.
－ 道元	- Dōgen
(『正法眼蔵』「供養諸仏」)	(*Shōbōgenzō, (Kuyō Shobutsu)* "Offering to all Buddhas")

My life at public school was juxtaposed with my monastic life. I went to kindergarten adjacent to the Buddhist temple, Antai-ji. Antai-ji belonged to the Jōdo or Pure Land School of Buddhism. It was located on the same hill as Hōsen-ji. The railroad cut through the hill and the track ran along the bottom of the two temple hills. A high bridge over the railroad connected the narrow path and I crossed over the bridge to go to kindergarten.

The old fashioned school oversaw fifteen to twenty children. The kindergarten section in Antai-ji was a large freestanding building divided into two large wooden-floored rooms. I do recall that the teachers were young women in their mid-twenties. They wore *kimonos* and solid dark colored *hakama*, like loose trousers, worn over a *kimono*. They wore a pair of white *tabi*, or Japanese socks, and *zōri*, or flat sandal shoes. Those outfits were probably passé even then since I never saw *kimono*-clad female teachers at other schools except on formal occasions such as New Year's Day. We also played on the temple ground adjacent to the kindergarten where a large pine tree stood in the center. We liked to play around the pine tree as a group but no one dared to go near it alone. The pine tree was known then as the "ghost" pine for its branches sagged like the arms of a ghost.

In kindergarten, I learned to sing and dance. I also learned to count and read some simple Japanese. The principal was the abbot of the temple, whom my mother called "Antai-ji-san." A thick black beard covered the lower part of his face and either his head was shaved or he was naturally bald. The contrast of his baldheadedness and thick bearded chin gave me the impression that his head was formed upside down by mistake, which frightened me. I made a few friends but our relations were limited. However, after a few weeks of kindergarten the boys formed a pecking order and the bullying began. I was not physically intimidating with my small frame, which placed me pretty low in the pecking order.

I can recall a few occasions later in my childhood years that were so piercingly painful or frightening that I still remember them. I also remember many joyous and pleasant events in my life, but those have not had the same riveting effect on my memory. It was through traumatic and life-threatening experiences that I learned of human frailty and impermanence. Perhaps we have an innate fear of losing our lives. I wondered at the time why we could not have prescient knowledge that would help us avoid such painful happenings. I learned in later years that painful experiences are related to the four vital sufferings of the eight sufferings in Buddhism. It is the classification of the Truth of Sufferings within the Four Noble Truths. Of course, I did not have access to that understanding in my youth.

Although my childhood memories are inexact as are those of most children, I have retained some acerbic incidents quite clearly in my mind. I had several such incidents. Some of the earlier episodes occurred when I was about five or six years old. It was probably in the late spring when my older sister, Minako, and two of her girlfriends went out to pick horsetail grass or wild dandelions near the Tempaku River about a mile and a half from the temple. The river had wide sandy banks on both sides and in the middle ran a clear narrow stream. I tagged along with them. Along the riverbank, they picked grass while I picked shiny round stones. I remember that I was not interested in field horsetails and dandelions, thinking those were for girls. We spent a long time there. My sister told me that they were going home and I must go home also. I trailed behind them for awhile. The road was actually a narrow path weaving through a vast rice field. The plants were slightly higher than a foot and a half and the soft young green plants in water-covered fields were pleasant to look at. Among them, green grasshoppers caught my eyes and I felt drawn to them. I wanted to find more grasshoppers in the field so the intensity of my search increased, as did my curiosity. I was totally engrossed with finding more grasshoppers. A while later, I realized that I was all alone in that vast rice paddy field, surrounded only by several farmhouses in the distance. My sister and her friends were nowhere to be seen.

That area was entirely unknown to me. I had never gone that far from home before, and I had no idea how to get home. It seemed I had come from far away and the area was all too strange. These farm-houses were unfamiliar. I stopped for a minute and thought carefully about which way my sister had gone. My heart was pounding and I was extremely frightened. I could not cry because some stranger might hear my voice and kidnap me. I began walking in what I per-ceived to be the right direction. I walked at a fast pace for what seemed like a long time. Still, the scene was alien and not a single landmark I knew appeared. I thought my life would soon end. Then, I saw a woman with a baby on her back walking toward me. She came closer to me. She was a stranger so I was afraid to look at her, thinking she might snatch me up and sell me to a faraway place beyond the vast sea where no one spoke Japanese and where nobody could find me.

Suddenly, the woman said, "Nii-chan (old brother), where are you going?" At that very moment, I ran. I ran away from her with-out breathing. I ran and ran until my chest hurt and I felt I could no longer breathe. As night descended, I noticed a flock of bats flitting about in the sky. Finally, I saw Antai-ji hill, my kindergarten, and its "ghost" pine tree. In that moment, the once scary "ghost" pine, with branches outstretched like a ghost's arms, seemed welcoming and handsome. Then I saw my friend Mabuchi's house at the foot of the hill. When I saw my house, tears streamed down my face. When I entered the house through the kitchen, I saw my mother, preparing an evening meal, and my sister, Minako, sitting near the cooking stove looking at a picture book. Without another thought I began sobbing. I felt I had to cry aloud to shake the dread out of my system and also let my mother and my sister understand how I felt. My mother came and hugged me tightly. My sadness reached its peak. She said, "Of course, you were sad. I understand. Oh, my, your hands are so cold and sweaty. But you are all right now, why don't you stop crying?" I looked at my sister. She was still look-ing at the picture book. She paid no attention to my catastrophe for which she was partially responsible. Many years later, I asked my sister about this incident but she did not remember it at all.

I got lost one more time in my life. It occurred at the Higashiyama Zoo in the eastern part of Nagoya. We took city trains to the zoo. It was crowded and I lost my mother in the crowd. I don't recall anyone else besides my mother being there at the time. Perhaps my mother's younger sister, Sada, who was taking care of my younger brother and sister, was there. My older sister must have been there, too, but not to my memory. I was probably five years old. Losing my mother in the crowd at the zoo was an acutely frightening event. The memory still remains deep within me, and I can easily recall its trauma. The zoo was located a far distance from home and we had had to take a long train ride to get there. Its distance from my home heightened the trauma's emotional impact. I thought I was lost in no man's land. Losing my mother at that age was almost like losing the entire world. It seemed that my childhood social circle centered on my mother and a few others with whom I was closely acquainted. I don't have any recollection of how my mother and I found each other there.

For a young child, losing your mother or someone whom you love, trust and need poses a threat to your subconscious sense of survival. According to Buddhism, such a dreaded emotional experience stems from one's self-consciousness and that ego emerges from what Buddhists called *avidyā,* or ignorance. Such suffering stems from ignorance of *saṃsāra* (the continual cycle of life and death), of which *pratītya-samutpāda* (dependent origination of existence), plays a key role. Ignorance is a hindrance to the right outlook on life. I learned much later that Dōgen carefully taught this fundamental concept of Buddhism in the Chapter of "Buddhism" or "*Bukkyō*" in his *Shōbōgenzō.* I was too young to know then and my suffering continued.

A few years later, as a second-grader at my primary school, I had another unforgettable experience. On my first school holiday, I took a trip to a large city-park with my sister Minako. The trip again ended in catastrophe. It was, I believe, a clear autumn day. Minako and I took a city bus to Tsurumai Park near the center of the city. My other sister and brother were too young to go along. My other memory of what we did at the park and at its famous pond, the Tatsuga Ike (or Dragon Pond), is overshadowed by an incident that occurred just before boarding our bus home. I accidentally broke my ticket in half. We both had a small ticket good for one ride. The ticket was rectangular in shape. It was about an inch and a half by one half-inch. It was made of thin paper. We had spent all our money at the park and we were penniless when we went to the bus stop. I held my ticket very firmly. It was folded in half. I was nervous being there with my older sister who was only a fourth grader. My hands perspired and the section of the ticket folded in half began to tear. I wet the spot with my saliva hoping to strengthen the ticket. But, on the contrary, it began to disintegrate and broke apart.

I showed the torn ticket to my sister and asked her what I should do. She said, "Oh, you did it again. When we get off the bus, you give the ticket to the bus conductor. Okay? Put more saliva on it and pressed down hard so that she won't notice it." I said to her, "You do that." She said, "No, you do that; you are the one who broke it." I was frightened just thinking about it. What would happen when the conductor found the torn ticket? She might lift me by the collar and toss me in the trunk. I couldn't bear it.

As we rode on the bus I was so worried I could look at nothing of the outside scenery. My sister softly told me, "Remember, act natural." Then the bus came to our hometown stop. I gave the ticket to a young woman conductor as it was, folded in half. I did not use any more saliva; it was still wet and seemed to have disintegrated a little further. She looked at the ticket, opened it and exclaimed, "What is…!" She held the ticket torn in two pieces and then looked at me. I thought the world would end right then. I thought death must be easier than that particular moment. I gathered all of the strength from my body and spirit to apologize to her and explain what had happened to the ticket. I almost crumpled helplessly onto the ground. But she only smiled and, to my surprise, said, "Don't use saliva next time. You understand?" My mouth was dry and my teeth clattered so uncontrollably I could not utter a sound. The bus left and I collapsed on the ground at the bus stop. My sister said, "See, it was all right, wasn't it?"

When I returned home I explained the entire ordeal but did not get much sympathy from anyone. Only my older sister shared the distressful experience of the episode. She actually told everyone that I had acted very courageously. When I met my older sister more recently in January of 2003, I asked her about it. She said she still remembered it vividly. Our recollections were exactly the same. I suppose this incident also caused a keen sensation in her.

***

While I was a student, the Japanese school system enforced wearing uniforms from primary school through the college level in public and private schools. I walked on the old Tōkaidō in my new school uniform. It took approximately fifteen minutes to get to school. The school buildings were long, rectangular-shaped and two-storied. Four of those buildings enclosed a large playground where we played ball games. Dodge ball was popular among the girls and baseball among the boys. School assemblies were also held there every morning. My primary school was called Yobitsugi School. My father, mother, uncles, aunts, Gyokusen, and cousins had all gone there. It was a big school. As the town of Yobitsugi grew, the school also grew to accommodate more children. Some children attended from long distances by foot. Behind the school, there was a wooded area and a large pond called *So Ike*, the "Pond So." It was a muddy pond with water-grass growing wildly. It was unfit for swimming but children did nonetheless, and often fished for catfish there. Tree branches overhanging the pond made a good diving board in the summer. The wooded area was a wonderful place in which to play. In autumn, we picked sweet acorns around the pond.

When I was in the second or third grade, I begged my mother to get me a baseball mitt and lied to her that everybody had one. She took me to a department store and bought me a mitt. While we were at the store lunchtime came. I told her I was so hungry that without lunch I would fall to the ground. She then took me to a restaurant in a department store and we looked at the display window of sample dishes. An item called "chicken rice" looked very pretty and appetizing. Chicken rice was sautéed chicken, onion, and a few green peas thrown together with rice and colored with ketchup. In a vulgar way, it was a dish of chicken fried rice smeared with ketchup, but it was red and green and served in a tidy round mound on a western-style flat plate. It came with a bowl of creamy delicious soup. It was a new experience for me to eat using a large metal spoon instead of chopsticks. Most likely that was the first time I ever used a western eating utensil. Furthermore, it wasn't the monotonous boiled vegetarian dishes we normally ate at the temple. I found a few chicken bits buried in the red rice and thought they were not as good as they looked. The unusual meal and my new genuine leather baseball mitt, together with a ball made of rubber were the highlights of my young life. I felt a bit uneasy having such expensive items. The mitt and ball were looked upon as far too excessive in the eyes of the neighborhood children. Despite my excuse to get that mitt, none of the neighborhood kids had a baseball glove or mitt to play with me. With only one mitt, we took turns using it—one mitt, and the rest with bare hands. I had mixed feelings. There was the happiness of enjoying the mitt and sharing with the other children. But there was also for me the hidden guilt of having taken advantage of my mother's kindness and trusting nature.

***

I mentioned earlier that Hōsen-ji was not a wealthy temple. However, for several years, the Kōbō Daishi statue that was placed within the temple helped to make it a popular place. Before the Second World War, among the general population, poverty was not unusual in Japan; still, some echoes of the early depression period lingered. Most of the people in Yobitsugi were no exception. I used to take a shortcut to school, which passed through a poor section of Yobitsugi. It was behind the woods of the Kumano Shinto shrine. On both sides of the road were rows of small houses. Buildings were sectioned into small two room apartments. They were oblong shaped without windows and seemed dark and humid. In some of those apartments, men and women shared one *kimono*. When a husband wore the *kimono*, his wife waited in the house and when the wife had to go out, she wore that same *kimono*. *Kimonos* are, after all, convenient clothes, cut to a size that will fit anyone. Although sharing a *kimono* between men and women was unusual.

If the townspeople are poor the temple they support will be poor as a consequence. Buddhist temples in Japan, like those in ancient India, were supported by *dānapati* or *dāna* in Sanskrit (donors, *danna* or *seshu* in Japanese) who believed in Buddhism. People of India supported monks and nuns with food, clothing and shelter. Over the years *vihāra* and *saṃghārāma* (monasteries for them to live and practice in) had been donated by *dānapati*. There were no set membership fees for Buddhist temples. They were supported entirely by people's good will and occasional honoraria from memorial services or funeral services given by priests. When the temple needed incidental funds the elected representative of the supporters solicited donations. The temples and priestly modes of life are, in general, quite modest. As Gyokusen taught me, monks must not possess any belongings other than life-supporting essentials. These are a bowl (to obtain food with and eat from), a sitting mat, and a set of three robes.

Hōsen-ji took in several youngsters to care for besides our four children. One of those was a young monk in his late teens from Kyushu, Hōzui Maruta, who practiced Buddhism during the day at the temple. In the evening he went to a Buddhist College in Nagoya called Bussen. There was also a girl, Kimi Nasu, who lived with us. She came from Niigata Prefecture facing the Japan Sea. Across the sea was Siberia. She came to work at a textile factory on the outskirts of Yobitsugi. However, she was only eleven years old and the factory, by law, could not hire her until she was thirteen years old. My mother thus took her in and she lived with us for several years. I remember that Kimi taught us all sort of things when my mother was busy. Also, at Hōsen-ji, everyone was expected to take care of her or himself, which included spreading their own bedding quilts or folding them and putting them into a closet. Kimi, who was older than my eldest sister, helped my younger brother Kengo complete this task. We became good friends of hers. Years after they left Hōsen-ji, both Hōzui and Kimi visited Hōsen-ji many times. My mother enjoyed seeing them as grownups. Hōzui Maruta became a Zen priest. He later became a resident priest of a temple in Kyushu. Kimi Nasu married a farmer in Niigata. She showed my mother pictures of her many children and, later, she showed the pictures of her grandchildren to my sisters when she visited Hōsen-ji.

***

Japan was and is a group-oriented society. Due to this cultural trait almost everything is regimented. The academic year begins on the first of April and ends on the last day of the following March. Schools, national and local governments, most banks and private companies use the same fiscal calendar. The first of June was the day all students throughout Japan changed their clothes from winter uniforms to summer uniforms, and the first of November was the day everyone changed clothes back to winter uniforms. I remember the entire school atmosphere changed on those days. Those dates marked for the seasonal changing of clothes goes back to the time of Lady Murasaki in approximately 1000 C.E. As the author of the *Tales of Genji,* Murasaki mentions this clothing change in the Chapter of "*Aoi*" or "Hollyhock." Not only in the schools, but in all walks of Japanese life, people followed suit. It was like American daylight-savings time; mistakes were not allowed. Today, the customs are a bit more relaxed, so many schools give students a week or ten days before or after those dates during which to switch their uniforms. But in those days, this thousand-year tradition was still very much intact and the date for changing clothes, regardless of the weather, was observed strictly and without exception.

Summer vacations were about a month and a half long, from July twenty-fifth to September seventh or eighth, for kindergarten through high school students. College vacations were a little longer. Summer vacations were not exactly full vacations. There were a few days when we had to go to school to report what we were doing. All teachers assigned homework. Everyone had to write a diary during vacation. I used to write the entire summer diary for forty-five days on the day before school began in early autumn. There was a section in which we had to record the weather. Had it been fine or rainy, hot or cold, etc., I copied from my older sister

Minako's diary. She didn't like that, but she always gave in and showed it to me.

The end of summer was elegiac every year, but it was not about my diary. I did not write or could not write my honest feelings in my school diaries. My summer vacations were filled with nostalgic memories. Everyday was a long, lazy, endless time with no school, swimming in the Yamasaki River, playing in the wide open fields, watching diabolic shaped nimbuses that brought a deluge of showers, tracing ants' trails, and looking for cracks in the dry ground—a make-believe fantasy. Although adults dreaded the heat of the day, day after day, for us children summertime was freer and nothing seemed to restrain us. As a monk in training, I had *obon* and other small duties, but I did not mind.

During the month of August, the temple spread out all the robes, kimonos, and paper scrolls to air them out. I had to help with that. This was called *"mushi-boshi"* and it took place in the Lunar Seventh Month according to the old Imperial Archives dating back to 787 and 811 C.E. This custom has become lax and is no longer practiced throughout Japan except at Tō-ji, Tōfuku-ji, Kennin-ji, and other famous temples where their archives need to be aired out. Both Japan's weather and people's clothing have changed so much that *"mushi-boshi"* is no longer a necessity. Still, in June and July, cold upper atmospheric air from Siberia remains over Japan. Warm moist air from the South Pacific pushes toward Japan creating a prolonged rainy season. During the rainy season, even wooden floors feel wet and sticky.

We had winter vacation from December twenty-fifth to January eighth or ninth. There was no diary assignment for this fortnight vacation. But at about this time all of Japan engaged in a thorough cleaning of one's house and property called *"susuharai,"* which fell before the New Year's season. No one could escape from "*susuharai*" or "national cleaning day." Formally it was on December thirteenth. When I was small, the temple did a thorough cleaning just as did all neighboring houses on that day. All *tatami* mats were put outside and all *shoji* screens were renewed with fresh paper. I didn't enjoy cleaning but I liked the commotion associated with it. Both my mother and my father, before his illness, participated. It was a peaceful event marked by concord and unity. People from the neighborhood often came to help clean the temple, and the temple in turn provided food for them. At times, my mother gave the clothes we had outgrown to the children of those helpful people.

Ms. Ōya, or Ōya Sensei, was my teacher for the first two years of primary school. She was a short, amply built woman in her mid-thirties. I don't recall much from those days except that she was a warm, nice person. She always wore a western-style dark-colored jacket, dark-colored below-the-knee skirt, and heavy black cotton stockings with dark gray sneakers called duck shoes. I thought she was quite modern. School days were Mondays through Saturdays. Saturdays were a half-day, until noon. Instead of taking the day off on national holidays, we had to observe them by putting on a clean school uniform with a clean handkerchief pinned to the left chest of the uniform. Our uniforms for primary schools were made of navy cotton with metal buttons. Trousers were cut above the knees. Girls wore a sailor blouse and navy skirt. Ōya Sensei carefully checked our hands and faces to see if they were clean. Some of the children had torn clothes and dirty nails. She told them to wash their hands but didn't say anything about their clothes. She had several white handkerchiefs and pinned them on their uniforms if they did not have one. After the inspection, we attended a ceremony. Often the Principal, in his formal "morning coat and striped trousers," gave a talk on the significance of the holiday. His ceremonial message never changed during all my six years. Afterwards, the school gave us a small flat box containing two three-inch-diameter-sized red and white *"rakugan"* cakes each with a large chrysanthemum emblem on it. *Rakugan* is a dry cookie-like substance made of roasted wheat flour and sugar. It is dry, chalky and never goes bad. As far as I know, even though we were hungry for sweets, no one really liked *"rakugan."*

In 1927, the Japanese Imperial Order No. 25 set ten national holidays. One of those holidays was *"Kanname-sai"* (Imperial Harvest Ceremony at Isé Grand Shrine). Emperor Hirohito always visited Isé Grand Shrine in his special maroon colored train. The Tōkaidō Line passed through the south end of Yobitsugi and all the school children nearby had to line-up along the side of the railroad to greet the Emperor. Ōya Sensei was especially careful to inspect her pupils on that day. We went to the railroad track and lined up, possibly an hour before the Emperor passed. About ten minutes before the Emperor's train was due another train passed, presaged to inform the bystanders of the coming of the Emperor. Our Principal called out in a loud solemn voice "Everyone, *saikeirei* (the most respectful bow)!"

There are slight, regular and profound bows. In *saikeirei*, you bend your body almost ninety degrees forward and remain in that position. We all bowed, facing the track. We remained in that posture until the Emperor's train passed. We were told every time that you had to remain in that posture and never peek at the Imperial train. I glanced at it once, but all I saw was the shiny reddish-brown train. I never saw the Emperor. The Principal was such an avowed imperialist he made us remain bowed for a few more minutes after the train had gone by. It was hard to maintain a deep bow for several minutes, but we did it. On that day, too, we received a box of red and white *rakugan* with the chrysanthemum emblems. At any age, the task of bending and maintaining stillness and silence in that posture is very taxing. We were all exhausted from our "rendezvous" with the Emperor.

I liked my life at Yobitsugi School most of the time. I enjoyed just about everything until the fifth and sixth grades, at which point my life turned into dire misery. Until then, I received good marks in all subjects. To adults' eyes I was a good boy and my mother told me that one neighbor told her that she named her son after me. Before my ordination, when I was still eight or nine years of age I was given a regular job of visiting approximately half of the members of the temple during the *obon* period. Since I did not know all the members' houses, Mr. Ruiji Ōya, an old plasterer about sixty years of age, took me to each house. While I chanted the verse entitled the *Kanromon,* or the "Gate of Sweet Dew Drops," at each household shrine, he waited for me. He spent a full three-day period from August thirteenth to August fifteenth from early morning to late evening with me. My knees gave way after visiting thirty or forty houses. It was extremely taxing on my body.

Obon is a long established Buddhist custom in Japan. There is a sūtra that discusses how one of the Buddha's disciples, *Moggallana* (in Pali, *Maudgalyāyana* in Sanskrit), dreamt his mother was hanging upside down in hell because of her previous wrongdoings. Moggallana asked the Buddha how to save his mother. Buddha advised him to invite all the *saṃgha*; monks, nuns, and lay people, to pray for his mother and thereafter enjoy the food Moggallana prepared for them. This was called "*kuyō*" in Japanese, or "to make offerings to buddhas, dharma, and *saṃgha*." The merit of this act would be transferred to help save all sentient beings. Moggallana did exactly that and his mother was released from pain. Along with Moggallana's story, there are several other similar stories attributed to *obon,* which correspond to Mahāyāna's way of the *bodhisattva.*

Commonly, people believe that all deceased people, or a family's generations of ancestors and relatives, come back to their home the night before *obon*, on August twelfth. In front of their residences, people burn small bonfires to greet the ghosts and invite them into their homes. During those three days in which ghosts occupy the houses, people prepare food for the dead. On the night of fifteenth, the last night of *obon,* people make a small boat of wood or bamboo, put the ancestors' names and some food on the boat, and let the boat float down the nearest river. In many areas of Japan, *bon-odori,* a communal dance, is part of *obon* activities. In my youthful days, *obon* festivals, especially the *bon-odori* dance, were big events. No one dared miss one. Popular belief in *obon* was mystic, dramatic and attractive to most everyone.

Traditionally, the day of August sixteenth was set for the "*Bon Segaki*" at Hōsen-ji, which was, and is, a special *obon* memorial service. All Zen temples do this "*Bon Segaki*" on their certain set date. For Hōsen-ji's service, a dozen priests would come from nearby temples to help. This was a reciprocal practice; in turn, I had to help other temples' services on their set dates. Consequently, the month of August was a very busy season for all Zen Buddhist priests and I was no exception.

***

At school, I worked quite diligently, never missing a day, from the first through fourth grades. My memories of third and fourth grade are quite vague because the memories from my fifth and sixth grade years eclipsed my prior memories. I experienced a most dreadful fear of my youthful life in the fifth and sixth grades and when I think about those days, poignant memories still haunt me. From the first to the fourth grades, classes were coeducational. When

I became a fifth grader, classes were separated into boys' classes and girls' classes. My fifth-grade teacher was a madman, Kusaka Sensei, of about mid-twenty years of age. He enjoyed beating ten and eleven-year-old boys with a heavy bamboo rod during almost every class. We were in a constant state of fear at school every day. Many boys were injured and I was no exception. One day I came home with several bumps on my head. My forehead was bleeding quite badly, and my shirt was soaked with blood. The reason for the punishment was that I had looked out of the window while Kusaka was talking, so I couldn't answer the question he asked me.

I wanted to conceal my injury before I returned home, but my shirt was bloody and impossible to disguise. My father asked me what happened and I told him. I didn't want a big commotion so I told him Kusaka Sensei was right to hit me. My father did not agree with me and went to school to talk to Kusaka, but there were no rules in place to prohibit teachers from using physical punishment. My father talked to the principal, but he too blamed me for my bad behavior. The principal was protecting his colleague. My father knew that my teacher was an extraordinarily severe disciplinarian from what other parents had said. In fact, many had asked my father to talk to the teacher before. He had done so on one occasion, but he couldn't correct the situation. After all, under a traditional Confucian system, respecting and obeying one's teachers was paramount. Furthermore, his militaristic discipline was in accordance with the zeitgeist at the break of the Second World War. My father's effort was to no avail. When he talked to me after he came home, he held my two arms with his hands and told me to grin and bear the situation. He said, "It won't last forever." I saw tears in my father's eyes.

My grandfather on my mother's side died in July 1940, when I was in the fifth grade. It was assumed that I would go to the funeral instead of going to school. But I was afraid of Kusaka's reproach and punishment if I missed classes, even for the reason of my grandfather's funeral. I told my grandmother and everyone that I had to go to school. My father assured me that nothing would happen if I missed classes. If I was punished, my father would go to the city superintendent and ask him to let me change schools. Although worried, I attended my grandfather's funeral. Upon return to school, to my surprise, Kusaka Sensei didn't say anything.

***

That was the year that Japan escalated the war by attacking Pearl Harbor. I believe it was in the morning of December 8, 1941. I was eleven years old. We were told to stand in line on the school ground before classes began. The principal and all teachers stood before us and told us that Japan had attacked Pearl Harbor that morning and that the assault had been successful. The seriousness of Japan's engaging in war with America and the Allied Forces, for me, was not realistic. Kusaka told us again later in class that Japan had attacked Pearl Harbor and it was a glorious victory. Japan was already engaged in war with China and there were shortages of rice, wheat, sugar, cotton, silk, shoes, clothes and other essential items. Even a sixth grade boy could feel the grave and somber atmosphere.

Kusaka Sensei continued his practice of corporal punishment that year and the next. He had all the power in the world and none of his pupils had any right even to disagree with him. Disagreement or any dissention might lead to further torture. Some of my classmates became unreasonably timid and submissive, and their academic scores were lower than those of other fifth and sixth grade classes. None of my classmates went on to first-rate middle schools. One of them died in an accident and one committed suicide before finishing the sixth grade. My classroom was, indeed, a dreadful place of perdition. This schoolteacher's impact on small children was so strong that all of my classmates were left with deep life-long scars.

I must, however, give one credit to Kusaka Sensei. For some reason, he introduced several of his pupils to a Zen master named Reverend Roshū Okajima, who not too long before that time had opened a Sōtō Zen temple on Mt. Sanage, about twenty miles from our homes. We went to the temple, Daihi-den, "the Temple of Great Compassion," during the summer vacation of 1941, for about two weeks. We were all eleven-year-old boys. We did exactly the same routine as the novice monks, waking up before dawn with the sound of a bell, meditating and chanting for morning service. We ate the standard Zen monastic breakfast of "rice gruel" in a formal setting every morning. We listened to talks by Okajima Rōshi about Zen Buddhism after breakfast. We even sat for hour-long evening meditation. However, some of my friends had difficulties sitting in a cross-legged position and very much wanted to go home. I, too, wanted to go home but I had an advantage over them. I knew the routine and could chant all of the sūtras. That was some consolation. We also had several hours of free time in the early afternoons.

We found a small waterfall about a half-mile away from Daihi-den. We had a wonderful time going under the waterfall and swimming in a deep clear pond created by the waterfall. The pond was cold and no one else was nearby. The area was for us entirely and we had an extremely good time every afternoon. During those afternoon hours at the waterfall we forgot everything and were totally carefree. However, while we had to sit in the right posture at meditation or sit correctly for chanting, everyone but me hated it. I did not mind the routine, but even so, being away from family was a difficult experience. The two-week session of monastic life was more than enough even for me and we were very happy to return home.

Kusaka gave me low evaluations for all classes since my father complained of his use of severe corporal punishment. From the first to fifth grades, I had been an A student. Then suddenly, from the latter half of the fifth grade onwards, all my courses dropped to D grades. Having graduated from Yobitsugi School with such low grades, I could not take the entrance examinations for prestigious middle schools. Besides, Kusaka had to recommend me to each of the schools I applied to. Finally and luckily, I was admitted to the Sōtō Zen founded middle school in Nagoya as a substitute student, not a regular student. I felt it was fair on the part of the examiner, yet my life course was distorted quite unfairly.

On the day announcing the results of the entrance examination, a cousin on my mother's side, Muneö Oda, came along with me. He was two years older and a student of a reputable middle school. Those who passed the entrance screenings were posted on the big billboard in front of the school. My examinee number was missing. Muneö asked a few times about my number but could not find it. Then, I found my number at the bottom of those rows of numbers as a substitute admission. Muneö assumed my agony and said, "It's all right. Once you enter, no one knows that you are a substitute student. Let's go and buy textbooks and the school insignia." I was markedly injured by this defamatory incident. I had never doubted that I would be successful in getting admitted because I was a Sōtō Zen monk and my father and Gyokusen went to the school. Muneö, an extremely kindhearted cousin of mine, likely felt what I felt and tried to console me.

After shopping, we returned to my temple. I told my father that I had been admitted as a substitute student. He was not surprised with the result at all. It was as if he already knew that fact. Instead of scolding my inability, he congratulated me by saying, "Well done, Kazumitsu. It's all over, now. I am very happy for you. Do you know the Zen expression, 'Originally, not a single thing'?" I said, "No, father." I was ashamed and upset with the day's event and not yet composed. My father said, "If I say it in an ordinary way, it means that we mustn't cling to anything. Let's not cling to this, all right? Let's concentrate on now. We only live now, and every now is our life. Why don't Muneö and you have a nice cup of tea. There are also a few sweets in the cabinet. Tea is a traditional celebratory drink and it will cheer you up." Muneö said, "See, everything is fine. You were caught up in a bad situation but you studied hard and corrected it." Both of them gave me kind words of consolation but I was so injured with the day's event and I gave them only slight nods.

Normally, those who were admitted and advanced to middle schools returned to their primary school to report their entrance examination results to the teachers. My older sister Minako worried but I did not go back to school to see Kusaka Sensei for that. Must I thank him for the past two years? I told Minako exactly what my father told me, "Originally, not a thing exists." Minako asked me, "Are you chanting a sūtra?" I said to her, "I don't cling to anything." Minako then said, "You are acting weird." I became happier while I was conversing with Minako.

At my new middle school, classes were organized by entry-level scores and I was placed in the class of lowest achievers due largely to my grammar school reports. It was indeed the price I had to pay for that karmic chain. The first two years in middle school were doleful and uneventful. I went to school and returned home after classes like the motion of a pendulum. It took about forty-five minutes by streetcar to commute one-way. However, I made several friends during those years and on several weekends I went out to the hills east of the school with them, and occasionally, I visited their houses.

***

I spent the third year of middle school at a monastery in Nagoya called Kyūkoku-ji monastery. Spending the third year at Kyūkoku-ji monastery was a requirement for those who are heading toward priesthood. During that period, I began breaking out of my doldrums and started to study seriously. I began enjoying all the subjects I studied from that time onward. Several months after the war, our classes were reorganized. I was placed in the top-level class. I became one of the high-achieving students thanks to Muneö's kindness, and to my father, who taught me to concentrate on the present moment in my life and to not dwell in the past. The churning of my karma continued and from the 1960s to 80s, I was an invited speaker several times at the middle school where I had once been a substitute student. When the middle school hosted an academic conference in 1974, I was invited to be the keynote speaker. In 1995, when I was the Dean of International Studies at Nagoya University of Foreign Studies, two teachers from the middle school I had attended came and took my photograph. They said that I was often mentioned as a role model for their students. It was most likely because I had started there as a low-achieving substitute student.

Since I started attending the Sōtō Zen founded middle school, my future seemed to be determined for monastic life as were the lives of my father and Gyokusen. I assumed that was my destination and had no doubts. Christians might say that it was my calling. Later, when I became a life-long teacher both at American universities and also at Japanese universities, Kusaka's handling of children gave me a valuable lesson: a teacher may give students immense advantage through beneficence or the teacher may harm students through mishandling. In later years, I read theories on education by Jean Jacques Rousseau, Johann Heinrich Pestalozzi, Jean Piaget, and other philosophers and educational reformers and learned that Kusaka's excessive punishment had no place in education. Unfortunately, most of my classmates in Yobitsugi ended their education at the compulsory limit of eighth grade. I was one of the few who had gone to a middle school. Here, I would like to explain the Japanese educational system of that time. In the American education system there were 6 years for elementary school, 3 years of junior high school, and 3 years of senior high school and 4 years of college (6-3-3-4). The Japanese education system then was 6 years of elementary school, and two years of compulsory school above elementary school. Middle school was 5 years above elementary school, followed by 3 years of college and 3 years of university. In other words, it was 6 elementary, 5 years middle school, 3 years of prep school for university and 3 years of university (6-5-3-3). For Kusaka, teaching small children was definitely not his métier. I learned later that Kusaka left Yobitsugi School and moved to the next prefecture, Mié, a few years after I left Yobitsugi School.

***

Three or four years later, I believe it was in 1947 or 1948, our fifth and sixth year class had its first class reunion at Yobitsugi School. It was after the war and I was a senior in the middle school. One day before the reunion, several classmates came to my house and invited me to come outside to talk. They told me that they plotted, after the reunion, to batter Kusaka in the woods near the So Iké pond. They were seething with still smoldering resentment after four years. I understood them but still I disagreed with the idea of beating him. Because of my study-pressed schedule, I was not planning to attend the reunion. Hearing of their plan I thought I had better go and try to stop my classmates' puerile attempt at revenge.

I thought we shouldn't rekindle the fire that we had once extinguished. I told them instead of battering him, we must tell him our honest feelings, so that he might stop torturing children. Even though we did not respect him as our teacher, hitting and injuring him would not heal our pain. The best thing for us to do, especially those that were Buddhists, was to try to forgive and forget the past indignities and pains inflicted upon us by Kusaka. I knew they didn't believe in Buddhism seriously but they listened to me. I told them that beating him would make us the same or even worse than him. It was also possible that the act of battering him would fuel our anger even more. I felt we should try to ignore the past and live in the present. I didn't know whether I convinced them or not. Until that time I had not met any of my classmates since I left Yobitsugi School. The war had destroyed many of their houses and, I suppose, most of them had left Yobitsugi. I lived there but I was involved in events at the temple and with schoolwork, and never had a chance to see them. When I told them that they were Buddhists, no one objected. Since I was a Zen monk with a shaved head, I had an advantage in convincing them that violence brings further violence. I told them that if one clings to the past, one becomes a slave to it. It creates a futile link of *karma*. Incidentally, Kusaka did not come to the reunion.

While I was a college student in Nagoya, I volunteered to assist teachers at Yobitsugi School for two summers since summer vacation for college students was longer. There was a serious shortage of schoolteachers because of the war. Basically, I taught a class under the supervision of a full-fledged teacher. I did that at Yobitsugi School and Kusaka's memories did not bother me at all. I enjoyed teaching, playing baseball and dodge ball and sometimes idling with the school children in the dry riverbed of the Tempaku River where I was once lost many years ago. Some children enjoyed picking horsetails grass and wild dandelions as they engaged in their day of play.

***

Many years later, in May of 1985, I met Kusaka. I was a visiting professor at Chubu University in Kasugai, north of Nagoya. I wrote articles on comparative cultures between the U.S. and Japan for the *Chūnichi Newspaper*, Monday through Friday, for the month of April. When the series ended, *Chūnichi's* editor called to tell me that someone named Kusaka had written to the newspaper asking for my address. I knew it was my teacher Mr. Kusaka at once and I was surprised he was still alive. I thought, as a fifth grader, he was well into his middle age. I was fifty-five years old and he must have been at least sixty-five years of age then. I did not know why he wanted my address. I said to the newspaper editor then and there, it was all right to give my address to him, but I was really puzzled as to why he wrote asking for my address after more than forty years. I wondered to why he wanted to see me now. Did he have a guilty conscience? A few days later Kusaka wrote and asked me to meet with him. Unpleasant memories came back to me for a few days. How could he see me now after he had given me such unjust and low grades, which affected me for many years thereafter? That evening as I began *zazen* in my apartment everything began to wane. The image of him gradually eclipsed and became simply prosaic. I remembered that once I had stopped angry classmates from violence by saying it was not the Buddhist way. I remembered telling them to detach themselves from clinging to past events. I decided to see Kusaka. Because of his advanced age, I went by train to visit him at his house in Matsuzaka, Mié, about two hours away from where I lived.

On the train to Mié I thought about time. Dōgen said of time: "Passing is a virtuous attribute of time. Therefore, it changes, such that today passes to tomorrow and today passes to yesterday. Yesterday passed to today and likewise, today to today" (Chapter on "*Uji*" or "Existence is Time," from the *Shōbōgenzō*). The events with Kusaka were what had happened yesterday and thus had passed. My belief was that "I am here now, not yesterday."

He was living alone in a small house. After an exchange of greetings, he told me that he had hesitated to contact me. He was afraid that I would be angry and refuse to see him. He then asked me if I was angry with him or not. I asked him why he asked that. He said that while teaching at Yobitsugi School, he had felt very awkward. His wife had left him. He did not mention his excessive physical discipline toward eleven and twelve year old boys. But I sensed that he was tormented by his past actions. I said to him that I was, like everyone in my class, more frightened of than angry with him in those days. I told him that after forty-five years, I still had feelings of ambivalence whenever I recalled those days. I did not elaborate this issue since it was long gone and it was nearly noon. I invited him out for lunch.

In the restaurant, he bid me to take a higher-positioned seat in the room while he remained in a lower seat. Japanese people have a distinct social rule about seating in just about every situation. If this had happened during the Second World War, while Japan was dominated by Confucian ethics, this arrangement would have been impossible. According to that ethic, once he had been my teacher, he was my teacher for my entire life. He told me he was sixty-five years of age then which was younger than I thought. The difference between us was only ten or eleven years. As a young pupil, I suppose, your teacher always seems much older. Looking at and talking to the aged Kusaka my murky feelings that survived the passage of time were on the wane. Needless to say, I withheld some of the unpleasant things in my mind while debating whether or not to say them aloud.

Our meeting was somewhat superficial and our conversation did not reach any depth due to the formality between a teacher and a student. But as I was leaving, he walked me to the railroad station and even came to the platform to see me off. I noticed tears tracing down his cheeks and he said, "Please forgive whatever I did that caused you anguish. Now, I can die in peace. I am so glad to see you, Katō-san." He smiled genuinely with tears in his eyes. There was no trace of the younger embittered man. "I, too, am glad that I came to see you, Sensei. We closed our gap, didn't we, Sensei?" I said quite sincerely. He put his two palms together and bowed to me as if he were praying at a shrine. I followed suit. As I was waving to him, I felt a flash of sorrow welling up inside me. A karma-tree that grew from zero to one—from two to endless branches—but that has now broken, I thought. It returned to zero, śūnyatā, again. I felt tears streaming down my cheeks. A few minutes later on the train I thought about how everything has a cause and effect in the cycle of saṃsāra. My existence today has a definite connection with Kusaka and if I had not had Kusaka as my teacher, I might have chosen a different course of life. My "now" embraces in its instant all my past as well as my future. The chain of karma is certainly curious—all my anguish, pain, pleasure, good and bad deeds created this present being.

That was the last time I saw him.

I told my older sister Minako that I visited Kusaka, several days after the visit. Then she surprised me by telling that Kusaka had been sending her New Year's cards for nearly thirty years. Minako had met Kusaka in the early 1960s at her class reunion. She told him that I was her brother. Since that meeting, he sent her New Year's cards asking about me every year. Minako was very impressed. Hearing that, I realized my memory of Kusaka had slowly deracinated from my mind. My memory of him was associated with my bringing shame to my father by not being selected to the middle school as a regular student. My notion of Confucian filial duty was deeply rooted in my mind. When I told him that I was admitted as a substitute student, my father held my hands and told me not to look back and concentrate only on what I was presently doing. It was the Buddhist way to look at situations but I did not understand that at the time.

When my classmates attempted to batter Kusaka after the class reunion, I stopped them, not because of Buddhist *ahiṃsā,* or "no violence," but perhaps because I was afraid to rekindle the fire I thought once extinguished. I felt sorry for Kusaka since he embraced the memory of me for years. It was the suffering he created by himself but for years he could not annihilate that cause.

In Buddhism, every action occurs in the combination of inner, outer, direct and indirect cause and effect. In that moment, we both seemed to realize this causal pattern, which led to *nirodha,* the cessation. At least I realized that I had reached *nirodha* for this karma chain. I felt good for visiting him. Having Kusaka Sensei as my teacher was, after all, a vignette in my long karmic sequence but it indeed contributed to my life in positive way. I had no idea I was learning so much from that experience at the time. All that I have become and much that I have not become are the result of my karma. Kusaka Sensei was certainly a part of the karma that is who I am.

Chapter 4

MY FATHER'S DEATH

いたずらに百歳いけらむは
うらむべき日月なり

かなしむべき形骸なり。
たとひ百歳の日月は、
声色の奴婢と馳走するとも
その中1日の行持を行取せば、

一生の百歳を行取するのみにあ
らず
百歳の他生をも度取すべきな
り。
一日の身命は、たふとぶべき身
命なり、
たふとぶべき形骸なり。

－ 道元

(『正法眼蔵』「行持」)

To live one hundred years in vain
would result in lamentable days and
months,
sorrowful body and frame.
Even if you live one hundred years
running around like slaves,
but among those days, just one day
of sincere practice
will befall not only one life of hundred years,
but also other people's one hundred
years.
Living of your life for one day will
lead to a meritorious life,
with a respectful body and frame.

- Dōgen

(*Shōbōgenzō, (Gyōji)* "Activities")

During the times when school was unpleasant, I spent more time at the temple. My father became my teacher of Zen after my ordination. He taught me new sūtras and explained brief meanings of the sūtras, although my comprehension of those sūtras was limited. Sūtra chanting is not melodic in most cases; rhythm is usually in even tempos accentuated with long and short syllables and the voice is carried in a sustained monotone. It sounds uninspiring to many, I suppose, but when the words are chanted, especially in chorus with several voices, it creates a natural polyphony and produces an extraterrestrial spirituality that is hauntingly beautiful. When I was walking alone, I often chanted the sūtras I liked. On a few occasions, other children overheard my chanting and teased me. Those incidents bothered me a little and I was careful when I chanted outside. In a relatively short time, I learned almost all of the essential sūtras from my father. Not only that, I also learned most of the *Lotus Sūtra* chapters, some rarely chanted in the Sōtō School of Zen. The meanings of those sūtras came to me much later—after I began serious studies of Buddhism. Nevertheless, I am so grateful to my father; he was gravely ill, yet he taught me those difficult sūtras even though my learning capacity was still limited. He also told me many stories from the sūtras in an easy way, such as the following:

When the Buddha was traveling, a woman who had recently lost her son came running to him and said, "You are the Venerable Buddha. Please let me see my son, even just a glance. For that, I don't mind any hardships." Buddha then told her, "Yes, I will let you see your son. But do what I tell you to do." The woman said, "Yes, I will."

Buddha said, "Go around this town and ask each household whether there has not been any death among its family

69

members or relatives in the past thirty years. If you find
such a house get a bit of ash from the hearth and eat it."
The woman went from house to house asking that question but not a single family had not experienced death in
the past thirty years. Sometimes, she even came across a
funeral. She returned to the Buddha. The Buddha said to
her, "Those who are born must die. No one can escape this
course. It is only in one's ignorance that one thinks he or
she can evade this truth. Only those who truly understand
this will achieve the true state of life and death."

The woman cast her illusion away. Her son's death actually
helped her understand the reality of human life and death.
Life and death show the impermanence of this world.

This story that my father taught me was an illustrated "*hōben*," or
upāya in Sanskrit, a skillful way of leading sentient beings to realize
the true state of existence. For my father, at that time, whether *hōben*
or not, death was an imminent reality; I realized that even then.

As I stated earlier, I went to the Sōtō Zen middle school from
where my father, Gyokusen, and many of my acquaintances had
graduated. In fact, I found out much later that Reirin Yamada
Rōshi (Zen Master), who was the head of Zenshu-ji in Los
Angeles, graduated from there. Yamada Rōshi later became the
President of Komazawa University and subsequently the Abbot
of Eihei-ji, the Head Temple of Sōtō Zen Buddhism.

Unfortunately, during my second and third years (eighth and
ninth grades) the war interrupted all my studies. For over a year,
all students had to work in the munitions factories. This was the
new wartime national policy.

Gyokusen, who had an extremely bad case of myopia and wore

thick, heavy eyeglasses, escaped military duty. Soon after I entered middle school, Gyokusen was promoted to some administrative position. His working hours became longer and he had to move away from his house near the temple to a new place closer to the university. Watching him leave I felt empty. He was the one who had conscientiously answered so many of my questions regarding Buddhism. But I congratulated him for the advancement in his career. He told me when we needed him at the temple he would come to help at any time. And he did return from time to time, even just to see us.

My father's illness had taken a turn for the worse. Diabetes-induced kidney disorder became extremely serious and his diet was very limited. His legs started to swell and at times he had difficulty moving. My jobs at the temple increased. I started going around to members' houses for their ancestral memorial services. Some came to the temple for the services and I took care of them after school or on my days off. If my father's illness had happened today it could have been at least slowed in its progress for some years. But in those days, dialysis had not been invented and getting appropriate medicines was impossible.

***

As mentioned earlier, my studies in middle school years had frequent interruptions because of wartime activities. The first and the early second years were relatively calm and we had classes normally. But after the middle of the second year, periodically for one or two weeks, students were conscripted into forced labor and sent to farms to help harvest or plough the fields. There was an acute labor shortage of young farmers. Later that year, all middle school students had to work in factories. Almost all young men were drafted and sent to the theatres of war. We had to wear gaiters over our trousers and our school cap was changed to one similar to the soldiers' training caps. Our navy-blue uniforms were ordered to be changed to a dark-colored khaki—the only permissible "*kokubō-shoku*," or "national defense color." We had to take martial arts courses and military training became compulsory. Even a Buddhist monk like me could not escape from the zealous zeitgeist. It seemed everything had been designed clumsily and in a hasty fashion. Time went by nonetheless.

Unfortunately, my father's illness was rapidly worsening, and from the latter part of 1943 on, he became bedridden until his death a year later. Dr. Hayashi came to see him periodically but couldn't help him at all. His lower abdomen began to swell because of the kidney disorder and difficulty in urination. His skin lost its natural luster and became a dull yellow. The back of his torso was covered with the lesions from extended periods of lying down. It was difficult seeing him in that condition. He still insisted on teaching me more sūtras and I learned more diligently at his bedside. My father knew his life was coming to a close. He told me many things about Hōsen-ji: its previous masters, the members, how to maintain the property, the land, the rental houses that belonged to the temple, and countless other matters.

One day when I went to my father's room to tell him I had returned from the school, I saw Nin'yū Yamasaki sitting beside my father's bed. My father told me to sit close by. I had been sitting in the corner of the room. He said, "Come near me." I moved close to him. He said, "I have asked Matsubara-san (my father called Nin'yū Yamasaki this name) to take care of the temple and you until you become a fully-fledged priest of this temple. He has kindly agreed and will help you from now on." I said, "Yes, father. I will obey Matsubara-san and I will study hard. Please don't worry about me. I will also look after my mother, sisters Minako and Junko, and brother Kengo. Remember, I am officially a Zen monk now." In a weak voice, my father said, "Thank you. That was well said." Then, he looked at Nin'yū Yamasaki. Before my father started to talk,

Nin'yū Yamasaki said, "Don't worry Hōsen-ji-san (he called my father this). He is a fine young monk. Your family is faultless. The temple members are intact. There is nothing more for you to be concerned about." My father nodded a few times and closed his eyes.

My father died on March 17, 1944. It was a cold, gloomy day. In Japan, people say, "both cold weather and hot weather remain until equinox." It was a day before the spring equinoctial week yet it was unusually cold. Although Zen Buddhists don't emphasize it, equinoctial week is generally considered the time of "*higan*," or the time to reflect on "the other shore." Special rituals are observed to remind us of the way to reach the other shore, that is, *nirvāṇa*. Some Buddhists who believed in *higan* might think it was a good time to die. But for Zen, there was no difference. It is time, it is life, and it is death.

My father was placed in a plain wooden coffin, and like Grand Master Genrin, he sat in a cross-legged meditation posture. Young monks from the neighboring temples came to help Hōsen-ji. Someone had posted an announcement in front of the temple announcing my father's death. Someone helped to clean my father's body with scented water, shave his head and face, put on fresh robes and place him in the coffin. He was very thin and seemed smaller, unlike his youthful days when he was regarded as a big man.

The Japanese custom is to observe wakes. People gathered to mourn together and watch over the body of a dead person on the night before the burial rite. His coffin was placed in the *hondō*, surrounded by many white chrysanthemums. People began to come to the temple to pray farewell to my father and to condole my family. For the vigil, we stayed awake all night. We performed the service on the day before the funeral, called *otsuya*. People arrived at Hōsen-ji continuously all through the night. Despite the shortage of food, the temple asked a caterer to serve some available food for those who stayed for the wake and some members donated rice and vegetables. My father's former peers from various monasteries and temples arrived the next morning for the funeral. I, as the head of the household and blood-related heir, had experienced a busy night constantly greeting a large number of people and had not had time to mourn for my father. Some of the monks began preparing the temple for an abbot's funeral. There were many long banners prepared. Each banner bore significant writings for this occasion. For instance, one red banner had "*Vairocana Buddha, pure Dharma-kāya*" written on it. The other colored banners of blue, yellow, red and white had inscriptions in the Classical Chinese, "*buddha, dharma, saṃgha,* and treasures.*" These banners were erected at each side on the *sanmon* gate, literally, "mountain gate," referring to the temple gate. The following are some of them:

Buddha: *The Tathāgata proved nirvāṇa.*
Dharma: *Life and death have been severed forever.*
Saṃgha: *If you attend to this matter wholeheartedly,*
Treasure: *You will attain the utmost bliss.*

The white banner at each side of the gate was inscribed:

Buddha: *Utmost Mahāparinirvāṇa [greatest nirvāṇa],*
Dharma: *perfect and clear that is eternal serenity,*
Saṃgha: *ordinary ones think this death, and*
Treasure: *uninformed ones attach to that and make it cessation.*

Another set of white banners at each side of the gate quoted from the *Nirvāṇa Sūtra*:

Buddha: *All things are impermanent,*
Dharma: *that which is born must die, that is the dharma.*

Saṃgha: *When the dharma of birth and death is fathomed*
Treasure: *the bliss of nirvāṇa will be realized.*

Also, a banner of my father's last poem before his death stood beside the ones above. I don't remember the exact wording of the poem but it was something like this:

Fifty years of life in one instant.
All are in the dharma world.
A drop of water circulates but flows back to the ocean,
The moon sinks yet is ever in heaven.

Monks and priests normally composed a last verse or poem before death. It was not usually formal teachings like the *Nirvāṇa Sūtra* of the Buddha but a way of bequeathing their own state of mind to their successor and the members of the *saṃgha*.

The funeral followed the orthodox procedures based on the oldest Chinese Zen monastic rules—*Chanyuan Qingqui*, the *Pure Rules for Zen Monastery,* written in 1103—and also on the *Chixiu Baizhang Qinggui*, the *Pure Rules of Baizhang Revised by the Imperial Decree,* written in 1136, and reflective of the Tang Dynasty Zen procedures. It was an elaborate ritual. I went through my Grand Master Genrin's funeral but I was only seven and did not remember much. Before the funeral a big drum, instead of a gong, was slowly struck 108 times. Gongs, along with most other metals, had been confiscated by the militarist regime this time. Then everyone made a queue in front of the *hondō* and observed the incense offering by an officiating priest. At the head of the procession were the banner carriers, followed by the musical instrument carriers, each with bells, drums and cymbals. Then, temple members carried in my father's robe and eating bowl, or *ōryōki,* as symbolic items of a Buddhist monk. In the procession, I carried my father's new wooden tablet bearing his full title and post-humous name. This was the custom following the Buddha's death. When the Buddha died in the *śāla* grove in Kuśinagara, India, his body was carried in a procession to the cremation site for *jhāpeti* (cremation in the Pali language). Here at Hōsen-ji, we solemnly and slowly circled clockwise around the open plaza in front of the temple. The *inō* chanted, "*Vairocana buddha, pure Dharma-kāya* (the pure dharma-body of the Buddha)," and everyone joined in the refrain. The *inō* then chanted, "*Rocana buddha, complete Saṃbhogakāya* (the complete reward-body of the Buddha)," and the chorus followed. He recited ten different buddhas' names and everyone followed.

I wore a black robe, with a *kesa* over it, and sandals without socks. *Kesa* is short for *kāsāya*, a Buddhist robe. After hot water and hot tea were offered to the deceased, I prostrated three times to the officiating priest. Then the *inō* prepared two torches. One torch was held by the officiating priest in front of the coffin and I held the second torch at the opposite side of the coffin. The priest drew a large circle with the torch clockwise three times and then counterclockwise three times. I did exactly the same. This symbolized the cremation and symboli-cally, I was the one to kindle the cremation fire since I was the heir. The actual cremation took place later at the crematorium.

***

In almost all cultures people dislike having close contact with the dead. Indians were especially averse even though they believed in reincarnation. According to an ancient Āryan custom that in-fluenced Buddhism, when one died, village mourners immediately carried the body to a cremation site. They formed a processional queue with elders first and young people last. During the march, some verses from sacred texts were chanted in chorus. After the

cremation began, the people circled around the fire while chanting the verses in a counterclockwise direction. After this, everyone went to a nearby river or pond to bathe before they proceeded
back to their village. This time, contrary to the earlier procession,
the younger people took the lead and elders followed. Three days
later, they formed in line again and went to the cremation site to
collect the ashes, which were scattered into a river or buried on the
land, and *ketiya* (the mounds raised over the ashes) were made over
it. Ten days later, they gathered together to offer rice balls called
piṇḍa and sprinkle the "water of liberation" around the *ketiya*. This
was to prevent the dead from being reborn into a beast, or *preta*,
which might haunt living human beings. They believed that the
piṇḍa would save them and also help the dead receive a new life
in the coming months or years. That ended their duty to the dead
in India. We had a procession honoring our Indian heritage in front
of the *hondō*. I carried an oblong tablet with my father's name inscribed, and we circled around the *hondō* in a clockwise direction.

***

After a funeral, Japanese Buddhists observe a period called *chūwu*,
translated from the Sanskrit word, "*antarā-bhava*," meaning a period
of intermediate existence. This is supposed to be the period between the
death of a person to the beginning of another life. It is forty-nine days
long and every seventh day, a memorial service is held to secure the former and latter lives for those who need to be guided. Tibetan Buddhists
call this period *bardo,* or the period in which the deceased would be released from his or her *saṃsāra.* A known Tibetan book, *Bardo Thodol,*
or the *Book of Dead*, recounts the experience of those forty-nine days
of *chūwu.* However, most Theravadan Buddhists do not believe in this
"in-between" period. Only the Mahāyānan Buddhists hold this belief.

Zen Buddhism discarded the idea of reincarnation. Observation of *chūwu* for forty-nine days was merely observing the custom. The time of forty-nine days serves to help the healing of the survivors.

During the fourteenth day to the thirty-fifth day, no one but Nin'yū Yamasaki and our family performed memorial services. Following the big commotion of the funeral, the temple suddenly became quiet. The loss of my father, then, was keenly felt. The forty-ninth-day memorial service was the first big gathering at Hōsen-ji after the funeral. Many priests and members came again to observe this day. If the eternal recurrence of life is believed, my father was supposed to be reborn into another being or arrive safely at the other shore, or *pāra,* the land of *nirvāṇa.* As a Zen Buddhist, I did not believe in reincarnation but I definitely did believe he was in *parinirvāṇa,* or the perfect quietude—the realm of *nirvāṇa* where neither illusion nor any residues of this fleeting world exists.

> As I sit on this flat rock,
> the waters in the gorge below
> are cold and icy.
> I quietly enjoy this happiness,
> this beauty.
> The empty grotto
> is lost in thick fog.
> It is a peaceful resting place.
> In the sun's slanting rays,
> shadows of the trees hang low.
> I contemplate my mind:
> a lotus flower
> rises from the mud.
>
> – Han-shan

Chapter 5

REACHING A STEP HIGHER

いはゆる諸仏とは、	All buddhas are
釈迦牟尼 仏なり。	Buddha Śākyamuni.
釈迦牟尼仏、	The Buddha Śākyamuni
これ即心是仏なり。	is one's mind itself.
過去、現在、未来の諸仏,	When you become the buddha,
ともに仏となるときは、	whether past, present, or future buddhas,
かならず釈迦牟尼となるなり。	you must become Śākyamuni Buddha.
これ即心是仏なり。	That is one's mind itself.
－ 道元	- Dōgen
(『正法眼蔵』 「即心是仏」)	(*Shōbōgenzō, (Sokushin-zebutsu)* "Mind is Itself Buddha")

On May 6, 1944, two days after the forty-nine day service for my father, I went through another important ceremony for a monk. I was fourteen years of age and this ceremony was held despite the war's increased intensity. This ceremony was called "*shuso hōza*" (dharma practice by *shuso*), or "*shuso hossen-shiki*" (the dharma combat of *shuso,* the head-seated monk), traditionally performed during the *kessei ango* period, or the ninety-day confined practice period. *Kessei ango* generally begins on April sixteenth or May sixteenth for the summer and on October fifteenth for the winter period. The ninety-day confined period was designated for Zen practitioners to study and practice in one place without leaving the premise.

Unlike today, in adhering to the old system, I had to practice several years from the time of initial ordination before I was able to proceed to this ceremony. Initially, my father's illness caused this acceleration. By the performance of this ceremony, I had reached the halfway point toward becoming a full-fledged monk. The main part of this ceremony was a "question and answer" ritual in which I was obliged to answer all questions regarding Buddhism and Zen Buddhism. When I had answered them all adequately, I would be, although my position was still at the apprentice level, placed one step higher in the monastic ranking and called *shuso*. *Shuso* literally means the head seat in the *sōdō*, or the meditation hall. I would be allowed to take a leading role in the ninety-day *ango* practice even though I was still a young and inexperienced monk. To achieve this level, I must first answer all questions the practitioners posed to me. I was also to spend a minimum number of years of practice, and participate in the confined monastic rituals during either the summer or winter *ango*.

My *shuso hōza* ceremony took place at Hōsen-ji. The official document was a part of the *ango* practice at Entsū-ji in Nagoya, the head temple of Hōsen-ji. The abbot of Entsū-ji, Reverend Kisan Yamada, was the official host of the *ango*. I was told that this ceremony was altered, but it was the best we could do considering the wartime circumstances. Originally, the *shuso hōza* was held at larger monasteries where many practitioners could be accommodated for a ninety-day-practice in confinement. *Shuso hōza* in local temples became a nominal affair and the ninety-day *ango* could also be nominal. Furthermore, in 1944, the Japanese government issued a firm fiat seizing all metal implements that were not essential to life, such as gates, fences, and metal posts. Precious metals such as rings, necklaces, pendants, etc. were also seized. Our school gates and a park border chain nearby were gone. Bells and gongs of Hōsen-ji were likewise confiscated. All such items except for a few handbells and small bells in the *hondō* were taken. Even if we had bells and gongs, we were prohibited from ringing them, for such sounds were to be used only for emergencies. Hōsen-ji kept a few handbells and small bells in the *hondō*. We were told that all metals were to be melted down to make munitions. In place of bells and gongs, we used drums.

In contrast to the cold winter day when I had been initially ordained, for my *shuso hōza* ceremony it was a beautiful spring day. The day was neither cold nor hot. The sun's rays glistened on the sprouting young leaves of just about every deciduous tree. My only regret was that my father was no longer there to see it. My father died on the seventeenth of March. My ceremony was two days after the completion of his forty-nine-day mourning period, including the day he died.

***

At the Hōsen-ji *hondō*, the members of the temple came and sat to wait for the commencement of the ceremony. Priests, young and old, also came, and sat waiting for the ceremony. The first phase of this ceremony was to introduce me as a candidate of *shuso* to all who participated. First, a wooden plaque was struck in three sets of seven, five, and three beats. Then Kisan Yamada Rōshi of Entsū-ji entered the *hondō*. After everyone was seated, Yamada Rōshi took me to the entrance of the *hondō*. He was called the *hōdōshi*. Literally this means the one who raises the banner announcing the *ango* practice. Inside the *hondō*, the *inō,* who was the master of ceremony in this case, together with other officers of the temple and I bowed face-to-face. This was the invitation to the *shuso* position. The *inō* called out the following loudly: "I now dutifully inform you, in this summer *ango*, we respect the compassion of the Head Priest and we have invited Wakō *Jōza* (my rank) to the position of *shuso*."

After that, a monk in charge of reception, the *shika,* came forward and bowed to me. I said to him, "I was recommended for this ceremony. I now humbly exercise my duty." He replied, "Your ability is suited to lead people. I reckon that this is an auspicious occasion."

He led me to the *hōdōshi,* Yamada Rōshi, who came back to his seat in the *hondō*. There, I was placed on the sitting mat in proper position. I then prostrated before the shrine three times. After that, the *shika* made a gesture for me to prostrate to the *hōdōshi.* After the first bow, I said to him, "A monk newly receiving precepts enters into this monastery. I am not refined in anything but received your invitation by chance. I fear for my compliable ability." Then, after the second bow I said, "It is a beautiful warm day. I respectfully think that the Head Master sets forth wellness and I congratulate the Head Master for that." Thereafter, I prostrated three times. Yamada Rōshi prostrated once at my third prostration as a reply. Next, the *shika* took me to both the upper and lower sections of the *hondō*. Then, he took me outside before leading me to the head-seat, or *shuso*, in the rows of seats where I stood. The *shika* returned to his seat. Thereupon the *inō* entered the room, bowed to the shrine and then struck the wooden stamp on the floor with a piece of wood and said, "Now we finish inviting Wakō *Jōza* and put him in the *shuso*. I respectfully pronounce this matter." He then struck the wooden stamp once more. After that everyone prostrated three times and retreated.

***

It was a solemn introduction to my new rank. The second phase would be to participate in a tea ceremony in which the Head Master of this occasion, Yamada Rōshi, announced the next phase of the ceremony. One round of the drum sounds signaled everyone to a seat in the tearoom. The Head Master and I wore a full set of robes. He then announced; "I am going to have Wakō *Shuso* lead tomorrow's *hōza* (Dharma practice)." Then he told his attending monk to put the *kōan* text on a tray and place it before me. I received it, prostrated three times to the Head Master and the Head Master returned my respect and bowed once at my third bow. I then took the tray and placed it in front of the Head Master for him to examine. The tea ceremony followed immediately after the introduction of the *kōan*. The tea ceremony was simple, not different from other monastic tea ceremonies. In place of sweets my mother prepared three tiny pieces of skewered cooked taro roots on a dish at the side of teacups. It was a wartime substitution for traditional sweets.

The preparation of the third phase of the ceremony began immediately after the tea. The white colored verse was written on a large red plaque then hung on the *hondō* wall. In the head master's room, on a tray, the text of a *kōan* was wrapped in a purple silk cloth. Beside it lay a bamboo stick of approximately three feet wrapped with thin strips of rattan and lacquered in black, called *shippei*. There was also a ceremonial fan tied with red and white symbolic threads.

The main part of this ceremony was the question-and-answer portion, the *hōza*. Gyokusen handed me a book to read in preparation for that. The book was called the *Record of Zangrong, Zangronglu,* or the *Shōyō-roku* in Japanese, a Chinese collection of a hundred *kōans* originally collected by Hongzhi Zhengjue in the early 1100s. The *Zangronlu* was annotated later by Wangsong [Wang-sung] in 1224. *Zangrong* (Repose, Serenity) is the name of a small hut where Wangsong lived. The *Shōyō-roku* was revered and studied by Sōtō Zen practitioners as the *Blue Rock Record* was to the Rinzai Zen monks. I spent many days diligently reading the book but I was ambivalent as to what to make of it. For instance, the seventy-third *kōan* reads as follows: "A monk asked [Master] Caoshan (Sōzan in Japanese), 'Why didn't you wear your mourning outfit [when your parents died]?' Caoshan answered, 'My piety is fulfilled [and I have no need to wear such a thing].' The monk further asked, 'What do you do after fulfilling your filial piety?' Caoshan replied, 'I'll get drunk.'" I asked Nin'yū Yamasaki what he made of this story, but all he said to me was, "That's what I am doing."

Gyokusen later explained it to me by saying, "First of all, the monk's question is not asking whether Caoshan wears mourning apparel or not. Caoshan's answer was on an entirely different plateau. In the original state of being, one needs not be bothered with such things as mourning apparel. Furthermore, there are no given days, such as forty-nine days or a year of mourning to fulfill one's filial piety. Every day is a fulfilling day. There is neither before nor after for that." I felt that I was left alone in vast barren field. I read the book a few more times and memorized several stories, but still, without thorough comprehension.

***

The day came for the main part of the ceremony. This ceremony was supposed to take place on May seventeenth but in my case, it took place several days earlier. At exactly ten o'clock in the morning, the large drum was struck in place of a gong. It was struck seven times, beginning with a slow, loud, even rhythm, gradually growing faster and softer. The monks who were participating in the preparation entered the *hondō* when the drum continued with five more slow strokes in even rhythm, gradually becoming faster and then quieter. I left the *hondō* with the official monks of the *ango* period: namely, the *shoki,* or secretary, *shika* the hosting monk, and *chiden,* the building managing monk. We all went to the Head Master's room. At the third set of drum strokes of three slow, even beats, the Head Master entered the *hondō* and those who had gone to his room to invite him followed in two columns. The drum sounds waned and silence swept over the hall. He offered sweetened water, other sweets and tea to the altar. Then, the participating monks began chanting the Heart Sūtra. At the end of the sūtra I unwrapped the silk cloth, opened the *kōan* text and in a loud voice stated, "I raise this," and read the *kōan*.

Then I said, "Here is a verse. This verse will be recited by a young monk." A monk, younger than me, recited the verse. I then re-wrapped the kōan text, *Zanronglu,* which had been presented the day before. I bowed several times at different places and seated myself. The attending monk took the bamboo stick from the Head Master's side and brought it before me. He then asked, "Head-seat monk, Wakō, (*shuso*), how do you use this *shippei* (bamboo stick)?" I answered, "I can kill or let live freely." I rehearsed these sections earlier so that question was easily answered.

I held the *shippei* in front of me horizontally with both hands and recited the verse dedicated to the *shippei* while I sat cross-legged on my sitting mat. I said, "This precious sword came to my hands from the Lion Seat (Bodhisattva Mañjuśrī). I can make the sword kill or give life to people. Now, you who are clever and capable come and test me in the dharma combat. Open your mouths and try to vanquish me."

Then, monks began asking questions. Some of those were: "Without using words, without drawing patterns, tell me your explanation of Buddhism?" I shouted with all my might, "Kaaa...h!" The fifth *kōan* of the *Shōyō-roku* had a similar question. A monk asked Qingyan, "What is the utmost importance of Buddha-dharma?" Without answering the question, Master Qingyan simply asked, "How much is the rice in Luling?" I answered with a loud shout, "Kaaa...h!" meaning, "You ought to know it."

Someone asked, "How are you going to improve matters regarding Buddhism?" I answered, "Willow trees outside are green and flowers are red." I did not find this question in any book. I answered of my own volition, using this ordinary phrase. What I meant was that everything is in its right place and we just need to see it directly. There were none others that even faintly resembled this question. A typical example of this *kōan* would be the following in the forty-second *kōan*: A monk asked Master Nanyang, "What is the true body of Vairocana-buddha?" Master merely said, "Bring me a pitcher of clean water." The monk brought a pitcher. The master said, "Go back to where you came from." The monk repeated the question, "What is the true body of Vairocana-buddha?" Master Nanyang said, "The ancient Buddha has long gone."

Reading the *Zangronlu,* or *Shōyō-roku,* a few times, I thought I had found the ways to answer questions even though my understanding was far from what the original dialogues actually signified. Someone else asked me at the ceremony, "There are flowers, a moon, and a beautiful temple." At this point, I interrupted him with "You lost your mind, beguiled by the scene before your eyes."

Someone again questioned my answer: "Zhaozhu once said 'some are manipulated by the twelve hours but I manipulate the twelve hours.' Can you use twelve hours?" I said, "Yes, I can." He then asked "How?" and I replied "I eat a bowl of rice-gruel in the morning and I go to bed after evening meditation."

I had observed a *shuso hōza* once before so some of the questions and statements requiring a reply were vaguely familiar to me. Yet all the questions and answers we exchanged were in the 700-year-old classical Japanese-read-Chinese, which was difficult. Furthermore, most Buddhists use the pronunciation for each of the thousands of Chinese characters found in the *"Go-on,"* or the "Pronunciation of Wu [dynasty] Chinese." My family and several of the members of the temple said to me later that they were very impressed with my handling of the language, although they did not understand what I was saying. At the age of fourteen, I somehow managed to respond to every question thanks to my father who had painstakingly taught me that language as well as sūtras and verses. It was like speaking Church Latin to an English speaking Protestant congregation.

After the last question and answer had ended I thanked everyone, of course, in that same medieval Japanese-Chinese. Thereafter, each monk came before me and congratulated me in the same language, ending with the exalted closing remark, "*Shishuku fujin*" (It is a time for great rejoicing!). Thus, my *shuso hōza* ceremony ended.

Following congratulations by everyone, I, the *shuso*, hosted the lunch, *tenjin*. It consisted of rice cooked with red beans, called *osekihan*. This was the next phase of my *shuso* ceremony. This may not seem important, but *tenjin* in Japanese has the same characters as *dimsum* (Chinese dumpling), meaning "to make you alert."

Shuso hōza ceremony at Hōsen-ji. May 6, 1944. Age 14.
Many monks attended this ceremony and asked questions
to test my ability as a *Shuso* (head-seated) monk.

To maintain a Sōtō Zen temple, it must have an abbot who oversees its activities. I am using the term "abbot" for a principal resident priest. I was still too young and had no qualifications to be a resident priest. My most closely related *dharma* relative was Genshi Yagi Rōshi of Fugan-ji, Nara. Genshi Yagi's dharma teacher was a dharma-brother of my grand master, Genrin. To explain it simply, Genrin and Genshi Yagi's dharma teacher were co-disciples of Genshi Yūgen, Hōsen-ji's seventh abbot. My grand master Genrin, my father's teacher, took the seat of the abbot of Hōsen-ji as the eighth abbot. Yagi's teacher had assumed the abbot position at Fugan-ji in Nara prefecture, a temple over six hundred years old.

The rightful candidate as the next abbot of Hōsen-ji after my father's death was Genshi Yagi, the dharma cousin of my father. The members of Hōsen-ji had officially asked Genshi Yagi to be the tenth abbot, after my father. Consequently, he became my official teacher on November 1, 1944 and I was assigned to study under him. Yagi Rōshi was extremely soft-spoken with a high-pitched voice and a gentle-sounding Nara accent. Now, with his acceptance, Hōsen-ji was to continue its dharma lamp. Hōsen-ji was a unique temple in that the temple lineage, or *garanpō,* from the founder down to the present time, and the lineage of priests, or *nin-pō*, who resided there as successive abbots, were one and the same. Genshi Yagi came to Hōsen-ji from time to time, but he wished to live in Nara and not in Hōsen-ji, even though he was a resident priest. Day-to-day activities at Hōsen-ji thus rested with me.

***

Nin'yū Yamasaki, a colleague of my father, asked Reverend Genshi Yagi to remain in the abbot position until I finished my practice and qualified as the abbot of Hōsen-ji. Yagi agreed. Meanwhile, Nin'yū

Yamasaki would also take care of the temple activities when I was occupied with other activities. I learned this fact much later on in life but Yagi Rōshi's temple, Fugan-ji, had experienced a glorious history. It was originally a Tendai School temple, probably built around the eleventh century. But when Zen Buddhism began to flourish in the thirteenth and fourteenth centuries, it became a Sōtō Zen temple. It was in the year 1384, when the second abbot of Fugan-ji was actively practicing Zen Buddhism there that a renowned Noh play actor, Zeami, came and studied under him. He took the Mahāyānan Bodhisattva Precepts as a Zen practitioner. Zeami's Noh plays, after his practice and study, began to reflect an otherworldly profound elegance amidst his scenes of worldliness.

In any case, Hōsen-ji was saved thanks to Genshi Yagi. Later, when I reached the time to transmit the dharma lineage, I took the lineage of Genshi Yagi, so that the Hōsen-ji lineage was intact from its founder.

I heard from the neighboring abbots that Nin'yū Yamasaki had undertaken monastic trainings and became a resident priest of a temple, but for some reasons he did not stay there for long, though I did not hear it from him directly. To me, connecting bits of his utterances over time, he was well-educated in government schools and had trained at various monasteries. He came to the Yobitsugi area because he knew several priests in the area and wanted to make a living helping with temple activities. He lived in a small rented house approximately a mile from Hōsen-ji and visited temples on his bicycle. He was thoroughly acquainted with all the rituals and the temples found him useful despite his alleged alcohol problem. He and my father became close friends. As he agreed to help, he came to Hōsen-ji on an almost daily basis. My father trusted him and discussed important matters with him prior to his departure from this world.

After Gyokusen left and my father became ill, I was alone most of the time taking care of the temple. I performed the morning routines but always in an abbreviated way. I had to study for middle school and visit the temple members' houses for memorial services. I also had to perform services when the members came to the temple. Needless to say, I was very busy. My mother had her hands full, raising four children including me. Although I was only fourteen, my mother depended on me in many ways, especially in matters concerning temple activities. Nin'yū's help and his long empirical wisdom were invaluable during those difficult days.

Nin'yū Yamasaki, besides coming to Hōsen-ji early every morning, began taking more of an active role in temple activities. Sometimes I had to stay at school for the wartime compulsory martial arts training or some club activity, and couldn't come home in time to visit the members' houses. Nin'yū came and helped me. That was a great relief for me since I also needed time to study. I suppose for Nin'yū, helping Hōsen-ji gave him a small but steady income. Hōsen-ji needed him when I couldn't be there all the time at the temple. Also, when the members wanted to hold elaborate services requiring several more priests, he arranged those flawlessly. I found that Nin'yū had his own followers, such as a wealthy *saké* brewer named Mr. Hirose, and a wealthy soy sauce brewer, Mr. Momiyama. He introduced me to them and I remember those wealthy households hosting wonderful lunches even in those days when such food was difficult to obtain. He taught me various comportments of rituals my father was unable to help with during his illness. Many people said Nin'yū was impossibly bad when he drank more *saké* than he should, but I did not witness this behavior in those early days.

***

One summer day, Nin'yū and I took a short trip to the peninsula south of Yobitsugi. We visited the tomb of Minamoto-no
Yoshitomo, who was assassinated by his own retainer while he was
bathing at the retainer's house in 1160. Yoshitomo was the father
of Minamoto-no Yoritomo, the first Shogun of Kamakura, and he
had been on the way to Kamakura to visit his son when he was
killed. He was only thirty-seven years old when assassinated. The
assassin, Osada, after beheading Yoshitomo, washed Yoshitomo's
head in the pond in the compound of the temple called Daibō. The
color of the pond immediately became blood-red or as Shakespeare
might have said, the color of incarnadine. People still call the pond
"*chi-no-ike,*" or "the pond of blood." At the temple, Daibō, a small
window was kept open which sold wooden swords as an offering
to Yoshitomo. The proceeds from those swords provided memorial services for him. We each bought a small wooden sword, quite
fresh and pale colored. The woman at the window said, "Here's a
brush and ink. You can write something on it."

On my wooden sword I wrote, "all forms are empty." Nin'yū
wrote on his sword, "the sword that kills also gives life." I remembered that phrase. I had in fact recited it at my *shuso hōza*
ceremony, holding the *shippei* (lacquered bamboo rod). We
threw our swords into the pond where hundreds of swords had
previously been thrown. Then we took a bus and train home. On
the bus, he asked me why I wrote "all forms are empty." I said,
"It is my sincere offering to Yoshitomo. Yoshitomo must have
been greatly chagrined and could not rest peacefully after his
tragic and violent death. All forms of existence, either natural
or man-made, are temporary and ultimately nothing remains the
same. Everything is evanescent and momentary. That is why it is
'empty.' I offered that phrase to him." Nin'yū said, "I am indeed
impressed." And I asked him, "Why did you write 'the sword that

kills also gives life?'" He thought for a few moments and then replied, "I wanted to remind you. That's why I wrote it. You said that at your *shuso* ceremony, remember?" "Yes, I remember," I said and continued. "It is a strange expression, since killing is the most offensive act and the first of the Bodhisattva precepts teaches us not to commit it."

Nin'yū Yamasaki replied, "That is quite true. To kill is to take everything away, life and death, buddhas and *nirvāṇa*, joy and suffering—it's the state of nothingness. To give life is the opposite— we are here now, surrounded by joys and sorrows, but in essence it is, as you have just said, fleeting. Therefore, both are no different, you know, being or non-being. That is why I gave this phrase to Yoshitomo. This phrase tells all. It's a Zen phrase that you are going to use later." And he repeated the phrase "*Satsujin-ken, katsujin-ken* (sword that kills is the sword that saves)." If the first precept of "do not kill" is interpreted that way, I wondered what happens to the third precept of "do not take alcohol." He might likely have said, "I am drinking, but at the same time I am not drinking." Our conversation continued in that vein as usual.

***

Public transportation in the late summer of 1943 became evermore inconvenient. The transfers seemed to take forever. This short trip took all day. Nin'yū Yamasaki did not drink any alcohol that day. We both enjoyed our outing in freedom from our daily chores. This was typical of my many outings with him. On one occasion, he said to me smilingly that in the common social norm, he was a failure due to his frailty. I thought that was a totally wrong assessment. He went through impossibly hard times in his life. I thought he was definitely strong and not frail at all.

Anyone who had gone through the tragedies of his life would likely be totally crushed. He had raised six children. Within a span of about twelve years he lost five of them in the quiet and long epidemic of tuberculosis. The only one to escape this illness was his youngest daughter. His other children died one by one from tuberculosis. Some died when they were not even ten years of age, though most of them died in their teens. The last of his children, the oldest son, died soon after he married in his mid-twenties. Nin'yū Yamasaki understood that this was an unfortunate natural process and he could not do anything to remedy the course. Medicine had not yet reached the stage where antibiotic drugs could cure tuberculosis. When one child died Nin'yū must have feared that the others would contract the disease and that it would take the same course. His worries were, unfortunately, correct. His children fell one after another, always after long struggles. I met two of his children; one was the son who was the last to die. Another was a teenage girl when I met her. She died a few years before reaching the age of twenty. When his son, the last victim of this illness, died around 1950, he was only five or six years older than I was. My mother said then, "Losing a child is most hurtful and as a mother or father, you would rather wish to lose your own life than that of your child."

When a family member dies, it is "you who at present must endure the pain of the loss of your beloved child, not speaking of the fear that the dying person experienced." The euphemism of death may be resting, sleeping, journeying and so forth but they are only euphemisms, far from the reality suffered by the survivors, especially parents. For instance, Sleeping Beauty is resting yet still in existence. But in death, where does that person sleep and how so? Is that person asleep in a timeless, immaterial realm? Does that person exist in any form, in any realm?

Every living being will eventually cease to exist; human existence presupposes the fact of death and that is an objective reality. The existence of an individual is only a passing point in a long continuum of human existence. Deaths must be the inevitable termini for all species. Some of that anxiety of impermanence is definitely associated with suffering. Death is, therefore, predictive for all of us and no one can evade it. It is indeed suffering. But when an understanding of the dharma-nature of life and death is reached, suffering will no longer haunt the person with fear and anxiety.

Nin'yū Yamasaki and his wife must have been devastated every time they lost a child. Human children take a long time to mature through learning to sit, to stand, to walk, to talk and to eat by themselves. During that time familial love and trust develops as parents watch their children grow through the stages of maturation in both sturdiness and frailty. There are endearing times, as well as painful times. Living is activity, which is also *karma,* and life is a continual chain of *karma.* Is an older, more accomplished person dearer and more valuable than a child who only lives a few years? For Nin'yū Yamasaki, the answer would be "no." He had lost a dear and most valuable child five times. In his life, his children were part of his existence and one by one they were chiseled out from Nin'yū Yamasaki's existence. As a human being how could he reconcile himself? I never found the words to console him and his wife.

I never understood his feelings while I was in high school. Even in my college days, I often forgot about his tragic experience. Of course, when my father died I went through degrees of suffering. Still, at the time of my father's death, after his long bedridden illness, thinking of his age, it seemed to be the natural order of things. That helped to heal my pain. Nin'yū Yamasaki's case was different. Natural order was reversed and those who were supposed to live longer had gone first. Nin'yū never said anything about the deaths of his children. He acknowledged their deaths but never mentioned his own feelings while I was still a teenager. Later, on the occasion when I took the seat of abbot at Hōsen-ji, he was elated and got very drunk. I asked him not to drink anymore. But he beseeched me by saying he was jubilant for that occasion and forgot everything else. I suddenly came to understand his personal catastrophes. He was a Zen priest, yet he was also very much a human being with innate frailties. He had personally encountered the truth of pain that the Buddha expounded after his enlightenment.

***

The relationship between Nin'yū Yamasaki and me, in my retrospective overview, was that of a master and a disciple, or in a more common way, a mentor and a protégé. He never scolded me but always patiently waited for me to learn the correct way when I was young. He was the one who convinced my mother to let me study and practice at Kyūkoku-ji monastery after my father's death and he also recommended and arranged for me to study at Kakuō-zan Nittai-ji monastery before I went to college. When I went to Kyūkoku-ji monastery he even helped put my bedding and books on a cart. Together we pulled it for about twelve miles to the monastery. He returned the same distance pulling the empty cart on the way back. Kyūkoku-ji was my first serious monastic practice. He had prepared me for my life there. I was fourteen years of age and it was only a few months after my father's death. I had observed the period of mourning and then I went through the *shuso* ceremony before I left for Kyūkoku-ji monastery.

My relationship with Nin'yū Yamasaki grew even stronger after Kyūkoku-ji, despite his several mishaps over *saké*. I did indeed have to apologize to temple members to save his face a few times. I, too, had many mishaps but in most cases he ignored them. On one particular occasion, however, after a wrongdoing of which I do not remember the nature, he made me sit in front of him. He asked, "What is good and what is bad for you?" I answered, "Good is a conduct which is..." I could not answer immediately. After a pause I managed to say, "Bad is a conduct which deviates from the right path of humanity." He asked, "What are those right paths of humanity?" I could not answer. Then he said, "We are Buddhist monks, a part of the *saṃgha* (Buddhist community). *Saṃgha* originally meant a harmonious and peaceful group. An Indian poet and Nobel laureate, Sir Rabindranath Tagore, once said that bad deeds disturb the harmony and peace of others. Buddhists concur with that criterion."

Nin'yū concluded by saying, "You recite 'I take refuge in Buddha, I take refuge in dharma, and I take refuge in *saṃgha*' every day, don't you? You must uphold what you recite. Don't disturb others' harmony. Rabindranath Tagore, for me, is a Buddhist." I recall that was the only time he seriously reprimanded me for my conduct. I pondered what he said for awhile after that occasion. Tagore's words stayed deep within me. I realized much later that what he said was part of the Bodhisattva Precepts that I had vowed to uphold at the time of my initial ordination ceremony, *tokudo*, just three years before: No killing, no stealing, no adultery, no lying, no slander, no insulting of others and several other precepts. They are all meant to not disturb the harmony of other people at their core. At that moment, I realized the real meaning of being a Buddhist.

My home has been on Cold Mountain
from the beginning.
Perching on these rocky cliffs,
I've severed the link
of worldly passion.
When my mind ceases,
 there's no trace of ten thousand things.
When it extends,
it flows out to fill the universe.
The light instantly shines,
illuminating my mind;
not a single *dharma*
appears before me.
Understand exactly
this tiny *maṇi* jewel:
a perfect sphere
without circumference.

– Han-shan

Chapter 6

KYŪKOKU-JI MONASTERY

あきらかにしりぬ、
結跏趺坐、
これ三昧王三昧なり。
これ証人なり。
一切の三昧はこの王三昧の眷属なり。

結跏趺坐は直身なり、直心なり、
直仏祖なり，直修証なり、
直頂寧なり、直命脈也。

－ 道元

(『正法眼蔵』「三昧王三昧」)

You must know
sitting cross-legged is
the king of *samādhi*
and awakening.
All other *samādhis* are kith and
kin of the king of *samādhi*.
Sitting cross-legged is
your body, mind, body-mind.
That is Buddha-patriarchs,
practice, enlightenment and your
blood-lineage.

- Dogen

(*Shōbōgenzō, (Sanmai-ō-zanmai)*
"The King of *Samādhi*")

Against this backdrop of World War II, I left Hōsen-ji to go to the Kyūkoku-ji monastery. My mother said to me, "A year will soon be over, so bear with the life at Kyūkoku-ji." I replied, "I won't give up, mother. Don't worry about me." That was my simple farewell to my mother. It was on May 12, 1944, six days after my *shuso* ceremony. I was fourteen years of age. Because of my father's death and mourning period, my entry to Kyūkoku-ji was approximately a month behind that of other *shintō*, or newly starting monks. The traditional ninety-day *ango* practice began, as explained before, on April 16 for the earlier group and May 16 for the later group. All the *shintō* at Kyūkoku-ji were part of the earlier group but I was an exception. The seventh-century Chinese Buddhist scholar, Xuanzhuang, mentioned the ninety-day *ango*'s starting dates twice in his renowned travelogue to India, the *Datang Xiyu-ji*, or *Great Tang Record of the Western Region.* He specified May16 and June 16 respectively, for the earlier and later summer *ango* periods. These records indicated that these *ango* had been considered vital components of Buddhist monastic practice as early as the seventh century.

I had to wear a prescribed traveling outfit as I did when undertaking mendicancy with Grand Master Genrin. For this occasion I wore a gray cotton kimono with a black cotton monastic robe over it. They were tucked into my belt at almost knee length. My arms were covered with old-fashioned white cotton arm guards. My legs were covered with white cotton gaiters and I wore long-range straw walking sandals. Over my robe I carried a basket to store my *kesa*, and my essential clothes, called *kesa-gōri,* and also my eating implements, called *ōryōki.* Both were wrapped in a dark colored cotton cloth hanging in the front and back, and supported by two straps over my shoulders. My head had been shaved afresh that morning and I had a large, hard-woven hat that had been hanging at the entrance of Hōsen-ji for years. The hat was to cover my head while traveling. Although I had not used it since my Grand Master died, it was needed for this particular occasion.

Nin'yū always wore a kimono with a robe over it, but for this day he, too, tucked-up his kimono and robe for our long trek. He was wearing a pair of wooden sandals, or *geta*, on bare feet, since it was a warm day. He covered his head with a towel. I imagine that, even for that time period in Japan, the sight of two monks with tucked-up robes pushing a cart on the city street appeared a bit strange.

Pushing the fully loaded cart of my belongings over a twelve-mile journey was exceedingly taxing, especially for Nin'yū, who was in his mid-fifties. It was not only the load of my belongings that was exhausting, but the distance. We crossed the Yamasaki River and thereafter passed rows of small houses and some small closed-down shops, since they did not have much merchandise to sell amidst the wartime rations. Although most of the city streets were paved with asphalt, some areas were sandy on the surface and in some areas scattered gravel gave us trouble. Nin'yū Yamasaki pulled the tail end of his kimono beneath the back side of his sash and looked as if he were a medieval palanquin carrier. People looked at him with curious eyes but he paid no attention to them. I was a little embarrassed. It must have been a very heavy task for Nin'yū Yamasaki.

We crossed the city of Nagoya pushing the cart. Hōsen-ji was located in the southern section and Kyūkoku-ji monastery was at the northern end of the city. This meant we had to travel all the way across the city. Nin'yū said, "You are lucky to have this opportunity to study Zen considering the present social conditions." That was very true. All able males up to forty-five or so were drafted for military duty and those who were not fit for military duty were rounded up to work for war-related endeavors. Young women, too, had to work in various factories. We could not act freely to pursue our own interests. Allotment of food, clothing, fuel, transportation and other essentials for daily living were arranged by order of priority. Monastic living was not even on the list of priorities.

***

On the way to Kyūkoku-ji, Nin'yū prepared me by telling me many things I had not yet learned. He told me that Zen monasteries do not officially accept anyone for five to seven days. At first, at the temple entrance, a *zantō*, or short-term resident monk who wished to practice in the monastery, had to prostrate himself from the standing position to fling his body to the ground such that knees, elbows and head touched the ground. I prostrated three times that way. Then, I, also a *zantō,* asked the receptionist monk to admit me to stay. Immediately after my arrival at Kyūkoku-ji, I was greeted in the room of the senior monk, who took care of *zantō.* I found out later that the senior monk who greeted me, *Godō,* oversaw our practice there. He led me to the abbot's room.

The abbot of Kyūkoku-ji monastery was Yūken Mizuta Rōshi who, after a brief greeting, gave me permission to stay in the monastery as a *zantō*. Nin'yū Yamasaki was right. I was led to a *tangaryō*. *Tangaryō* literally means "a room to pass a night until morning," or a temporary station for an applicant who had not yet been formally accepted to the monastery.

Tangaryō was originally a guest room for journeying practitioners who passed through the monastery and stayed for only a night or two. But it was also used to test monks who sought to practice there before official permission was granted to determine whether or not the monks could endure monastic life. It was exactly as Nin'yū had described. I had to sit cross-legged and practice *zazen* alone in the room. The *tangaryō* was simple, perhaps the size of ten by twelve feet, with a window made of paper screens over a light wooden frame *shoji* on one side letting faint light into the room. Two other sides of the room had light brown earthen walls and the fourth side was the entrance to the room, also with *shoji* doors. I sat there for five days. During those days, meals were brought to me. I was only permitted to leave the room to use the toilet.

Even though I had been informed of the *tangaryō* sitting, the fourth and fifth days were very difficult. I tried not to think about anything but it was very difficult. My mother's face and voice stayed with me while I was sitting alone in the room. I had a keen sense of yearning, especially when the late afternoon sunlight filtered through the *shoji* screen, and tears ran down my cheeks. When I noticed the tears, I shook my body and head and said to myself, "I won't give up. I'll bear this." Somehow, after that, a sort of renewed courage grew within me and changed my nostalgia into a different sensation. I was fourteen years of age and I had just started my third year at middle school (ninth grade). Arrangements had been made for me to continue school while practicing at the monastery.

The most difficult thing about this initial test of the *tangaryō* was sitting alone in a room all day and night with only six or seven hours of sleeping time for the entire period. We were conditioned as children to live by the clock. Here in the *tangaryō*, I did not have a wristwatch. I had a Seiko wristwatch when I entered middle school, but in those days if the hands of the watch moved continually, it was miraculous, and my watch was not so miraculous. At the beginning I had to adjust it every hour or so. It looked good on my wrist but other than that it was useless so I abandoned the idea of wearing it.

***

Without a watch or a clock in the *tangaryō*, I was totally imprecise in my measurement of time. I soon found out that my circadian rhythm was utterly inaccurate. At first I observed the change of brightness, though it was filtered and opaque coming through the *shoji* screens in the room during the morning. I watched the silhouette of building rooflines outside on the *shoji* screens in the afternoon to measure time. Time experienced alone in the stillness of a *tangaryō* room was different from any other time I had experienced. Time crept by as slowly as if it were standing still. The *tangaryō* was an extramundane cul-de-sac in the bustle of the world around it.

As I mentioned earlier, images of my family and friends occupied my mind in the first few days. I longed for every one of them. Time passed relatively swiftly when my mind was occupied but at other times it passed all too slowly. On the second and third days, time, if I ever understood what it truly was, passed slower and slower. It became a jittery vigil. I felt my own blood stream pushing through my veins one cell at a time. I felt every inhalation of breath as it passed through my body before I exhaled. My face began perspiring, yet my hands and feet were cold. Sitting alone in the evening hours by the dim lamplight scattered my thoughts. I felt time had been unmercifully augmented, for it did not move fast enough toward the close of day. The minutes felt like hours and the hours like a compacted eternity. On the fourth day, I began to realize that I had survived three days and probably could sit two or three more. This notion encouraged me and kept me from insanity.

While sitting alone in the room during this seemingly endless period, I was ill at ease. Are we not all children of a civilization that regards mechanical, or clock, time as real time? Clocks tell us that a certain length of time has passed. But if we speed up or slow down a clock without letting the observer know, the observer is beguiled by different notions of time. We measure time mechanically and physically, yet there still remains subjective and private time, which is difficult to measure. In the *tangaryō,* I experienced time as subjective, private and idealized.

What, then, is time? The past, present and future cannot be measured, for time does not have a system by which to measure itself. Yet, as I was told to sit in the *tangaryō* for the duration of five days, I experienced every passing instant with minimal or no visible change to my surroundings.

Time passed quietly, imperceptibly, into the future. *Dharma* (existing phenomena) also constantly and imperceptibly takes on new forms. We categorize a certain period of time as long or short. If we are bored, we say that time drags on and if we are engaged, we say that time flies by. Were the *tangaryō* hours boring only because they passed ever so slowly?

I spent five full days in the *tangaryō,* sitting in a full or half cross-legged lotus position. I survived this seemingly timeless temporality by realizing that the true measure of time was the flow of my consciousness. I experienced every second of sitting in the *tangaryō.* From this experience I realized that I was time and also the dharma, or in other words, essentially everything in existence. *Shoji* screen and *tatami* mats exist in time, just like mountains, clouds, the sky, rivers, and seas.

To the contrary, could we say time is mere illusion? I realized that time is immeasurable, and should not be sectioned off into discrete intervals. In that way, I was experiencing the moment and no other. I was surrounded by the seemingly unchanging dharma. It became absurd to think that such-and-such happened three days ago. The past occupies the present, as do pleasure and pain, life and death. In retrospect, I had experienced a momentous time, which was not boring in the least.

***

After breakfast on day five, I was guided by the *shika,* or hosting monk, to the *inō,* the managing monk, who held a written permission document on a tray before him. It was called the *kata-jō,* the letter granting permission, or "to hang one's bag of clothes and eating bowls on the wall of the *Sōdō,* the Monk's Hall." *Kata,* or to hang one's implement, means to stay there as a practitioner. It was a simple protocol for admission. The *inō* then took me to the *sōdō* where I prostrated before the shrine of *Mañjuśrī-bodhisattva.* He showed me the layout of the building and explained the monastic routines. I was now officially admitted to live in the *sōdō* where I would sleep, eat, and practice *zazen* for at least 90 days. The period of 90 days was called *varsa* in Sanskrit, translating to "rainy season." The *sōdō* was an independent building facing east on the northwestern part of the monastery grounds, facing the rear section of the *hondō.* The entrance to the *sōdō* was on the eastside and a corridor connected it to the *hondō.* The floor of the *sōdō* was a black shiny stone. At the center of this building stood an enshrined *Mañjuśrī-bodhisattva* statue on a pedestal. Three sides of the *sōdō* had approximately two-foot high platforms where *tatami* mats were laid lengthwise. Each *tatami* was approximately three by six feet in size. In front of it there was about a foot-wide wooden edge called *jōën* forming the frame of the platforms. Practitioners place their *kesa* (robes) and *ōryōki,* (eating implements) on the *jōën* when they eat and sleep, so monks do not step or sit on it. Every time practitioners step onto their *tan,* they place neither their buttocks nor their feet on the *jōën.*

The *inō* stopped at one place, pointed, and said to me, "This is your *tan.*" The *tan* is the practitioner's personal space for living, sleeping and *zazen.* At the end of each *tan* was a small closet for personal belongings at the opposite end of *jōën.* The closet was approximately four or five cubic feet. Above my *tan,* my name

"Wakō" had been freshly written in white ink on a black lacquered plaque hung over the *tan*. After the *inō* showed me the *tan,* I went to the abbot's room where I prostrated and offered incense. In return, he offered me a cup of tea. With this ceremony I became an official *shintō*, or a newly arrived monk at Kyūkoku-ji Monastery. The monastery had a relatively small *sōdō* compared to bigger monasteries but it could still hold approximately 25 monks. Kyūkoku-ji monastery did not have an outside *zazen* practice space called *ga-ïtan,* or outside-*tan*. It just had one room of *naïtan* or inside-*tan*.

I only had two sets of clothing, a monastic robe and a western-style school uniform. It was extremely simple living there but those things never bothered me. At the *tangaryō* I had been alone, but now I was fortunately with several others who, like me, were permitted to go to school after our morning routines. There were fifteen practitioners in all. Eight of us were students either fourteen or fifteen years of age. Besides the abbot, *inō, godō*, and *tenzo* (the monk in charge of the kitchen), there were only three young monks. Two of those were drafted to military duties a few months after I was admitted there. I had been performing monastic routines all along at Hōsen-ji, so my life there was not unfamiliar. However, Kyūkoku-ji monastery was stricter and everything had to be carried out in an exact manner. After all, my teacher at Hōsen-ji had been my father. Even though Kyūkoku-ji was rigid and strict, the teachers, such as the *inō* and *godō*, were not young and energetic, which made it less rigid compared to the monastic practices of previous times. Furthermore, the *inō*'s left hand was paralyzed, but he skillfully managed just about all of his chores. The *tenzo* was also old and we took turns helping him in the kitchen.

I discovered that the morning meditation at Kyūkoku-ji began at four o'clock, earlier than at Hōsen-ji. Nin'yū had already kindly briefed me on monastic routines, so I knew the *shinrei* (awakening bell) would be around three forty-five, with fifteen minutes to prepare for the morning *zazen*, called *gyōten-za*. We called it by an abbreviated expression, *gyōten*. We sat for about fifty minutes, which was followed by a morning ritual, or *chōka,* of approximately forty-five minutes. Thereafter, all monks carried out the *samu,* or daily devoirs, which for us meant thoroughly cleaning the monastery before an hour-long breakfast. The breakfasts at Kyūkoku-ji were like other Zen monasteries: rice gruel and *miso* soup every morning without fail. The *tenzo* made us carryout lunches for those who went to school after breakfast. Our lunches always consisted of boiled oats-and-rice with one or two boiled vegetables, such as lotus roots, *daikon,* carrots, or eggplant, seasoned with soy sauce. And, without fail, there were three slices of pickled *daikon.*

***

Days bearing fours and nines, such as the fourth, ninth, fourteenth, nineteenth, twenty-forth, and twenty-ninth, were called "*shi-ku-nichi,*" meaning "the days of fours and nines," or "*hōsan,*" the days where we were excused from morning and evening *zazen* and rituals. Those were the days we stayed in bed for about thirty minutes longer and used the extra time for bathing, shaving our heads, and other personal tasks. All of us needed this time for laundering, writing, studying and so forth. However, a *shintō,* or newly arrived monk, was not permitted to leave the monastery. This was a period of *ango,* meaning a confined ninety-day practice period. Middle-school boys were excluded from this confinement only to attend school. *Ango,* or *uango* was initially practiced during India's rainy season, *varsa.* This *varsa* was carried out as a 90-day confinement at the monasteries.

Those monks who attended middle school had to attend the Saturday afternoon and Sunday lectures. Regular school classes ended at noon on Saturdays in Japanese schools. We had Saturday lectures at Kyūkoku-ji called *naïkō*. Those lectures were usually given by the *godō,* in place of the abbot, Yūken Mizuta Rōshi. The Saturday lectures were geared toward student-monks like us. Lectures on Sundays were called *honkō* and were given after breakfast by the abbot. All monks attended those lectures. The lectures varied from time to time but often dwelled on *sūtras* such as the *Lotus sūtra,* the *Prajñāpāramitā-sūtra,* or the *nirvāṇa-sūtra.* Also included were the vast records of Zen masters' writings and sayings such as the *Shōbōgenzō*, the *Zuimon-ki,* the *Shōyō-roku*, the *Blue Rock Record,* the *Gateless Gate,* and the *Transmission of the Lamp of the Jingde.* There were no examinations for either *naïkō* or *honkō* but somehow whenever you were puzzled, questions came upon you. When you lacked understanding the advice was invariably, "You need to practice more. You will then attain that state."

***

Most Japanese Buddhists rarely give sermons at regular or special services except for a few Buddhist schools. Generally, Buddhist priests are to perform rituals for occasions such as the days of the Buddha Śākyamuni's birth, enlightenment, and death, as well as *obon* and *higan,* the rites for spring and autumn equinox. Individual families' memorial services are also an important part of their activities, but sermons or *dharma* talks are not part of their role. The Buddha Śākyamuni spoke and taught in India, according to the sūtras that recorded his teachings and activities. During the long course of Buddhist transmission from India to Japan, Buddhism assimilated native cultures as it was adopted. Indian Buddhism was transformed in China, in turn becoming uniquely Chinese and then, in Japan, uniquely Japanese. Cultural idioms of each country transposed and appended Buddhism in that process of integration into each cultural milieu.

***

In Japan, Buddhism encountered a cultural idiosyncrasy in which public speeches were very uncommon before the modern era. That trait might have been ascribed to the agrarian nature of its society, in which individuals collaborated with others and formed a group-oriented society. In such a communal society, conveyance of "one's" own idea, as opposed to a group consensus, was not cherished. This collectivistic societal fabric starkly contrasts historically individualistic societies, such as the ancient Greek *polis* (the root word of city, policy, and politic) and Roman *civis* (city, civic, citizen). Perhaps, in Japan, dialogues and dialectical discourses did not develop fully before the modern era for that reason. In the pre-modern periods, oratory was not considered vital to the role of Buddhist priests. Instead, communal rites played an important role in Japan's history. The word *matsuri* means "religious rite(s)" as well as "public rite(s)." Emperors performed *matsuri* when they attended political affairs. People enjoyed *matsuri* when they were at festivals.

Religious rites connect the people who participate in them. These rites *bridge* communications between the sacred and the profane involving prayer, worship, sacrifice and mystery. Japanese Buddhists had to follow them in order to establish their roots in the land. Rituals, therefore, played an essential role in Japanese Buddhist activities. If Buddhist priests were to deliver sermons, they could, I am certain, because they had to study and practice

Buddhism for the attainment of priesthood in appropriate Buddhist schools. However, almost all Japanese Buddhist schools placed a vital weight on rites; oratorical expertise was reserved for only a small number of priests.

***

To be a monk in the Sōtō Zen tradition, we have to practice meditation and learn rituals, including sūtra-chanting for all occasions. All of our activities are carried out as extensions of meditation. In *zazen*, we clear our minds, or, as we say, make our minds zero. We cannot imagine zero in our minds or think of its particular form. Zero does not have content in concrete or particular matters. Some might refer to zero as the freezing point in Celsius. That zero is simply a particular meeting place between positive and negative integers. We set our minds to zero and do not allow any numbers, positive or negative, to connect to zero before or after. Nothing comes from nothing. As a non-Buddhist, Lucretius, said in his *De Rerun Natura*, "*ex nihilo nihil fit*." But if you imagine one, which easily extends to two, and then three, four and so forth, your mind will develop until you exhaust your ideas. That is not *zazen*—it is merely imagining or a replaying of past experience, in a sitting position. *Zazen* practice cuts all reasoning processes of the intellect and excludes extraneous or inner thoughts; thereby the practitioner becomes one with *zazen* and nothing else. Zen does not coincide with the Indian meditation practice like the Yoga's *dhyāna*, although the zero was scrutinized by Indians and equated to *śūnya* or *śūnyatā* (meaning nothingness, or emptiness).

***

In his *Bendōwa*, or *A Discourse on Practicing the Way* [of the Buddha], Dōgen said:

> We say that in the practice of *zazen,* a person in a given moment becomes one with all existing matter and is omnipresent throughout time. For this reason, a practitioner is practicing and disseminating the Buddha's way within the unlimited phenomenal world and within the continual flow of time from the past, the present and into the future. The one who practices [*zazen*] and the world becomes one practicing body and one enlightened body. It is not enlightenment because of sitting but it is the resonating sound of striking *śūnyatā*, not only at the time of striking but before and after. In its resonance, marvelous music ceaselessly permeates places.

From the *honkō* and *naïkō* lectures, I was frequently reminded by the abbot and *Godō* about the significance of *zazen*, which Dōgen passed down. In our everyday *zazen* practice, we practitioners were told to make our minds *śūnya* while sitting. We sat, just sat, but did not wish to have the resonating sound of striking *śūnyatā*. Wishing itself becomes paradoxical from the perspective of zero-mind. *Zazen* must have no purpose other than *zazen* itself.

Occupying the *tan* next to mine was a tall, thin monk, Keidō Satō, who was a student attending the same school as me. Although he belonged to a high achievers' class, his *tan* was next to mine and on *shiku-nichi,* the days of fours and nines, he shaved my head and I shaved his. A special bond formed between us. Little by little he told me about his life. He was born in Los Angeles and when his father became the abbot of Sōkō-ji in San Francisco, he moved to San Francisco. When he was still in fifth grade at a San Franciscan grammar school, his father sent Keidō to his temple in Mié prefecture, near Nagoya, for a Zen education. Keidō's father, Ken'itsu Satō, went to Zenshu-ji in Los Angeles initially in December of 1929, and stayed until 1937. Reverend Hōsen Isobe was the founder of both temples. Residing at Sōkō-ji from its beginning in 1934, Reverend Hōsen Isobe decided to return to Japan and Ken'itsu Satō took over his position at Sōkō-ji. When Keidō returned to Japan his father was serving as the abbot of Sōkō-ji.

Ken'itsu Satō did not stay long at Sōkō-ji. His tenure at Sōkō-ji was cut short since he contracted tuberculosis while there. He, too, returned to Mié, Japan, to recuperate from his illness. That was a few years after Keidō's return. I had heard that San Francisco, before the war, experienced an occurrence of tuberculosis on almost an epidemic scale. Reverend Satō returned to Japan in late 1941; the Second World War broke out in the blink of an eye after that. Keidō then came to Nagoya, the nearest large city near his temple, for his middle school education and monastic practice.

Keidō and I exchanged stories of our "glorious" pasts whenever we had a few minutes of time. He talked about the San Franciscan streets on pea-soup-fog nights in the winter and how the fog moved over the city from the ocean in summer afternoons. Sometimes he mentioned things that I did not know about, such as butter, cheese, hot chocolate, hot biscuits, sausage, bacon, and much more. While he was talking about those things, he gazed at the sky with dreamy eyes as though he were fantasizing. Of course, I had never tasted any of the things he was mentioning. I could not even imagine the color, shape, smell, taste or consistency of cheese. My experience with western food was the "chicken rice" my mother once treated me to at a department store and the "curry rice" I shared with my sisters at my aunt's house. I was afraid that my ignorance led Keidō to sheer boredom since he had lived abroad as well as in Mié for a few years. His experience seemed unimaginably vast. I told him about *"chimaki,"* which was rice-flour kneaded with sugar, wrapped in bamboo leaves and steamed. *Chimaki* was a special treat for us on May fifth, one of the five seasonal festivals. I don't remember whether he knew *chimaki* or a few other delights that highlighted my life or not. Nonetheless, we shared our secrets and smiled at each other as if those were our ciphered signs. This exchange of our precious past continued until the middle of autumn 1944, about six months into our monastic lives.

***

At the time of *obon,* our *ango,* or the ninety-day practice period, ended. However, the *ango*'s ending did not mean much to us. Our monastic routine continued the same as before. At school, the second term began at the beginning of September. Keidō and I stopped our cozy chitchat. Our conversations had lost their luster and became lifeless clichés. We realized that we were repeating the same stories again and again. In reality, regardless of our enchanting past, the *banka*, or evening chanting, *yakuseki*, or simple evening meal, and *yaza,* or evening *zazen*, always awaited us. The abyss between our fantasy and our reality was so great that our efforts to create a stimulating conversation became futile. The ambrosial food that we had enjoyed in the past was not comparable to what we had at Kyūkoku-ji. The war forced the monastery to trim down our staple food. Often we had a bowl of rice gruel with a few strips of radish or some other vegetable julienne for dinner. Perhaps Keidō and I learned in a natural way that if we attached ourselves to our past, our present reality would be harder to face. In scrutinizing our own experience, we also learned that life is constantly changing without a moment of stillness. Our past would never come back. Attaching ourselves to it would be utterly pointless, especially if both of us were here at present practicing in a monastery. As the *Heart Sūtra* explains:

Avalokiteśvara-bodhisattva, when deeply practicing *prajñāpāramitā*, clearly saw that all five aggregates [all physical, mental, and other elements in this world] are empty and thus became relieved of all suffering ... Sensations, perceptions, formations and consciousness are also like this [devoid of essence].

Therefore, everything is empty. It is empty because all earthly phenomena are impermanent. The world is impermanent because everything constantly changes and the present is inconceivable, or always just out of reach. Furthermore, things seemingly exist only by means of interdependence with other things, including the element of time. There is no eternal and unchangeable substance in them. Instead, there is *"mu"*—nothingness, emptiness, thusness, suchness, zero or *śūnyam*, *śūnya*, *śūnyatā* and many other such terms attempting to describe the nature of reality as groundless. Our questioning the existence of such states does not lead us to peace of mind. One must experience it firsthand through the practice of *zazen*.

***

At Kyūkoku-ji, each of us took turns for just about every role in monastic conducts. Sometimes, I took the role of *inō*, and sometimes the role of *dōan*, an assistant to the *inō*. We used small gongs and bells that had escaped the wartime confiscation. We used wooden instruments in chanting and designated activities. In the monastery, silence is always respected. Percussion sounds signaled certain activities. I also assisted the *tenzo,* or the chief cook of the monastery. Every *shintō,* or newcomer, grew wiser as time went by. We unknowingly acquired confidence in performing rituals in a relatively short time.

Beside Keidō Satō, there was another monk who attended the same school. His name was Keishi Doi. Doi (we called him by his last name) was a year older than Keidō and me, but he failed the examinations and repeated the first year to join our class. The school was quite strict. Nearly a dozen students flunked each year. Doi was of medium build, a tough-looking lad. Since he was a "repeater" his hearty appearance made him a target for bullying by older students. The school's hierarchical system prohibited younger students from any resistance to harassment by those senior students. Doi was often badly beaten and had bruises on both sides of his face. I felt sorry for him, but he was an independent soul and thus quite able to tolerate bullying. Perhaps his arduous life at school helped to make him an obedient and assiduous worker at the monastery.

Doi came from the Shizuoka prefecture, between Tokyo and Nagoya, on the Pacific Ocean coastline. One day in late autumn, he went to his temple and came back to the monastery with a sack of tangerines. He said his temple had an orchard of tangerine trees. He wanted to surprise all of the monks by treating them to "orange marmalade." With a big grin, quite unlike him, he invited everyone, including the older monks, to the kitchen tables one afternoon before *banka,* the evening rite, for the "orange marmalade." Teacups were placed on a long table. We sat beside the table, and he brought out a pot full of hot, orange-scented liquid and began ladling it into each cup. Although it smelled very good, it only tasted like hot water with a faint flavor of tangerine. He laboriously squeezed tangerines and boiled the juice in water without sugar. It was his meager version of "orange marmalade." There was no sugar any-where at the time. I thought this unimpressive liquid to be genuine orange marmalade with simply too much water. Keidō Satō, who had initially told us about the word "orange marmalade," didn't say this was not orange marmalade; he just sipped the drink without any expression on his face.

Years later, in 1952, on the ship to San Francisco from Yokohama on an American cargo line, I ordered "orange marma-lade" at mealtime. The waiter was a bit puzzled but brought me a jam-like substance. I could not believe it and thought he didn't understand my English or rather my less-than-pidgin, so I asked again, "I ordered orange marmalade; please bring it to me." The waiter insisted that was it. I did not pursue the matter further, and just thought the waiter did not know what orange marmalade was. The impressionistic impact of the "orange marmalade" that Keidō and Doi gave me was penetratingly strong, so it took a while to undo it.

***

The middle school system in Japan was in disarray after the war. Many of my classmates did not return to school after the war. Some of them had died and some had lost their houses, or could no longer afford schooling.

The American school system imposed on the Japanese educa-tional system was quite odd. Five years of middle school seat-time was shortened from five years to four years in 1945. Then, after a few years, it was called "high school," and extended to six years including three years of junior high school. Japanese colleges had two years of preparatory school before the three-year university. We were caught in a great confusion during this mixed-up period.

Many students left at the end of four years but I remained in the old middle school system and stayed for five years. I met Keidō Satō occasionally, but I don't remember meeting Doi after Kyūkoku-ji until much later. I knew Keidō Satō went to Komazawa University. After graduating, he headed for the Sōtō Zen priesthood.

Every now and then I thought about Doi's future since he appeared as a tough guy without an academic penchant. In spite of his outward appearance he was a warm and sincere person. I met him in the summer of 1968 when I returned to Nagoya, where my middle school mates had convened a class reunion for the occasion of my return. Quite surprisingly, Doi came all the way from Shizuoka to the reunion. He wore a Zen robe. He had succeeded in becoming a Zen priest. He was then calm, warm, and soft-spoken. His face, motions, and composure had metamorphosed. I couldn't find a trace of the fearless Doi of our middle school days.

When he saw me, he came to me right away and said, "I had to come here today. I heard that you have become a college professor in America besides the role of *kaikyō-shi* (overseas priest). I thought you would become someone like that. Of course, I thought of the connection between you and Keidō. That's very good indeed. I am very happy for you." I replied, "That's so kind of you to come all the way from Shizuoka!" He said, "Yes. Oh, you remember I was from Shizuoka. Of course, I told you that at Kyūkoku-ji, didn't I?" I then asked, "How have you been, since then?" to which he replied, "I left the middle school after the fourth year. You know, academics are not my forte. Then, I went straight to Kasui-sai monastery for four years. After that I went to the Head Temple Sōji-ji for three years. I became the resident priest at the temple where I grew up." I asked, "Do you have family?" He said, "No, I decided to stay celibate. You know, after Kyūkoku-ji, I scrutinized my life with Zen and decided to stay a monk. I am glad I did it.

It's a befitting life for me." He then let out a big laugh. He kept smiling and said, "Do you remember when I made 'orange marmalade' at Kyūkoku-ji? It wasn't good but you said, 'that was a *daigo-mi*'(extraordinarily good taste)." I replied, "Did I say that?" Doi said, "Yes, you did indeed. Your word lifted my spirit. And you added that it was the best taste, equating it to *nirvāṇa*." I didn't remember that remark.

But he added, "Later, I studied the word, *daigo,* and you were right. It was in the *Nirvāṇa-sūtra* and *daigo* (the highest grade and best taste of a milk product) was a metaphor for the state of *nirvāṇa*. I was so impressed with what you said." He smiled and continued, "You know, I make a glass of 'orange marmalade' with the '*daigo*' every morning.*"* I asked, "What is that?" He laughed and said, "I mix tangerine juice and a few spoonfuls of yogurt. It's marvelous. Emperor Daigo was a clever man to name himself 'Daigo,' don't you think?" We laughed together. Indeed, *daigo* is the translation of the best of milk products and, perhaps, yogurt-like substances. Apparently, the "orange marmalade" Keidō taught us made a deep impression on him. I have not seen him since.

***

I met Keidō Satō once after we graduated from middle school. It was at Sōkō-ji in San Francisco when Reverend Tobase was the head of the temple. Keidō visited me there. I, who had heard about Sōkō-ji from him at the Kyūkoku-ji, had become an assistant resident priest, following in his father's footsteps. I pointed to his father's picture hanging in the office; Keidō smiled at me and nodded. This might well be a curious chain of *karma.* Keidō Satō was wearing a handsome business suit and gave me a card indicating his whereabouts. He was the president of an advertising firm in

Tokyo. He told me his father had died in Mié a year after we left Kyūkoku-ji monastery. The temple immediately needed a priest to take his place but Keidō was not ready to assume the abbot seat there. Although Keidō went to Komazawa University and studied further at a monastery, he did not go back to the temple because there was no position for him. Not too long after our meeting at Sōkō-ji, I learned that Keidō died of some unusual illness common for young Japanese adults. Keidō did not even reach his father's age when he died. He was still in his mid-thirties. My brother-in-law, Emi's older brother, Masuó, also died from this unusual illness at age thirty-nine in San Francisco. Some Japanese medical professionals said that this illness was attributed to the prolonged malnourished conditions during our developmental years. No one is certain of what triggered the illness even today.

***

Now, I return to my Kyūkoku-ji days. In October of 1944, due to the war, the middle schools in Nagoya were closed and students were sent to work in factories. My group was sent to the Mitsubishi Aircraft Company in the northernmost edge of Nagoya, not very far from Kyūkoku-ji. It was a large factory comprised of many large rectangular buildings with gray slate roofs and similarly colored walls. I worked in one of those buildings as a lathe operator shaving small metal cylinders day after day. I had to shave them to an exact size; no mistakes were allowed. Concentrating on such minute sizes required serious attention but after awhile it became easy. After three days, everyone was covered with an opaque colored metal cooling liquid with shards of metal pieces. We literally looked and behaved like robots behind our large goggles. Private whispering was strictly prohibited. I simply thought it was one way to meditate. I did my work and paid no attention to others, just as in meditation.

Even though students were forced to work at the Mitsubishi Aircraft Company, there was a special intensive *zazen* practice period at Kyūkoku-ji in December of 1944. If we wished to participate in that we would be excused from work. It was a seven-day *Rōhatsu Sesshin,* or "continual *zazen* from the morning of the first of December to the early morning of the eighth," in commemoration of the Buddha's enlightenment. It was continual sitting except for a short time to eat and a short time to chant. No percussive sounds—from bells, gongs, or wooden boards—were heard during those seven days. The monastery was silent. We were even told to refrain from bathing for the entire period. I was apprehensive about my capability. I was not sure if I could continue to sit for the entire period or not, but I decided to participate. So did Keidō and Doi.

The *rōhatsu sesshin* at Kyūkoku-ji began after the morning routine on December 1, 1944, around eight in the morning. The wooden board in front of the *sōdō* was struck slowly. Thereafter, a cymbal that escaped confiscation was struck to designate the beginning of *rōhatsu sesshin* and then another wooden board was struck several times. Next, the entrance to the *sōdō* was closed with heavy cloth shades. The *inō,* or supervising monk, announced formally, "From this time on, *sesshin* begins."

We began sitting day and night meditating in our *tan* for the period of eight days. The monastery was enfolded in total silence. It was a total quietude yet not at all in repose. I heard the soft cold wind rustling the frosty pine branches beside the *sōdō*. The sound of a breeze soon vanished unknowingly. I could neither hear other practitioners' breathing nor any sound of motion. Silence fell. The walking of a *junkō,* or a monk on duty to go around correcting postures or waking those who had fallen asleep, could not be heard.

The experience was like sitting in the realm of the genesis of the timeless universe and intuiting its primordial scene. I beheld the world's absolute stillness, as though I were getting in touch with the very source of all existence. This was the way my first *rōhatsu sesshin,* or uninterrupted, intensive and extensive *zazen,* began.

***

During the day we did a short slow-walking extension of *zazen* called *kinhin* every hour or two. Short breaks, called *chūkai,* followed after that for about eight to ten minutes. Once a day, I believe in the afternoon, we chanted short prose pieces such as the *Fukan Zazen-gi* or the *Universal Recommendation of Zazen and its Significance.* During this period, I found the second to fourth days to be the most difficult. My legs and spine ached from the prolonged sitting position. In addition, sleepiness and an occasional hallucinating sensation bothered me in the early days of sitting. I also had feelings such as a precarious trajectory between "I-ness" and "other-ness." That is to say, the subject merges with objects; objects entered me and I became those objects. At times, both were wholly fused. In the late hours of night, I slipped away and slept for three or four hours. But at two o'clock in the morning, we were awakened by the muted sounds of our signal to resume *zazen.*

A kind member of the monastery donated a dozen kilograms of genuine wheat flour noodles for the practicing monks. Such an item was extremely difficult to obtain at that time. Around midnight during the first three days, we were served hot noodle soup. The circumstances of sitting in a frigid night amplified the taste of steamy hot noodles; this is for me a savory remembrance. Unfortunately, during the rest of the nights, no noodles were served, since the supply had run out. Considering the wartime food scarcity, we had been lucky just to have noodles on those three days.

December in the *sōdō,* especially in the Nagoya area, was tremblingly cold, particularly in the early morning hours. Furthermore, when we practiced *kinhin* barefoot over the frigid stone floor of the *sōdō,* walking slowly numbed my whole body. My feet were pierced with pain over every little granule or crevice in the floor. Everyone breathed quietly in and out. Each monk's breath was visible—white with vapor. The daylight grew shorter in the early December; daybreak was almost seven o'clock in the morning and the sun set before five o'clock. But to me, sitting still in the *sōdō,* the high contrast of *chiaroscuro* had lost its significance. There was no other pattern in life but my one sitting position.

On the sixth and seventh days, it seemed that I had found my sitting meditation and became congenial to and better integrated with it.

On the eighth day, around one o'clock in the morning, the end of *rōhatsu sesshin, daikaijō,* or the completion of sitting, came. Immediately after the *daikaijō,* the special commemorative service of the Buddha's enlightenment followed. We chanted the sūtra, *Ryōgon-shū,* in Sanskrit transliterated verses. I did not know a word of it, but it had a beautiful and joyous sound. According to the *Pure [Monastic] Rules of Keizan,* the *Keizan Shingi,* these verses have been chanted ever since the founder of the Northern School of Ch'an (Zen), Master Dadong Shenxiu of the late seventh century, chanted them for the safety of confined practice. While chanting it, I had a great feeling of relief, accomplishment, pride, and joy for my first *rōhatsu sesshin.* I thought I had experienced real human time, neither augmented nor diminished. I thought I must carefully keep this feeling alive and tell my mother and N'inyū Yamasaki.

I looked at Keidō and Doi in the dim light. They, too, emanated expressions of relief, joy and visible traces of fatigue.

We went to bed around one thirty on the morning of December 8th. I had to be back at the factory that same day. I left Kyūkoku-ji with Keidō and Doi around seven o'clock. It was a cold, gloomy morning and the streetcar was very congested with passengers. The air inside was steamy as usual.

In the streetcar I told Keidō about my elation after the *rōhatsu sesshin*. Keidō said, "I was going to say exactly the same." We smiled at each other in the crowded cabin of the tram. Although Doi was quiet, we felt a kind of camaraderie among us. Neither the gloomy weather nor the crowded cabin could affect us at that time. Before parting at the factory, Keidō said to me, "My only wish now is to sleep, sleep, sleep, and sleep." I suddenly realized that I, too, wanted to lie down and sleep. I replied, "I feel like that, too. Oh, it sounds so good. Sleep, sleep, sleep." Doi vigorously nodded his head up and down a few times, echoing, "Sleep, sleep," as if he were humming a tune. We really needed a good night's sleep after that eight-day continual meditation.

Rōhatsu sesshin generated a strong affinity among all participants. I participated in two more *rōhatsu sesshins* while I was in Japan; but they did not have as much impact on my life as my first *rōhatsu sesshin* at Kyūkoku-ji. Perhaps this was due to it being a first time experience, and besides, I was more impressionable at fourteen years of age.

***

Ten days after the *rōhatsu sesshin,* on December 18, 1944, the Mitsubishi Aircraft Company where we worked was bombarded in the early hours of morning. Squadrons of Boeing B-29 bombers destroyed the factory almost entirely. In that bombing, I lost a shoe and a sock, and my trousers were torn such that my thigh was exposed, possibly by the blast. The impact of the blast had left one of my thighs blackened without internal injury. However, it did not wash off for two or three days. The explosion was like lightening, a deafening din, and a jolt of earth shaking with a tempestuous wind, all at the same time. Sitting in the air raid shelter for the duration of the bombing seemed like an eternity. Ten or fifteen minutes after the bombing began, my teacher said to us, "The factory is targeted by American bombers. These shelters won't stand the magnitude of the blasts. Let's get away quickly. Listen, when you run to the north, there should be Yahagi River and beyond that will be a vast farm. It will probably be safer there. Let's go. Go quickly!" Then he stood at the mouth of the shelter urging us to run away. He kept shouting, "Go! Go!" and shoved us out. I ran away with several of my classmates. We crossed a bridge over Yahagi River but we did not stop. I heard bomb blasts behind us in the direction of the factory but we kept running madly. The air raid waves ended in about two hours. We stayed in the rice paddy after the raid ended for another hour or so. We then returned to the factory to report that we had survived. Tumbled down buildings stood at the factory site.

Our middle school teacher had been waiting for us at the entrance of the factory and was checking our names. He told us to go home immediately. Some of us had left our belongings inside but the teacher told us not to go back there because of the danger and atrocities that we would see. City streets on the way home had not been affected and people looked upon my appearance, torn trousers and a shoeless foot with curiosity. When I returned to Kyūkoku-ji from the factory, the *inō* said to me, "I heard on the radio that your factory was bombed. I was worrying about you. I'm very glad that you are safe. Your temple is in Nagoya. Why don't you go home and show your healthy face to your family. Don't worry about things here." I went home and everyone was amazed that I had escaped the bombing that day. It was already dark. I told the story of how I escaped the atrocity. No one said anything. Everyone knew it was coming sooner or later, sensing from the earlier Tokyo bombings and the gradual retreat from the warfront by Japanese forces.

The day after the bombing, I went back to the factory at the usual time. Although our air raid shelter was not directly hit, the next shelter where the girls' school students hid was bombed. I saw a large hole and shards scattered around the edge of the large hole created by the blast. I learned that approximately thirty of the students were killed. The section of the Mitsubishi Aircraft Company where we worked had been totally demolished by that air raid. By sheer chance, no student from our school had died from the bombing. Our role now was to help collect the body parts of those who had died during the air raid. I had to pick up body parts of young boys and girls from the ground and shelters. It was an utterly macabre scene. It was cruel to have early teenagers pick up the body parts of their peers. It was a horrific act of violence. Perhaps, I thought, there were not enough adults to do the work or something was very wrong. I felt an unspeakable sense of sadness under a dark and heavy wintery aura. While working, the sūtra the *Verse of Homage to Buddha's Relics* spontaneously came out of my mouth:

With wholehearted reverence we bow
to the relics of the true body
of the Tathāgata Śākyamuni,
who is fully endowed with myriad virtues;
to the dharma body which is the fundamental ground;
and to his *stūpa*, which is the whole universe.

Our awful task was halted mid-afternoon for some reason. We were then ordered to clean the shards off the ground. The Mitsubishi Aircraft Company factory was bombed once again a few months later, but the second time we were readied and left the compound for nearby rice paddies, so the casualties were nil. After a few months we cleaned the ground as well as we could and then our work stopped. The power lathes and power grinders were totally useless and most machines were exposed as they remained in buildings without roofs. They were covered with rust within a few days. Almost all buildings were inoperative. There was an absence of electrical power.

***

On February 11, 1945, or the twentieth year of Emperor Shōwa, Japan celebrated year 2,605 of the country's founding with a little fanfare. In the morning students lined up on the ruined factory site and listened to the Emperor's address on the radio. This day, February 11, was my last observance of the *Kigen-setsu,* the Country Founding Day. The whole city, or rather the whole country, celebrated this day despite the obvious destruction in some parts of Japan. We still sang the song specially composed for this day. The whole event occurring on such desolated ground was to me pretentious and narcissistic. Yet to some, this event was lively. The event leaders hoped to lift our spirits. This was particularly true for an old military officer assigned to our school who was extraordinarily chivalrous. It was indeed a sad scene, as the officer stood alone on the scraps and shards to display his false bravado to a group of teenagers.

Five years earlier in 1940, the Japanese calendar year February 11 was 2,600, which was set as the mythical Emperor Jimmu's day of enthronement according to the *Ancient Chronicle, Kojiki,* and the Japan Chronicle, *Nihon Shoki.* In 1872, the conservative faction of the Meiji government decided on this day as "Country Founding Day." 1940, or the year 2,600 in Japan, was a big event and the whole country celebrated. 1945 happened to be year 2605, a good commemorative year. But the celebration of this year was an un-gesticulated event. We did not receive the good old *rakugan,* chalky cookies. After the war, this event was banished from the calendar entirely.

I returned to Kyūkoku-ji after a few days at Hōsen-ji and stayed there for a few months. My first monastic practice ended near the beginning of March 1945. Kyūkoku-ji had to close down all its monastic activities due to frequent bombings. Acute shortages and rationing of food also added to its closure. A few months after we left, Kyūkoku-ji was burned to the ground.

In March or April of 1945, students were sent to a small airfield, called Nakajima Airfield, in the Peninsula south of Nagoya. The airfield was located nearly an hour-and-a-half by train from Hōsen-ji. Our role was nothing important. We laid patches of grass on a bare, flat field. I suppose that the plan was to create an area of lawn where airplanes could fly in and out. We were machine-gunned by Grumman fighters several times while working there. Fortunately, none of us were killed in those raids. When we saw the fighters, we ran to a nearby rice paddy. On a few occasions, Grumman fighters targeted us but they didn't chase us for long. When we left Nakajima Airfield, the naked ground was diminished but the covered area had still not filled-in enough to give the appearance of a lawn. I also saw a number of holes on the same ground made by the bombardments.

127

What's so distressing about life?
This world moves on,
following the law of causation.
Days and months pass away like waves,
time is a spark off the rocks.
Let heaven and earth shift about!
I'll sit joyfully among these cliffs.

– Shih-té

Chapter 7

DESOLATION DURING THE SECOND WORLD WAR AND ITS AFTERMATH

山も時なり、海も時なり。	Mountains exist in time, seas exist in time.
時にあらざれば	If time does not exist,
山海あるべからず	there must not be mountains and seas.
山海の而今に	At this time of mountains and seas,
時あらずとすべからず。	one ought not think there is no time.
時もし壊すれば	If time ceases to exist,
山海も壊す。	Mountains and seas also cease to exist.
ー道元	- Dōgen
(『正法眼蔵』「有時」)	(*Shōbōgenzō, (Uji)* "Existence in time")

A little over two months had passed since I had left Kyūkoku-ji and returned home to Hōsen-ji. On May 17, 1945, an incendiary bomb had destroyed Hōsen-ji completely.

Japanese houses at that time, made from wood and paper, ignited easily, and were incredibly combustible. For centuries, infamous conflagrations that wiped out numerous lives have been recorded in the early Edo (Tokyo's old name). The same was true in all other big cities. Many earthquakes triggered big fires, which destroyed more of a city than the earthquakes themselves. Narrow winding streets were a good defense against the foot soldiers' invasions but during a fire they were a hindrance to defense. The common Japanese saying, "Most fearsome of all calamities are earthquakes, thunder and lightning, fire, and father." Fathers were no longer fearful disciplinarians after the war, thanks to the post-war worldwide disposition. Earthquakes, thunder, lightning and fire still threatened Japanese lives. Japanese houses, despite their fragile appearance, had withstood many earthquakes but were not fireproof. Lightning also ignited fires. Hōryū-ji temple in Nara, which was built in 607 CE and Shōsō-in, built in 756 CE, are wooden structures that have withstood earthquakes, fortunately escaped fire, and are still standing today.

A few weeks before the May 1945 bombing, extremely strong earthquakes shook the area. My mother told me to go and see how my grandmother was doing even though it was quite late at night. My uncle was drafted into the military service so she was living alone in the house. She was doing alright, but as I was making her makeshift bed on the ground in her backyard away from the house, I remember her saying, "This might be a bad omen." Bad omens seemed to be everywhere those days but I didn't pay much attention to them. However, for some reason I believed her on this occasion. A few weeks later in an instant, an incendiary bomb destroyed our temple, which had withstood numerous typhoons, earthquakes and social upheavals for nearly two hundred years. My grandmother's house, as her omen had predicted, did not escape the resulting fire.

I was still working as a "student draftee" at the Nakajima Airfield when Hōsen-ji was destroyed. The inferno it created was so devastating that eighty to eighty-five percent of the houses in Yobitsugi were destroyed by fire. It was a night raid. The sounds of sirens alerted us. There was a radio announcement that a fleet of Boeing B-29s was approaching the Nagoya area. It was the first time that ordinary households in this area were targeted. In the beginning of the raid, the B-29s approached from a high altitude and dropped incendiary bombs, but after a while, they swooped lower and the planes' silver bodies reflected the color of the flames beneath them. Incendiary bombs split midair into smaller bombs that carpeted a large area. There were so many bombs that even though we had been trained to extinguish fires, it was impossible to stop them all. As we managed to stop one fire, many other bombs ignited and our efforts were utterly useless.

The air raids caused widespread misery. People had to guess where their houses had once stood because the landscape had completely changed after the firestorm flattened the area. Many were searching for lost ones and many others created makeshift signs to tell someone where they could be located or how they could be contacted. Both sides of Tokaidō Road in the town of Yobitsugi were flattened; no buildings escaped the conflagration. Because of the fire, a panoramic view on the south side of the town opened up and continued to the Bay of Isé. Many places that had special value for me were gone. The Kumano Shintō Shrine, Antai-ji and its nursery school, and other Buddhist temples of different sects where I had often visited were gone. Yobitsugi Primary School, where my family members and I had attended, was also gone.

The Yobitsugi Theatre was gone. It had been located at the midpoint between Hōsen-ji and the Yobitsugi School. The theatre had been a place where the townspeople enjoyed offbeat and country-style acting groups. Yobitsugi Theatre was the place where old films had been shown at a third of the regular admission prices. The theatre was definitely rustic. It had a *tatami* floor and theatergoers had to give their shoes to a checker before entering. The entire hall was *tatami*-floored and there were two bridges from the front of the audience to the stage. Often, actors and actresses moved from the stage to the audience section on those bridges in bold gestures of bravado, which people enjoyed immensely. On cold winter nights, people rented cushions and *hibachi,* or small charcoal burning earthen braziers, in which we, although prohibited, cooked sweet potatoes or rice-cakes while watching the show. I have heard that some children occasionally enjoyed innocent escapades like throwing two or three garlic balls into the hot charcoal, which permeated the entire place with a very strong odor. In those days, garlic was not a part of standard Japanese fare, due to the Buddhist influence, and people eschewed it. Buddhist temples usually had a stone post, stating, "Onions, (garlic also), and *saké* should not enter." Anyway, I had been fortunate enough to have a few chances to go to the theatre with my cousins. I remember on the day or two before my theatre-going days I could not sleep because of the excitement. I thought it was one of the most gorgeous places on earth. Now it was gone.

There was a bathhouse called Fukuju-yu, or "Fortune Bathhouse," beyond the railroad station. I had visited it once or twice when my friends asked me to come with them. It was a typical public bathhouse, I suppose. The building space was divided into two sections—one for men and one for women, divided by a six or seven foot wooden wall. I am guessing though because I never went to the women's section. Each section had one large and one small bath made of tile. The large bath, about eight or nine feet in diameter, had clear hot water and the small one had some sort of herb bag floating in it. The color of the water in that tub was dark brown and had an offensive smell. Dressing rooms for each section were in the front with wooden lockers at each side against the wall. A man or woman collected fees to use the bath and oversaw both sections from that seat. Like the Yobitsugi Theatre, this was a communal place and sometimes three or four neighbors went together to bathe. They enjoyed bathing and chatting on these occasions. Bathing in warm water perhaps gave them the relaxation they needed. Hōsen-ji had a bath so I had no reason to go to the public bath. In my limited knowledge, I still think of Yobitsugi's public baths, or the "Fortune Bathhouse," as an auspicious place. That was gone, too. Those places were not major cultural institutions but I still felt regret for their obliteration. They had been important institutions for the community. The town had lost its precious establishments for socialization. When I first revisited Yobitsugi upon returning from America in 1958, the four bathhouses had been reduced to only one. Someone told me that the last one would soon be closed.

***

Fortunately, my mother anticipated the bombing of Hōsen-ji and had asked some workmen to dig a large enough cave in the west slope of the temple hill for an air raid shelter. The cave was secured by heavy timber. The ceiling and walls were partially covered by wooden boards. The ground was also covered with wooden boards. Straw mats were placed on top of the boards. In front of the cave's entrance there was an earthen and wooden boarded wall, three feet thick, ten feet wide and six feet tall. It was a blast screen to protect the cave. She had also arranged for someone to carry selected documents and temple treasures to the cave, such as the founder Gentō Sokuchū's handwritten *Shōbōgenzō*, and three large bronze seals once used by him, all nearly 200 years old. She was determined to save them from destruction. All these things were done while I was still at Kyūkoku-ji or working at the factory or airfield. In spite of my mother's best efforts, family photographs and her best clothing were not saved in this unimaginable situation. I felt odd because I was officially the oldest son and thus responsible for household affairs. Nevertheless, this shelter saved the important documents and implements of the temple from strafing. The Hōsen-ji temple of my childhood, photographs of events and precious artifacts, and our family memorabilia, no longer existed after the temple was bombed.

When I was lying on the floor in the dark air raid shelter looking at the bare wooden board ceiling, many thoughts about our whole existence entered my thoughts. Ontological ambiguity set deeply in my mind. All of existence might be in imagination only. It might be frames in a bad dream. Our situation seemed so hopeless. I fantasized that our lives were in actuality someone else's dream. Someday that person might wake up. Then, our devastated lives would disappear upon his awakening. I was often drawn into this sort of kaleidoscopic fantasy.

***

Change is inevitable. Despite this devastating change of scenery, this colossal destruction did not entirely alter our lives. At Hōsen-ji, all buildings, the *hondō,* main hall, *kuri* (living quarters) and *kōbō-dō* had been burned down to the ground. All we had left were a few small items saved in the cave shelter. Thanks to my mother, a few pots and dishes were saved. The cave was unfit for prolonged living; it was too small for the four of us to live in. It was, after all, eight feet deep, five feet wide, and perhaps four feet high. On top of that, dense moisture inside the cave created musty air, which made it a difficult place in which to live. We lived in those conditions with hopes for enduring peace.

Fortunately, this unbearable condition changed. A few months after the bombing, my mother asked aged workers who were beyond the draft age to help move a small hut belonging to the temple onto the temple grounds. Curiously, it had been in the back of the rental house and escaped the fire. Following Nin'yū Yamasaki's advice, the hut was positioned away from the burned site where we had had no time to clear out the crumbled tiles and earthen walls. Also, the hut was built half-buried in a shallow hole. Our ingenuity was at its best at that time. We thought perhaps it might be saved if there were any more bomb-blasts.

The hut was large enough to place four and a half *tatami* mats inside. The size of a *tatami* mat is approximately three by six feet; therefore, the *tatami*-covered area was about nine square feet. My mother added a small six-by-nine foot wooden floor so that the four of us, soon to be five with my younger brother returning home from dispersal, could be accommodated. It was better than what most people had in those days. However, a 136 square foot area was far too small for my mother and her four almost-grown children. The small hut had no bathing facility, so we had to bathe nightly at the house of my mother's older sister, Aunt Hidé, nearby. Aunt Hidé's house was also burned but since her husband was an oil retailer, they made a temporary bath out of a large oil drum. It was fun to see our cousins and they seemed to enjoy our company.

***

To my knowledge, the summer of 1945 was the only year in the history of Hōsen-ji to not honor the tradition of *obon*. Several weeks after the devastating fire, a truck came to the town with a dozen military police on it. I did not witness this but I was told that they came to arrest Nin'yū Yamasaki. Nin'yū was an outspoken critic of the war. His occasional tirades against the military government made him the town's cause célèbre. He told people that the effort people had spent for that cause was totally wasteful. He said that sincere believers of Buddhism throughout the ages have never taken arms to become aggressors. In the thirteenth century, Muslim invaders massacred almost all Indian Buddhists and destroyed just about all Buddhist sites. The Buddhists did not resist. Buddhism still survived elsewhere. Peaceful resistance was better than the armed aggression that the Japanese military government had instigated in other Asian countries. Furthermore, Nin'yū thought the Japanese military government's aggression was a delayed effort at colonialism and should never have taken place. When Germany had tried colonialism in South East Asia, it was an anachronism. Nin'yū was quite eloquent in elucidating these points. Nin'yū insisted that all Buddhists must uphold "no killing," the first precept of Mahāyāna Buddhism. That was the essence of his criticism. Unfortunately, people were afraid to even listen to him. Soon, he was spotted by an authority and taken to an unknown destination. It was a sudden and unexpected happening that threatened our way of life in this small town. Suddenly, I felt that the world had shrunk and become hostile to such an extent that it was even difficult to breathe. I sincerely feared for Nin'yū's life. I was silent but in my heart I agreed with Nin'yū Yamasaki. "No killing," or *ahiṃsā,* was a justified motto for a small island country like Japan. Furthermore, older men and even the impaired were drafted: men with full dentures, men of extreme myopia who could not read road signs without glasses. Soldiers with false teeth or limited sight did not constitute, in my mind, an élite corps.

Chapter 8

AT HŌSEN-JI

「芭蕉」は、 地水火風空、 心意識智慧を 根茎枝葉、 花果光色とせるゆえに、 秋風を帯して秋風に やぶる。のこる一塵なし、 浄潔といひぬべし。	A banana plant is made up of earth, water, fire, wind, air, heart, mind, consciousness and wisdom— these exist in its roots, trunk, branches, leaves, flowers, fruits, brightness and colors. When the autumn winds blow through, Not a single dust is left. You might say it is clean and clear.
－ 道元	- Dōgen
(『正法眼蔵』「画餅」)	(*Shōbōgenzō, (Gabei)* "A Painted Rice-cake")

Approximately two weeks after the war ended, Nin'yū Yamasaki was released from military incarceration and returned to Hōsen-ji. He mentioned neither his arrest nor the prison where he had spent those months. Once I asked him about his ordeal. He merely replied, "Oh, that? That came to an end when I returned here. I had no *mea culpa* to repent. Everything is clear." For him, he merely adhered to the *bodhisattva* practice; after all, it was in the past and held no significance whatsoever to the present.

My younger brother, Kengo, came home from the mandatory school dispersal program in Kariya, a small country village east of Hōsen-ji. He came home around August twentieth or twenty-first, 1945, several days after the armistice of the Second World War. We were living in our hut trying to figure out what to do next, and how to survive. The temple's members were dispersed and we had a myriad of things to do; yet our foreseeable future was hopelessly in disarray. We welcomed Nin'yū Yamasaki all the more. In order for the temple to be revivified we would need him for its recovery. At the time, we needed a mature monk's wise guidance.

After the war, due to infestations of fleas, lice and ticks, typhus fever swept through Japan, killing tens of thousands of people. My mother often boiled our underclothes in an effort to eradicate lice and tick infestation. It was a losing battle. We picked up fleas, lice and ticks from schools, crowded streetcars, buses, any place where we had contact with people. The United States issued DDT (Dichlorodiphenyltrichloroethane) to cities and villages. In turn, local governments sprayed DDT in various places. They also sprayed our bodies at stations and schools. They sprayed the powdery substance onto us through the openings of our clothing. I was thus completely dusted white with DDT repeatedly. I can recall its chemical smell even to this day. It was a substance to kill insects, but at the time no one knew it was so toxic to human beings as well.

Despite those efforts, my mother contracted typhus and was sent to a segregated hospital. A district worker came to our house and dusted with DDT inside and outside—even in the ditches. I don't remember how many days it was, but my older sister, Minako, then seventeen years of age, visited our mother every afternoon to help and comfort her. Many people were afraid of contracting the disease and my mother was literally isolated in that hospital for over a month. She eventually recovered from typhus and came home. She said many had died there because they were malnourished and their immune systems failed. The typhus epidemic lasted for more than a year. The shortage of food, medicine, and housing, and of course, a related lack of cleanliness, prolonged that epidemic. Those times, I felt, were immutable and the end was not even imaginable.

***

In late 1946 or early 1947, the temple's rental house became vacant. The people who had rented the house decided to go back to their rural home. At a time when building material was impossible to obtain we were fortunate to have our rental house vacated. My mother asked workers to move the house to the site where the *kōbō-dō* had once stood, leaving an open space for a large main hall and living quarters, in case a chance came along to rebuild the temple.

Our activities as a Buddhist temple had halted when the temple was destroyed. But with the relocation of the rental house to a new site on the temple ground, we hoped to resume its services again. It was not a big house but much bigger than the cave or the ad hoc hut in which we had been living. It had six rooms, an entrance area, and a kitchen. The usable area was about seven-hundred-fifty square feet. In the largest room, we created a shrine so that we could recommence temple functions. We felt, after the house was settled on the site and we began living in it, that we had regained breathing space. We could entertain people there. That had not been possible for several years. My older sister Minako's classmates began visiting us and spent some time with us. They were of college-bound age and their presence in the summer nights brought merriment to all of us. They discussed their idealistic aspirations for their future lives with eyes of unrestrained glee. Some were hoping to go to medical school—one of them, in fact, became a medical doctor. Some hoped to go into engineering—none made it. Nonetheless, everyone present was filled with hope. I enjoyed listening to their discussions and wished them future success.

***

General Douglas MacArthur came to Japan on August 30, 1945, from the South Pacific as the Commander of the Allied Forces. The Japanese government became entirely under his control. Those who believed in communism or socialism were purged from public offices completely in what was called the "Red Purge." For a while people pointed fingers at each other, hinting that so-and-so was a "red." It was a mad period. Perennial shortages of food and other essentials continued and there were no visible signs of improvement. People in towns, cities, and the country were wandering aimlessly. Poverty was commonplace, unforeseeably striking even the upper and middle classes.

Every spring during those difficult years, the temple's bamboo grove sprouted thin but tender bamboo shoots. Day-in-and-day-out, we ate those sprouts. At school, friends teased me, saying I was eating real bamboo. We were unaware of pandas then. The bamboo shoots sold in stores were large and pale yellow in color but ours were different. The ones we ate were greenish-yellow and thinner than those but were wonderful and filled our stomachs. Moreover, we enjoyed their succulent taste. Those bamboo shoots helped stave off our hunger. The shortage of foodstuff forced people to eat residues of soy, after squeezing out oils and other nutrients and some weeds such as joint weed (*polygonum*). The shops wherein we were supposed to get our rations had burned down and our vouchers were useless at other shops which were located miles away. Of course, if you had money or connections, you could buy rice from the *yamiya,* or black marketeers. I did not see any signs of hope at that time, let alone the affluence that Japan would have just fifteen years later.

***

A month or so after the armistice, a large number of American military men began appearing in the mid-city, Nagoya. Military headquarters occupied the city's largest Western-style hotel. The inflation rate in those days was phenomenal and the government had to devalue the yen several times. That also caused confusion since yesterday's one-hundred yen became today's ten yen and it was extremely difficult to cope. The devaluation was so quick that the government did not even have time to print new notes, so postage-stamp-sized stickers were issued to paste on the monetary notes.

The Hōsen-ji compound had a large area. Approximately half of the land was unusable for cultivation but my mother, who had no previous farming experience, cleared shards away from the area and began planting maize, wheat, pumpkins, peas, sesame, and all sorts of green vegetables as well as tomatoes. Not all were successful but these crops were enough to sustain us, and we shared any excess with our neighbors. This was in the early summer of 1946; I was still in middle school. A classmate from Yobitsugi Primary School who came home from the naval air force often visited me. He had only been a few months away from being assigned to a suicide plane attack, *kamikaze.* Those assigned to this task were only fifteen or sixteen years old. He told me the predicaments of his naval group. His seniors, only seventeen and eighteen years of age, left the airfield after receiving only enough fuel to reach their target, but not enough to get back. He romanticized those awful stories as if telling me an adventure plot.

It was indeed an absurd time. Honest people worked diligently at companies and their salaries were so meager that they were unable to support their families. Those people's salaries were called "old money." But there was a new type of people with less personal pride, who were engaged in all sorts of black marketeering; they were unbounded legally but immoral. They were called "*yami-ya*," or people of the "business of darkness." The *yami-ya* enjoyed lucrative profits from the "new money." For some people, hunger clearly compromised their sense of morality.

One summer night I heard an unfamiliar noise in the area where we cleared and planted our vegetables. I went out to see what was causing the noise and I saw a man who was leaving hurriedly. I caught up with him. He had a bag full of pumpkins and eggplants. To my surprise, he was one of the old members who had helped the temple selflessly before, during and after the war. He and his family were hungry and he wanted to pick a few vegetables for them. I sincerely regretted that I had caught him taking vegetables from the temple and was embarrassed, too. He put the bag on the ground and began apologizing to me, a young lad barely a fourth of his age. I wasn't sure what to do but I started to pick a few more maize ears and put them into his bag. I probably said, "It's all right. It's all right." I had no words of consolation for him. I remember that moment vividly. When I returned to the house, my mother asked, "Wasn't that Tomi-san? Why didn't he come in?"

I told her what had happened. My mother said, "How sad. Oh, they were hungry. He wanted to feed his wife, too. My goodness,

his family has belonged to this temple for so many generations."
She paused for a second and then continued. "They were in one
of the wealthiest groups before the war. How sad it is. What can
we do to help him?" I said, "I think we should just keep quiet and
do nothing." My mother said, "I wonder if they would come here
if I invite them for lunch in a week or so. In any case, I shall send
him vegetables." Tomi-san was one of the honest people who now
had only a very meager "old money" income. His old money was
not enough to buy food to fill his stomach and that of his wife. He
and his wife were semi-retired and had a small shop manufacturing
straw hats. Their two sons were killed in the early part of the war.
Perhaps the straw hat business did not earn enough to sustain their
lives. He was one of many people who were in a similar dilemma,
which was not an unusual predicament of the times: to choose to
be ethical and suffer starvation or to be amoral and survive. When
I was thinking about his situation, images of a *yami-ya*'s roué posture came to my mind. I thought to myself, what a contrast to that
of Tomi-san's modesty.

Human beings learn ethical norms from the communities in
which they live. It is like an understanding of the color spectra
while growing up in a familiar language. That is to say, how and
what color words are included in the languages of their communal
systems. Acquiring a particular ethic works like the Sapir-Whorf
hypothesis; by living in a given language-society, an individual
learns particular ethical parameters defined by its communal ethos.
Those people consciously accept those premises. The communal
society molds each individual into a moral being and in return each
is protected by the community and given a comfortable sense of
solidarity. Many envied the wealth of the *yami-ya*. At the same
time they shunned them because of their disrespect for communal
ethics. The *yami*-ya and their new money did not adhere to the

communal bonds, so they were "outcasts." I could imagine how Tomi-san's sense of pride had been hurt since he was a respected elder among our townspeople.

In any case, the only thing I could think of for Tomi-san to rid himself of this stigma was to seriously practice Buddhism. Of course, he could not quench his thirst or relinquish his hunger but he would come to know where our desires come from. He would come to understand the weakness of humankind. In my own life I had experienced this teaching found in the "Eight Enlightenments of Great Human Beings," while living at Kyūkoku-ji. Gyokusen first told me of this but at that time it was only a theory. I later realized its meaning through my experience living at the monastery. The "Eight Enlightenments of Great Human Beings" was taken from *The Last Teachings* [*of the Buddha*], the *Yijiaojing,* or in Japanese, *Yuikyō-gyō,* the essence of the *Nirvāṇa-sūtra,* in which the Buddha summed up all of his teachings. Dōgen, according to his disciple Ejō, also rewrote this in his last teachings. A concise summary of Dōgen's treatise "Eight Enlightenments of Great Human Beings" is as follows:

"I call this 'the eight enlightenments of great human beings,' because they contain the enlightenment of all buddhas who are great human beings. To realize these would be the foundation of enlightenment."

The gist of the "Eight Enlightenments of Great Human Beings," compiled in the last chapter in the *Shōbōgenzō*, is as follows:

The first is to <u>have less desire</u>. In the realm of the five desires (relating to eyes, ears, nose, tongue, and body), one must not have many and must not pursue them.

The second is to <u>know that what you have [now] is enough</u>. To already have embraced [enough] in the dharma world (world of existence) and to limit getting [more]; this is to know you have enough.

The third is to <u>enjoy quietude</u>, in which you disallow others and [even] yourself from disturbing this state of being and live solitarily in space [to liberate your mind and body]. This will enable you to eradicate the cause of suffering.

The fourth is to <u>practice assiduously</u>. That means practicing all dharma diligently without rest. Even a small drop of water can make a hole if it is constantly dripping.

The fifth is to <u>uphold the dharma and not let it escape</u>. If you do not lose the dharma, there will be no place for "worldly desires," or *kleśa*, to enter.

The sixth is to <u>practice meditation</u>, or *dhyāna,* which is to dwell on the dharma and not let it be interrupted. [That is the constancy of the state of meditation in which you and the world are one.] That state is called "steadfast concentration," or *samādhi.* If you are in *samādhi,* you will realize the comings and goings of the world [dharma nature].

The seventh is to <u>practice [and acquire] "true wisdom,"</u> or *prajñā.* If one holds *prajñā,* he practices neither attachment nor rejection. He is liberated within the realm of dharma.

The eighth is to <u>detach oneself from [ordinary and intellectual] understanding</u>. When we can thoroughly penetrate the true forms [of the world], we can detach ourselves from [ordinary] understanding.

Thereafter, we can enjoy [blissful] quietude.

Each of these eight enlightenments is interwoven with the others; therefore, altogether there are sixty-four, but more broadly, they are infinite. The Buddha taught this last discourse, according to the Mahāyāna tradition, on the fifteenth day of the second month [lunar February fifteenth], the day of his *Parinirvāṇa,* the complete *nirvāṇa*, meaning his death. Even though I was instructed about this teaching, I did not know what to say to Tomi-san to ease his embarrassment. I had neither the eloquence to explain, nor the diplomacy to lecture a man over sixty years of age. Tomi-san stopped coming to the temple for nearly a year after that incident. I visited his house, chanted before his family shrine once a month as I had done before. Each time I brought a small bag of vegetables from our yard and left them on the table at his shrine. It was awkward at first but the situation eased as time went by. His wife once thanked me by bowing her body on bended knee for a long time. We were so glad when he came back to Hōsen-ji. For me, this teaching was a great help when I myself was facing serious predicaments, such as attachment to the ghosts of mundane matters while living in the monastery. When I attached myself to the ghosts, I paid less attention to the true reality of life around me. I was obsessed with the attachments themselves. I became a slave to the ghosts. Yet those things I desired were not easily obtained, especially in the monastery. Buddhist teachings, at times when I went astray with my unceasing desires, were especially precious in my experience. "Peace of mind," or *anjin,* is the term denoting acquisition of quietude after extinguishing the passion of "worldly desires."

***

I was learning Buddhist teachings through my life experience. It may sound simple but it was not at all. I was an ordinary young teenager growing up in war-torn Japan, where nothing was easily obtainable and no place was easily accessible. Largely pre-war American and European films featured utopian idols who lived in unreachable fantasies. The dreams for all people in those days were unaccountably fantastic. My dreams were no exception. Without knowing, I was entrapped in what Francis Bacon called "*idola*" ("prejudices" and "misconceptions") in his *Novum Organum*. I wanted comfort with clothes, food and other provisions for living like those people in the films. However, those were phantom desires that had to be chased away. I chased them, but I came to the point where the chases were useless. Even if I had obtained what I was chasing, the ghosts would recede only temporarily. The same problem recurred and in the end the problems would prevail. There was no repose. Perhaps I had *idola specus,* or misconceptions from living in a cave-like confinement. All of us are creatures entrapped in our own little world. For me, homage to the Buddhist tenets seemed a natural course since I was living in a monastic environment.

However, the monastic environment of Hōsen-ji was not a sequestered enclave, but in the middle of the hustle and bustle of the unenlightened world. It took some years for me to reconcile this polar discrepancy. Several years later when I was engrossed in Dōgen's major works, the *Shōbōgenzō,* or the *Treasury of the Eye of the True Dharma,* I found that he spent great effort to teach his students what mind is and what the diversity of nature is. Some of those chapters are: "Mind is itself Buddha" or "*Sokushin Sokubutsu*," "Body and Mind Studying the Way" or "*Shinjin Gakudō*," "Ancient Buddha Mind" or "*Kobusshin*," "Three Worlds are One Mind" or "*Sangai Yuishin*." One of those chapters, "Expounding Mind, Expounding Nature," or "*Sesshin Sesshō*," of the *Shōbōgenzō* states the following:

> All in all, the merits of all dharma ancestors are nothing but the expounding of mind and nature. There is ordinary ex-pounding of mind and nature, and also that of walls and tiles [that have no mind]. That is to say, the mind arises [first] and all other existence arises after. If the mind ceases, then all other existence ceases. However, arising and ceasing of the mind occurs; yet on the other hand, mind and nature are one in "expounding" (of the Buddha-dharma, or the truth of everlasting existence).

Dōgen then introduces the anecdote attributed to a Chinese Ch'an (Zen in Japanese) master, Dahui Zonggao (Ta-hui Tsung-kao):

> Later, a person named Zonggao, the Ch'an Master Dahui of Mt. Jing (Jingshan Ching-shan) said, "People today like 'expounding mind and nature' and discussing profound and difficult issues. Therefore, their attaining of the Way [of Buddhism] is slow. One must discard both mind and nature, and forget about the profound and difficult. When both do not arise (reaching the state of non-discrimination), you will have proof of attainment. This understanding is ignorant of the Buddha-ancestors' teaching and ignores the noble teaching of Buddha-ancestors."

From the last sentence, we know Dōgen did not recommend Dahui's practice of Zen. That is to reduce the movement of mind and nature to nil by intentionally discarding them. Movements of mind and nature are essentially free and we cannot discard them. Dōgen contrasted Dahui's thought on mind and nature to that of Huike's. Huike was the disciple of Bodhidharma, the first dharma-ancestor of Zen in China:

> Once, the First Dharma-Ancestor (Bodhidharma) said to the Second Ancestor (Huike, Hui-ké), "You must stop any relations with the outside [world]. Your mind must not succumb. Keep it like a wall and tile [which have no-mind] and enter into the Way.

> The Second Ancestor attempted the state of "expounding mind and nature" yet he did not reach that state. One day, however, awakened suddenly, he told the First ancestor, "Your disciple, for the first time, stopped relations with the outside."

> The First Dharma-Ancestor knew it right away, so he did not ask further questions. He merely asked, "Did you cut [yourself] off completely or not?"

> The Second Ancestor said, "No, not at all."
> The First Ancestor asked, "What is that?"

> The Second Ancestor said, "I know [everything] clearly all of the time, so that I cannot describe it in words."

> The First Ancestor said, "That is the mind which is conveyed from all the buddhas and dharma-ancestors. You now have hold of it. Keep it with you and guard it."

Dōgen's view on mind and nature is free, like the experience of the second dharma-ancestor, Huike. We are alive and making our life in this world. We cannot cut ourselves off from the surrounding world. It is important to experience every relationship with the outside yet not attach to *idola*. Someday, I sincerely hope I can get out of my *idola specus* (perceptual illusion of caves) so that I can relate to all existence without any hindrance.

In my Buddhist studies, I learned the stance of my being. Buddhism teaches that our human existence is a condition based on a twelve-link chain of causes-and-effects, or *dvādaśānga-pratitya-samutpādah*. They are as follows:

(1) ignorance (2) innate power to create (3) consciousness (4) name and form (mind-body) (5) six sense faculties (eye, ear, nose, tongue, body, mind) (6) perception, objects of the six sense faculties (7) inclination and impulse toward something likable (8) attachment to something likable or aversion toward something not likable (9) attachment (10) continual existence (11) birth [of the next stage of life] (12) old age and death

Each of the above categories depends on the previous category, just as the previous category creates the condition for the later categories so that our own beings are interconnected. For this reason, if the previous category ceases to exist, the latter category naturally ceases to exist as well. If indeed it is true, would I be free of any predicament? What were the causes and conditions that led to the predicament? I am not free as long as I have not relinquished the causal links.

Buddhism has taught me to realize that I am here now, being just as I am. My present being is the result of previous links. First, an unknown force creates an innate power to become a being. A sort of selection process works next. As a result of this selection process, I was born as a human being. Solidarity of name (*nāma* or mind, known only by name) and form (*rūpa* or color, visible body) have now been created. Immediately, my six sense faculties of eyes, ears, nose, tongue, body, and mind begin to develop and connect me to the world. Through these senses, I have learned that some things are agreeable and some things are not; some things are pleasant and some are not. Some of this I learned through direct experience (*hetu*, primary premise), and some through someone else's guidance (*pratyaya*, contributory causes), such as that of my mother or father. All karmas occur in connection of *hetu* and *pratyaya*. My existence now is the result of those causes and conditions. My character was being formed and molded into a particular being through these continual recurrences of actions, or *karma*. I shall undoubtedly continue to create causes that form my future being—which is also myself in the present moment. This is the chain of cause-and-effect, which further leads to the perpetual repetition of life-and-death. Shall I be able to unfold my disposition and, thereby, theoretically, be able to banish a good many of the ghosts that had been haunting me? In Zen, this categorical interpretation of human suffering is only accepted as a part of the general Buddhist tenets. We thus hear that our suffering is based on our ignorance—the first of this chain of action. But as long as we are here, our present existence is already the result of the causal chain; we cannot deny having perceptions through the six senses. Can we discard them, as Dahui taught his students? Isn't Huike's experience of knowing everything but not attaching to it better? Is the theory of the causal chain, which presupposes dire life or death consequences, incompatible with Zen's belief in reincarnation? Furthermore, if reincarnation *(saṃsāra)* is not accepted, sequential and perpetual recurrence of life and death does not occur; this would free us from life and death, and thus from *saṃsāra*.

In those days, learning Buddhism was an eye-opening experience for me, yet at the same time Buddhist teaching was an inconceivable enormity to grasp. I felt as though I were removing a thin
flat piece of ice from the surface of an iceberg. But I was destined
to continue the monastic course as I was trained to that point and
my family and temple members remained firm on that idea.

***

Now, let me return to post-war Japan. American educators dismantled
the Japanese educational system, which had been in use since 1873.
A new American educational system was installed in 1946. Certain
existing courses were thought to be incubating militarism and fas-
cism. They were banned immediately. One of the first courses the
American educators prohibited was on Confucian morality, which
was considered feudalistic. I did not believe it was a good idea to
omit ethics from the curriculum, but the American educators must
have believed that those ethics were oppressive to children's growth.

The society, nonetheless, continued molding each individual
into a moral being even with the absence of express moral teaching.
American educators implemented quite a few ideas in the Japanese
educational system. One of those ideas was the "homeroom" arrangement, which allowed teachers and pupils to convene on a
regular basis. Corporal punishment was condemned. They also encouraged class discussions and voting exercises.

At the time, these ideas were foreign to the Japanese tempera-
ment. Japan was accustomed to Confucian hierarchical arrangements
between teachers and pupils. At first, discussions using the parliamentary system were handled quite clumsily by the children and their
teachers. Their voting and choosing a delegate among themselves
were both difficult tasks. Teachers were accustomed to assigning

roles in the class. As for making public speeches, that was torture. The candidate had to convince the voters by saying, "I am good, so vote for me!" This program of acculturation rather than reform of the educational system went against a long-entrenched grain. American music was introduced into the school system. It was perfectly all right to include a wide variety of subjects but I thought it was a bit strange to include several popular American hymns as part of the new music program in Japanese primary school curricula. Transition from the old educational system to the new was totally unexpected and awkward.

As mentioned earlier, I stayed in the old middle school system and graduated after five years. It was 1947 and I was seventeen years of age. When I was about to go to college, higher education had just been transformed into a new system. But the system did not change overnight; the students who had already matriculated in the old system had to finish their courses within that system. Thus, the two systems coexisted for several years. The country's educational system had to absorb students in the old system and repatriated soldiers who were college students before their conscription had to be readmitted. The transitional period was confusing. For one year, in 1949, a special examination for sophomore-year entrance to a government university was given. Why the second-year entrance? Had the change of system created vacant seats?

I never really found the answer. But I fortunately had the chance to matriculate in the sophomore year. The university system lasted three years after the five-year middle school and the two-year high school in the old system. The new system was 6-3-3-4 years, counting from primary school to the university, respectively, and the old system was 6-5-2-3. The total number of years of education in both systems did not change.

***

Aside from the university system, in the summer of 1945, people of Yobitsugi had curious times. Retrospectively, one episode was quite amusing. On the outskirts of the town of Yobitsugi on the north side, deposits from the Yamasaki River created alluvial earth near the river. That was the lowest part of the town. The area was not much higher than sea level. Right before the war, a wealthy man named Ogasawara started a frog farm on part of their land. My understanding was that a shady businessman lured Mr. Ogasawara into this business. The initial idea was to export frogs to France for food and, if possible, cultivate Japanese peoples' palates for that food. Ordinary Japanese citizens had never heard of eating frogs. Mr. Ogasawara had a large pond in his backyard and the area was fenced in with thin wire, much like chicken wire; this designated space became his farm. Then the war broke out and he could not export his frogs for use in French cuisine.

After a while, the wire rusted and rotted away. Large bullfrogs began escaping from the farm and invaded a section of town. In that peaceful town, people slept on sweltering summer nights without closing windows and doors. At first, I liked the humorous appearance of the frogs and their low-pitched baritone voices. Then, on several occasions, my sleep was interrupted by cold, soft, heavy and rubbery frogs landing on my face.

Japanese people use firm comforters, *futon*, to sleep upon their *tatami* mats. The floor is raised a foot or slightly higher with steps. Those frogs invaded most houses in Yobitsugi and wrought tremendous havoc. The temple was on high land and was dryer than the low area where Ogasawara's farm was located, but still some frogs came up the Hōsen-ji hill and entered the house through open windows. Several yards from the living area of Hōsen-ji on the south side, there was a small pond that might have attracted frogs. The whole town cried out because of that frog invasion. Frogs, although large and ugly to many, were beneficial and did not harm humans in any way. Still, they were a nuisance. People had a lot to say to each other and the topic of their conversations always centered on the frogs' intrusion into their lives.

Contrary to Mr. Ogasawara's dream, frogs still had not entered into the Japanese people's dietary imagination. The people of Yobitsugi tended to be naïve in general, far from the vanguard of culinary adventure and were bound by small-town cultural constrictions. Mr. Ogasawara was Gatsby-like and his antagonistic stance created a high barrier, such that no one in town could complain to him. I don't even know whether he was a connoisseur or if he had ever consumed frog legs. His house was burned down in the war and he did not come back to Yobitsugi. I don't even know whether he had a family or not. I had never met Mr. Ogasawara. I don't know anyone in the town who knew him. He was a rich, mysterious person and his house gate was always closed. Because he was rich and reclusive he could get away with ignoring the townspeople.

In social settings, it seems sometimes that the very top people and very bottom people have much more freedom than those who fall into the middle classes. A policeman stationed in the town was caught barbecuing frog-legs in his backyard by a neighbor and the rumor spread overnight. People began looking at him and his wife with unfriendly eyes because they ate frogs. Frogs had never, for some reason, been included in the Yobitsugi people's tray of hors d'oeuvre or menus of entrées. In those days, the majority of the nation was malnourished. People had pale complexions and were extremely underweight. Many had died from malnutrition. Yet, they did not consume any of the frogs that had invaded our town.

Years later, in San Francisco, my wife and I were invited to a friend's house for dinner. One of the food-containers had what looked like chicken legs. I picked one up and while I was starting to eat, the host came near us and said, "Do you like the frog legs? They are good, aren't they?" I almost dropped the frog leg I had attempted to put in my mouth. All my memories of frogs came to mind at once, especially that summer frog invasion. I looked at my frog leg and pondered whether I should eat it or not. It looked very much like a small chicken leg and it was covered with a crust and fried, resembling fried chicken legs. In fact, I had been tempted to eat it because I picked it up and put it on my plate. I had an aversion to eating frogs like the Yobitsugi's townspeople, but I did eat the frog leg. A few minutes later, I realized how misleading our senses could be and how easily misunderstandings occur. The frog leg was delicious after all. They might have saved quite a few lives in Yobitsugi or for that matter in Japan.

***

Asian sub-continent Indians have many stories regarding superficial misconceptions that divert people from their true identities. They tell us of people who mistake a rope for a snake. Then there is a story of the three blind men touching different parts of an elephant. One understood it to be a rope when touching its tail only. Another understood it as a pillar when touching the leg. During our lifetimes we might unknowingly misidentify many objects.

Mahāyāna Buddhism supports the notion that everything we see and touch has no lasting substance. The *Diamond Sūtra* or *Vajracchedika prajñāpāramita Sūtra* states:

> All existing dharmas [things] of *saṃskāra* [something which has risen],
> are like dreams, fantasy, foam, or shadows,
> and also they are like dew drops or like lightning.
> You must view things in this way.

It expounds emptiness, or *śūnyatā*, which is essentially *prajñā*, or wisdom. Is there any difference between frog legs and chicken legs if both are in *śūnyatā*? That might be the reason why the Buddha ate everything he received as alms from ordinary households during his entire fifty-one years of travels before and after his enlightenment. In mendicant practice there is no luxury of discrimination regarding food, clothes or habitation.

So I ate a frog leg. It had a light, sweet, delicate taste. My bygone aversion to frogs faded away. Every experience such as that reminds me of the tenets of Buddhism, which I have acquired over the years and have often solved my predicaments or suffering. Those teachings come quite naturally when I start to face a problem. This time with the frog leg, I had also realized the primary teaching of the Buddha—the Four Noble Truths, or *ārya-satyāni catvāri*. The Four Noble Truths were the primary contents of the Buddha's enlightenment after six years of rigorous ascetic practice. The above cause-and-effect chain was appertained to the Four Noble Truths. They are:

All existence is suffering,	*Duhkha*
the cause of suffering is illusion and desire.	*Samudaya*
Nirvāṇa is the realm free from suffering.	*Nirodha*
This is the way to attain *nirvāṇa*.	*Mārga*

I then understood that our sufferings inevitably come from our own ignorance. Illusions and desires were leafy boughs branched out of our ignorance, *prima facie* cause of suffering. I saw things as having a momentary existence, like an instant flash of lightning, and as having no more substance than a shadow. It was the most sensible solution to eradicate the causes of our suffering. It was in that moment that I lived and that moment was too expeditious, with no time for cause-and-effect.

The post-war continuum in Japan pervasively remained for four or five years. Transportation systems were slowly repaired and began to run on a normal schedule. The gaps in the qualities and provisions of the system were an entirely different issue. When I visited a few friends in Tokyo, it took over eight hours by express train to cross the distance of two hundred and fifty miles. And trains were, to say the least, overcrowded. Once I moved my leg in one position, I could not move it into any other position for awhile; moreover, I was almost suffocated by the lack of air in the crowded cabin. Such scenes were common and signs of improvement were slow coming. It remained a tumultuous period, despite the people's hope for the dawn of a better time.

Dissolute young men and women were roaming around everywhere, ignoring the ethos. Some of them had no family, no job, no money, no decency, and no moral criteria. I had the experience of getting roughed up on several occasions by those rascals and my meager pocket money was taken away by them. Once, I came home with black eyes and swollen lips. My mother at that time asked me why I was injured. I could not answer truthfully and told her I had bumped my head on a pole. She did not pursue it any further, as she knew better. What little I had learned in martial arts could not help at all. Gangs of thugs who wore oversized zoot suits or loud-patterned "aloha-shirts" were suspicious and we could not go near them. Some young women became prostitutes. I suppose they desperately needed income for survival. Some pretended to be risqué in their motions but they could not hide their tender age in speech and smiles. Unlike the typical chignon hairdo worn by most Japanese women of that time, those women had short, permed hair. They wore décolleté blouses with long flared skirts to hide the fragile ingénue. They hung about the railroad stations to pick up men. They were called *pan-pan,* which came from American G.I. jargon.

Some desperate ones even pulled on my school-uniform sleeve at the railroad station. I was in my late-teens then.

Many people could not recover from their incredible sacrifice and the loss of those who had been consumed by the bombs and fires. Shortages of food, clothing, and shelter remained for a few more years. A lack of ethical sense lingered on among some of the population. The agglomeration of ordeals resulting from the war and its holocaust effects were so unimaginably large that people were unable to fully realize all that had happened. It was more real and crueler than Dante's *male bolgia,* or the inferno of infernos, in the *Divine Comedy.* The old established Gemeinschaft ethos was gone. The outlook of the country and our surroundings was bleak. Due to famine and illness, we did not know whether we would survive until tomorrow.

One of those hopeless times was when I saw a framed copy of calligraphy on the wall at my classmate's house. It was a Japanese Rinzai Zen master, Ikkyū (1575-1645), who wrote the word "Dream" in bold brush strokes before his death as his last verse. Then he added in smaller script the following:

One hundred years, thirty-six thousand days.
Are there Bodhisattvas Maitreya or Kwanyin?
It is a dream and yet it is not a dream.
Maitreya is a dream and Kwanyin also is a dream.
Buddha said, 'one must see that way!'

Ikkyū was seventy-three years of age when he wrote it. Did he think of human life as a moment of a dream in the lasting reality of this all embracing cosmos wherein our life comes and goes? If in fact that was so, what I thought of as "I," or "reality," or the "time" I spent could not be real. The previously quoted *Diamond Sūtra* tells us that every existing thing is a dream or foam that instantaneously appears and disappears. "All existing dharmas [things] / are like dreams and foams / or like thunder and lightning."

The sūtra is not intended to prove physical existence but instruct one to view the entire physical world in such a way that the viewers will not attach themselves to any part of the dharma world. We are living in the world of things and those things are, in fact, the contents of our life. There is no place wherein things do not exist. Even when we think of a vacuum, the vacuum is a positive presence encapsulating a void.

What about time? I often come to this question and have dwelled on this subject before. Does time exist as is? I must say yes, when we think of time, we translate time into certain events or things around us. That is why we keenly feel the existence of time when we return to the silhouette of our homes in the evening dusk; that is a vivid reminder of time between daylight and darkness. When we wake up in the dead of night, or when we celebrate New Year's Eve at midnight—between the last year and the next, we feel some sort of ambiguity about ourselves in the midst of our awareness of time change. Without time we cannot conceive of things outside or within our own minds; however, we then realize time is also an object to us. Our perception of time is our own "human time," a subjective time. Our commonly used time is the "clock time" upon which our civilization is based. It is quantitative, objective and regular, whereas our human time is qualitative, subjective and often irregular. We perceive all things as objects—things outside of us, and those inside of us such as our perceptions and imaginations. In our perceptions, we can also imagine things, or the "idea of things." We idealize time, color, speed and temperature; yet these exist as concepts, not things. Our ambiguities about the concept of time-change are mere fabrications of our minds. Our ideas of an outer and inner world are organized into sequences of time, which present us with our perceptions of "order." Those ideas are the very fabric of ourselves and translate into our "time."

Time does not pass evenly between individuals. We use time in our daily life as the time we need to do something or how much time we have until a certain occurrence happens, not a physicists' measured time. Our life centers on our constant awareness of outer and inner changes and movements—that is time. We cannot conceive of a timeless world. Ikkyū's poem suggests that one hundred years or thirty-six thousand days are dreams.

As far back as I can remember, possibly from five or six years of age, I recited the *Heart Sūtra* at Hōsen-ji day in and day out. It contained a passage, "O Śāriputra, all dharmas are marked by emptiness—they neither arise nor cease, are neither defiled nor pure, neither increase nor decrease. Therefore, given emptiness, there is no form, no sensation, no perception, no formation, no consciousness; no eyes, no ears, no nose, no tongue, no body, no mind; no sight, no sound, no smell, no taste, no touch, no object of mind; no realm of sight... no realm of mind or consciousness." I did not understand the meaning of these words but the question lingered on for years. Many years later, I believe in college, I asked Gyokusen why everything is denied its existence in the sūtra. His answer was that since everything is in a state of perpetual change, we are unable to grasp the true nature of reality. Therefore, what we see or touch is not the true state of things. It is just the glimpse of a form in a fleeting moment. Material objects are thus called "emptiness," because they are only a passing state and not the true form of existence. Again, I asked Gyokusen, if things are evanescent then would we still perceive them in their momentary existence? What about our perceptions of that instant, which we see and touch? He did not answer my question on that day but days later he gave me meticulously written notes consisting of about fifty pages. Gyokusen was an ineloquent speaker and not terribly persuasive so he often prepared notes when he explained my questions. He gave me the note saying the question is only of academic interest so just read it as such.

He mentioned the question of time had been continually pondered since the dawn of civilization in the West but not much in the East. He then told me that Aristotle presented two arguments. The first is that time does not exist since the past no longer exists and the future, which has not yet arrived, does not exist either. In this framework, time appears to not exist. Then the question follows—what about now? He explained that the now we are experiencing would be a different "now" from the "now" that has just passed. Time, however, exists universally and in seemingly absolute intervals. We can measure time intervals of events and that interval measurement remains constant regardless of person or place. If time did not exist, movement and change could not exist. We would generally think that the very nature of movement and change inevitably entails time-intervals. But Aristotle did not include time in his argument on motion and transformation. Change consists in a substance or matter but not in time as such. Time apparently exists independent of spatial changes. Furthermore, his paper explored Isaac Newton who believed, like Aristotle, that the existence of time and space is absolute. Thus, time for him is independent of space. Gyokusen explored St. Augustine, Bergson, Heidegger, and many other people who elaborated on the theory of time. Bringing Aristotle and other western philosophers in to interpret the content of my question was extremely generous. But my initial question was from the *Heart Sūtra* specifically, so I felt a bit awkward. Besides, it was too difficult a concept and I did not understand his generous interpretation thoroughly. I imagine he spent a lot of time preparing to answer my question. On his notes, he wrote if my question on time was in Dōgen's teaching of time; western philosophy did not give clear answers for its purpose was on an entirely different plane. Western philosophies began as *philos* (love) of *sophia* (knowledge); historically, philosophers randomly investigated all phases of ideas and matters irrespective of their academic or social significance. On the other side, Dōgen's concept of time and space was clearly directed to give peace and freedom in life.

Didn't Ikkyū point this out by writing "dream" in his last statement before his death? When a child plays, the child is absorbed in the act of playing. When people are absorbed in reading, they have no notion of themselves. Similarly, when one is listening to music or looking at an art object the listener or viewer often loses the notion of self. This state is the state in which subject and object become one. However, once one recognizes that "I" am listening or looking, or "I" is identified, the subject and object are separated out from each other. If one is constantly in that undifferentiated state, there would be no notion of "I"; thereby life or death would not pose any problem.

Likewise, neither the past nor the future exists for there is no fixed notion of time. In this way, we realize that the concept of time in our minds is conditioned on the premise of having an "I." The word "dream" that Ikkyū wrote in the last moment of his life was truth, realized after one casts off the common sense of reality. In that state, there would be no Maitreya or Kwanyin. Both of them are "dreams" and so are one hundred years.

I had recited the *Diamond Sūtra* countless times since fifth grade. But in the midst of the unrealistic devastation and futile deaths of the war in my everyday physical reality, it was extremely difficult to see the world as "dream." Thinking about Ikkyū's simple verse, my mind became a ball of tangled flax. If this life were a dream, my dream had colors, shapes, weights, substances, some likable and some not, and my life, death, laughter and tears—all existed as real. They were not dreams, nor foam, nor lightning; but if not, then what was my real life?

***

I have been describing the dark side of our lives in the *après guerre* or the post-war period but there were also bright spots that sprouted up in that era. I was always fond of reading prose and poetry, and thanks to the publication of those works by some writers and poets immediately after the war, I had no shortage of reading material. Furthermore, although I could not attend, there were plays and musical concerts in Tokyo. It was as though they were waiting for the war to end so that these activities could resume. Every time I saw advertisements for those events in the paper, I was envious of the artists' enthusiasm and tenacity in pursuit of their goals. These events were mostly in Tokyo. Nagoya had to wait several years until the cultural milieu in the area returned to normal. Travelling to Tokyo to see those performances, for me, was too decadent to even think about.

On December 26, 1945, several companies of actors got together and performed Anton Pavlovich Chekhov's *Cherry Orchard* in Tokyo. It was only four months after the end of the war. The theatre they were going to perform in had escaped the war's destruction. It was perhaps an opportune time in Japan to lift spirits (or some might see it as an anachronism) but I saluted the ardent pursuit of artistic interests. I had never seen the play, but I read it. The landowner, Ranevskaya, faced ruthless time changes and had to sell her cherry orchard to Lopakhin. After obtaining the orchard, Lopakhin destroyed it and erected houses. As the Ranevskaya family prepared to leave, there were echoes of an axe chopping down cherry trees offstage. I did not know how well this play was evaluated. But it might have pierced the audiences' hearts with pathos by reminding them of the social changes they were facing. The play depicted changes occurring over time; in Japan, there were mass retreats of old Ranevskyas and the coming of new arrivistes, Lopakhins.

The *après-guerre*, or post-war period, was the word used in Japan to describe that rapidly changing era after the war. Much of the amoral activity went unpunished, and was instead written off as *après-guerre*. The zoot suit men and *pan-pan* girls were a few of the *après-guerre* phenomena. *Kasutori* (a low-grade distilled alcoholic drink) and *hiropon* (a pick-up drug) induced writers' Zolaesque personal stories in *kasutori* magazines. They, too, were facets of the *après-guerre* phenomena. However, a quite large number of serious writers who couldn't publish their works during the war began publishing independent books or serialized works in literary magazines after the war. Those were indeed refreshing cases since cultural activities had been in limbo for so long.

One particular novel impressed me in those days. It was Takeyama Michio's the *Harp of Burma* that appeared in the children's magazine *Akatombo*, or the *Red Dragonfly*. It was serialized and published from mid-1947 to mid-1948. Although it was published in the children's magazine, it was suited for all ages. The author Takeyama Michio was a repatriated soldier and professor of German literature. I suppose he was intending to write a fairytale-like story. The protagonist of the *Harp of Burma,* a Japanese army corporal, Mizushima, was fond of the Burmese hand-held harp. Once on the theater of war facing the British army, he played the tune "The Last Rose of Summer" and an Irish air, "Home Sweet Home." His company of soldiers began singing the tune and,

amazingly, British troops facing opposite them also started singing the tune. This was the fairytale-like plot. His gentle narrative
touch and Corporal Mizushima's warm personality made this story
into the author's intended form of *Märchen* (fairytale). Corporal
Mizushima saw abandoned corpses in the jungles of Burma. This
carnage inspired him to join Buddhism. When the Japanese army
repatriated at the end of the war, Mizushma remained in Burma
to take care of the victims of the war. In the last scene, clad in a
Buddhist monk's robe, Mizushima stood behind the crowd to see
his comrades off at the pier.

It was a very moving and befitting story. I was impressionable
at seventeen years of age when I first read this story. Mizushima
severed himself from his own country and family to do what he
wanted to do. It was exactly what Buddhists did throughout history.
Takeyama's novel was like other *Märchens*, or fantasies filled. Yet
narration, characterization, temporal arrangement, motif, etc. were
all realistic enough to impress me deeply. I read it twice. When I
finished reading the *Harp of Burma* I associated this *Märchen* with
the "Parable" of the *Lotus Sūtra*. The "Parable" is one chapter of
the *Lotus Sūtra,* which is also beautifully written. Both "Parable"
and Takeyama's *Märchen* are dreams, unreal in essence.

Several years later, I read another "war-time" novel based on the
author's personal experience as a drafted soldier. In reality, he was
seized in the Philippines by American forces as a prisoner of war.
The novel *Nobi,* or *The Fire on the Field,* by Ōoka Shōhei, also left
a keen impression on me. There was a scene in the novel when a
Japanese soldier found an American soldier off-guard in close rifle
range on a theater of the war. The American soldier did not notice
him. The Japanese soldier aimed his rifle at the American. After a
moment of hesitation, he decided to let this opportunity go. It was on
the battleground where the norm was to kill or to be killed. Yet, he

realized that he is a human being and could not kill another human; thus he abandoned his duty as a soldier. His realization was certainly that of Buddhist *ahiṃsā,* or no-killing, a first and essential bodhisat-tva precept to all Mahāyāna Buddhists. The humanistic theme of the story gave me hope in the bleak *après-guerre* era.

> The road ascending Cold Mountain
> never ends:
> stone upon stone in the long gorge,
> broad stream rank with weeds;
> no rain has fallen but the moss is slippery,
> the pine trees cry even without the wind.
> Who can transcend worldliness
> and sit with me
> among the white clouds...

> – Han-shan

Chapter 9

NITTAI-JI MONASTERY

身すでにわたくしにあらず、
いのちは光陰にうつされて
しばらくもとどめがたし。
紅顔いづくへかさりにし、
たづねんとするに蹤跡なし。
つらつら観ずるところに、
往事のふたたび
あふべかあらざるおほし。

－ 道元

(『正法眼蔵』「恁麼」)

My body is no longer my own,
my life is passed onto time
and it cannot stop even an instance.
My red cheeks are gone
and cannot trace it.
I think about those things,
we will unlikely meet
those bygone days.

- Dōgen

(*Shōbōgenzō*,(*Inmo*) "Question")

Nin'yū Yamasaki continued helping Hōsen-ji as well as other temples in the vicinity. He spent more time at Hōsen-ji than any other temple. Every now and then, he talked to me in depth about issues concerning Buddhism. Some of his remarks were quite critical of present-day monks and their practices. He was also critical of Buddhist organizations saying that the institutional systems altered the essential tasks of Buddhism. One day, several months after his release from military prison, he said, "My life was spared because

I was an old monk. Those soldiers often listened to me as if they were attending my lectures. I asked one of them to get a few books on Buddhism for me. I gave him some titles of the books. He did get those books and I had ample time to read all of them. Those soldiers, all draftees, you know, were good people but conscripted into the army. I had taught the military police the precept of non-violence, or *ahiṃsā.* Buddhists practiced pacifism and, as a result, Indian Buddhism was completely wiped out. Those Buddhists did not take arms to defend themselves in conflicts. The Muslim invasion was awfully destructive, wholly destroying Buddhism down to the last bastion. In retrospect, even without that invasion, Buddhism in India was destined to wane."

I asked why it was destined to wane. He continued, "Buddhism then had powerful and wealthy supporters and they were comfortable. In my assumption, they concentrated on developing unrealistically complex abstract philosophies. Their works were too far exalted from ordinary people's lives. As you know, every morning we recite our dharma-ancestors' names to pay respect to them. You know Nāgārjuna, whose theory of nothingness, *śūnyavāda,* and the middle way, *mādhyamika,* or Vasubandhu's theory of "knowledge only," *vijñāptimātratā,* was way beyond the average populace's comprehension. Nāgārjuna and Vasubandhu were two of the most respected patriarchs in Zen. They became eminent patriarchs not only in Zen, but also in the Pure Land and other Mahāyāna schools. Average Buddhists could not fully grasp their theories. For those reasons, they were already losing the support of the populace before the time of the invasion. Buddhism in India, Afghanistan, and Pakistan continued to wane and eventually disappeared. Fortunately, by then, Buddhism had spread southward to Ceylon and northward to China."

Nin'yū became enthusiastic on this issue, explaining that, "When you come to their precise treatises, only a handful of academic specialists understand. Yes, they were not written for ordinary people to read. To simply read those treatises would require a lot of time. Furthermore, they were too voluminous and required exhaustible effort, knowledge and free time. I respect the determination and effort of writing those works. I admired their devotion to theorizing the Buddha's simple teachings. They had spent manifold effort, I am certain, and an enormous amount of time. I wondered every now and then whether the purpose of those patriarchs' scrutiny was solely for the salvation of those who were suffering? Or were those scholastic minds simply getting carried away to create those involved theories for their own sake?" Then he said in a different pitch, "Yet, on the contrary, some of us think that because of those dharma-ancestors' untiring efforts in theorizing, Buddhism survived when supporters were diminishing." Nin'yū Yamasaki might well have been right to ask these questions. His knowledge of Buddhism was amazingly thorough.

***

I believe it was a summer evening in 1947 when Nin'yū Yamasaki came to Hōsen-ji, quite intoxicated. The first thing he said was, "Japanese Zen Buddhism is nearing its end." I asked why. He said, "I just came from Sakura (a town east of Yobitsugi). My acquaintance had hosted a special feast for his priest who has just been promoted to a higher rank. He can now wear a yellow honorary robe. What do you think of that? In addition, those and several others are going to buy him a set of those silk robes and gold lamé *kesa* (robes) at an exorbitant price on the black market. You know, Kazumitsu-kun, people are starving. It is ludicrous. People are struggling to get their own clothes. What nonsense would that be? Indeed, it is absurd." He continued, "I don't believe in the monastic rankings. What sort of thing did he do to deserve to be promoted? Does a higher ranking of their priest mean anything to them? I only respect Dōgen's natural selection, based on the length of monastic practices, not by arbitrary and high-handed organizational authority." This was his usual way of introducing a question he had been thinking about.

He sat on the *tatami* floor and began explaining why he was so upset over a yellow robe. He said, "Our great founder of Sōtō Zen, Dōgen, studied under the Chinese master Rujing, you know. The *Record of Baoqing* (*Hōkyō-ki*) has this dialogue, with Dōgen asking Rujing: 'Why is it that you have never worn a *kesa* with multicolored patterns since you are the abbot of this monastery?' Rujing said, 'I suppose, because of my frugality. Buddha Śākyamuni and his disciples preferred to wear *kesa* made of pieces of discarded cloth and used eating bowls which had been thrown away." This was the first time I learned about the *Hōkyō-ki*, or the *Record of Baoqing.*

Nin'yū's fervor continued, "The Buddha and his disciples only wore *kesa* made of discarded cloth. The original *san'é* (three essential pieces of clothing) were worn for warmth and protection from adverse weather conditions. That was enough! Zen Master Dōgen wore only a simple black robe throughout his life. When the Chinese emperor presented an honorary purple robe to Dōgen's master, Rujing, he refused to wear it. Dōgen, Rujing's dharma heir, never wore a gold embroidered robe. He never rode in a palanquin with a canopy over it. Remember that Buddhism, from the time of the Buddha, revered egalitarianism. There is no place for a progenitor so-and-so, or a disciple of a magnate so-and-so. Kazumitsu Wakō! You must remember it. A Buddhist monk's robes should not be used as objects of one's desire, nor should they be used to impress others. Understand?"

I said, "Yes." Then, Nin'yū Yamasaki paused for a moment.

He continued the next topic in a somewhat somber tone, "Oh, yes! Wakō, I recommend that you go to another monastery, hopefully Eihei-ji, where Dōgen established the Sōtō School of Buddhism. But just go for a year or two and no more. Learn only the essence of Zen. That is all you need to learn and that is enough. There are some monks who stay in monasteries for a decade or longer and they only become wiser. All they care about is the style and façade of the rituals and, of course, their own monastic rankings. The longer you stay the cleverer you'll become. No need for that. So, stay just a year or two. Understand, Wakō?" I said, "Yes. I understand." Nin'yū nodded a few times, "That's right. Spending excessive money to buy a higher status or for robes is vanity. It is conceit out of incompetence." He concluded this tirade over the robes with his usual waggish laugh, and a breath of calmness returned. Then he said he was getting tired and wanted to go home. So, he left. I was always amazed that his anger was so fleeting.

***

Nin'yū Yamasaki became more and more isolated from other priests. This was due largely to his drinking and his unabashed criticism of some priests' behaviors. One day, when we were sitting together at Hōsen-ji, I said to him, "I have heard that when people grow older, they become mellower, but why don't you get that way? It would be much easier for you to get along in this community." He looked at me and said, "When Karl Marx was living in a small London flat, Friedrich Engels, a collaborator of the *Communist Manifesto,* approached Marx and said to him the same thing you have just said to me. Marx approached Engels, grabbed his jacket lapel and said, 'Would you? Would you?' Do you understand Kazumitsu? Whether or not you agree with what Karl Marx professed is not the question here. Whether or not this is a true story is not the question either. What Marx wanted to point out was that his mission was not completed yet. He wanted to convey that to Engels. Kazumitsu-kun, my mission is not finished and I don't have much time left." Thus, he vetoed the idea of becoming a genial character, and adamantly upheld his principles. He was not a recalcitrant, but a maverick who tried to walk the path his Zen predecessors walked without yielding to the system.

On another day, when he was heavily intoxicated, I boldly said to him that he was advocating the principle of nonattachment, which is the key to eradicate suffering, yet his actions contradicted that principle. He replied, "Do you recall that on our day-trip to the Daibō's Blood Pond I wrote 'killing sword, saving sword' on the wooden sword?" I answered, "Yes, I remember that." That had been on the rare occasion that we took a short trip to the Chita peninsula and visited the tomb of Minamoto Yoshitomo at Daibō. That had been three or four years before, but I still remembered it vividly.

He said, "My action is exactly that. I'm killing them and also saving them. I'm sure you understand that. I am not as angry as I look. Do you see my compassion when I am angry? Both are there. It's like a flash of lightening, instantaneous. It doesn't leave any trace within me. It is an attachment yet at the same time, non-attachment. Wakō, suffering is to let your feelings linger on by keeping and clinging to them. If you practice a little more, and your practice and your actual life become inseparable, you can become *śūnyatā* at all times. By the way, you said I am contradicting myself, didn't you? Yes, I am contradictory—that is life. But, remember, I am not attached to that contradiction either. When you are experiencing 'emptiness' of your mind, in that moment, you are one with the universe. But you are still living in this mundane world filled with unavoidable particulars. Life is continual attachment and detachment, and they are linked by the chain of cause-and-effect. There is plenty of room for contradictions, even to attaching yourself to the idea of detachment. The key is not to let it linger on. Let it disappear like lightning. That is the teaching of Zen. Am I lecturing you again? If so, take my advice with a grain of salt." Then he paused a moment and said, "I still think that you must go to the monastery to experience that." He evaded my question and lectured me on a different subject. Drinking was his biggest weakness and that topic was not open for discussion.

***

On the south side of Hōsen-ji, beyond Tokaidō Road, there was a lower plateau. Beyond the flat land, there was a hill similar to Hōsen-ji hill. A Sōtō Zen temple named Byakugō-ji stood on top of that hill. Byakugō-ji had been built a few hundred years earlier than Hōsen-ji and was bigger and busier. A young monk came from Hokkaido to live there and help at Byakugō-ji. His name was Kitamura-san. He was a tall, thin and handsome person. He had a slight Northern accent. I don't remember exactly when I first met Kitamura-san, but for as long as I can remember, he was a full-grown man. He was five or six years older than me. When I was a fifth-year student in middle school, he was attending college. His college was called Bussen. It was an evening school specializing in Buddhist studies. Most of the students, according to him, had been priest candidates. He called me *rago,* which means "son of a Buddhist priest" in the ordinary sense, and he used it that way. The actual meaning came from the name of Gautama Siddhārtha's son, *Rāhula.* That was before Siddhārtha renounced the worldly life to become an ascetic seeking the release of human sufferings. Whether Kitamura-san knew it or not, *Rāhula* literally means "obstruction." Kitamura-san apparently came from a lay family, like many others that I knew who assisted the Byakugō-ji abbot.

Just about the time I finished middle school, he came to Hōsen-ji one night. He told me that he had been asked to take the position of abbot of Byakugō-ji but he needed monastic training to be qualified. The abbot of Byakugō-ji had no *rago* (son) of his own to succeed his position. Kitamura-san had no previous monastery experience. He came to Hōsen-ji to ask me what it was like at the Kyūkoku-ji monastery. My experience was not an encompassing one. It was a Zen middle school program and had been interrupted by my attending public school and the war. I told him of the routines, *rōhatsu sesshin*—the taking of turns for the many roles necessary to carry out priestly duties. He said he was planning to go to Kakuō-zan, Nittai-ji Monastery to study and practice Zen.

The next morning when Nin'yū Yamasaki came to Hōsen-ji, I told him about Kitamura-san's intention to go to Nittai-ji monastery. He asked me, "You are going to graduate from middle school next year aren't you?" I said, "Yes, next March." I was 16 years old. He seemed to ponder for a moment, and then said, "Traditionally, since this temple was founded by the Fiftieth Abbot of Eihei-ji, every generation of this temple has practiced at Eihei-ji at least once. I was thinking about it. You know the post-war situation made it so difficult. Hōsen-ji has burned down and it needs you here now more than ever."

This conversation took place in late 1946, only a year and several months after the end of the war and the country had already, though ever so slowly, shown some signs of recovery from the war-torn desolation. Amazingly, however, there were coffee shops that had opened in the city and saccharine-sweetened candies were already available. If you could afford to buy black-market sugared sweets, they were also obtainable. Hōsen-ji's only income was anything I made while visiting members' houses or when members came to the temple for services. But the temple had other expenses too, such as when Reverend Yagi came from Nara, as the temple had to pay his fare and offer him an honorarium. Even Nin'yū's assistance had to be paid by the temple. Nin'yū was aware of the financial difficulties of our temple and that it would be hard for me to go and practice at Eihei-ji. I had several acquaintances that went to Eihei-ji and I had been thinking about going there for a year or two; however, I knew that I could not impose any further financial burden on my mother. It would be easier if I went to the nearby Kakuō-zan, Nittai-ji monastery, where Kitamura-san was planning to enter. Additionally, after the ninety-day confinement period I could come home and tend to the temple occasionally. That would somewhat ease my mother's worries. I had lost my entire outfit to be worn at the monastery in the fire during the war. I was not certain whether I could obtain a new set. Talking to him about all of these reasons, I decided to go to Kakuō-zan, Nittai-ji monastery. Nin'yū agreed with my decision.

***

Kakuō-zan, Nittai-ji was a unique temple built for the commemoration of the Buddha's remains, *sarīra,* which had been presented to Japan by the King of Siam (Thailand) in 1901. Initially, the *sarīra* was kept in Kyoto, but in 1903 they were moved to Nagoya and the temple was built to enshrine it with the collaboration of all Japanese Buddhist schools. The temple escaped bombing as it was located in the east end of the city. Nittai-ji means "the temple of Nippon and Thailand." Kakuō-zan or Mt. Kakuō means the Mountain of the King of Enlightenment; *kakuō* is an epithet for the Buddha. The temple, on its large temple compound, had many impressive buildings. They housed the Buddha's ashes as well as gifts from the King of Siam; also, a golden Buddha statue, books of sūtras, and a gold-studded brocade were enshrined in its storehouse, the *Hōan-den*. In 1914, Nittai-ji built a pagoda, or *Hōan-tō*; the main building, or *Daiyū-hō-den*; the phoenix hall, or *Hō-ō-dai*; the activity hall, or *Kōshaku-dai*; the Master's Living room, or *hōjō*; and the Monk's Hall, or *sōdō*. The temple was managed by one of the Japanese Buddhist sects for several years in turn. However, the *sōdō* (monastery) section was entirely managed by Sōtō Zen monks, and they had almost no contact with other sections of the temple.

On April 10, 1947, a few months after I graduated from middle school, I left Hōsen-ji for Kakuō-zan, Nittai-ji with Kitamura-san. Nittai-ji temple sits on the hilltop plateau of Kakuō-zan: the hill was named after this temple. Kakuō-zan was one of the high hills in the otherwise mostly level city of Nagoya. Streetcars climbed over a mile to the top of the hill before reaching Kakuō-zan station. From the station, Kitamura-san and I walked toward the temple, approximately three quarters of a mile. It was an uphill path. Both sides of the pathway had shops catering to the temple visitors. It was like the famous path to Tokyo's Asakusa temple. We went to the *sōdō* section of the temple, bypassing all other buildings. It was a nice, quiet place in spite of its location within the famous and busy temple where visitors came from all over Japan. I was quite nervous before entering the receptionist area of Nittai-ji. Like Kyūkoku-ji, we met the *inō,* or managing monk, who led us to the abbot at his *hōjō* [abbot's] room. We were allowed to stay in the *tangaryō,* the temporary staying room, for five or six days. Nittai-ji was much bigger than Kyūkoku-ji. During the stay there we practiced *zazen* uninterruptedly from four o'clock in the morning to nine in the evening. Unlike at Kyūkoku-ji's *tangaryō*, I was not alone. There were two of us this time, which made it easier. I did not yearn for my mother and siblings as I had upon entering Kyūkoku-ji years before.

When no one was nearby the *tangaryō,* Kitamura-san began whispering to me. He spoke of benign matters. In the beginning, I listened to his talk, but not too attentively. Soon, I began to meditate more deeply and my responses to Kitamura-san were less focused. I suppose he realized that, and stopped whispering to me. We continued sitting in the increasingly silent *tangaryō.*

***

The weather of mid-April was neither hot nor cold, so the window with the *shoji* screens was opened halfway. A cool breeze came into the room, softly warding off my dismal torpor. In a short while, serenity brought a harbor of peace that encompassed our ensemble of two novice monks. Our sitting environment at Nittai-ji *tangaryō* was a small *tatami* mat on the floor beside which nothing was placed. The area around us was idyllic. The silhouette of dark pine branches nearly touched the eaves of the building. The spring sun reflected on light green shades of deciduous tree buds. It was totally still, as if time had stopped. A soft stroking wind gently touched us, also in silence. It was the only moving part of our environment and that connected us to the rest of the world. The wind moves everywhere; across high mountaintops, over vast oceans, through inner cities and now it was connecting us to the world by caressing our whole body and mind. After a while, I unclasped my legs from the sitting lotus position and did a walking practice, or *kinhin.* I was mindful to follow exactly as Dōgen's Master Rujing had instructed Dōgen. The notion of the wind vanished. Excerpts of that instruction from the *Record of Baoquing* or the *Hōkyō-ki* are as follows: "If you wish to do *kinhin,* upon getting up from *zazen,* you should walk in a straight line, not a circle. If you wish to make a turn after having taken twenty or thirty steps, always turn to the right, not to the left. When you [begin to] walk, first move your right foot [forward] and then your left." And in another section: "When you stand up and begin walking after having done *zazen,* you should definitely follow the method of proceeding a half step with each breath. That is to say, when you take a step [forward], you should not exceed half a foot length. [At the same time], you should always inhale and exhale once with each step." I followed this instruction earnestly but the room was a bit too small to walk straight for thirty steps. I walked about twenty-two to twenty-three steps, turned right, and with each half step, I breathed in and out. While I was doing this, I completely forgot Kitamura-san who was sitting next to me, facing the wall as required in Sōtō Zen. I must add this important note here. The Sōtō Zen School always recommends that practitioners sit facing the wall when practicing in the Monk's Hall, or whenever engaged in the practice of sitting. The tradition of sitting and facing the wall came from the legendary Bodhidharma's sitting practice. According to the legend, he sat facing the wall for nine years. Dōgen mentioned this in his chapter entitled "*Gyōji II*" from the *Shōbōgenzō*.

While I did the slow walking practice, Kitamura-san joined me and we did *kinhin* together. Shortly after my *kinhin,* I began having the feeling of wholeness—not only with myself but with everything around me. My body, my mind, Kitamura-san, the room, trees, breeze and entire world became one whole entity. The "I" as a subject had been absorbed in the objective world. Or, it might be that my mind embraced the entire objective world. I practiced *kinhin* for five or six minutes then I returned to my seat and continued *zazen.* Kitamura-san followed suit. The *tangaryō* sitting practice went on for five days. After that, we were led to the *sōdō,* or the monk's hall, and were given a *tan* (a three-by-six foot living space, where we practice *zazen*). Kitamura-san and I were not next to each other, and in fact he was given a *tan* on the opposite side of the hall from mine.

The *sōdō* at Nittai-ji was larger than that of Kyūkoku-ji and it had an outside sitting platform, *gaïtan,* on the front, or eastside, and also on both north and south sides. The inside hall, or *naïdō,* was like Kyūkoku-ji. The floor was made of black shiny stones. In the center of the building was a statue of the Sacred Master, or *Shōsō,* placed on a pedestal. It was the statue of Bodhisattva Mañjuśrī on the pedestal since the *Tōjō-Garan-ki,* or the *Record of Sōtō Temples*, mentions that they usually place Mañjuśrī as the *Shōsō.* In the long Zen tradition, the statue of a Bodhisattva Mañjuśrī is often attired in a monk's robe similar to that of practicing monks. The word "wisdom" symbolizes Mañjuśrī. The Mañjuśrī-bodhisattva statue also appears in the set of the "Three Venerables of Śākyamuni" with Samantabhadra-bodhisattva positioned at the right. Mañjuśrī-bodhisattva is transliterated into Chinese as *Wenzhushili Pusa* (or Wen-chu Shiih-li P'u-sa), *Monjushiri Bosasatsu* in Japanese.

I still remember the first formal teaching, or *honkō,* we received from the abbot of Nittaiji, Tesshin Yoshida Rōshi. Despite his small stature, Yoshida Rōshi had a resounding voice and clear diction. He appeared to be in his mid-sixties. He told us the story of Mañjuśrī. Abbot Yoshida said it was an anecdotal *kōan* about Mañjuśrī from the first of one hundred *kōans* in the *Shōyō-roku* or the *Record of Shōyō-hut* (*Zongronglu* or *Tshung-jung-lu* in Chinese). Before he started to recite a *kōan* he told us that Mañjuśrī represents "wisdom." The *kōan* was from "The First *Kōan*: The Bhagavat (the respected one, the Buddha) Ascended to the Dais":

One day the Bhagavat ascended to the dais [where an assembly of people gathered to hear him]. Mañjuśrī struck the tree stump to signify [the opening of the event]. Mañjuśrī said, "You have witnessed the Buddha's dharma. The Buddha's dharma is just that!" Hearing Mañjuśrī's words the Buddha descended from the dais.

Yoshida Rōshi repeated this short *kōan* two or three times so that I memorized it. Then Rōshi added a poem dedicated to this *kōan* by Lay Master Wansong (Bansho in Japanese). It praised both the Buddha and Mañjuśrī. Yoshida Rōshi concluded that in this *kōan*, the Buddha's very presence, not the words he spoke, took precedence. He said it was not a mistake for Mañjuśrī to address an audience with a closing remark instead of an opening statement, which is supposed to be, "People of dragons and elephants (the superiors), now you will see the primary significance [of Buddhism]." He added, "In any case, the Buddha's dharma cannot be heard or seen. It can only be acquired through your own diligent practice. That is why Mañjuśrī is enshrined as the Sacred Master in our *sōdō*." Yoshida Rōshi said that Master Wansong added the poem using the Buddha's teaching as if it were the true wind. Thereby everyone in the *sōdō* breathes in and out that true wind of the Buddha. Suddenly I recalled the cool breeze that permeated the *tangaryō* where I sat before I had been officially admitted in the *sōdō*. The wind circulates the world over without discrimination, touching everything and everyone. It is the catalyst that changes the temperatures and weather. That is Manjuśrī.

181

At times it brings wrath and other times, it brings a cool comfort to the earth. Rōshi's *honkō* was, I thought, as precious as the breath of Manjuśrī-bodhisattva.

***

One day, Abbot Yoshida spoke at his *honkō* about a Chinese monk named Wenzhu. His name happens to be a transliteration of Mañjuśrī. Of course, this monk was not the Bodhisattva Mañjusri. This time he quoted from the *Blue Rock Record* or *Biyanlu (Pi-yen-lu), Hokigan-roku* in Japanese, which is the thirty-fifth *kōan*. A Zen monk called Wuchu took a journey to a famous Buddhist site, Mt. Wutai, where he met an accomplished Zen monk, Wenzhu:

> Wenzhu asked Wuchu, "Where are you coming from?" Wuchu said, "From the south." Wenzhu further asked, "How is Buddhism in the south? How do they maintain it?" Wuchu said, "Those *bhikṣu* [monks] in this 'degenerate' period do not practice [all] the precepts." Wenzhu asked, "How many *bhikṣu* are there?" Wuchu said, "There may be 300 or 500." [Then,] Wuchu asked [Wenzhu], "How do you maintain Buddhism here?" Wenzhu replied, "[We have] the sacred and the profane in the same place, dragons and snakes mixed." Wuchu asked, "How many are there?" Wenzhu answered, "Before, three-three and after, three-three."

Then there is the poem:

> A thousand peaks are protruding close to each other, their color is [deep] blue.

Who said, Wenzhu had a conversation there.
Laughable is the one who asked
how many monks are on Qingliang [mountain].
It's "before, three-three and after, three-three."

Abbot Tesshin Yoshida, after addressing us with this old *kōan,*
laughed aloud, saying "Before three-three, after three-three. What
is this? It's nonsense. Mañjuśrī, to whom we revered as a sacred
master, but this…huh… is also nonsense." He spoke and laughed as
though we novices understood it. Someone laughed with the abbot
but I could not laugh. I did not understand the meaning of this *kōan.*
After all, Wenzhu is the transliteration of Mañjuśrī, a homonym,
and we don't distinguish between the two in pronunciation. I did
study this *kōan* later, however. It came from a time when Mañjuśrī-
boddhisattva worship at Wutai-shan [Mt. Wutai] was at the height
of its popularity and Wutai-shan attracted many veiled stories. In
any case, Wuchu answered Wenzhu's questions in a literal way but
Wenzhu's answer to Wuchu's question was very different. There
were not 300 or 500 *bhikṣu* (monks), but mountains, rocks, trees,
and all are buddha-dharma. If the question was about their existence,
their quantity did not have any significance. To the other question,
"How do you maintain Buddhism here?" Wenzhu's answer was "sacred and profane in the same place; dragons and snakes [are] mixed."
What Wenzhu said was that the idea of maintaining Buddhism did
not deal with illusion or superficiality. There is no such nonsense as
sacred or profane, let alone dragons or snakes. "Before, three-three
and after, three-three" puzzled me at first, but I think it might mean
that the numbers create further illusions and in this context, simple
numbers signify nothing. Yoshida Rōshi simply laughed openly.

As you might have guessed, I did not understand the significance of the role of *kōan* in the practice of *zazen.* I understood

it superficially but I did not experience *kōan* with my body and mind. I rather felt as if I had been thrown into a murky pool of confusion. Even to this day, I do not completely put this particular *kōan* into practice. Other literary sources numerously stated in chorus that Wutai-shan had protruding peaks and was covered with lush vegetation. It was also affectionately called the *Qingliang*, or the Green Peaks. I wondered if this *kōan* was a sort of criticism of the flourishing craze of Bodhisattva Mañjuśrī worship at its peak.

Wuchu's question of "how many [practitioners] are there?" was definitely an ordinary question. Since he asked for numbers, Wenzhu answered, "before three-three, after three-three." Wuchu, likely, did not recognize that in Zen, the entire universe is dharma and numbers are only used for convenience, which is *upāya*, or skill-in-means. In more penetrating ways, one includes all, and all are in one. Wuchu did not grasp that, and could only see it in his own limited world-view. A mouse can only see the world of mice. Those who only think of food can only see things from the point of view of food. Wuchu and Wenzhu were a world of difference in this case. If this anecdote was a legend, it was one well-suited to study.

This anecdote reminded me of another from the *Transmission of the Lamp of Chuandeng Period* or the *Jingde Chuandeng-lu,* (*Ching-tê Ch'uang-têng-lu*), the *Keitoku Dentō-roku* in Japanese, Vol. 19:

> [Master] Yunmen (Yün-mên) addressed [the assembly of monks]:
> "Before the fifteenth, I do not ask you, but after the fifteenth, bring me a phrase."
> [Before anyone said a word,] Yunmen said to himself, "Every day is a fine day."

This was a delightful story; Yunmen had asked and then answered his own question. If every day is a fine and perfect day, nothing should obstruct Zen practitioners. Therefore, there is no need to distinguish between before the fifteenth or after the fifteenth day. There is no reason to regret the past or hope for the future. If one lives each moment attentively, that is the only time in which he or she is living—neither before nor after any one point in time. Each and every "now" is fine and perfect. Once your life's journey has started there will be no turning back. We shall continue living in the here and now in the ebb and flow of the seemingly realistic world without ever stopping, until we cease to be altogether. One might be reminded of the phrase, *"carpe diem"* from Horace's *Odes*, "seize the day."

Mañjuśrī symbolizes wisdom and is considered a great influence on Zen practice. Many glorious stories are attributed to Manjuśrī, but at that time they did not affect me anymore than my presence in the *sōdō* where I prostrated before Mañjuśrī as part of our prescribed ritual. I put my palms together before his statue every time I passed before it. Hence, when I meditated and ate my meals in the *sōdō,* or Monk's Hall, in the presence of *Mañjuśrī-bodhisattva*, that presence did give me an enlivened, comfortable feeling, even though I did not know the exact reason for it other than that it was a part of my daily life at Kakuō-zan monastery.

I memorized many Zen *kōans* by then but what I was to heed to most was the passage I had recited aloud when I was initially ordained into Buddhism—the *tokudo*. It has remained in the back of my mind. To this day, I recite it occasionally. It is the story about Bodhidharma's encounter with the Emperor Wu of the country Liang:

When the Emperor Wu of Liang asked Bodhidharma, "What is the primary meaning of the sacred truth?" Bodhidharma answered, "Everything is in its right place and I don't see any sacredness." The emperor asked, "Who is the person facing me?" Bodhidharma answered, "I don't know." The emperor was bewildered. Bodhidharma thereupon left the court, crossed the river and went to the country of Wei.

Emperor Wu [later] told Zhigong about the incident. Zhigong asked, "Did the Emperor know that person?" The emperor replied, "No, I didn't." Zhigong said, "He is Kwanyin who brought the proof of the buddha-mind." The emperor was remorseful and attempted to send a messenger to invite Bodhidharma back. But Zhigong said, "Don't do that. If you send a messenger, or even if you send an entire country's people, he won't come back."

When you memorize a story like this at a young age, it often stays with you for the rest of your life. Emperor Wu neither saw Bodhidharma nor understood the answers to his questions. When the emperor asked him who he was, Bodhidharma answered, "I don't know." The sympathizer of Buddhism, Emperor Wu, had asked the primary meaning of Buddhism first and then his name. Bodhidharma did not give conventional answers. Bodhidharma said that everything is in its right place and also that a person's name is only a mark, label, or tag, which is not attached to anything substantive. Obviously, Emperor Wu did not grasp Bodhidharma's answers. But were there any better answers to the emperor's questions if you are a known Ch'an (Zen) practitioner? Bodhidharma answered the core of the Zen Buddhist belief that everything is in its right place, such that one needs neither to seek anything further, nor worry, nor regret. One can simply rejoice in his or her present state. Unfortunately, the emperor had not reached Bodhidharma's plane. Bodhidharma demonstrated the unique traits of Zen in his encounter with the emperor, unlike that of Nāgasena's encounter with the Greek king Milinda (Menandros), which demanded a lengthy explanation. Perhaps, as Nin'yū Yamasaki had said to me, I had to live in a monastery and acquire Zen with the entirety of my body and mind. It was not simply a mental acquisition that was needed for understanding but a total empirical experience was required to reach the Bodhidharma's plane.

***

Two months after my *ango* or the ninety-day confined practice, a month long rainy season (*varsa*) began, which perhaps befitted *ango*. *Ango* originally was a rainy season practice that confined monks and nuns in one place. Temperatures rose in the summer. The Monks' Hall was built on the tree-covered landscape of the monastery and the shade made by those trees helped make the heat bearable. Furthermore, the building's high ceilings and thick walls created a much more comfortable condition than in most places. I enjoyed the chanting, meditation and cleaning. I enjoyed the Nittai-ji monastery. However, contrary to its serene surroundings, I was having an indefinable experience of impending perplexity. My youthful energetic inclination for learning the meaning of Zen and Buddhism remained unanswered. My inexpressible yearning for something that I could neither imagine nor define stayed within me during my early *ango* days. I did what I had to do as a novice monk but I was nonetheless in a state of limbo. I felt I was not securely held in place and these precarious inward irresolute notions tormented me for the first few months; however, this slowly went away as I became familiar with my daily activities and listening to Yoshida Rōshi's *honkō* lectures. Instead of explaining the meaning of Zen, he stopped his lectures abruptly at random points, which posed a number of questions in my mind. I used all sorts of references to simply grasp outlines of his lectures.

There were some differences between Kyūkoku-ji and Nittai-ji in terms of daily matters. The former followed the formality of the Head Temple, Sōji-ji, whereas the latter followed the formality of the Head Temple, Eihei-ji. Between the two, there was a slight difference in the wearing of robes and also in ritual comportment. It bothered me a little at first when I went to Kyūkoku-ji. Hōsen-ji followed the formality of Eihei-ji. By the time I began living at Nittai-ji, those differences no longer bothered me. It was like "before three-three, after three-three."

I returned to Hōsen-ji briefly in autumn for some temple matters and my mother said, "You look well. Is everything alright there?" The Hōsen-ji members also said that I had grown to be a fine monk. Some even said that I chanted sūtras with confidence. I didn't think so, but it was very nice of them to say those kind things about me. What I appreciated most was that the people began to acknowledge my presence as a young adult.

My mother prepared some candies made of sweet potatoes for me to take back to Nittai-ji. I carried them and when I walked along the narrow path from the Kakuō-zan station to Nittai-ji, I noticed that there was a row of sweet shops selling similar items. My mother had never been to Nittai-ji and probably didn't know of the shops. Near the end of the year, she was making sweets again and I told her they could be bought. She said, "I didn't know that. But this is my *kuyō* (veneration) to you and your fellow monks. You must enjoy them as monks receiving *kuyō*." I shared the sweets with my fellow monks and they all enjoyed them. *Kuyō,* the offerings to the Buddha, dharma, and saṃgha, are a long-held tradition in Buddhist countries.

Many of the monks at Nittai-ji came from distant areas. Some were there just to add years of practice to their résumé and, when they finished their required time for a particular qualification, they made plans to leave. Some were interested in learning rituals, such as how to enter the main ceremonial hall and how to strike gongs and wooden drums. For some, correct deportment alone occupied their entire practice. In fact, there is the *Standard for Deportment,* or the *Gyōji Kihan* in the Sōtō Zen School. Every rite must follow from that text. The text is essential for coordinating rites by large numbers of monks; otherwise, the rites would be discordant and chaotic. So, we studied and practiced the correct deportment. In the case of the *Standard for Deportment,* the term *gyōji* is used as "deportment," but the primary meaning of *gyōji* is "practice and retention." As Dōgen said in the chapter entitled "*Gyōji I*" from his treatise, the *Shōbōgenzō*:

> The great way of the buddhas and patriarchs was the utmost [fulfillment of] 'practice and retention, *gyōji.*' That is, making a circular circuit so there would be no severance. In Buddhism, practice, *bodhi* (enlightenment), and *nirvāṇa* must have no gaps between them. That is the circle of *gyōji.*

In the same chapter, he said:

> Our compassionate father, Śākyamuni Buddha, practiced and retained [what he has practiced] from the dharma-age of nineteen. When he reached the age of thirty, he had 'practice and retention' of great enlightenment together with all sentient beings on this great earth. Thereafter, until the dharma-age of eighty, he maintained the state of 'practiced and retained' on mountains, in forests and also at various *vihāra* (temples and monasteries).

He never returned to the palace [of his birthplace], never possessed the wealth of the country, wore only one robe [*saṃghāti*—a robe for traveling and delivering sermons] throughout his life without replacement. He had one bowl without replacement. He lived [with other monks] and never lived alone, not even for one day. He did not accept meaningless veneration-offerings. He endured defamation and abuse uttered by nonbelievers. The Buddha's teaching was "practice and retention," or *gyōji*. His practice of wearing pure cloth and acceptance of alms was the buddha-practice and that was the *gyōji*.

In the above passages, [the term] *gyōji* is meant as "practice and retention" of what one has practiced. It is not limited to the correct deportment one uses in rituals. In Buddhism it is homologous with another common deportment, meaning "manner, event, or function." Even those entering Buddhist practice pay little attention to the differences between the two, although the two words are not homonyms. Most of those monks focused their practice on ceremonial comportment, neglecting retention as Dōgen said above. This is indeed regrettable.

At the time I entered Nittai-ji, I was already accustomed to monastic practices from my upbringing in Hōsen-ji and my training at Kyūkoku-ji. They had become second nature to me. There, among fellow monks, unlike at Kyūkoku-ji, I found no congenial companions. Fellow monks at Kakuō-zan seemed to have had definite goals that were somewhat competitive among the fellows, whereas at Kyūkoku-ji, we were younger and simply lived a scheduled monastic life. At Nittai-ji, I spent a lot of time studying—various sūtras, the Buddha's life, Indian philosophy, history of Buddhism in India, China and Japan, and other schools of Buddhism. I borrowed books from senior monks incessantly since I could not leave the monastery to buy books freely. After the *ango* period, we were allowed to leave as many as two times in a month and each leave had to be less than three days. Whenever Hōsen-ji needed me, I used those permitted leaves of absence. While I was at Hōsen-ji I had to buy books since the temple lost all of its books in the inferno. There was a bookstore in Ōsu, Nagoya, named Kichū-dō, specializing in Buddhism and related books. Although I could not afford to buy books every time, I still stopped by as often as possible even just to browse through their fascinating bookshelves. Nin'yū Yamasaki often looked at the books I bought and suggested some others that he admired. The books he suggested were often out of print or somewhat dated, having been written in a pre-war phonetic system.

Almost immediately after the Second World War, the Japanese government changed the then traditional phonetic spelling to a vernacular speech-like form and some of the *kanji* (Chinese characters) to newer, less-complicated varieties. Spelling became simpler as it was changed to reflect more closely the way we spoke. The system of writing had to be adjusted to natural euphonic changes that had occurred over the years. However, the linguistic changes puzzled many people, especially those who had been using the old system for a long time. There were always people who resisted any change adamantly and those people kept using the old system. At the time I lived at Nittai-ji, that transition was just about complete and people were getting used to the new way of writing. I switched from the old to the new writing system during my fourth year of middle school. Switching to the new writing system en masse took four to five years. Of course, there are some stubborn people who have refused to change even to this day. One serious drawback to this system was that most Buddhist sūtras and its treatises were written in the old *kanji,* which required an extra step for those who studied them under the new system. Of course, anyone who studies the archives also needs to know the old system.

***

I don't remember the date exactly, but perhaps in the summer of 1948, a surprising episode occurred in my life. It was before my transmission of the dharma-lineage and I believe I was still at Kakuō-zan. It was a warm day, and I happened to be at Hōsen-ji when Reverend Kataoka, the old abbot of Tenshō-ji, a mile north of Hōsen-ji, dropped in casually. We offered him a cup of tea. He began asking me how long I had stayed at the monastery and what my plans were. Then he said the reason he had come to Hōsen-ji was that he wanted to retire from his position of abbot and was looking for a suitable successor at Tenshō-ji. My mother was sitting beside me and the abbot was looking alternately at both my mother and me. My mother said to him, "Your temple, Tenshō-ji, is a long-established and large temple situated in an affluent neighborhood. You don't have to worry about an heir-priest." The Reverend Kataoka then said, "This may surprise you but I came here today to ask Wakō-san to be the next abbot of Tenshō-ji. This temple has Abbot Yagi and he is still young enough to wait for Kengo-san to become the abbot here. What do you think? This is an important matter. Please consider it seriously. I have thought about it for a long time and Wakō-san is the most suitable person to become the abbot of Tenshō-ji." His offer was very sudden and totally unexpected. I told him that I would think about it and answer him in several days.

The next morning when Nin'yū Yamasaki came to the temple, I told him of the offer made by the abbot of Tenshō-ji. Yamasaki made a serious face, folded his arms and said, "It's a generous offer and I am pleased about it. Tenshō-ji is a much older and much bigger temple. This is a fine prospect for you. But this temple needs a real abbot. Reverend Yagi only comes when we invite him to come. Coming from Nara and having to arrange his schedule is hard on him too." A few minutes later, he said, "Let me think about it. This is a serious matter." While he was saying this, I had decided not to accept the offer. The prospect of becoming the abbot of a bigger and wealthier temple did not really attract my interest. I could not accept it because the members of Hōsen-ji expected me to follow in my father's path and become the abbot there. Once, in his sick bed, my father had held my hands in his hands and told me to work hard at school; otherwise I wouldn't be a fine priest for Hōsen-ji. My mother was also eagerly hoping for me to succeed Hōsen-ji. I liked the gentle old Tenshō-ji abbot, Reverend Kataoka, and I did not want to decline his kind offer. But for me, there was no other answer. Before Nin'yū Yamasaki opened his mouth, I told him my decision. He was surprised but pleased. In fact, he said he was thinking that would be the best solution. My mother was also pleased.

I went to Tenshō-ji the next morning and told Reverend Kataoka my decision and the reasons for it. He said that he understood my reasons and actually praised my decision as a sound one. He said he had been thinking about me for a few years, not just a few months, before he made that offer. I had a sincere appreciation for his consideration in choosing me as his temple heir. Surprisingly, our congeniality grew after this episode. He never showed me any ill treatment because of that. Instead, he treated me in a sort of paternalistic manner. I reciprocated on my part. He taught me things I didn't know. I helped him when he needed a young helper.

I sincerely hoped that he would find a nice monk to take over his temple seat so that he could be free of his search for an heir.

***

Some new and important books relating to Buddhism were beginning to appear on the shelves of bookstores during the late 1940s and early 50s. These included the books of Hajime Nakamura and D.T. Suzuki. I did not disregard Nin'yū Yamasaki's suggestions, but the pre-war editions of his suggested books were so difficult to find in those days. Buddhist books were a lot slower in changing to the new writing system during that transitional period; however, most publications, including newly annotated works of Buddhism, switched to the new writing system. There had been Zen Buddhist texts published during the war by such scholars as Hakuju Ui and Sokuō Etō, but they were on such poor quality paper and with such flimsy bindings that I had to handle them very carefully or they fell apart. However, while I was at Nittai-ji, those books gave me a great deal of help in my practice. Many of the sūtras I chanted in the morning and in the evening began to have a profound meaning for me. Some members said that my chanting had changed after I went to Nittai-ji. Still, there were many sūtras I was merely following the formality and convention of, without understanding the content of what I was chanting.

As I studied the sūtras more, I organized some of them in my mind, such as the sūtras of *Prajñāpāramitā* or *Saddharmapundarīka (the Lotus Sūtra)*. In those days I had nearly mastered classical Chinese, especially the literary styles of the Han Dynasty [c. 200 BCE] to the end of the Qing Dynasty [c. 1850 CE]. Also, I began learning Sanskrit little by little. The works of Professors Hakuju Ui and Hajime Nakamura fascinated me in many ways. Professor

Shōson Miyamoto's approach to Buddhism reminded me of my dharma-uncle, Gyokusen.

The Zen Masters' *teishō,* or the "Zen masters' dharma-lectures," were also being published around that time one by one. A memorable one was that of Ian Kishizawa Rōshi's *Tenzo Kyōkun,* the *Teachings for the Tenzo* (cooking monk) and Kaiten Nukaruya's *Sanzen Dōwa, Teaching of Zen Practice.* Later, I read a book with the same title as Nukariya's, written by a lay Zen practitioner, Seiran Ouchi. I also read Rinzai Zen masters' *Teishō* during those days. One was Shisan Ashikaga Rōshi's *Rinzai-roku Teishō,* or the *Teaching of the Record of Rinzai's Sayings.*

The readings of Zen texts augmented my understanding of the "free-spirited talks" of our Rōshi, Tesshin Yoshida, at his *honkō.* His lectures were uncommonly free and his talks often digressed from the main topics. He talked about everyday issues, sometimes agreeing and sometimes not, but the conclusions always had a refreshingly Zen tone. He seemed to enjoy lecturing and interpreting anecdotes from old texts.

One day, Rōshi quoted an anecdote of Tongshan, the eighteenth *kōan* from the *Gateless Gate* or the *Wumenguan.* A monk asked Tongshan, "What makes Buddha the Buddha? Tongshan replied, "Three pounds of flax."

After his animated laugh Rōshi said, "What a wonderful exchange this is. By the way, this same episode was recorded in the twenty-second *kōan* of the *Record of the Transmission of the Lamps of the Jinde Period,* or the *Jinde Chandenglu, Keitoku Dentō-roku* in Japanese, as follows:

A monk asked Tongshan, "What makes Buddha the Buddha?" Tongshan said, "Three pounds of flax." Master Suangquan listened to this [dialogue] and said, "When you face south, you will see bamboo and when you face north, you will see trees."

"Isn't this a wonderful story?" The Rōshi then laughed again and said, "Three pounds of flax… huh… huh… worthless. But what does make Buddha the Buddha? Are buddhas more valuable than a small amount of flax? Have you had a chance to read the big plaque in front of the Monks' [Meditation] Hall? It says, *Senbutsu Dōjō,* doesn't it? '*Senbutsu*' means 'selecting buddhas,' and '*Dōjō*' simply means the place [to practice]. So, all of you are going to practice to be selected as buddhas. Never mind whether it is three or five pounds of flax or none at all, all dharmas (things) have the buddha-nature. Don't ask questions like what makes Buddha the Buddha. If you do so, you will certainly fail to grasp a grain of flax seed. The true Buddha will likewise slip away from you. That's why to make Buddha is three pounds of flax." After the Rōshi's *honkō,* it usually took me a whole week to grasp the significance. This *honkō* was no exception.

Yoshida Tesshin Rōshi was, as I mentioned before, an older man, small in stature. He usually wore a big *rakusu,* a simplified garment over a robe. Because of his stature, the *rakusu* looked too big for him and made him look somewhat humorous. Despite his size, he had a very strong voice with clear diction. I still remember to this day that his pleasant laughter echoed in the large main hall. But, in those days, more than the echo of his voice, the whole experience of his *dharma* lectures reverberated in my mind for a long time after each talk.

What is the difference between buddhas and flax? The Rōshi once used the wonderful phrase, "Be with the time before your parents were born." That is the very state which is earlier than when you were born, and earlier than when your parents were born. That is to become absolutely "non-discriminating." Even then the entity or essence of humanness is still intact within. It is the original nature of man and woman. This is called "buddha-nature," or *buddhatā,* and it means one whose essence [very nature] is buddha. In Japanese it is called *busshō.* Mountains, rivers, grasses, trees, flax, and all other things have buddha-nature, or *buddhatā*; as Dōgen interpreted the phrase from the *Nirvāṇa Sūtra, 27,* "Every existing entity possesses *buddhatā* without fail." That is three pounds of flax. When the Rōshi said, "you are going to become buddha" he meant that you are going to become one with flax, for that is *buddhatā* as well. Master Suangquan's south or north, bamboos or trees, all are *buddhatā.*

Dōgen interpreted this as, "everything, including all living beings, are *buddhatā."* I am *buddhatā,* the Buddha is *buddhatā,* all buddhas are *buddhatā,* flax is *buddhatā,* north or south is *buddhatā,* cats and dogs are likewise *buddhatā.* Any discrimination becomes, in that case, utterly absurd. After all, flax came from plants that had needed sun, wind, rain, and air to exist just like human beings needed them. We are living in a world where we rely on other elements to survive. Consequently, humans and flax are connected without a doubt in the chain of interdependency, not to speak of its products of thread, rope, and cloth from its stems or oil from its seeds. The existence of flax itself, without a doubt, might well have influenced human lives. To be one with flax is a sound notion. Both are *buddhatā.* I am *buddhatā* and so is flax. Then why should I seek Buddha if I am already Buddha and exist in the sphere where a myriad of *buddhatā* are coexisting?

When the monk asked, "What makes Buddha the Buddha?" Tongshan recognized that the practitioner was asking about personal enlightenment to become a buddha. To respond Tongshan could have pointed to just about anything, not just three pounds of

flax, to remind the monk that the whole gamut of existence is buddha, including Buddhist practitioners.

I really enjoyed Tesshin Yoshida Rōshi's "wonderful story"
and the time I spent there, even though I was not yet able to
internalize my experiences. Nonetheless, the Rōshi's teachings had a profound impact on me. I thought, "I shall definitely
meditate on Zen, and one day I shall acquire its subtlety." My
experience of Zen practice as the "place to select buddhas," or
Senbutsu Dōjō at Kakuō-zan, Nittai-ji, under the abbotship of
Tesshin Yoshida Rōshi, was an inexpressibly important period
in my life. Although Zen practice there was a period of monastic
discipline and was therefore supposed to be very strict, I found
the altruistic, kind, and gentle side of Zen practice at Kakuō-zan.
Most importantly, I began to acquire Zen with both my mind
and body, not just intellectually, which made Zen practice quite
congenial indeed.

> Clouds and mountains
> are heaved in thousands of layers.
> Deep on the dark ravine path,
> human footprints cease.
> By emerald cascades and clear streams
> are many beautiful spots.
> Sometimes birds come,
> murmuring in harmony with my mind.

> – Shih-té

Chapter 10

TRANSMISSION OF THE DHARMA

昨夜たとひ
月ありといふとも、
今夜の月は昨月にあらず、
今夜の月は始中後
ともに今夜の月なりと
参究すべし。
月は月に相嗣する
がゆへに、
月ありといへども
新旧にあらず。

Even though you say that
there was a moon last night,
the moon you see tonight
would not be last night's moon.
Tonight's moon,
whether early, middle or late,
still is the moon of tonight.
You must understand
that the idea of moon is the moon,
neither new nor old.

– 道元

- Dōgen

(『正法眼蔵』「都機」)

(*Shōbōgenzō*, (*Tsuki*) "The Moon")

I believe it was a short while after the *Rōhatsu Sesshin* in December of 1948 when I received a letter from Reverend Genshi Yagi, informing us that he was coming to visit. It was highly unusual for him to visit Hōsen-ji without an invitation, so we were unsure about the reason for his visit. Normally, we asked him to come to the temple for some special occasion; he had never initiated a visit before. There was no telephone at Hōsen-ji in those days, nor was there one at most temples. I stayed at Hōsen-ji and waited for him. He arrived midday. After he prostrated at the shrine, he looked around inside and out, and told us that the temple and surrounding ground had become quite nice over the years. I felt that he was going to say something very uncomfortable and was just stalling for time.

Reverend Yagi asked me, "How old are you now?" to which I replied, "I am nineteen, Reverend Yagi." He said, "Oh my, time flies like an arrow, doesn't it? How old were you when your father died?" "I was fourteen, Reverend." He looked at me and said, "Oh, five years, five years have passed already, how swiftly time passes!" I asked, "Are you in good health, Reverend Yagi? You look very well." Then he broke into a big grin and said, "That's it. That's the reason why I came here today. Oh, yes. We had to pass through those difficult years. And, you know, you are the successor of this temple. Everyone is waiting for you to succeed here as soon as possible. When you reach the age of twenty, you will be able to attain the position of abbot. You are almost there. I am going to prepare all the necessary documents so that you can ascend to that seat. Wakō-san, you are lucky to be the abbot of a small temple, for which the qualification will be easier. Your monastic and priestly qualification will soon be completed. Isn't that right? It is better for this temple if you become the abbot as soon as possible."

Then he began telling me about his busy schedule. He added that despite his age and all, his health held up. In addition to his temporary abbotship at Hōsen-ji, he was helping Sango-ji in Osaka. Sango-ji, and by extension Hōsen-ji, was a temple of his dharma relations. The Sango-ji abbot caught tuberculosis and was therefore unable to take care of his temple. His young son was not ready to take care of the temple activities, so Reverend Yagi had to take care of them. I sympathized with him; it must have been a big task to travel back and forth between two remote locations in those days. Trains were crowded and infrequent everywhere.

He asked me about the total time I had spent at monasteries, including Kyūkoku-ji. He also wanted to know about my schooling at the Zen-founded middle school. After a while he said I was ready to assume the position of abbot at Hōsen-ji and that he would take all the necessary steps to bring this about. In fact, he had requested many necessary forms from the Sōtō Zen Administration Headquarters and they were already filled out. He told me to put my personal seal on them as a sign of my compliance. He said that I was qualified to go through all of the necessary procedures anticipating my completion of practice at Kakuō-zan. I was totally dumbfounded by his painstaking effort to prepare everything. This was the beginning of a series of very important procedures—my last course of monastic order. Reverend Yagi requested from the Headquarters to obtain the necessary forms for transmission of the dharma lineage (*shihō*), to change the color of my robe (*ten'é*), and to get permission to visit and pay respects to the two head temples of Sōtō Zen (*zuisé*). I was overwhelmed by his kindness.

***

Only a few weeks after his visit, it seemed that he had swiftly taken care of several important matters, such as *dempō*, or the transmission of the dharma, and *sanmotsu*, or the inheritance of the three items. Reverend Genshi Yagi, who had been the tenth abbot of Hōsen-ji from November 1, 1944, was my official dharma transmission master. I was thus going to receive the dharma lineage from him. The chapter entitled "*Dhāraṇī*" from Dōgen's *Shōbōgenzō* states:

You have a master from whom you [learn to] become a monk and you have a master from whom you inherit the dharma. The master from whom you inherit the dharma is the true master of your monkhood.

Personally, I did not know Reverend Yagi very well since I had met with him only occasionally after my father's death. I had been grateful to him for accepting the additional abbotship of Hōsen-ji despite his busy temple schedule. Our meetings were so limited that I did not learn much from him, but without his help Hōsen-ji could not have continued its existence. Moreover, without his help I would not have inherited the same dharma-lineage of my father and my grand master Genrin. Reverend Yagi happened to be the closest relation of the same lineage. Inheriting the dharma from Reverend Yagi would thus mean that I was transmitting the buddha-dharma from my father, my grand master and all the patriarchs to the very source: the Buddha himself, Śākyamuni.

It was ironic, I thought, that I was ahead of Kitamura-san who was older than me and eager to finish the basic training course in order to become abbot. I had not been thinking about it at all. But now, just a few months after I left Nittai-ji, I was on the path to ascend to the rank required to become the abbot of Hōsen-ji. I wondered what others might think about my course. "Oh well," I told myself, "Others are not me."

***

The day came when I was to officially receive the *sanmotsu*, or the three essentials, together with the dharma transmission. It was February 6, 1949. It was cold but the fresh air felt bracing and exhilarating. It was just a month before I left Nittai-ji monastery. I took a leave especially for this occasion. A few fellow monks had heard of this and congratulated me as I was leaving the monastery in the early morning. I was to receive the transmission of the dharma lineage from Reverend Yagi. It was the right course since my father was no longer there to be my dharma-lineage master.

Reverend Yagi was quite serious. He seemed a bit nervous. He and I went to a room usually reserved for services and daily activities. The room was in a section of the main hall, or hondō. All the doors were closed. This room was temporarily made for master-and-disciple special instruction. It is called *shicchū*, which in Zen literally means "inside the master's room [to transmit the dharma]" and is reserved for important events such as this. Dōgen personally received the utmost important instruction from his master, Rujing, in the master's room, face-to-face.

Carefully choosing the right words, Reverend Yagi said that I was in his estimation ready to inherit the three essential items, or *sanmotsu*, and therefore qualified to change the color of my robe from black to more subtle colors. He told me that we were going to perform a simpler ceremony and briefed me with the procedures. It consisted of multiple prostrations and careful listening. He reminded me that the dharma transmission had always been from mind-to-mind, not in lengthy writings. That had been the tradition of Zen from the seven past Buddhas (including Śākyamuni) to twenty-eight Indian patriarchs, and then to the twenty-three Chinese patriarchs to Dōgen who brought the dharma to Japan. Reverend Yagi then talked about the *tanden*, the single transmission of the dharma from a master to a disciple. All heirs of Dōgen followed that heritage of transmitting the dharma from master to disciple, or in Reverend Yagi's expression, from mind-to-mind. That meeting in the *shicchū* with Yagi Rōshi was not a casual tête-à-tête or face-à-face affair. Yagi Rōshi stressed the way of Sōtō Zen as being oneness of teaching and ritual, and also of practice and realization of dharma—and that I should never ignore the importance of this interconnectedness. I also remembered that he explained the meaning of the three essential items, or *sanmotsu*, just before he bestowed them to me. The three essential items were a set of the three lineage charts referred to as *sanmyaku*. Those are: *shisho*, meaning the lineage chart given from master to successor as a proof; *daiji*, meaning the chart signifying Sōtō Zen; and finally, *kechimyaku*, or the dharma-transmission lineage-chart. After he explained the *sanmotsu*, he began to recite two sūtras in a soft voice: *The Harmony of Difference and Equality* and *The Precious Mirror Samādhi*. I joined him in unison. Then he said, "You must study these verses I have just recited. I wish I could explain them to you but I cannot; you must study them yourself."

With my receipt of the three essential items, my *shihō* was thus successfully completed. According to the official rules of the *shihō* (also called *dempō*) ceremony, it would take seven days, but the actual *shicchū* ceremony took only one day, even with Reverend Yagi's Nara accented and extended articulateness. Of course, he could not take seven days from his busy schedule and I, too, had a month of practice left at Nittai-ji and was on leave from there. I welcomed the shorter version of the ceremony, although he had just told me that the rituals are just as important as other Sōtō Zen teachings. This was a very private ceremony between master and disciple. There were probably no rigid rules applying to its nature. However, in addition to the official rules of the Sōtō School regarding this ceremony, there was a text precisely stating its significance and the procedure to be followed. A prominent Sōtō Zen master during the Edo period, Menzan Zuihō, wrote the *Discourse on the Private Teaching for the Transmission of the Dharma* (the *Denpō Shitsunai Mitsuji Monki*). Most likely, Reverend Yagi had referred to this text, yet the ceremony was a simplified version of it.

Simultaneously, I received permission to change the color of my robe, or *ten'é*. Reverend Yagi carefully planned not to waste any time. I finished one step to become *oshō* from the rank of *zagen*, which I was prior to that point. *Oshō* or *upādhyāya* in Sanskrit is a teacher who has the authority to bestow the precepts to those who are willing to take them. *Oshō* may also connote a teacher who could instruct disciples and teach them throughout their lives. Most significantly for me, at the time, was that an *oshō* is qualified to be the abbot of a regular Sōtō Zen temple. I had now reached that rank. On April 2, 1949, I officially received permission to wear a colored kesa. I still needed to visit the two head temples, Eihei-ji and Sōji-ji, to pay my respects, or *zuisé*.

***

Kitamura-san and I completed the two years of practice and left Nittai-ji monastery. Our final departure was, I believe, a few days before the spring *higan* on the equinox day of March 21, 1949. The reason why I remember that day was because I went to Higashi-Betsuin, the largest Jōdo-shin temple in Nagoya, with my cousin Muneö. I had my head shaved. I wore a Sōtō Zen robe over a kimono. I did not think anything of visiting a Jōdo-shin (Pure Land) temple. Muneö treated me to a bowl of Chinese noodle soup at a restaurant in Ōsu, the busy commercial district near Higashi-Betsuin. However, I could not stand to eat the thinly sliced pork or bean sprouts in my soup. I had never seen anything like the thin-sliced pork encircled in red-colored rind or intestinal-worm-like bean sprouts. Muneö laughed and took all the pork and bean sprouts from my bowl and ate them as if he were a genuine gourmand. I told this experience to Nin'yū Yamasaki. He said that I must learn to eat anything, just like the Buddha Śākyamuni, who ate everything that was offered. He was surprised that I had not eaten those before. I never had them at Hōsen-ji.

I actually missed my life at Nittai-ji, even before I left there. The monastic life would be difficult for some people, but when you have accustomed your body and mind to a daily routine of simple patterns following the sounds of bells, drums and wooden boards you can act naturally and be at ease. I missed my co-practitioners with whom I shared every bit of my life. But again, as with any other memories, it was necessary to discard my strong partiality to monastic life and face the reality of my present life. Dōgen expressed this in his chapter entitled "*Uji*," or "Existence is Time," from the *Shōbōgenzō*.

In his "*Uji*" chapter, Dōgen wrote: "A six-foot-tall golden statue is time. It is time; thus it is also the light from the decorative gild, which shines in time." Yes, time and I are the same; and I am constantly changing with time. At every coming moment, my psychosomatic system acts and reacts. Sometimes I cannot stop it. Stopping is an act also. Attachment to a specific past would be dwelling on the past in the present time. The past occupies the present. Therefore, such an attachment is unrealistic because the reality that is present is simultaneously absent.

Two years prior to this time, Kitamura-san and I traveled the same route to enter Nittai-ji. This time, on the way home from Nittai-ji, I was on the same streetcar with Kitamura-san. Sitting on the streetcar seat, I felt a bit of nostalgia although I kept quiet. I was actually enjoying that feeling when Kitamura-san asked, "You look sad. What happened?" I replied, "You know, I feel nostalgia for Nittai-ji." He looked at me in surprise, "To that place? Cut that off. You have longing for that place? Aren't you happy that you finished and can go home for good?" I replied, "No, it's just a flash of nostalgia." At that moment, I realized that I was thinking of the time we had just spent there. That time had passed and was no longer in the present. He reminded me of that. I replied, "You are right, Kitamura-san. Let's talk about something else. By the way, what are you going to do from now on?" Asking that question, I immediately realized that I was contradicting myself. The future is also not in the present.

Nonetheless, I revered and treasured the experience I had at the Nittai-ji monastery. Kitamura-san said, "I am soon to be qualified as a fully-fledged priest. I'd like to complete all the necessary steps and finish all of the requirements." I asked him, "Are you planning to become the abbot of Byakugō-ji?" He answered, "I don't know but I hope so. The present abbot is still in good health, so I will continue to assist him." When he said that, I understood his circumstances at Byakugō-ji. He was not a *rago* (son of a priest) like me. He needed to find a secure position, possibly at a well-established temple—most ideally at Byakugō-ji. This was why he called me a *rago* during our conversation in an envious tone. I then began to admire his courage in maintaining composure and a gentle-mannered attitude despite his precarious stance. I thought he was a worthy person and I would, if the present abbot asked me, strongly recommend him to be his successor at Byakugō-ji. As our conversation continued on about mundane matters, my nostalgia for Kakuō-zan, Nittai-ji waned and soon faded.

I would like to add a note here about the -ji in the Japanese temple names I have mentioned, such as Hōsen-ji, Kyukoku-ji, and Nittai-ji. "Ji" is used as "Buddhist temple" in Japanese today. However, the word "ji" originally referred to the government office where the government entertained foreign officials. For instance, when two Buddhists, Kasapa (Kashō) Matō and Shirukasen went to China in 65 C.E. they stayed at Pai-ma-ssu (Hakuba-ji in

Japanese), meaning "The White Horse Inn." Thereafter -san or -ji came to mean "Buddhist temple."

After returning to Hōsen-ji, I began visiting the members' houses. Nin'yū Yamasaki did not seem to have changed much, maybe because I saw him on and off whenever I visited Hōsen-ji from Nittai-ji. My monastic practice at Nittai-ji developed in such a way that became easier over the years. I suppose the war's shortage of monks and other essentials somewhat eased the strict adherence to monastic rules. The simple excuse that I was needed at Hōsen-ji had been accepted as the reason for my leaving Nittai-ji. For its members, I was a fixture at Hōsen-ji. After all, I was born and had grown up within the temple's realm. A member once told me that my absence made the temple feel incomplete.

***

My brother, Kengo, who was four years younger than me, had polio when he was a small child, but still managed to follow in my footsteps and was attending the same Sōtō Zen Buddhist high school in Nagoya. It was quite natural for us to follow the course that tradition dictated. For him, also, it would have been awkward to go into courses in commerce or technical training. Although as the second male-child, he could have taught or gone into a professional field had he not chosen the priesthood. But it was natural for him to take on a Zen curriculum by attending the high school founded and supported by the Zen Buddhist organization. He started middle school when I was in my fifth year. We had the same teachers in some basic courses and shared comments about those teachers. He was also surrounded and influenced by a Zen atmosphere in which he incubated no ambition other than to become a Sōtō Zen monk.

Nin'yū Yamasaki came to Hōsen-ji every day. He gave me all of the necessary news about the other temples nearby, filling the gap of my two-year absence in no time. After only a few weeks of idling, Nin'yū Yamasaki brought me a newspaper early one morning. He pointed to a notice of a national university's mid-year entrance examination. He said hastily, "This is a grand opportunity for you. Take this examination. The national university won't cost much. In fact you might be able to get a scholarship or a grant. I'm certain that you will pass the examination. I saw you studying very seriously before you went to Kakuō-zan." I was surprised by this unusual announcement. It gave opportunities for many young people, including repatriated soldiers who missed the chance to matriculate. Nin'yū continued after a pause, "You will need a college education in the coming age. Hōsen-ji will need a college-educated abbot hereafter." He had decided that I should take the entrance examination, even though I was a bit apprehensive, due mainly to the lack of precise information and its abruptness.

I took the special examination to matriculate into the sophomore class of a national university. It was in the middle of the academic year. Fortunately, I was one of several applicants who passed the examination and was accepted. I spent a year and a half on the three-year course before graduating from the college. I saved almost two and a half years counting all school levels in that curious transitional period. I cannot evaluate whether I gained or lost time. From the position of paying tuition and my personal time, it might have been a gain. But from the point of educational concern, I lost that time for learning. Aside from the loss or gain, I had spent almost two years at Kakuō-zan, Nittai-ji monastery. That was the equivalent time I saved in public education. Personally, I felt it was indeed very good timing.

Chapter 11

UNIVERSITY

仏祖の葛藤は皮肉骨髄の命脈なり。 拈花瞬目、すなはち葛藤なり。破顔微笑、すなわち皮肉骨髄なり。さらに参究すべし、	Entwinement of buddha-patriarchs involves their skin, flesh, bone and marrow. Buddha Śākyamuni held a stem of flower and smiled(at Mahākāsyapa). A broad smile was returned that was the entwining of branches, leaves, flowers and fruits.
葛藤種子すなはち脱体の力量あるによりて、	You must further study that the seed of vines have the power of casting off self-notion.
葛藤を纏繞する枝葉花果ありて	There are branches, flowers, and fruits interposed around the vines.
回互不互回互するがゆへに、仏道現成し、公按現成するなり。	This is the transmission of Buddhism, the standard of Buddhism realized.
－ 道元	- Dōgen
(『正法眼蔵』「葛藤」)	(*Shōbōgenzō, (Katto)* "Entwinement")

Thus far, I have written about my schooling and monastic life as they occurred. I had two parallel processes of learning; one was in the public educational system and the other was in Zen monastic practice. The two processes were intertwined in my daily life. The temporal arrangement of events by chronological order may pose some confusion for readers. While attending university my monastic training included visitations to the two Head Temples after my transmission of the dharma-lineage. The following are some episodes from my university days.

My university days passed swiftly but there were some notable events. I paid for my university tuition with private tutoring. Students called those moonlighting jobs *arubaito,* from *arbeit*, the German word meaning "work." As for my *arbeit*, I tutored two children whose father was the Toyota Motor Company founder's son. I did this for nearly two years. I was paid quite well, so that was sufficient for my tuition, books, and a little spending money. I also received a small monthly stipend from the university because I was working on a teaching credential. Every time I received money by giving services at Hōsen-ji, I gave it to my mother. My mother never mentioned financial matters and I didn't know our financial condition, but I did know my mother was having quite a difficult time feeding four teenagers, all students.

***

Hōsen-ji was not a busy temple and I had plenty of time for reading. In fact, it was a period of intense reading for me. I majored in Japanese literature at the university where I met Professor Ishikawa; he was a professor of Japanese medieval literature. I enjoyed his classes. A few months after our initial acquaintance, he invited me over to his house. I visited him a number of times thereafter. I unwittingly made him one of my role models. He lived in a regular middle-class house, which had an amazing number of books in the study and in the small drawing room. Professor

Ishikawa and his wife had no children. Both of them came from Tokyo and both had distinct *Yamanoté* accents, which is a pronunciation peculiar to the upper-middle residential district of Tokyo. He was a very handsome man and his wife was very beautiful. They were very different from the way I was brought up, and for that matter, from anyone I knew. While associating with them, I began to idolize them. They were urbane and distinguishably intellectual. Even though his field of specialization was Japanese medieval narrative literature, he had the aura of a chic European intellectual persona. In contrast to her husband, Mrs. Ishikawa was unequivocally Japanese, yet with modern frills suggesting a self-effacing grace in her speech and motions. When she focused in on some interesting topic of our conversation, she gave a hint of her bluestocking-like side.

Professor Ishikawa introduced me to countless western novels, philosophical treatises, and works of poetry from Germany, France, England, Russia, Italy and Spain as well as America. That experience was entirely new to me. I devoured book after book and often discussed my readings with Professor Ishikawa. He explained what Naturalism was to me through the writings of Zola, Stendhal, Balzac and Flaubert. He taught me about Classicism, Romanticism, Dadaism and Surrealism. On such occasions, Mrs. Ishikawa brought us English tea, then sat beside us and listened. From him I learned methods of reading and analyzing literary works, such as theme, plot, narrative voice, temporal arrangement, characterization and motif, which were entirely new to me. I enjoyed those occasional discussions more than his formal lectures on Japanese medieval literature. The experience with Professor Ishikawa opened my eyes to areas of culture I had not previously encountered.

On several occasions, he invited me to see movies, including

European and American films. Against the grain of Japanese gender roles at the time, his wife usually accompanied him to the cinema. On the way back from the cinema, we stopped at his favorite coffee shop and discussed the films. His comments often surprised me. One such comment regarding a cinematic aspect was that when the film was narrated from the point of view of a teenage boy, the stance of the camera was always at the boy's eye level. I realized that only after he pointed it out to me.

One day, while visiting at Professor Ishikawa's house, I met Eishō Hyūga, who had been a co-practitioner of mine at Kyūkoku-ji monastery several years back. He was attending the same university. I did not know until that time that Hyūga was a student of Professor Ishikawa. Hyūga later went to graduate school at Hokkaidō University. At Kyūkoku-ji, his *tan* (place of practice in the meditation hall) was located opposite of mine. Therefore, he was not as close to me as Keidō or Doi. I again met Hyūga in the 1980s when I visited Nagoya for a short time from the United States. He had left the priesthood and become a television producer. He worked at Nagoya's largest TV station as a program director. We met and had dinner near his station headquarters. We exchanged mutual experiences about Professor Ishikawa. He told me that he too had felt the strong impact of his influence. He told me that his experience of vast readings with the professor influenced and led him to his lifework of TV production. I did not doubt his assessment.

Professor Ishikawa also taught me how to read and write the Heian period scripts, or *sōgana*. At first, he handed me a fifteenth-century photocopy of the *Tale of Genji* and told me to learn it. He said that knowledge of it would help me in the future. About a week later, he sent me a letter in that very script style and I had to read it with no one to lean on. I struggled and finally managed to read his letter. He sent me another, and then another. After six or seven letters, I replied to him in that same script. After learning the script, I thought it was not so difficult. One evening, after I had mastered the script, Mrs. Ishikawa invited me to dinner at their house. At the dinner table, she said, "You learned the Heian script. Congratulations! It wasn't difficult, was it? It's wonderful. Ishikawa (she referred to her husband this way) said the script itself is not so important today, but you will be able to use it when you have need for it. Actually, you can learn whatever you need to learn if you have need for it—especially with your willpower, and with someone like him to push you." Professor Ishikawa simply smiled and listened.

Earlier, Professor Ishikawa told me the script would help me in the future. He was right. As a student of Buddhism, my knowledge of that script helped me on many later occasions. Whenever I faced the original written script or photocopies in that style during my research, I benefited immensely from knowing it. I also helped several people who could not read that writing. Professor Ishikawa was quite correct that knowledge of that script would be of great assistance throughout my academic career. I even taught the script to some of my graduate students in the United States and in Japan. Professor Ishikawa vastly influenced my cultural and intellectual endeavor.

While I was attending the university, before and after my classes and on weekends, I still had to visit Hōsen-ji members' houses as well as nearby temples for occasional services. I also tutored the Toyota family's two children, as mentioned earlier. Looking back to those years, I had overly idealistic thoughts framed in fragile sensibilities. Without Professor Ishikawa's influence, I would probably have just been content to live within my sheltered niche. I was inexperienced in the real world, yet I fashioned the carefree attitude of a university student. All in all though, I enjoyed my fruitful university days.

***

Much of my monastic activities occurred in tandem with my university studies, but, as you well know, they were not at all similar. Soon after the transmission of the three essential items and the granting of permission to change the colors of my robe, I arranged to visit the two Head Temples to offer my reverence.

These visitations, called *zuisé*, are also part of the requisite for the rank of *oshō*. I don't remember precise details of the days during which I visited the two temples, but I do remember I started with the head temple, Eihei-ji, on the Fukui prefecture on April 26, 1949. Looking back, I remember that on the way to Eihei-ji in the local train I met an elderly Sōtō Zen priest who asked me whether I was going to Eihei-ji for *zuisé*. At first, he gave me the impression of a matured and composed, if somewhat impassioned, priest. He calmly told me that he was from Shuzen-ji in Izu. I told him that my father practiced at Shuzen-ji for nine years. After I said that, his attitude changed, saying that fact was remarkable. He then began talking about the ways in which Shuzen-ji had changed over the course of forty years. He had heard about my father many times as a fine *tenzo*, or cooking monk. When I bade him farewell, he reaffirmed my choice to follow the monastic life. It was good seeing him on the way to Eihei-ji.

I arrived at Eihei-ji and informed the reception monk that I had come for the "reverence visit," or *zuisé*. I waited a few minutes at the entrance while he was informing others about me. Another monk came holding the handle of a paper lantern with large visitation letters of *zuisé*. This young monk who held the lantern offered me a

pair of nice slippers and led me to a room reserved for *zuisé* visitation. He then introduced himself with the following greeting: "My
name is Shōdō Kondō. I am your attending monk and will take care
of you." While I stayed there he attended to me, which included giving me instructions of what I was supposed to do at the hondō the
following day. It was a large and simply arranged room where he
offered me a cup of tea. Shōdō-san was about my age, with a similar
physique as mine and a very affable personality. My role at Eihei-ji
was to pay reverence to the founder of the school by officiating at
a service just as if I were an abbot of Eihei-ji. This was scheduled
for the next morning. Shōdō-san treated me courteously without a
soupçon of disdain. Occasionally monks stressed ritual procedures
and comportments so much that they became conceited and haughty
to others who were unfamiliar with them. I was a practicing monk
and had never had such a reception before this time. I was elated
and wished my mother could see me. I asked Shōdō-san what to
do, when to do it and other questions, which he answered precisely.
I thought I knew these things, such as how and when to enter the
naïjin (the central part of the main hall), bow at certain signals, and
move around the interior of the main hall. Thanks to the Kyūkoku-ji
monastery, we had learned most rules by taking on different roles;
however, this was a special occasion at the Head Temple and I was
unsure of how to conduct myself. With Shōdō-san's kind help, these
concerns lessened and I felt somewhat at ease that night. I slept well.

The next morning, Shōdō-san told me that the time had come
and I should get ready for my part in the ceremony. I put on my
robe and he led me into the main hall of Eihei-ji with the third
set of bells, just as the presiding priests, or *dōshi*, do. My role for
this day was to act as *dōshi*. The main ceremonial hall of Eihei-ji
was enormously large. The practitioners and the seasoned monks
were on each side of the hall, standing in a line face-to-face, called

ryōban. The other parts of the main hall were filled with those who came to worship. Perhaps, I thought, there were several hundred. When I entered the *naijin* (central section of the ceremonial hall) my legs began to shake with nervousness and I had to stand firmly to control the shaking. When I had to walk, I concentrated so as not to tip over and fall. What a shame, I thought to myself. After all, I had practiced since the age of six or seven, and yet I was irrationally nervous that morning. I held the ceremonial whisk, or *hossu*, but the handle was wet with perspiration from the palm of my hand. I don't know how it went for the first several minutes. I exerted my utmost effort just to calm myself. But once the chanting had commenced, I held myself together and my nervousness became somewhat controllable. Time moved ever so slowly though, as if the ceremony continued on for hours.

When I had finished my officiating role at Eihei-ji I was embarrassed about my tenseness. As soon as we returned to my room, to my surprise, Shōdō-san said, "That was very good. You did it very well. Congratulations for completing this." I said, "I am embarrassed. I suddenly became very nervous at the *naijin*." He replied, "Everyone becomes nervous when they stand there, even monks of forty or fifty. Don't be embarrassed." While we were finishing our conversation, Reverend Mokudō Katō came into the room. "Ah, Kazumitsu-san (my childhood name), I observed the ceremony. You did very well. It was very good, indeed. After you finish here, would you like to come to my room? Shōdō-san, could you bring him to my room?" Then he left.

***

Reverend Mokudō Katō was the abbot of Hōzō-ji, a temple approximately two miles from Hōsen-ji. After I had been ordained, I helped his temple on many occasions. Although he was the abbot of Hōzō-ji, he spent most of the year at Eihei-ji, and he held an office there. He originally came from a wealthy fabric manufacturing family near Nagoya but after the age of twenty-eight, he had decided to become a Sōtō Zen monk and practiced under Chōdō Katō at Fukuju-in in Nagoya, about five miles from Hōsen-ji. He became the abbot of Hōzō-ji in 1945. Hōzō-ji was a small temple and its members were fewer than Hōsen-ji. It was therefore ideal for Mokudō-san to spend a good part of the year at Eihei-ji and later he became Kan'in, managing the whole Eihei-ji on behalf of the Abbot. Every time I helped him, he offered me a fancy cake and before I returned home, he always gave me half a dozen delicacies to take to my mother. He repeated the same phrase over and over again in his strong Nagoya dialect: "These are for your mother. I take it that she is well. You take good care of your mother, Kazumitsu-san." He always spoke very softly. Mokudō-san never married.

Shōdō-san took me to the room of Reverend Mokudō Katō. It was a large room, furnished with a low table and a few sitting-cushions. One side had a large alcove wherein a black-ink stroked picture had been hung and underneath that a stalk of a faint white flower in a vase. It was a simple scene and gave me a forlorn feeling. Mokudō-san was sitting in front of the alcove and when he saw me he said, "Ah, come in, come in. Sit here with me." He pointed to a cushion and offered me a cup of green tea that is used in tea ceremonies. He commented that I had grown to be a fine monk. He asked me about my forthcoming plans. He also asked how my mother was and so forth. I stayed in his room for about forty-five minutes. Then, I returned to my room one more time and thanked Shōdō-san for his help. We exchanged addresses and promised to see each other in the future.

I took a long, slow train back to Hōsen-ji. Coal-burning loco-motives pulled the trains so every time the train passed through tunnels smoke permeated the cabins. The cabins were fairly crowded on this line. But I did not mind that at all. I felt relieved about finishing the big task of being a one-day-abbot at Eihei-ji. I suppose I was smiling. Two local elderly women were sitting facing me in the cabin. One looked at me and said, "You look very happy, I can tell. Are you going to get married soon?" I said, "Oh, no, no. I am not going to get married soon or ever." The other woman then said, "You visited Eihei-ji, didn't you? You look clean. Did you shave your head today?" I nodded but said, "I shaved it yesterday. I just finished an important cere-mony at Eihei-ji." The first one said, "That's why you look so happy. That's good. But I think you should marry. It is no good if you are unmarried, *kozō-san* (Mr. Little Monk)." Then the other woman said, "I wish I had a daughter your age, but mine are too old for you. If I had a young one, I would surely have her marry you, *kozō-san*." I didn't know whether or not to thank them for that comment. I was thinking about Mokudō-san, whom I deeply admired and who had never married. The two old women were laughing aloud looking at each other and at my blushing face. Teasing a young Zen monk about marriage and women in con-versation was once a taboo but such a lazy conversation on a slow local train could be an exception. I did not hold a grudge against them. Instead, I laughed with them.

***

On August 29, 1949, several months after my Eihei-ji journey, I visited another head temple, Sōji-ji. If I were to travel there today, the trip would take an hour and forty minutes by bullet-train, but back in those days it took seven or eight hours from Nagoya to Yokohama on the Tokaido train. Like the Eihei-ji visit, the trains were still pulled by a coal burning locomotive, which filled the cabins with smoke whenever the train passed through tunnels. I rode in the coach cabin filled with passengers. The interior was unbearably hot in the August weather; air-conditioning was not available on trains in those days. But this time too, I did not mind that condition at all. I had a mission to accomplish and that determination prevailed over discomfort on the train. Similar to the arrangement at Eihei-ji, I arrived at Sōji-ji in the middle of the afternoon for the next day's ceremony.

During this visitation one small incident occurred when I passed through the entrance. An attending monk brusquely told me to take off my shoes (which were sandals), wrap them and take them to my room. I understood that the temple had a problem because of the large number of visitors every day. In Japanese houses everyone takes off her or his shoes when they enter and step onto the raised floor. Sōji-ji being the most traditional place of all, everyone was expected to remove her or his shoes before entering the temple's interior. Keeping so many shoes in order must have been difficult. But *zuisé* visits were not common. These shoes alone should not have posed a big problem, or at least that was my thought at the beginning. Many decades later, I still remember the impatient way in which the attending monk told me to pick up and wrap my shoes—even though I was visiting to pay my respects and to act as an abbot for one day. A decade later I became the abbot of Fugan-ji in Nara, which was founded by the abbot of Sōji-ji in the mid-fourteenth century—making Fugan-ji a direct branch temple of Sōji-ji. It was a curious turn of events in my life but I did not know that when I visited Sōji-ji.

Zuisé was a requisite to attain the rank of *oshō*, which in turn gives credibility to become an abbot of a Sōtō Zen temple. My *zuisé* officiating in the ceremony went well since I had already had the experience at Eihei-ji. It was the same as Eihei-ji. My role was finished in the morning and since I had no acquaintances at Sōji-ji, I left promptly after the ceremony for Tokyo. I had a few friends in Tokyo whom I visited for the rest of the day since I was near there. I left Tokyo on the night train back to Nagoya. I went both ways on an all-night train. If you could find a seat on the train, you were lucky. Otherwise you had to stand all the way to your destination for seven or eight hours. I don't remember whether I found a place to sit. But I was relieved by the fact that I had completed the *zuisé* at the two Head Temples.

The two Head Temple visits, or *zuisé*, completed the requirements for my rank of *oshō*. Since I have mentioned those in detail, I shall now explain the priest ranking system. The priestly ranks of Sōtō Zen are as follows: *jōza*—one who has been ordained to be a priest and been entered in the Priest Registry; *zagen*—one who has been *jōza* and has completed the *risshin* ceremony in a ninety-day confined practice; *oshō*—one who has been *zagen* and has completed the *zuisé* (with a special visit to the two Head Temples, Eihei-ji and Sōji-ji;) and *dai-oshō*—one who has been *oshō* and has set up the dharma banner by leading a period of confined practice, or *kessei ango*. I believe it was after my transmission of the dharma-lineage, or *dempō*, when I was promoted to the erudite ranking of the second rank teacher, or *nitō-kyōshi*. To become a Sōtō Zen priest, one must have both the erudition ranks and the monastic ranks. I had finally attained my qualification for being a resident priest of Hōsen-ji.

Genshi Yagi Rōshi arranged for me to assume my tenure as an abbot at Hōsen-ji in a timely manner. Nin'yū Yamasaki helped him, quite naturally. I hoped that their responsibilities could now be lightened; yet it did not change much for Nin'yū Yamasaki. From the time I became the resident priest, he was still coming to Hōsen-ji almost as his regular procedure. As for Genshi Yagi, he had both his own temple and one in Osaka in addition to Hōsen-ji. Travelling from Nara to Nagoya alone consumed a good deal of his time. The task of helping to care for extra two temples must have been taxing for a man of his age. I am certain he was eager to end his responsibility at Hōsen-ji. It was ungrateful and presumptuous of me to guess their reasons for pushing me to be an *oshō*, and consequently, a fully qualified resident priest. I was sincerely grateful to both of them for taking care of me for seven years, especially during the chaotic war years.

By now I had reached my twentieth year of age and was just waiting for official permission to become the resident priest of Hōsen-ji. The notification from the headquarters of the Sōtō Zen School came as I expected. I became an official resident priest of Hōsen-ji on December 7, 1950, a few months before I graduated from the university and exactly a month before I reached the age of twenty-one. I promptly visited nearly a dozen temples nearby to formally inform them of my new role. Thereafter, I visited prominent members of the temple to tell them the news. The resident priests of the temples and all our members congratulated me. Reverend Kataoka, the abbot of Tenshō-ji, also congratulated me despite our earlier episode. I thanked him for his warm support and understanding. He held my hands for a long time and said, "Your mother must be very happy about this. Have you need of any help, don't hesitate to ask me."

December 7, 1950. Far left: Reverend Kuki (abbot of Chōraku-ji);
third from left: Zen Master Mokudō Katō; center: Kazumitsu Wakō
Katō (with whisk); fourth from right, back row: Kitamura-san (resident
priest of Byakugō-ji); second from right, front row: resident priest
of Jōdō-ji (name unknown); others - names and titles unknown.

My mother, my siblings, and my relatives, including my maternal grandmother, all congratulated me. Nin'yū Yamasaki said,
"Congratulations! Now you are a fully endowed resident priest. You
ought to be one of the leaders among all humans and all beings under
the heaven, *ninden no dai-dōshi*, oughtn't you? Yes, you ought to be
a leader, above and below the heaven, *ninden ganmoku*." Although
those words were old clichés in Zen circles, they struck a sentimen-
tal chord for me. Hearing those words reaffirmed my new position.
However, Hōsen-ji was historically not a rich temple and I had no
idea how to make it stay solvent. I had no experience or knowledge
of how to lift its financial condition. The country was slowly recovering but inflation rates were still at an annual two-figure level since
the end of the war. "*Takenoko seikatsu*," literally meaning "bamboo

shoot living," was a common term for those whose income was insufficient to cover their living expenses, and had to sell their clothing one layer at a time to feed themselves, like bamboo shoots. Layers of coats and kimono had to be shed one by one, but unlike "*takenoko*" their ways of living were unnatural and undeserved. No one I knew had any real hope for the future of the country.

Besides the economic crisis, my main concern was my own qualification. I asked myself, "Am I really qualified to be an abbot? Am I qualified to be a full-fledged *oshō*?" Nin'yū Yamasaki's phrase, "a leader among all humans" sounded attractive but also burdensome to me. What do I really know about Zen? What do I really know about Buddhism? Am I living in accordance with the precepts that I vowed when I became a Zen monk? Am I able to follow the precepts throughout my life without misconduct? Or if someone asks me what Sōtō Zen Buddhism is, can I answer that question reasonably well?

The reason for my concern was my own self-effacement. As Dōgen said in the *Shōbōgenzō*, in the chapter on "Inheritance [of the Dharma]" or "*Shisho*":

Every buddha had to inherit the dharma from every [preceding] buddha.

Every dharma-ancestor had to inherit the dharma from every [preceding] dharma-ancestor. This is the proof and the single transmission [of the dharma].

It is the utmost wisdom coming from enlightenment [i.e. *mujō-bodhi*].

Should you not be a buddha, you would not have been permitted to have inherited [the dharma].

Should you not inherit [the dharma], you will not become a buddha.

I felt the weight of this heavy statement. It was a serious concern for me, more so than the economic conditions of the temple. After all, economic problems were likely temporary; furthermore, it should not be the concern of a monk. I received all the necessary training for the qualification but they were only nominal. I had no confidence even to emulate those qualifications. As the third patriarch of Chinese Zen, Sengcan (Séng-ts'an), wrote in *Believing on the Mind, Xinxin-ming*:

> Reaching the Way is not difficult,
> if you have no dividing [mind] of good or bad.
> If you have no love or hate,
> you will be clear and unaffected.

I thought I was still not even reaching the portal of that Way. The economy, at that particular time, imposed on me an extra divisive force. As a head of the temple and a fully-grown adult, I was supposed to ease my mother's responsibility by managing financial matters. It was not the same dichotomy stated by the third patriarch, Sengcan, in the above poem. Later, when a Zen master Zhaozhou (Chao-chou) cited the above lines, a monk said to him, "You said that reaching the way is not difficult if you have no mind to divide good or bad. How do you make a no-dividing mind of good or bad?" Zhaozhou said, "Above the earth and under heaven, I am the only revered One." According to the traditional story, this statement is said to have been uttered by the Buddha just after he was born. The monk further asked, "Isn't that still having a divided mind—into good and bad?" Then Zhaozhou replied, "You fool! How do you make a non-divided mind good or bad?" Zen is exactly like that. The monk asked a further question after judging that Zhaozhou had fallen into a dichotomy, but his subsequent question fell into that same dichotomy. Zen points the way to that which is beyond dichotomy, above aesthetics or ethics, and untrammeled by contradiction.

Could I live every minute of my life above dichotomy? This world is filled with dichotomies, polarization, dualism, genders, ethical or esthetical appraisals, syllogisms, and so on in our daily lives. As a young Zen monk, these questions posed a serious dilemma for me. In my case I had no solutions in sight to eradicate them.

While I was tormented by the whole ordeal, Nin'yū Yamasaki was elated; he told everyone that I had officially become the abbot of Hōsen-ji. But I was not enjoying the role since I did not have any confidence or sound plans other than to just continue visiting the members' homes. As Dōgen said in his chapter entitled "Prostration and Obeying [the Master]," or the "*Raihai Tokuzui*," from the *Shōbōgenzō*: "Women also study under their masters diligently and acquire [right] knowledge. They can become leaders among the realm of humans and heaven, *ninden no dai-dōshi*."

This phrase, "study under their masters diligently and acquire [right] knowledge," came from the legend of the Second Chinese patriarch Huike's diligent study under Bodhidharma. Dōgen was right. Men or women who study diligently under the right masters could become leaders. Had I studied diligently under a master or masters? Yes, I had, but the problem rested on my own ability. What could I teach Hōsen-ji's elderly members? I was much younger than those who had many more experiences in this world. As I thought about this, the outlook for my future turned somber.

One day on the way to Hōsen-ji from visiting a member's house, I saw Nin'yū Yamasaki. It was a bright summer day. We met on a path in the vegetable field. He said, "What are you worrying about? You don't look well. Are you all right?" I said,

"I am alright, I suppose, except that, uh…. I don't know what I must do as an abbot." Then he said at once, "I knew that was what you were worrying about. You try to get something by stretching out your hands and arms but you cannot reach it. Is that right? If you are worrying about your new title, don't be foolish! A title is only a title and nothing more than that." He continued as we both walked, "Some time ago, I believe you were still at Kyūkoku-ji, you said that to attach yourself to your past makes you unhappy. You are attaching to the future. That future has not yet come. Why worry now for time which does not exist?" I said, "Ah, attachment."

Suddenly this word dawned upon me. It was true. I was helplessly attached to non-substance that was not present in the now. "Ah, yes, I am attached to…" He interrupted me and said, "You are indulging in a flight of fancy. Would you be a prisoner of your mind? Kill them. Get rid of them right away." He laughed aloud. At that moment, suddenly, Shih-té's poem came to my mind:

> What's so distressing about life?
> This world moves on,
> following the law of causation.
> Days and months pass away like waves,
> time is a spark off the rocks.
> Let heaven and earth shift about!
> I'll sit joyfully among these cliffs.

In the chapter on the "Existence in Time," or "*Uji*," from Dōgen's *Shōbōgenzō*, he reminds us that "Life is time, Buddha is time." We are supposed to live in one instant, the now, and no other time. I am here only in this instant. I am time, just like the Buddha is time. Nin'yū Yamasaki's simple words struck me. I invited him for a cup of tea at the temple but he declined and said he was already invited to his friend's house for a barrel of sake. He smiled and said, "I must kill my attachment too, mustn't I?" Again he laughed and then left without looking back.

***

To kill your attachment is very difficult indeed. What if your dearest attachment is involuntarily taken away from you by external forces, such as bombs or an inferno? Hōsen-ji's members were scattered after that devastating inferno, which destroyed that which is dearest—their lives and their belongings. Only about forty or forty-five families remained in the area. I was told then that to support a Buddhist temple through memberships alone would call for more than one hundred and fifty families. Hōsen-ji had less than a third of that number but had several wealthy members who generously supported the temple. My daily visits to the members took only a few hours of my time and then I was free. I waited eagerly for the weekend to visit various temples for *segaki* so that I could meet with Kitamura-san and other priests to exchange some news. However, it seemed that everyone was so busy that the topics were often limited to superficial and non-essential matters. We rarely conversed on a deeper level with other priests except for Nin'yū. Whenever I needed him he always managed to share his time with me.

***

Nin'yū Yamasaki was an indispensable priest for almost all neighboring temples during those activities for he arranged the *segaki* ceremonies such that they did not overlap one another. Nin'yū did

228

not mind those arrangements. Despite his busy schedule, he was very generous with his time with me. He also informed me of the news regarding Sōtō Zen activities as well as the news of the temples in the vicinity.

I believe it was the year 1948, Nin'yū told me, Ōryu-ji, a temple located about a mile east of Hōsen-ji, and Ryōsen-ji, another temple located about two miles west, started a day-care nursery. Those nurseries were operated by the wives of priests with a few helpers. I thought it was an excellent idea for those temples. It was nice for those temples to help and serve the community. The kindergarten I attended at Antai-ji burned down and no longer operated. Hōsen-ji, unfortunately, had neither the funds to build a nursery nor the space on the temple property. Furthermore, I was too young and unable to undertake such a responsible task.

I continued my role as a resident priest at Hōsen-ji, performing simple daily activities. One old member, Ruiji Ōya, a retired plasterer in his late 60s, came to the temple every day in the early morning to clean and weed the temple compound. My job cleaning and weeding at the temple was lessened with his help. Thanks to Ruiji, I enjoyed languorous days like the long hot summers of my childhood. I spent a great deal of time reading various genres of literary works, perhaps eight to ten hours a day. I enjoyed exploring all sorts of fields other than those I had studied at the university.

***

I still languished in recovering from the scars of adversity. I was told, though perhaps it was only hearsay, that people first fill their bellies and only then visit temples. Despite those rumors, there were often nearby temples that held a service called *segaki* on Sundays. *Segaki* or *segaki-é* literally means a "ceremony of making oblation to the hungry spirits," but in reality this was an elaborate memorial service. The host temple needed at least eight priests to perform this ceremony, and young priests were especially useful for preparation and cleaning afterwards. I was the youngest and therefore quite busy helping just about all of the neighboring temples.

The tradition of *segaki* came from several legends inherited from Indian and Chinese Buddhist texts. Some of those sources were from the *Nirvāṇa Sūtra*, in which *bhikṣu* (monks) and *bhikṣuṇi* (nuns) offered food to gods and devils everywhere. Also, the *Vinaya* (*ritsu* in Japanese) text includes an allusion to the Buddha hearing that a devilish woman, *Hārītī* (or *Kishi-mojin* in Japanese), ate human babies for her food. The Buddha offered *Hārītī* wholesome food, which changed her into a guardian of children. The legend that influenced Japanese Buddhism the most was from the sacred text *Dhāraṇī,* and was entitled "*Dedicated to Demons whose Mouths were Burning [and thereby could not eat]*," or *Yankou-egui Tuoluoni-jing* in Chinese and *Enkū-gaki Darani-kyō* in Japanese. This sūtra is about a hungry demon whose mouth was bursting with fire every time it wanted to eat, thereby preventing it from doing so. He asked Ānanda, the Buddha's close disciple, to heal this condition. Ānanda asked the Buddha what to do about the demon. Afterwards, he was instructed by the Buddha to prepare a bowl of food and offer it to the demon while reciting the "*Dhāraṇī for the Retention of Food and Drink,*" or "*Kaji-onjiki-darani.*" Ānanda did this, at which time the bowl of food conjured out an abundance of attractive delicacies. The food was for the demon but also for all other sentient beings. The recitation of the sūtra relieved their hunger and thirst. Despite the story depicting the time of the Buddha, most likely this text originated in China. There were a variety of *segaki* ceremonies, such as throwing food into a pond or river. In this way people could save those who were suffering on the path of evil. In Sōtō Zen, Menzan Zuihō directed the ritual in the *Rite of Segaki* or *Segaki Sahō* in the latter part of the 1700s. The essential meaning of this rite was the practice of "giving," or *dāna* in Sanskrit. *Dāna*, or *fusé* in Japanese, is the act of "giving [material or spiritual]," and it must be a selfless act. It is one of the six practices by which *bodhisattvas* (those practicing to become buddhas) are able to attain Buddhahood. The six practices are called *ropparamitsu* in Japanese or *ṣaṭ pāramitāḥ* in Sanskrit, and they are as follows: *dānā* (giving), *sīla* (keeping precepts), *kṣānti* (endurance), *vīrya* (diligence), *dhyāna* (meditation), and *prajñā* (correct perception of dharma). *Segaki* is supposed to remind all Buddhists of the bodhisattva practice.

***

One day in the mid-summer of 1949, at an annual temple activity, I had helped to air out various temple textiles, such as robes, kimonos, and picture scrolls. I found the "war-chest," a large wooden box of valuables which had been protected from the destruction of the war. I nonchalantly brought the chest to a breezy part of the temple floor. The articles contained therein had been selected and stored by my mother, so I did not know what I could expect to find in the chest. Among them I found the Eihei-ji edition of Dōgen's *Shōbōgenzō*. It was a surprising moment. At the monasteries, I had heard parts of Dōgen's *Shōbōgenzō* many times in the *rōshi's honkō* and other dharma talks. I remembered many excerpts and phrases from it but I had never held the *Shōbōgenzō* in my hands. I was hoping to find the *Shōbōgenzō* in the original writing style. That day my effort was unavailing. I looked at it carefully. This edition had been originally published in June of 1924. The one I had held in my hands was the eighth printing, published on June 25, 1943, two years before the temple's destruction. The Head Temple edition was considered to be the most authoritative text of the *Shōbōgenzō*. Not only that, but there was also an inscription by Kumazawa Taizen Zenji (a Zen Master), the Head Priest of Eihei-ji, dedicated to Hōsen-ji. The inscription took the form of a poem:

> *The skin and flesh of our dharma ancestors is still warm*
> *   today.*
> *The blood-vessel [dharma transmission] will not cease.*
> *It will continue on to dharma heirs ceaselessly.*

Kumazawa Zenji became the Head Priest on February 8, 1944. He resided as the Head Priest of Eihei-ji for twenty-five years. The inscription was dated only months before May 17, 1945, the day the temple was burned.

My mother found me looking at the book and said, "I thought you would find it useful someday. It was given to Hōsen-ji by Eihei-ji, when we donated the handwritten *Shōbōgenzō* of Gento Zenji, the founder of Hōsen-ji. I think you know that episode. We didn't know whether we could safely keep a book of such value. We were afraid that fire or water might damage it." I said, "Of course, that was the right decision at the time." My mother continued, "There was a priest from Kenkon-in named Tōgen Sumi who came and told us that giving the book to Eihei-ji was the best way to keep it safe." My mother made the right choice. I understood why the Head Temple edition of the *Shōbōgenzō* was in the war chest with the poem of a newly seated Head Priest (*Zenji*) of Eihei-ji. For my mother and me at that time, Eihei-ji was to us like the Vatican is to the Catholic faith, adorned by the presence of radiance. It was the spiritual summit and the domain of Sōtō Zen's standard of excellence.

My reading shifted to the *Shōbōgenzō* from that day forward; I completed all ninety-five chapters. My copy of the text had been published during the Second World War and the quality of the book was very poor. I had to handle it with special care at all times, otherwise the paper would tear and the binding would fall apart. With the inscription by the *Zenji*, specifically for Hōsen-ji, I could not read it carelessly. Every time I read it, I sat in the formal *seiza* position, on the *tatami* floor. I sat before my desk and placed the *Shōbōgenzō* on it. I had heard excerpts from various *rōshi* (Zen masters) and thought I understood them. I found it extremely difficult to read and understand them, but I tackled them anyway. I sat in the same position for so long that my mother began worrying about me. I said to her, "It's all right. You know Bodhidharma sat in the cave for nine years. Just a few years won't hurt anyone." My mother said, "A few years? Are you going to do this for such a long time? Why don't you walk around somewhere? You move only when you visit members' houses?" I did not listen to her. I earnestly read it chapter by chapter, yet I understood very little. Then I began reading it aloud, just like chanting. Even though I did not understand it, I wanted to experience the resonance of it. I discovered that the *Shōbōgenzō* was exquisitely written and finding it was as if it snapped me out of my reverie. After almost a year of reading it, I began to feel the essence of what Dōgen wanted to convey through the power of his sentences, words, and tones. I was still nowhere near a sound grasp of the *Shōbōgenzō*. In the beginning, Nin'yū seemingly approved of my intense reading. I once asked him whether or not he read it but he merely replied, "I started to read it at about your age, but I still haven't finished it."

I often asked Nin'yū Yamasaki random questions from my reading. One early autumn evening, he unexpectedly came to Hōsen-ji. When I saw him, I immediately asked, "What is the meaning of 'the whole world is one fist'? Or 'red-heart (yourself) is the endlessly clear world. I just pounded out marrow from the bone'? How could one fist equate to the whole world?" Nin'yū tapped his head with his fingers a few times and said, "It is the true self, self of no disposition, self of no artifice, the self before you think of what self is." I continued, "You are not answering my question. I am not asking about 'true self,' I am asking about 'one fist'." Nin'yū, upon hearing that, shouted at me: "I answered your question but you didn't get it. You are a two-year-old, very green! Just to be born won't make you a human being. Practice! Practice makes a man out of you. Practice Zen, practice life, and practice death! Then you understand the one fist. Your head is walking in front of you." When he was leaving, he said his last words: "The Buddha Śākyamuni said at his birth, 'Above and under heaven, I am the only venerable one.' I hope you understand that phrase some day!" He left abruptly, giving no chance for me to talk further.

I continued in the same mode of life, completely drawn into the *Shōbōgenzō*. I enjoyed every minute of it. Dōgen's use of words, sentences, and tonal quality were amazingly beautiful. Every phrase and sentence had a hypnotic influence on me. This turn of events in my life opened an entirely new vista of the world. Dōgen's views on time and space were entirely different from anyone except Nin'yū. I thought Nin'yū was eccentric and capricious in his behavior. I was wrong. We were taught at school how to think in terms of dichotomies: subject and object, right and wrong, beautiful and ugly. We conceptualized matters using so-called logical and relative reasoning. Teachers discouraged wish-washiness. Dōgen's world, however, extends beyond what we conceive of as the world. The world he showed me was original and essential to my existence. I spent more time on the chapters I thought would be useful for my life and less on others. I began recognizing passages from the talks of various *rōshis* and doing so brought me unspeakable delight and reassurance. Such feelings further generated my desire to undertake the entire book. It took a long time for me to understand Dōgen's vision of space—like a fist encompassing the whole world, like a life not entrapped by notions of numbers, qualities and quantities, such as near or far, large or small, and heavy or light. Dōgen's *Shōbōgenzō* was the clear and incisive critique of my life in this dualistic world.

***

I don't remember exactly when, but it was a cool and crisp late afternoon when Nin'yū Yamasaki came to Hōsen-ji. He came to the room where I was reading. He sat near my desk and looked at the page I was reading. He said, "Do you know Kawakatsu?" I replied, "No, I don't recall his name." Nin'yū said, "He is a city councilman from this neighborhood. He lives at Kashibata (the river-side), you know, across the Yamasaki River." I recalled his name vaguely when he said that. I had read or heard his name somewhere, but I had not paid much attention to his area of expertise. Nin'yū continued, "There will be a new school in his district and it needs a teacher next year. Are you interested?" I said, "This is the first time I am hearing of this. Would you please tell me more about the school?" Nin'yū continued, "You told me earlier that you took some courses in education, which leads to obtaining a teaching credential. Besides, you have been a bookworm for quite some time. You have become attached to whatever you are reading, whether it is Dōgen's work or not. Attachment is attachment. That's why I am telling you this. The school is named Honami School, a brand new school. The construction is almost finished and the school is planning to open this coming spring. They need teachers, although some have already decided to come from other schools. The principal of this new school is Mr. Seian Tanaka, or rather Reverend Seian Tanaka, a Sōtō Zen priest. I met him a few times. He may be similar in age to Gyokusen or he may be a few years younger." Nin'yu said that the experience would be good for me. I would learn of a different society, and my worldview would be broadened. In addition, I would learn how people think and act in different circumstances. I thanked him for his concern and said that I would think about it.

I had obtained a regular teaching credential when I graduated from college. It was, as Nin'yū said, a good idea to know society outside the Zen circle or priest-and-member relations. I decided to meet Kawakatsu-san. His house was not far from the temple; in fact, it was less than half a mile. I found out that "Kawakatsu" was not his name but the name of his shop. He owned a small dry goods store. Fortunately, I found him in the shop when I stopped in. He was a man of about fifty-five, not tall, fairly heavy set, and wearing a navy blue pinstriped three-piece suit. His hair was clipped short at the sides and maintained long over the top. It was parted in the middle and groomed with glossy pomade that had a strong scent. He was a bit pompous for a shop owner, I thought. Since he was a city council member, I suppose he had to act and dress accordingly.

He knew who I was. He knew my grandparents as well as my mother and her family, since they were all longtime residents of this area. My acquaintances were limited only to my peers and fellow Zen practitioners, and of course, the temple members. Kawakatsu-san was not a Hōsen-ji member so I had no occasion to meet him until this time. He said that the Honami School was

236

in his district, and that he had the authority to recommend me as a teacher. He added, "You know, Hōsen-ji-san (he called me this), every teaching certificate holder wants to teach in the city of Nagoya. The city teachers get better pay than in rural areas. This is a position that is sought after by many teachers. You just graduated and have no experience teaching. Well, I'll do my best to secure your position."

On the way back home I took a detour to Honami School, just to glance at it. It was a nice looking two-storied school. The school was built in an L-shape and its large grounds were enclosed with a three-foot high fence. At that moment, I made up my mind to endeavor to learn a new pattern of life. Nin'yū was correct. I needed to know how people earned their living. If I continued to be ignorant of people's arduous lives, how could I teach them Buddhism? If I were uninformed of people's joys and suffering, how could I extend my help to them? The essential tenet for all Mahāyāna Buddhists is to let other people reach the shore to *Nirvāṇa* before you cross that river. Thinking about this, I made my decision. I had no regrets in taking the job, if the job was offered to me. One small reservation was that I was bit hesitant about asking Kawakatsu-san for the position. My mother, sisters, brother and Nin'yū of course, were all happy about my decision to take the job and hoped that the prospect would come through. The following day, I visited Kawakatsu-san's house carrying something my mother prepared for him. Fortunately, he was there again. It was not bad at all. Kawakatsu-san treated me courteously and gentlemanly this time. I felt ashamed of the thought that had occurred to me about him the day before.

In my afterthought, this opportunity was a great experience for me. I was truly grateful for Nin'yū, whose guidance helped me in the right direction at this turning point.

The beauty of mountains and streams,
ascending layer upon layer,
veiled in smoke and mist.
The stream of mountain air
dampens my gossamer hat;
dew moistens my thatched coat—
on my feet, traveling shoes,
an old wisteria branch in my hand.

Once again
I contemplate this world of dust
from the outside:
What is it?
Only a land of dreams...

                              – Han-shan

Chapter 12

A SEED PLANTED

諸仏諸祖の受持単伝するは、古鏡なり。	Many buddhas and patriarchs transmitted this old mirror.
同見同面なり,	When anyone stands before it, they see their own faces.
同像同鋳なり、	When one sees the mirror, one sees himself.
	When anyone stands before it, they see their own statue.
同参同称す。	When anyone participates, it proves exactly.
胡来胡見、十万八千	When Hu (northwestern people/Mongolians) appear, eighteen thousand
漢来漢現、一念万年なり。	Han (people of China) appear,
	One thought includes tens of thousands of years.
古来古現し、今来今現し、	Ancients come as ancients, and contemporaries come as contemporaries.
仏来仏現し、	When buddhas appear, they are buddhas.
祖来祖現するなり。	When patriarchs appear, they are patriarchs.
－ 道元	- Dōgen
(『正法眼蔵』「古鏡」)	(Shōbōgenzō, (Kokyō) "Old Mirror")

On April 1, 1951, I began working at the Honami School in Nagoya. The school was located about a mile west of Hōsen-ji. The district had a mixture of both poor and relatively affluent families who lived in that part of Nagoya. My role at the school was that of a specialist teacher. I taught occasionally when some teachers were absent, but most of the time I was doing research on an experimental methodology; in addition, I occasionally demonstrated the research result in classrooms before other teachers. My assignment was a desirable one. I had no classroom responsibilities except for the occasional substitute assignments. It was a job for an experienced teacher, but the principal, Mr. Seian Tanaka, kindly assigned me to the job despite my limited teaching experience. As I mentioned before, Mr. Tanaka was trained as a Zen Buddhist priest as well as a school principal. Luckily, my work ended around half past three in the afternoon so I had plenty of time to attend to temple activities and still more time for my continuous reading of the *Shōbōgenzō*. It was a fitting job for the priest of Hōsen-ji.

One day during summer vacation in 1951, near the end of August or the beginning of September and after the busy *obon* period, Nin'yū Yamasaki came to Hōsen-ji looking for me. As soon as he saw me he said, "There is some good news for you. Listen carefully! I just met Hodō Tobase at Iō-ji, you know, Baidō Satō's temple." I replied, "Of course, I know Iō-ji, and I like Reverend Baidō Satō, but who is Hodō Tobase?" Nin'yū ignored my question and said, "I went to Iō-ji. I needed to talk to Baidō Satō. Satō was eating noodles in the room with this monk, Tobase Hodō. They knew each other from Eihei-ji monastery. They had *ango* (the ninety-day confined practice period) at the same time. Satō invited me to have some noodles with them, so I did. To my surprise, I was told that Tobase was the resident priest of Sōkō-ji, a Sōtō temple in America, located in San Francisco. Tobase said he needs an assistant priest there." I said, "That is interesting. Did he find an assistant priest?" Nin'yū continued, "No, not so far. He said there was a likely candidate from Tokyo, but he needed one more assistant. Sōkō-ji must be a busy temple. Tobase told me that there were only two Sōtō temples in America, one in San Francisco and the other in Los Angeles." When he said that, I immediately recalled Keidō Satō with whom I had spent a year at Kyūkoku-ji monastery in the middle of the Second World War. In his youthful days, he had told me many wonderful stories about San Francisco.

I had also heard about experiences in America from Reverend Dōkō Ōtsuka, an abbot of Bucchi-in in Yagoto, Nagoya. He was also the principal of Aichi Middle School, a Sōtō Zen supported school that I had attended in my youth. When I went to Bucchi-in to help with temple activities, he had told me of his experiences in California. Reverend Ōtsuka was an exchange student chosen to go to Zenshū-ji in Los Angeles by the Sōtō Zen Administrative Office. He went to Zenshū-ji in 1932, ten years after the temple was founded in Los Angeles and a year before Sōkō-ji was founded. His account of America was quite different from that of my friend Keidō. Keidō spent his childhood years in San Francisco whereas Reverend Ōtsuka was an adult and a mature student in Los Angeles. My knowledge of America led me to believe it was an exotic and almost utopia-like place, which was certainly enough to arouse my curiosity. After all, it was immediately after the Second World War. No one I knew, except for those two, had any direct experience living in America. Furthermore, there was a disparity between the level of American affluence and the people of war-torn Japan. America was definitely the envy, though unspoken, of the silent majority. Reverend Ōtsuka told me about "Little Tokyo" in the center of Los Angeles. He also told me about the universities, such as the University of California, Los Angeles and the University of Southern California. He told me that Los Angeles City College opened a few years before his arrival in Los Angeles. He told me about several other places that were impressive to him, including the city of Pasadena (where I would later live). His portrayal of Los Angeles sounded very inviting. He also told me about Sōkō-ji and San Francisco, as well as his visits to the University of California, Berkeley and Stanford University. He mentioned the Buddhist movement among the Japanese-American communities. He did not say much about the conditions of Sōkō-ji.

Dōkō Ōtsuka Rōshi was a priest with a wordly manner, soft spoken and often smiling. He later ascended to the position of *Fukukanin*, Vice-Manager of all Affairs, at the Sōtō Zen Head Temple, Eihei-ji. What I heard of his quiet descriptions about the Californian culture and its modes of life generated my interest in knowing more about it and perhaps experiencing it for myself. Though I did not have wanderlust, those ideas of California from my two acquaintances generated my curiosity about the American way of life.

While he was talking about Los Angeles, Reverend Ōtsuka went to the back of the house and brought back a large, heavy brown leather trunk. It was filled with photographs and documents in English. He read some of them in English and I was amazed by his fluent use of the language. I had never heard Keidō Satō speak English while we were together during the Kyūkoku-ji days. It may well be because during the Second World War the English language was banned entirely. I assumed Keidō could be like Reverend Ōtsuka. I envied Reverend Ōtsuka's extraordinary experience and high level of English language fluency. When Reverend Ōtsuka told me of his American experience, I had already been exposed to numerous Western writers' works and had some basis of understanding them, thanks to Professor Ishikawa. They were not all American works but their worlds were similar in many respects to America. All of those were available in Japanese translations. They were scattered by that plethora of dazzling attractions, and for me, all were forbiddingly gravitational. I learned many foreign words, but those words were without practical application. For instance, "put a piece of *chōzume* into her mouth," literally means, "put a piece of 'stuffed intestine' into her mouth" in Japanese. I did not know what a "stuffed intestine" was, but the literal passages were still veiled in exotic romanticism. I accepted "stuffed intestine" as some sort of delicious food that literary heroes and heroines enjoyed, not as a grotesque substance. The post-war Japanese translated *chōzume* to "sausage." Many other words, such as "blackberry jam," "wiener sausage," "cheese," "butter," and "lamb" imaginatively referred to items without any basis for empirical knowledge of their substance.

Interestingly, such phenomena already existed in Buddhism, and I was amazed at the recurrence of that historical trait. In the early seventh century, a Chinese Buddhist monk named Xuanzhang visited India via Kashmir. He studied Buddhism and the new Indian culture there. When he returned to China, he brought back many new words. Some words, such as *dadhi*, the finest milk product in India, did not exist in China; instead, only the word for the "marvelous taste [of milk]" or its variation, "marvel," entered the Chinese lexicon. This word in Japanese is *daigo*, which later became synonymous with *nirvāṇa*. A Japanese emperor later named himself using that very word, without substance.

***

In 1945 or 1946, the United States began to help starving Japanese citizens by providing food supplies such as various canned and dried foods. At that time, quite a few people in urban Japan had died of malnutrition. I witnessed some who had died from that condition; it was a slow and lamentable death. We could not help everyone who was struggling to get a spoonful of food during those rough years. The starving ones had dull yellow complexions, bony bodies, and often had swollen, bloated abdomens. They slowly lost mobility and died.

Hōsen-ji was delighted to receive this American aid but it only came once or twice. One item was a can of granulated pink colored sugar with a fruity scent. My mother used it to prepare vegetable "sushi" with a strawberry scent. We all enjoyed the sweet taste for we had not partaken in sweets for over four or five years. Later, I found out that the can of pink sugar was actually "Jell-O." Another item was a quart and a half can with a beautiful picture of a pineapple pasted on the outside. We all sat around the table with a bowl and chopsticks. My mother opened the can and dipped a ladle into the can but she couldn't scoop up any pineapple. She said, "Something is wrong. There is no pineapple in the can." I looked at the picture of the pineapple on the label. It was a can of pineapple juice. Even I understood that word. We were disappointed to say the least at that moment of hunger. We had not heard of such a thing as "pineapple juice." Before the war, we had eaten a can of pineapple but did not know about pineapple juice. Now we had experienced both Jell-O and pineapple juice. We learned later that we were lucky to have received pineapple juice instead of grapefruit juice. Grapefruit juice was bitter and a totally unfamiliar taste, which was not native to Japan.

Quite possibly, my unspoken gratitude to Americans, who helped starving Japanese even in the wake of a war that drew such hostile enemy lines, promoted my curiosity about America. It was also my simple curiosity to experience something previously unknown to me. Every item Reverend Ōtsuka mentioned in his American journey whetted my appetite. Had I ever seen Americans up close or had I ever talked to them? I had no experience of that sort yet.

One afternoon when I was in middle school, I went to see an American film with a few friends. I don't remember the title or the plotline of the movie, but one scene that unfolded in a bar left me with a puzzling impression. I believe it was Edward G. Robinson who was sitting on a barstool. A silvery-blond girl came through the door, swinging her hips in a risqué fashion. Edward G. Robinson said to her, while he had a large cigar in his mouth, with the Japanese translation, "Young lady, you are genteel." The "young lady" moved on to the back of the bar still swaying her hips with her handbag over her shoulder. We were all shocked by his statement. This was a mistranslation, of course. We were too naïve to catch the true meaning. We discussed American esthetic criteria and came to the conclusion that their taste in clothing and manners were ostentatious. Their mannerisms were unmistakably idiosyncratic.

Years later, I saw the same film on a "late-late show" on television. "Young lady, you are genteel" was actually, "Baby, you've got class." Poor translations appeared all over Japan, from menus in coffee shops, to instructions on how to cook prepackaged food and shop signs. Even Japanese films introduced into the West had poor subtitles.

I suppose these phenomena happened many times over in the process of cross-cultural transition. Idiosyncrasies in early Chinese Buddhism also occurred, since dissimilarity and foibles between Indian and Chinese culture prohibited the spread of Buddhism for nearly 300 years. Foibles were corrected by reverting to original Indian terminology. Aside from the problems associated with translation, my curiosity about America remained undamaged.

I wanted to find out what America was like in reality by experiencing its culture directly, so I asked Nin'yū Yamasaki to arrange a meeting with Reverend Hodō Tobase. I needed more information about Sōkō-ji and San Francisco. If he had to leave Iō-ji that day, I could come to wherever he wanted to meet. Nin'yū said, "Don't tell your mother about this yet; she might have a heart attack." I said, "I haven't decided yet. I need more information about the temple." He did not ask further, and went to Iō-ji again. While I was waiting for him I began regretting my request. I realized that going to America was a huge event that would affect everyone around me. I had no idea what I would do with the temple in the case of my departure. My younger brother Kengo was still a sophomore in college. He had not yet decided to go into the priesthood. In fact, he had undergone no monastery training up to that date. What if he said that he did not want to be a Zen priest? Kengo observed the temple conditions while growing up at Hōsen-ji. Many adverse thoughts haunted me while I was waiting for Nin'yū.

Nin'yū came back to Hōsen-ji an hour or so later and as soon as he saw me, nodded a few times and smiled. He whispered in my ear, "He is going to stay overnight and wants to see you after dinner tonight, say around seven thirty. You must go see him. You don't have to make a decision right away. In fact, you mustn't just yet. Listen to him carefully, and ask any questions you have tonight." Then he said loudly, "Good night everyone. Don't let the mosquitoes bite you," and left. After supper, I told my mother, "I am going to Iō-ji to see Reverend Tobase, who is the abbot of a San Franciscan temple, Sōkō-ji." My mother asked, "What about? Do you know him?" I told her, "No, Mother, Nin'yū just told me that he is visiting Reverend Baidō Satō. Both of them practiced at Eihei-ji at the same time. I would like to hear about San Francisco and, of course, Sōkō-ji." She said, "That's good. San Francisco must be a nice place. It would be a nice opportunity to hear about it directly from someone who lives there."

I left Hōsen-ji around 7:00 o'clock in the evening, summer time. There was still light in the sky. "Summer time" meant it was "daylight-savings time." This was part of the effort to embark on the post-war reconstruction of Japan by the American government or the Occupied Allied Forces in those days. Late summer heat still lingered around town and there was a hint of cooking odors from the houses. I walked to Iō-ji at a normal pace, though I was quite serious about the meeting with Reverend Tobase. I arrived at the entrance of Iō-ji about ten minutes before 7:30, where tiny Mrs. Satō greeted me and led me into a guestroom. Both men were sitting on tatami and in front of each was a teacup stand on a wooden saucer.

At the entrance to the room I knelt down, put both hands in front of me on the tatami and bowed to them. Reverend Satō said, "Oh, Kazumitsu-san. Welcome, welcome; come in and sit down. A cup of tea will come soon." He looked at Reverend Tobase while he was still talking to me, "Here is Reverend Tobase, a good friend of mine from the Mountain (Eihei-ji). He was kind enough to visit me because he is going to Sōkō-ji in America. I hope not, but possibly, this will be for good. We don't see each other often, but this time he has come to say farewell." I said, "On such a precious evening, I feel awkward interrupting your meeting." Then Tobase said, "Oh, no, no. I wanted to see you. I met Yamasaki Rōshi several hours ago and I told him about my new assignment at Sōkō-ji in San Francisco. He mentioned that to you, didn't he? He also said that you wanted to hear about the life and conditions over there. I am definitely delighted to see you." He smiled.

Reverend Hodō Tobase was sitting on a cushion but I could tell he was chubby and not too tall, perhaps five feet two inches. I had expected to see him in Buddhist robes but he was wearing a white shirt and a black necktie. He rolled both of his shirtsleeves to his elbows and his pale hands were resting on his thighs. His charcoal-gray jacket was folded and placed beside him. He was wearing a wool flannel suit in the sweltering heat of a humid Japanese summer. Despite the weather he was very cheerful and laughed often throughout our meeting. As always, Reverend Satō, with a similar physique to Tobase but wearing a priest's robe, was quiet. A few of his front teeth were missing and the empty spaces created a hissing noise when he spoke. For an aged Zen monk practicing vegetarianism, it was exceptional for him to have retained some of his teeth. The Zen diet is strictly vegetarian with neither animal nor milk products. Reverend Tobase was almost bald but, to my surprise, he was beginning to grow his hair long. It looked as if he had a half-inch of hair on each side of his head.

"Do you know anything about Sōkō-ji or San Francisco?" Tobase asked me. I replied, "Not much Sir. I have heard some stories from Keidō Satō, the son of Reverend Sato, who was an abbot there before the war." Tobase opened his eyes wide and said, "Ken'itsu Satō? What a coincidence! He was the second abbot of Sōkō-ji. I chant his name every morning. Oh, what a coincidence." I continued, "I have also heard about America from Reverend Dōkō Ōtsuka." Then Tobase interrupted, "Reverend Dōkō Ōtsuka? Yes, he was also there before the war. I believe both Satō and Ōtsuka met each other in America. What a coincidence; oh, what an astounding event this is." I was stunned about how many of my acquaintances were also acquainted with Tobase. His verbalization of "coincidence" resonated with my own feelings at the time. Suddenly, he exclaimed loudly and between laughs, "Wakō-kun, you are the right person to come and help me at Sōkō-ji. Sōkō-ji awaits you. People there need a priest who has qualifications such as yours." He chuckled and nodded his head a few times, lost in thought.

He told me San Francisco did not have hot summers. The weather was usually cool, but not too cold, and never hot except for a few days of "Indian summer" in late August. He looked at his wool jacket and pointed to it, explaining, "I wear Western clothes over there; the members want their priests to look like regular gentlemen, so I only wear robes when I perform rituals. I am also growing my hair long. If you come to San Francisco, you will do that, too, Wakō-kun. If you wear a robe with your head shaved, nobody will sit next to you in the streetcar because you look so strange." In those days, short-sleeved shirts were not worn under a suit, I suppose, even in San Francisco. Tobase's rolled sleeves were common in Japan but his wool suit was quite unorthodox even in the late summer. I liked Reverend Tobase's openness on this first meeting at Iō-ji. I learned that his tenure at Sōkō-ji had only started several months prior to when I met him. He had come back to Japan to prepare for a long stay in San Francisco. He also said he wanted to find an assistant or two during that trip, who would be willing to stay there for a long time.

Before I left, he formally asked me to help out at his mission in San Francisco. I said to him, "I have just heard about this; I have not yet had a chance to think about it. I think it is a wonderful opportunity for a young priest to go and work there. If you please, Reverend Tobase, would you give me a few days to think it over? Besides, this is such a big decision I cannot decide it unilaterally. Is there any way to contact you in Japan? If not, can I write to you and send a letter by air-mail?" Tobase said it was a good idea to think carefully and consult temple members. He would be in the Nagoya area for one more day. After that he would go to Tokyo and stay there for a week to ten days before he left for San Francisco. He gave me an address in Tokyo where I could reach him.

As I left Iō-ji for Hōsen-ji, warm moist air enfolded me in the darkness. Everything had moved so swiftly, and I was keyed-up by the thought that I might go to San Francisco. This was an event I had never dreamed of before. When I heard the stories from Keidō or Reverend Ōtsuka, I never imagined that they would come to me that way. As I walked nearer to my home, I suddenly realized that I would have to explain this episode to my mother, and eventually to the temple members. I stopped for a moment and thought carefully, but I hadn't a clue as to how to go about it.

When I got home, my mother was with my sisters and brother in a room near the kitchen. I still had no idea how to tell her about the possibility of my going away. I did not know how she would react if I were to go to America. Would she think that I would be abandoning her? I decided to give a good deal of thought to this before telling her. I said, "It was a pleasant evening at Iō-ji. The priest from America is a nice person. I have heard many things about America." My mother said, "That is good. I am glad that you had a good time." Soon after that conversation, I retired to a small room near the entrance, which I used when I read the *Shōbōgenzō* and other books. I thought about *kaikyō-shi*, the overseas priests, in San Francisco over and over again. I even picked up a piece of paper and drew a line down the center dividing it into two sections—one side of the line was for and the other was against going to America. I began jotting down any ideas for either position. I was skeptical, thinking "Does this judgment of dichotomization have any significance? What conclusion do I get from this polarized diagram?" But, for consolation I weighed pros and cons in this way to help make my final decision.

Besides deciding whether or not to go to America, this was in fact the first time I had given serious thought to my life and my future. Did I really like my prearranged course of life to become a priest at Hōsen-ji? Or would I prefer some other course of life?

This thought had never before occurred to me. I thought, "If I stay at Hōsen-ji, what will my future be?"

Up until now, Dōgen was my guiding principle. He had been my inspiration ever since I discovered the *Shōbōgenzō* in the chest. Dōgen had brought over a pure form of the Sung Dynasty monastic practice from China. But his teachings were for monks willing to practice in a monastery their entire life. He had nothing to say for ordinary priests or laypeople who supported local temples. Reading the omnibus of Dōgen's thoughts on Buddhism, I found nothing about local temple management. In fact, many of his statements contradicted my service to the lay members.

In his *Wholehearted Practice of the Way*, or *Bendōwa*, Dōgen wrote, "Practicing Zen is casting off one's body and mind, which will be attained only through sitting. Burning incense, prostrating, repentance and chanting sūtras are not necessary." His teaching of "only sitting" would not help my situation, whether I stayed at Hōsen-ji or went to America to serve at Sōkō-ji in San Francisco. I carefully considered how Dōgen and his close disciples started their new Zen Buddhism in medieval Japan and what made it flourish so.

***

At this critical juncture in my personal narrative, it seems important to discuss some aspects of Buddhism and the early development of Sōtō Zen in Japan. Those interested in the early history of Sōtō Zen may benefit from reading the following section. If not, I ask my reader to bear with me because the following is an important facet of Sōtō Zen, which greatly influenced the course of my life. Studying and reflecting on the life and thoughts of Dōgen, I reached a new level within myself and gained strength for the long journey of my life.

Dōgen had inherited this pure form of Zen, stressing "sitting" more than other provisional activities, from his master Rujing during his stay in China. He even criticized the popular Zen manual of his day—the *Pure Rules of Zen Monasteries* (or the *Chanyuan Qingguei* or *Zennenn Shingi*), as being too modernized. He thought it necessary to return to the earlier untainted way of the *Pure Rules of Baizhang* or *Baizhang Qingguei*, which are called *Hyakujō Shin-gi* in Japanese.

These texts were in essence monastic rules about how to live and practice Buddhism. However, a monastery cannot support itself without the laypeople's support. Let me explain this tension in detail. From Buddhism's early roots in India, the *dāna*, or donors to the Buddhist cause, were recorded in the Pāli text, the *Dighanikaya*. Their presence was an integral part of the continuance of Buddhism; without *dāna*, or the laypeople's material support, Buddhism would not exist up to the present time.

Around the time of the Buddha, India experienced a blossoming socio-religious climate. Social norms were established for the people to seek the Dharma (Religious Law and Tenets) in order to be liberated from never-ending *saṃsara* (the life-and-death cycle). Those who sought the Dharma were revered and people offered them food and clothing in return for their guidance. Of course, during the time of the Buddha, domiciles of monks and nuns, called *vihāra* or *saṃghārāma,* were living in forests and caves with minimal needs. They received food from the *dāna*, and their customary practice was to eat it almost immediately, or at least before noon. I suppose that was part of their practice of asceticism and was, I assume, also followed so the food would not spoil in the tropical zone. They possessed only three articles: three pieces of clothing, one bowl and a sitting mat. The three pieces of clothing were the *antar-vāsaka*, the daily work and sleeping robe; the *uttarāsaṅga,* the robe for rituals, listening to lectures, and the days of *uposatha* (the days designated for meetings); and *saṃghāti*, a large outer robe for special occasions such as visiting villages for mendicancy. The last robe is considered formal attire. All clothing was the color of *kāṣāya*, yellow ochre or neutral colors, since no bright colors were allowed. Practitioners used the bowl for accepting food and eating only. Dōgen upheld this tradition and he instructed practitioners on the twelfth day of the third month, in 1245 at Daibutsu-ji (Eihei-ji's former name), that the bowl and the robes (*kesa*) were the most important items Buddhists inherited from the buddhas and dharma ancestors.

***

Time and society have changed, as our lives have become increasingly complex. The arena in which we move around has expanded many times over. The society in which we live has warped from a mutually trusting communal society, or *gemeinschaft*, to an impersonal benefit-oriented society, or *gesellschaft*. The economy has changed from a basic farming livelihood to a more complex fabric of capitalistic manufacturing, distribution and services. In the Buddha's time monks and nuns could simply survive with alms given. Today, the maintenance of even unembellished temple buildings calls for sizable monetary support. Priests could still wear three simple sets of clothing in neutral colors but the mores of our social hierarchy mandate colorful and finely textured robes to be worn in rituals as status symbols. In the midst of all this upheaval, still I found the *Shōbōgenzō* was the best way to find peace of mind.

As I mentioned before, Dōgen brought a pure form of Sung Dynasty Zen monastic practice over from China. His form of Zen

Buddhism did not sail smoothly in medieval feudalistic Japan, at least not during his lifetime. The year he returned from China in 1227, he first stayed at Kennin-ji, a Rinzai Zen temple in Kyoto. Kennin-ji was Japan's oldest Zen temple, built by Eisai in 1203. Dogen's new way of practicing Buddhism disturbed the Tendai School group in Mt. Hiei and they decided to banish Dōgen from Kennin-ji. That pressure might not have been the only reason for his relocation. In 1229, he decided to move to an interim temple, An'yō-in in Fukakusa, a hamlet south of Kyoto. In 1233, he moved again to Kannon-dōri-in Kōsho-ji in Uji, also south of Kyoto. A group of serious practicing monks under Dainichibo Nōnin, an active Zen advocate, joined Dōgen after their teacher Dainichibō died in 1234. One of his students, Koün Ejō, first joined Dōgen. Then in 1241, Ekan, Tettsū Gikai, Giyin, and Giën joined Dōgen's Kōsho-ji monastery. All of them had a deep respect for Dōgen's sincere practice of *Shōbō Zen*, the true-dharma Zen.

The lord of Echizen (or the Fukui prefecture of today), Hatano Yoshishige, invited Dōgen to come to Echizen. Dōgen accepted his invitation and in 1243, moved to Shibitani village in Echizen. Dōgen was then forty-two years of age. The initial temple where he and his group settled was named Daibutsu-ji. Later the name was changed to Eihei-ji. (Koün) Ejō and (Tettsū) Gikai followed Dōgen. The Sōtō School was formally founded at Eihei-ji. Ejō, Jakuën (a Chinese monk), Gikai, Giën, Giün and Donki were prominent practitioners in the early days of Eihei-ji. Ejō painstakingly edited and compiled the *Shōbōgenzō* while Dōgen was still alive and then after his death. Later Ejō transmitted Dōgen's dharma-lineage and succeeded Dōgen to become the second abbot of Eihei-ji. In those days, Eihei-ji had only two or three buildings and Ejō thought it needed a more suitable environment for the practitioners. He sent Gikai to study the long-established Chinese Zen monasteries. Gikai stayed in China for four years and then returned at forty-four years of age.

Gikai was given Ejō's dharma-lineage and became the third abbot of Eihei-ji. This was five years after he completed his Chinese studies. During his tenure as abbot, he built the new temple gate based on what he studied in China. Also, he introduced innovative activities and rituals. His revisionism was not all accepted smoothly and invited disputes from other monks, especially from Giën. Giën had to resign from the abbot position at Eihei-ji. The former abbot of Ejō had come back to Eihei-ji from his retirement. Gikai then simultaneously received an invitation from a Shingon School monk who resided at Daijō-ji in Kaga, approximately forty miles west of Eihei-ji. A Shingon school priest named Chōkai revered Gikai and urged him to come to become Daijo-ji. Keizan Jōkin, a practitioner and admirer of Gikai, followed Gikai to Daijō-ji. After Gikai's resignation from Eihei-ji, Giën became the fourth abbot of Eihei-ji. Giën was a peer of Ejō and Gikai, and studied under Dōgen from the early days. While Giën held the helm, he did not have outside support and Eihei-ji's existing buildings began to deteriorate.

A Chinese monk, Jakuën, who aspired to study with Dōgen, followed Dōgen to Japan in 1228, four years after Dōgen's return. He studied with Dōgen until Dōgen's death in 1254. Eventually, Jakuën transmitted the dharma from Ejō and founded Hōkyō-ji, not far from Eihei-ji. His dharma heir, Giün (not to be confused with Giën), who studied with him for twenty years, became the fifth abbot of Eihei-ji after Giën. When Giün became the Fifth abbot of Eihei-ji, as mentioned above, Eihei-ji was getting rundown and needed maintenance. Giün was sixty-two years of age but he energetically worked to restore the temple even using some assets from Hōkyō-ji. Fortunately, he received the support of Lord Hatano Michisada and obtained the large gong for Eihei-ji. After

Giün, twenty more successive abbots of Eihei-ji were from the lineage of Jakuën and Giün.

Now, returning to Keizan Jōkin, who followed Gikai and became the founding monk of Daijō-ji. Keizan was only twenty-two years of age at the time. After a while, Keizan left Daijō-ji and visited many Buddhist masters. When he was thirty-one, his master Gikai asked him to come back to Daijō-ji to help him. The following year, Keizan began lecturing the practitioners there. One of his major works, the *Denkō-roku*, or the *Record of the Transmission of the Light*, was based on those lectures. According to the record, his master Gikai sat and listened to his lectures. Keizan diligently upheld Dōgen's teachings, but he began adding new dimensions such as teaching lay people—including women. He received the purple robe from the emperor, as did Dōgen. Dōgen did not wear it, instead wearing only a black robe, but Keizan wore the robe. Keizan adopted esoteric teachings of the Shingon School by enshrining esoteric deities, or *myō-ō* or *vidyā-rāja*, and the heavenly beings (*tenjin* or *devāta*), including *Brahma, Indra*, and so on. He recited *Dhārani*, the mystic syllables regarded as the quintessence of the *sūtras*. Some of them took the form of *mantra*. *Dhārani*'s verses were believed to embody a mystical power. *Dhārani* literally means that which sustains something, or *sōji*, which is the teaching of the Buddha in esoteric Buddhism. Keizan's broad approach to the teachings appealed to laypeople, and as a result his temples flourished. Keizan founded many temples—among those were Sōji-ji, which became the Head Temple of the Sōtō School later along with Eihei-ji. Today's Sōtō Zen is the mélange of those two traditions: Dōgen's strict monasticism and Keizan's all-encompassing practice.

***

Is there any inspiration to draw from this chronicle of early Sōtō development? I thought, from the history of Sōtō Zen, I could learn some new modes of innovation. I am a distant dharma-heir of Dōgen and Keizan, and a student of the *Shōbōgenzō* and the *Denkō-roku*. I always had the conviction that I was learning Buddhism through Dōgen and his successors.

Dōgen's practice was strictly for monks through-and-through and he believed that only monks could become buddhas. He said:

People do not need to worry about how close or not close [they are to Buddhism]. I only recommend that one takes the precepts as a monk. Do not regret that you might ebb away [from Buddhism]. Do not worry whether your practice is effective or ineffective. This [taking of the precepts as a monk] is the true dharma of the Buddha.

(*Shōbōgenzō*, "Virtue of Leaving Home," *Shukke Kudoku*)

It sounds as though Dōgen avowedly discriminated against laypeople who had not taken the precepts, but this is not so. Considering the circumstances of the time in which he lived and wrote, Daibutsu-ji (Eihei-ji) was still in its embryonic stage, and had only a small number of devoted monks. There was no likelihood of laypeople being able to practice there. Eihei-ji was, and is, located in a remote area, and, in those days, it was not easily accessible for short visits. Only determined monks could carry out their rigorous and steadfast practice in the isolated location of Eihei-ji. Perhaps Dōgen, being the keenly discerning person that he was, felt that he needed to firmly establish this new form of Buddhism in Japan and thus had to train and educate the future leaders of this new school of Buddhism.

Dōgen wrote about many of his predecessors who had diligently practiced Buddhism. One practitioner he admired was a

Chinese monk named Guishan (Kuei-shan), who had transmitted the dharma from Baijang. Guishan climbed a mountain, now named Mt. Gui (Kuei), or Guishan, alone and lived there for forty years. He practiced Zen, eating only acorns and chestnuts. He did not even have a hut to protect himself from rain and snow. Dōgen wrote about him in the *Shōbōgenzō*:

> We must meditate on his [way of] practice quietly. Imagine that you are living on the mountain, or the Guishan. Torrential rain comes in the middle of the night—it is so strong that it not only washes moss away from rocks but also breaks rocks with its force. On snowy winter nights, even animals won't visit him. How could people in the villages know that he was practicing there? If he had not preferred this practice more than his own life, he could not have sustained such a [way of] life. He neither cut weeds nor betook himself to construct [living quarters]. He practiced. He only practiced. We must have empathy for this dharma-ancestor who transmitted the true dharma. He never bothered with the difficulty of living in the midst of the mountains.

(*Shōbōgenzō, Gyōji* Part II, *"Continuous Practice"*)

Dōgen definitely esteemed Guishan's rigorous yet diligent practice. When I read this section, I too, admired Guishan. I even felt a desire to exchange my life for such a worthy cause. I reflected long over this issue, but decided I could not abandon my temple for a monastic life of meditation. Even so, I was tempted. In spite of his austerities, Guishan attracted many students, and founded a new Zen School, Gui-yang School, with his student, Yangshan. The school was named after Guishan and Yangshan.

Dōgen also wrote about another dharma ancestor, a diligent practitioner by the name of Nanyue Huairang (or Nan-yüeh Huai-jang), who attained enlightenment after he practiced under the Sixth Patriarch, Huineng, for fifteen years. About him, Dōgen wrote:

The ancient master's [Nanyue's] footsteps are especially admirable. Fifteen autumns of wind and frosts must have bothered him often. Regardless, he single-mindedly practiced. He is a paradigm for those who followed him in later days. On cold nights, he had no charcoal burning in the hearth and he lay down alone in an empty room. In the cool night of autumn, he had no light to brighten the room, but practiced *zazen* by the moonlit window. Even if he had not acquired wisdom or even half an understanding, this is [still called] the unapproachable practice. This is [Zen] practice.

(The *Shōbōgenzō, "Gyōji"* Part I, *"Continuous Practice"*)

It was not a half-baked practice. He said laypeople could not attain Buddhahood because true practice requires all of one's devotion, time and energy. Laypeople, if they wished to practice, had to abandon their livelihoods and family ties. For Dōgen, the monastic life must be more significant than one's ordinary life. He wrote the following in "Continuous Practice" from Part I of the *Shōbōgenzō*:

It is difficult to know what life is, whether living or not living, whether aged or not aged. Everyone views a thing in different ways, so we must not mind such views. We must earnestly and steadfastly practice. When we practice, it is that the practitioners see life and death within practice; it is not that practitioners practice in life and death. People of

259

today live to the age of fifty, sixty, seventy, or [even] eighty, and think practice is no longer needed. It is foolish to calculate how many years and months have passed since one's birth. These are only the numbers we count to measure life, not to measure the soundness of our studies. You must not think about your age, whether you are middle-aged or elderly. You must think about your study and practice single-mindedly. One must study shoulder to shoulder with Parsva [who practiced for three years without lying down].

The above chapter, "Gyōji II," was completed on the fifth day of the fourth month of 1242, a year before Dōgen moved to Daibutsu-ji, the former name of Eihei-ji.

I have often envied those who heard Dōgen speak personally. I imagine they must have been moved by the depth of his Zen practice, insight, and brilliant force emanated with grace. If I had been given the opportunity, I would not have had a moment's hesitation in vowing to study under him.

**

I return now to my concern at the time: what was I going to do with my life? This question was mine, but it is also the perennial question of every person. While we live in this world we face all sorts of pain and anxiety. The question of "Who am I" and "What am I?" might well be the very core of our existence. Our pains and anxieties are bound up with our very existence. Does enlightenment eradicate our pain and anxiety? Dōgen recommended that we just practice *zazen*, which on its own will lead to the very source of life. However, if you pursue enlightenment as an object of practice, it will vanish, and you will never grasp it. In his chapter on the "Manifestation of Reality," or "*Genjō Kōan*" of the *Shōbōgenzō*, Dōgen said:

When all things are the buddha-dharma (in this case, "all things in their natural setting") there is confusion, enlightenment, practice, life, death, buddhas and sentient beings. When the ten thousand things [all things] rest in selfless states, there is neither confusion nor enlightenment, neither buddhas nor sentient beings.

In my humble opinion, Dōgen did nothing other than practice buddha-dharma. That is, he never left the buddha-dharma during his entire monastic life. While practicing, he reached the purity and blissfulness of *nirvāṇa*. This state, in his words, was "oneness of practice and enlightenment." His accomplishment was, for me, the most ideal form of enlightenment. His wealth of Buddhist knowledge made him an ageless master and the epitome of a buddha among buddhas. I wondered if I could follow in his footsteps while taking care of Hōsen-ji and its members. Could I be free of worry about the temple buildings? Did I have the tenacity to devote my entire life to the practice of Buddhism alone? Did I have the courage of Dōgen? If not, in what state of mind should I occupy the seat as abbot of Hōsen-ji? I recalled that Dōgen once instructed his students thus:

Students! Don't expend the effort for [obtaining] clothes and food. In this small country located on the fringe [of the world], those who reached a prominent level earlier or later in both esoteric and exoteric schools [of Buddhism] never had an abundance of clothes and food. All of those people endured poverty and paid no attention to other [mundane] matters. They [steadfastly] practiced the Way [of the Buddha]. Therefore, they became prominent. For this reason, students must disregard worldly matters and not seek them. Those [students of the Way] must not be wealthy.

(*Shōbōgenzō, Zuimon-ki*, I, 4)

I was occupied with these thoughts about Dōgen while my ordinary life fared relatively well. I was searching for some sort of solution in order to rest my mind. I had studied how the Sōtō lineage must be maintained without deviating from strict adherence to Dōgen's norm. How did the school survive in spite of Shogunate control and economic deprivations? I needed to learn any and all of those ways in order to keep Hōsen-ji afloat. A Japanese proverb says, "A drowning man will grasp even a floating straw," and my state of mind was close to being that of a drowning man.

Keizan's foresight into a new Sōtō Zen practice was unique. His temple, Daijō-ji, joined Sōtō Zen after the original Shingon priest, Chōkai, was swayed to the teaching of Gikai from the Shingon esoteric Buddhism. The temple, Daijō-ji, thenceforth became the center of Gikai and his disciples' activities. Gikai had a progressive approach to teaching Sōtō Zen Buddhism. He started such a movement at Daijō-ji. Among Gikai's disciples, Keizan opened Yōkō-ji and Sōji-ji, which were both on the Noto Peninsula along the coast of the Japan Sea. Keizan had keener aspirations of broadening Sōtō Zen teachings, as I mentioned before, and he energetically worked in that direction. Thus, Daijō-ji became the center of Sōtō Zen under Keizan, and his two pre-eminent dharma-heirs, Meihō and Gasan, further disseminated Sōtō Zen to almost all parts of Japan.

Eihei-ji had received the support of the clan of Lord Hatano when Dōgen was alive and the clan's patronage continued for many years thereafter. The fifth abbot of Eihei-ji, Giun, was also supported by the Hatano clan and revived the once dilapidated Eihei-ji. Those powerful and resourceful warriors and lords countenanced Dōgen's approach to Buddhism. When Daichi, a dharma heir of Meihō, was about to open a temple in Kaga, not far from Daijō-ji, Lord Fujiwara Shigemune donated land for the temple. Kangan Giyin, a dharma-heir of Koün Ejō, received support from

Lord Kikuchi of Higo (in Kyushu). Kikuchi not only patronized Kangan, but also supported Daichi. When Gikai opened Yōkō-ji, Lord Minamoto Yoriaki became his benefactor. Within a relatively short period of time, Sōtō Zen temples sprouted up rapidly and thrived in many parts of Japan. Nearly all laypeople backed the Sōtō movement from the beginning, including Dōgen.

One of the reasons for the expeditious expansion was the advent of a simplified and popular form of ritual not seen in the days of Rinzai's five main temples of Kyoto. Also, those who could not afford an expensive funeral and other memorial services under Tendai, Shingon, or Rinzai, took refuge in Sōtō Zen. Aristocratic Rinzai monks continued to study in China. But comparatively speaking, fewer monks of Sōtō studied in China. For that reason together with Dōgen's intention, Sōtō Zen had much less connection with the power holders in the central Kyoto government. Also, in order to serve a broader and multilateral populace, Sōtō had to have close relations with old Buddhist schools, especially with those of the esoteric schools. The esoteric Buddhist transmission of the three items, or *sanmotsu*, and precept-giving among Shingon and Rinzai sects were both limited to only a few people, but Sōtō made these accessible to all walks of life. In those days, people commonly said, "Rinzai is for the Shogun and Sōtō is for the farmers." This saying may have come from the conventional and historically delineated practice of each school.

***

Regardless of the Sōtō School's prevalence in those days, Sōtō monks still practiced seriously during the summer and winter months. They held *kessei ango (gōko-é)*, or the ninety consecutive days of confined practice. The *rōhatsu sesshin*, or eight days and nights of *zazen* practice, was strictly observed from December first to the early morning of the eighth. Daily, monthly, and yearly practice of *zazen*, chanting, and other monastic activities was unabated from the time of Dōgen. A reformer, Keizan, wrote the *Pure Rules of Monastic Comportment*, or the *Keizan Shingi*, the standard for monks practicing in Sōtō Zen monasteries. It is a detailed text, which set the criterion for Sōtō Zen activities. In addition to daily, monthly and yearly schedules, there were occasional veneration services, or *segaki*. So, while Keizan and his dharma heir flourished throughout Japan as the Sōtō's fountainhead, they maintained strict adherence to the pure Zen practices of Dōgen. Contrary to their burgeoning, Eihei-ji kept itself the repository of Sōtō Zen in the wake of the Keizan group's flowering. Eihei-ji and Sōji-ji remained the Head Temples of the Sōtō School and thus the heart of all Sōtō Zen.

It seems paradoxical when you consider Sōtō's early movement. If Dōgen's pure approach to Zen Buddhism had existed solely without the novel approach of Gikai and Keizan, it would likely have remained very small, if not ceased to be altogether. Eihei-ji, if it had survived, would have been a very quiet place where only a few people lived and practiced without involving laypeople. Not only that, but without outside patronage, practitioners would have to pay room, board, tuition, and maintenance expenses. If in fact that were the case, could Dōgen's pure form of Zen be known today? Where would the practitioners get the money they needed, if their interests were only to practice Zen in a hidden mountain temple? Retrospectively, Gikai, Keizan, Meihō, and Gasan's expansion of Sōtō Zen by involving lay members in active roles was, like those days of the Buddha, a step in the right direction. Without those progressive monks' visions and efforts, today's Sōtō Zen would not exist.

I did not have either Dōgen's tenacity or fervor for practice, or Gikai, Keizan and his disciples' perception and sagacity to undertake a novel form of activity. My situation at Hōsen-ji at that time seemed like a deadening predicament. I was dispirited by the thought of spending the rest of my life simply visiting a few members here and there, and occasionally performing memorial services, like the tedious motion of a pendulum. I did not know of any other activity to launch at Hōsen-ji. Was I permitted to leave Hōsen-ji? Could I become something else? I thought I was in a dead-end situation, or what Greek philosophers called an *aporia.*

With all of those thoughts, my commitment as a resident priest of Hōsen-ji became shaky despite my responsibility to the temple members and the temple's long lasting light of the dharma lamp. Due largely to my affinity to Dōgen and his dharma heirs' activities, I was totally disenchanted with the status quo. The post-war social condition in Japan further added to my perplexity. I was not certain whether or not Hōsen-ji's memberships would return to support the temple, let alone build a pre-war sized temple or even a decent sized Dharma Hall. These thoughts brought further questions to my mind. I thought of the choices I might possibly make to simply follow the destiny set by other people. I realized for the first time that becoming a priest at Hōsen-ji might not be my only choice. The people close to me had blueprinted my course of life to become the resident priest of Hōsen-ji, as if no other course would ever be deemed worthy to them. There seemed to be no doubt in anyone's mind that I would take this course. My mother eagerly waited for me to become the priest of Hōsen-ji. My decision to leave would gravely disappoint her. Was I being rebellious if I changed my mind and did other things? Was it against filial piety? Against my dear members' good will? Many questions flitted through my mind, again and again.

***

The idea of going to America was an entirely new concept and also a staggering one to me. I thought, at times, this could very well be a new phase in my life. That night, like a sunflower rotating to face the sun, my mind fixated on the idea of going to San Francisco as a priest. What would I do with my life there? Contrasting the war-torn scene of Japan, San Francisco life seemed rosy. At the same time, there were still too many enigmatic elements in San Franciscan life to draw a concrete picture. I could not even focus on a central idea. Tangled chains of thought never left me. On the night after my meeting with Reverend Tobase, I was lying on the bedding-cushion turning right and left aimlessly almost all night. Then just before dawn, I decided to confer with Gyokusen, Nin'yū, my uncle Ennosuke, and Professor Ishikawa. They might give me some ideas and insights. That decision somewhat consoled me for the moment and I finally slept for a few hours.

During the next few days, I kept busy visiting people and seeking their advice in making a decision about my future course. I wanted to give a definite answer to Reverend Tobase before he left Japan for San Francisco as to whether or not I would go to America. If I decided to go, I needed to talk to him about the many other things that were on my mind. I did not know what to take with me to San Francisco other than a few sets of robes and essential personal items. How much money would I need to take with me? There were many questions that needed answers before I set off on a journey that would possibly last for years.

My questions to Professor Ishikawa, Nin'yū Yamasaki and other people, however, were not only about going to America, but also what else I could do if I didn't go to America. I wanted to consider all possible courses by listening to other people's opinions. I wanted different views and insights about my future.

Professor Ishikawa, being a professor of Japanese medieval

literature, related to my case with an example from the medieval folklore collection, the *Uji Shūi*, or the *Folklore of Uji*. He quoted the phrase "one who had been completely drawn into [the aura of] China" to illustrate that foreign cultures have a certain magnetism. He said it would be a great idea to go to America with one reservation—of not being drawn completely into Americanism. His father and brother studied French literature and lived in France. Their ways of thinking and modes of life were very much affected, in imitation of all things French. He said they became biased against things that were not French. That was why he studied Japanese literature instead. He was looking at the ceiling for awhile as if he were thinking of all the possibilities before giving me his thoughts about this very important decision.

The professor then turned to look directly at me and said, "Katō-kun, there are three types of reactions in facing foreign cultures. The first type is being totally immersed in the target culture and one's own culture is viewed as inferior. The two cultures are always in comparison. The second type is the opposite of the first. This reaction is possibly a result of some sort of disappointment. For this type of person the target culture is not what was expected, therefore anything related to that culture is viewed as negative. Those people often become ultra-conservatives and single-minded nationalists adamant in the belief that their own culture is superior." He then smiled a bit cynically and said, "You know, we experienced this more than enough during the war. Low-level patriotism also falls into this dangerous type of thinking. The third type goes beyond the dichotomy, with people who can understand both old and new cultures, and can judge them both fairly for the virtues of each. The third group views each country from an unbiased stance. Professor Ishikawa smiled and said, "I think the third type is ideal and truly international. If one reaches that level he can be named a renaissance man or a man of all seasons. Katō-kun, whether or not you are going to America, I want you to become like the third group of men. Isn't that what you hold in Zen?" He paused awhile and then continued, "If you are going to America, you must absorb everything you see, hear, smell, taste and touch. Use all of your senses to absorb the culture. And, of course, you must acquire the English language while you are there. If you have knowledge of English, it will be very useful to the future of Japan." He then nodded a few times and continued, "I have mentioned the three types of people reacting to foreign cultures. But they can be applied to just about everything in life. Don't you think so?"

Mrs. Ishikawa sat with us after serving tea, listening to our conversation and then said, "Katō-san, my husband is sometimes jealous of his father and his brother when he faces a situation related to France or Europe. Actually, he studied English quite seriously when he was young just to compete with his brother, didn't you?" She looked at the professor. He said a bit defensively, "Well, I was fascinated by some of those English writers." Mrs. Ishikawa did not reflect on that statement. She continued, "It's wonderful to go to America, Katō-san. Why don't you go to a graduate school while you are there? Why don't you get an M.A., or even a Doctorate in Literature? My, what a wonderful idea! What a splendid opportunity for you, Katō-san!" Both of them assumed that I would eventually return to Japan after some years of stay in America. I did not get clear answers of anticipated depth and breadth, or any assistance in regard to help in my decision of whether or not to go to America from Professor Ishikawa. Furthermore, they did not comprehend my position as a Buddhist priest and a Japanese. Nonetheless, they were generous to spend the time thinking about my future there with me. Perhaps they thought I came to simply inform them that I was going to America. Whatever I made of their response, Professor Ishikawa's third example of a cosmopolitan person attracted me. I immediately thought of non-dualism in Zen. I liked Mrs. Ishikawa's suggestion and encouragement that I should get an M.A. or a Ph.D. It was a novel and enlivened idea. Without her hint, I would have never have thought of it then. However, I didn't have the slightest idea of what fields I would fit into. Also, I had no idea whether or not I had the ability to cope with a higher level of academic endeavor.

That conversation opened up a whole new trajectory for my future, but I enjoyed the visit with both of them. On the way home I realized that I was intrigued by his idea about the three types of people. Many people after the war became the first type who idealized America, though only superficially, by comparing the gap between affluent American life and meager existence in Japan. Dazzling Americanism aroused xenophobic tendencies among many Japanese people toward their own culture. They fell into the first type. In any case, the first two types are dualistic. Viewing the current social conditions in Japan at that time Professor Ishikawa's premise did seem to create a dialectical inevitability. My thoughts continued on this subject until I returned home.

As young as I was, I thought my mother's younger brother Ennosuke was somewhat naïve. His way of drawing conclusions was straightforward, but not sophisticated. However, I valued his intuitive opinions, which occasionally surprised me with their keenness and unconventionality. Also, some of his opinions, though tested empirically, were clichéd. Unfortunately, this time when I consulted him he did not surprise me at all. He was all for my going to the rich and prosperous America because it dominated the world by winning in the Second World War. It was, therefore, wise to go to America now, and take any chance for advancement. During and after the Second World War he was drafted into the

Japanese army and sent to the Philippine islands where his unit was defeated. He was captured by U.S. forces and became a prisoner of war. That experience may have been the basis for his advice to me. He probably witnessed the well-fed and well-equipped American military. Seeing the contrast between the starving Japanese army and the well-heeled Americans was, I thought, a materialistic basis for his decision. He was a textiles merchant and his clothing concepts were naturally inclined toward pragmatism. I did not ask many questions while I was talking to him for I could foresee his answers. Instead, I said to him, "I haven't decided whether I am going or not. But if I do go, could you please take care of my mother, brother and sisters?" He said laughingly, "Of course. I know you came to me to say that, I know. You don't have to ask me. I will. I will take care of them. You don't have to worry about that at all."

After talking to Professor Ishikawa and my merchant uncle, I was still in a state of deep puzzlement. Each of these men had kindly given me their advice, drawn from their own experience and social circumstances. Despite his army experience in the Philippines, my uncle's vantage point was from the town of Yobitsugi. Yobitsugi, a small corner of the city of Nagoya, was his world, whereas Professor Ishikawa's world was Japanese and also faintly European. It was always pleasant to hear Professor and Mrs. Ishikawa's idealistic thoughts, and though they were not accountable, my life was at stake. There were so many unknown factors and variables. Their views were a reflection of their own experiences. That may well be a natural human tendency, but I thought it was a bit distressing that they did not have a truly cosmopolitan but instead an empirically limited view. Their ideas entertained only my journey to America but did not consider the possibility and circumstance of my not going to America. I immediately thought of Dōgen's "Mind is mountains, rivers, and great earth. It is also the sun, moon, stars and time" (*Shōbōgenzō, "Sokushin-ze-butsu"* or "Mind is Itself Buddha"), which sets forth a completely unbiased cosmopolitanism. Unfortunately, we are the products of our own cultural milieus and cannot easily depart from our self-created cocoons. Nevertheless I continued my search for reasonable help with the decision.

My father's dharma-brother Gyokusen often gave me sound advice though it was sometimes a bit pedantic. He advised me to go to America without hesitation. He said that the Buddha was an Aryan like white Americans. I didn't know whether or not that was true and if it had any bearing on my leaving Hōsen-ji. He reminded me that I was the thirty-third dharma heir of Dōgen and I must devote myself to teaching Buddhism to Americans and if necessary, bury my bones in America. This was new to me also. I never thought I was going to America for good. He did not give any hint about my foreseeable welfare in the new world. When I mentioned my concern about life there he said, "I have heard that in America everyone can eat well even just by doing a 'dish washing' job. Buddhist monks need only a bowl of gruel. Don't you worry about that." He was exhilarated by the idea of Buddhism taking root in America. Indian Buddhism had moved eastward to China and further eastward to Japan. This time, it was moving eastward again to America. He was elated by this thought and said excitedly, "Wakō, you happen to be the eighty-fourth generation from the Buddha, don't forget that. It is a well-chosen role to help pass Buddhism eastward to America. My dharma-nephew will be the banner-carrier for this new movement." Idealistically, his reasoning sounded convincing but I, the person at stake in this case, was somewhat absent from his thought. He mentioned my name, but how well I would fare in the United States was not entering his mind, even as a motif in his salient saga of the "Eastward Current of Buddhism." After listening

to Gyokusen's jubilant opinion, I was again appalled by his elation
that "Wakō is going to America!" His idea was also unrealistic and
failed to emerge from its self-created cocoon. I thought to myself,
"All three of them just gave me a one-sided view."

Soon after I met them I was beginning to realize that I, too, was
the selfish one falling into the same subjectivism. It was because
of my ignorance that I expected an eye-opening idea from them, as
if I could evade the painful process of big decision-making. I was
hoping someone would give me sound advice and sensible judge-
ments. This was my dilemma, but I was depending on them. The
desire for other people to take on the burden of making my own
decision was definitely selfish on my part. I felt bad for criticizing
all three good men.

***

Nin'yū Yamasaki dropped by Hōsen-ji around ten o'clock in the
morning on the day after I talked to Gyokusen. He looked at me
and whispered, "Have you decided?" I said, "I haven't yet, but …
almost. I would like you to give me your opinion about it." He
nodded and said, "All right, all right. I've been thinking about it
all night." Then, after a pause he said, "I am the one who started
all this commotion and I feel very responsible for it. In fact, I have
played an imposing role ever since your father asked me to take
care of you and this temple. I fashioned you to become an abbot as
quickly as possible by arranging your *risshin* (a head monk in the
kessei ango—the ninety-day confined practice), the *ten'é* (change
of robe colors), *shihō* (transmission of the dharma-lineage) and the
zuisé (visitation to the two head temples for veneration) and many
other small things. I knew that after the war Japan would change,
although I could not foresee the destruction, the rapid pace of

change, and the magnitude of metamorphosis. For the past several years, everyone has cried, *'après guerre* this*'* and *'après guerre* that.' You know they needed a scapegoat. Old intellectuals are quiet and 'black market operators' are briskly walking on the main roads in bright daylight. Everyone's life has changed. Temples also have to change. You know, I thought of you as my own son, and I have always wished you to be a good Zen priest despite all the changes— because that is the only course of life I know. I still think there is no other life worth living. I have watched you for some time and I can see that you are not satisfied with the activities at Hōsen-ji. Yes, the temple has been eclipsed and no longer has the affluence of the *oharami daishi* days. The temple members have been scattered by the war and many have not come back. Many people are occupying themselves with just gathering food and don't even glance at temples and shrines. Spirituality, it seems, comes after satiating most people. They can live without Buddhism but not without food."

He was talking to me but he looked into the sky as if he were talking to himself, without awaiting my answer. His monologue continued, "You know, it might not be a bad idea to go to the United States for a few years. Your life is guaranteed. You will see different people; you will learn how they think and behave and what their value systems are. By the way, I have heard that an American writer, Ernest Hemingway, writes novels reflecting his idea that everything has a price tag. To make a piece of merchandise, there is the cost of material, labor and the expected profit all used to determine the product's value from the manufacturing and mercantile side. But there is a consumer price, too. If items are too costly, no one buys them. Also, there is a price that reflects the period of time and the place in which they are sold. Everything you do has a price tag and everything you receive also has a price tag. I cannot say this nicely, but it is a very interesting thought to me. I wonder when a Buddhist priest gives a service, whether that has a price tag. If so, then, how much would it be? If you extend a kind gesture to, say, an old woman, how much is that kindness worth? The idea that everything has a price tag is an interesting observation. Being a Buddhist, I don't believe in pricing. You know *dāna*, or 'giving,' is a selfless, one-way act. I am afraid that the fabric of Japan might change to that mode of two-way economic exchange in the near future, I think." I interrupted, "But, Matsubara-san (I always addressed him with this name), Zen teaches us to discard a price tag, so why..." Nin'yū looked at me and simply said, "That is why you are going there."

I did not know what to say to that dialogue. The theme of his talk had digressed and I thought it had virtually no relevance to my future. He was talking about the composition of American values as expli-cated from his interpretation of his readings of Ernest Hemingway. I said to him, "Does Hemingway's notion of values have any bear-ing on whether or not I am going to America?" Nin'yū immediately replied, "Oh, yes, of course. I am not talking about any particular value system. What I am talking about is the whys and wherefores of American human behavior. It may well be Western behavior in gen-eral. It might stem from the individualism, which you and I, living in Japan, have never experienced. While I was talking to you, it dawned on me that democracy is based on that individualism. Collectivism, you know, the very fabric of Japan's communal society, has not produced constituents for democracy. General MacArthur imposed democracy upon us. Yet, we are behaving in a feudalistic frame of mind so that democracy has never been fully understood here. Now, everyone is talking about democracy and freedom, but they don't really know what those words mean. It is a great opportunity for you to learn all those things in America." I interrupted him by say-ing, "I think you have drifted from the main topic of our dialogue." He denied that again by saying, "No, I haven't. Japanese people in the last three hundred years have acted collectively and Buddhism's survival has up to now been in that environment. My forefathers and my neighbors supported Buddhism so my family and I support Buddhism. That is the way everything has drifted until now. Yes, drifted. But if the tide shifts in a different direction, that might not be the case. You might have to convince individuals to understand Buddhism." He stopped and looked at me. He had most likely noticed that I was not following his discourse.

It was true. I did not understand his reasoning thoroughly, especially in regard to my situation, but I understood that he was telling me to explore societies based on different social systems. He concluded by saying, "It is a good idea to spend a few years in a foreign country, especially America. You are still young; the experience will help you grow. It will be a grand opportunity to open your eyes to the world. Besides, the people in San Francisco need you. I strongly recommend that you go. Don't worry about Hōsen-ji. I'll take care of it."

His last sentence consoled me. Nin'yū had been taking care of us and the temple since my father's death. He had visited and talked to members, and sometimes soothed some small disputes among them, or consoled them when a family needed it. All his services were performed without reticence. In addition, the Hōsen-ji family survived on his assistance during those years. He helped us selflessly. He had small desires; therefore he needed little. In that sense, he was a sincere Zen monk living with Dōgen's ideals.

***

After days of thoughts, recurrent emotions and reasoning, I finally made up my mind to go to San Francisco for a few years, hoping to acquire English proficiency. I decided to go to San Francisco as an assistant to Reverend Tobase, and assume whatever duties were required at Sōkō-ji. I thought I could cope with any hardships. I told Nin'yū of my decision. Nin'yū stared at me for a moment and then said, "Well, let's go to Yamadai-san, the head of Hōsen-ji's supporting members. Let's not waste time. If he says it is agreeable to him, there will be no problem with the other members. You are the abbot but he must approve the idea first." He then hastily added, "We don't have much time; let's go there right now." We visited Yamadai-san. Nin'yū had a tendency toward quick action when his mind was made up. I stopped him by saying, "Wait, I must talk to my mother about this." But he said, "If Yamadai-san supports you, I know your mother will do the same."

Yamadai-san was a recently retired second-generation proprietor of a brewery that made soy sauce and *miso*. He was a gentleman to the core. His unpretentious appearance, gestures, tastes, and the way he spoke exuded gentility that was quite rare in this small town of Yobitsugi. He was born into a well-to-do family in the city of Gifu and had married the daughter of the founder of the Yamadai Brewery. People in the town called him, "Taka-sama." "Taka" was his name and -sama is the same word as—san but signifies a special class of people; it is an honorific suffix. Many years later, when I returned to Yobitsugi and visited him with my wife and children, my wife commented that Taka-sama was very refined in his manners and she had never encountered a person like that in her life.

Taka-sama was probably in his late fifties or early sixties when I consulted him. He had just retired from his business in order to give the proprietorship to his son-in-law. He then moved from his main house to a villa nearby. Nin'yū, Taka-sama and I strolled along the path in the well-attended garden in his villa. He had arranged for water to be sprinkled before we arrived so that the faces of stepping-stones were refreshingly moist. The green moss around the stones was incredibly green and the multi-colored leaves of shrubs glittered with dew. It was a subtle yet blissful scene. While we were strolling in the yard, I recalled Chapter III of the Lotus Sūtra, entitled "The Parable":

> There are always the sufferings
> of birth, old age, illness, and death.
> They are like flames
> raging endlessly.
> I have already left
> the burning house of the three worlds.
> I am tranquil and peaceful
> on the ground sprinkled with dew.

Indeed, the Buddha's teachings are the peaceful grounds sprinkled with dew where people in the burning house (the mundane world) can retreat. While we were strolling, Nin'yū said, "Taka-sama, every time I visit here, I feel so tranquil." He looked at me once and then continued, "This reminds me of a parable in the *Lotus Sūtra*." Nin'yū was thinking exactly what I was thinking. He explained the gist of the parable to Taka-sama; a rich man's house was burning and there were still several children and servants in the burning house. The man lured them out to safety with a skillfully composed story, or *upāya*. He led them to peaceful ground covered with dew. Nin'yū then reaffirmed that the garden reminded him of the parable.

While Nin'yū was explaining the *Lotus Sūtra* to Taka-sama, I thought that the "ground covered with dew" might be the essence of religions. Many forms of religion advocate a god or gods, together with their ethical tenets, which eventually lead believers to restfulness. Worship, meditation, recitation of sacred texts, observation of rituals, and even elaborate temples, church buildings and grounds all help members achieve peace of mind. I shall call that "noble serenity" to differentiate it from a momentary calm. Japanese Buddhists call it *anjin*, literally meaning "peace of mind."

Taka-sama whole-heartedly agreed with my plan to go to San Francisco. He encouraged me to go without reservation. He also said that I need not worry about the temple or my family. He further encouraged me to spend at least several years there. Like many others, Taka-sama assumed that I would return to Japan eventually. When we left the villa my mind was firmly set on going to America to work as an assistant priest. I, too, was planning to come back to Japan after I completed my tenure at Sōkō-ji.

On the way home I mentioned my thought about "*anjin*," or peace of mind, to Nin'yū. He said, "When you are facing fear or crisis, do you cry out for help to God or Buddha? Is that an act of seeking peace of mind?" I answered, "Yes. It is similar to that." Nin'yū continued, "When you feel a moment of happiness or felicity, do you wish to express your gratitude to someone, possibly to God or to Buddha? Is that action still called peace of mind?" I replied, "Yes." Nin'yū continued, "What about God, Brahman, or Prajāpati (creator of the world in Indian parable) or whoever has omniscient power, knowledge and skill to create this well-balanced universe? The creation was surely beyond human capability. Is there a god or some super-human who has unimaginable power to do that? Where is that scenario? Is there a place for peace of mind?" This time, I said to him, "I don't know whether it was someone's infinite power or just a natural process that helped the evolution of the universe. Still, creating gods or Brahman or whoever as creators shows the ingenuity of humans to lead people towards peace of mind. If you and I believe, remember I said 'believe,' that god or someone created this world, embracing that faith, we feel comfortable living in it. This, too, leads to peace of mind." I was excited with what I was saying. Nin'yū said, "That's very good! You are more mature than

I thought. I am confident that you will be all right in San Francisco. But just remember, and I said 'remember,' that you are a Zen monk and an assistant to Reverend Tobase there. You must be humble at all times. Remember humbleness is a great virtue."

Conferring with my mother was unexpectedly easy or else she had already had some sense of the decision from my jittery behavior. She said, "It is your life and you are old enough to think about your own future. Our family and I will be alright. I will ask Nin'yū Yamasaki to take care of the temple until you come back. The temple will be alright, as he has already been helping us for many years. If Yamadai-san said it is alright, then the whole membership will say it is alright. Don't worry about us. You take good care of yourself." I was certain that she would feel lonely losing her oldest son. Six years ago, she had lost her husband. This would be her second time losing an immediate family member, but she bravely accepted this course of her destiny.

***

That evening, I rode my bicycle and visited Reverend Dōkō Ōtsuka at Bucchi-in temple in Yagoto. I told him of my decision to go to Sōkō-ji in San Francisco. He was very surprised at the sudden news but a moment later he told me he was delighted about the news of my life. Reverend Ōtsuka said, "If I did not have so many responsibilities here at this temple, I would have stayed in Los Angeles longer. I am, nonetheless, very glad that I went. I am certain that you will feel the same later. When you go there, don't let your mission slip away. Just do what you have to do. Watch your step at all times. Do you recall the sign at the entrance of the monasteries stating 'Watch your step!' That does not mean 'watch out there is a step higher or lower'; it means 'mind every second of your time.'

It is the reminder that you are living only in this moment. Life in America won't be easy but don't lose your way of life. If you become a full-fledged priest at Sōkō-ji, that will be fine. If you want to go to school and master whatever you are studying, that will be better, too. I imagine, by now, Sōkō-ji needs an English-speaking priest." Then he began to smile like the opening of a flower. He lifted his index finger right in front of his face to signify the importance of his following words: "I am going to give you something very useful. It's a large trunk I took to the United States in 1932." I knew immediately what he was talking about. It was the trunk he had shown me once. In it he stored the records of his trip to the United States. He went to the back room and soon returned carrying the brown leather trunk. While he was emptying all the contents of the trunk onto the floor he said, "Don't mind this; I will store all this in some other container." I thought the trunk had been a treasured reminiscence of his youthful days. I was not expecting this gift at all. I thanked him sincerely and left Bucchi-in. I had visited him on my bicycle so I tied the big ocean-liner size trunk firmly on the rack behind the seat.

When I was going around the big pond in front of his temple, tears streamed down my cheeks. Whilst I was pedaling the heavy bicycle I cried aloud, "You are Ōtsuka Rōshi, true man of no attachment!" The trunk tied on the carrier above the rear wheel was probably forty by thirty inches and twelve inches thick. It was made of thick cowhide and all the corners of the trunk were reinforced with the same leather. I imagine that the trunk was in vogue in 1932, twenty years ago, for an elite exchange student. It had aged gracefully. There were only a few fine cracks on the surface. It weighed at least ten pounds and looked extremely sturdy. The entire thing had an air of romanticism reflecting the time between the two world wars. Having it, I felt as if I were an elite exchange-student. Then,

I wondered if Reverend Ōtsuka might have been whiling away the time with his reminiscence.

When I arrived at Hōsen-ji, it was past nine o'clock. While I was unloading the trunk from the bicycle, my mother came out and immediately understood the gift. I saw her wiping away tears.

> Not going, not coming,
> originally
> deep and clear;
> residing
> not within, or without,
> nor even in-between:
> one jewel
> of water-essence,
> never cracking or clouding;
> its light fills
> heaven and earth.

> – Shih-té

Chapter 13

DEPARTURE FOR THE UNITED STATES

もし画は実にあらずといはば、
万法みな実にあらず。
万法みな実にあらずは、
仏法も実にあらず。
仏法もし実なるには
画餅すなはち実なるべし。

If the picture is not real,
everything would not be real.
If everything is not real,
Buddha's teaching would not be real.
To make Buddha's teaching real,
the rice-cake in the picture must be real.

－ 道元

- Dōgen

(『正法眼蔵』「画餅」)

(*Shōbōgenzō, (Gahei)* "Rice-cake In the Picture")

I visited Reverend Hodō Tobase to convey to him my decision to go to the United States. He was staying in a small temple in the Arakawa District of Tokyo. While I was in Tokyo, he introduced me to Tatsugen Satō, who was four or five years older than me. He was a Zen priest and also a graduate assistant at Komazawa University, where he was specializing in the field of *Vinaya* (code of disciplines) in Chinese Buddhism. Tatsugen kindly invited me to stay in his father's temple in Mukōjima, not far from Asakusa in Tokyo. His father's temple did not escape damage from the war. It was burned down. The temple I stayed at was still a provisional temple. His father told me that he was originally from Nagoya. It was a coincidence that his son Tatsugen and I, who had our origins in Nagoya, had aspirations to go to San Francisco to help Sōkō-ji.

At my meeting with Tobase, I asked him many questions of importance to me. Some of my questions included: What would my daily duties be? How many people belong to the temple? Does Sōkō-ji have a dormitory or some sort of accommodating facility for a priest? If not, then what is average rent for a small apartment in San Francisco? I was also anxious to know what my remuneration would be, but did not ask, because it would have been improper to do so. He laughed and said, "I don't know the answer to your questions." He did say, however, that Sōkō-ji had ample space to accommodate me, and that I need not worry about such things. He told me about the weather, the number of temple members, and also what his and my various routines would be. As I was talking to him I realized his personality was such that he did not worry about such small and transitory matters as living costs or my remuneration. Nonetheless, I began having precarious feelings about my future at Sōkō-ji, since I had only fragmentary information about the practical matters of my upcoming life in San Francisco.

Reverend Tobase promised to send me the necessary papers, such as an official temple invitation to be a priest there and also a letter guaranteeing my ability to sustain a living while in the United States. Each piece of correspondence between Sōkō-ji and me by airmail took approximately six to eight days. If there was procrastination on either side, it easily took ten days for a one-way correspondence. When I was told by the American Embassy in Tokyo to furnish some documents, by the time they came back to me for submission to the Embassy, three or four weeks had already elapsed. During that time I waited nervously for documents of all sorts, such as Sōkō-ji's status as a religious establishment recognized by the State of California, its statement of solvency, and so on. Needless to say, overseas communication took a long time. I was not certain when I could go to San Francisco. I wrote to Tobase about my anxiety but his reply was, "Don't worry; your worry does not solve anything now. Just stay put."

I told Tatsugen my concern about my future's ambiguity since Tobase's information was sketchy in areas where I needed information the most. He told me that he was experiencing the same feelings. He also told me that his mind was not yet made up to go to San Francisco. The reason was that he wanted to become a professor at Komazawa University in the future. If he left his position now, he would have to abandon hope for that to even happen. It was, for me, too late to change my plans. In addition, I did not want to change my mind after the serious consideration I had given to reach this decision.

Nonetheless, Tatsugen and his father courteously extended an invitation for me to stay in their temple while I was in Tokyo for the business of getting a visa. Tatsugen did not pursue getting a visa. He decided to stay in Tokyo and stay on track to obtaining a professorship at the university. I went back and forth between Nagoya and Tokyo, filling out all the necessary papers. Finally I received my visa and green card, which gave me permanent resident status in the United States. It took several months, but in those days this processing was considered relatively fast. An officer at the American Embassy, Fuyusaku Katō, who happened to be a person from Yobitsugi, Nagoya, and an old member of Hōsen-ji, helped to expedite the process. I visited Mr. Katō's house in Zaimokuza, Kamakura a couple of times to thank him for his help in this matter.

By the time everything was completed, including the purchase of my ticket on the President Line steamer, it was mid-May in 1952. My passport from the Japanese government was issued on April 4, 1952. The passport cover was made of handsome black genuine leather, and inside written in beautiful calligraphy was the signature of the Minister of Foreign Affairs, Shigeru Yoshida. Getting a passport and exchanging currencies from Japanese yen to American dollars in 1952 was still an uncommon occurrence in Japan, and I had to go through many cumbersome steps.

***

While I was waiting for the necessary paperwork to be processed, I continued my employment at the Honami School until the end of March, 1952, exactly one year after I took the position there. Principal Tanaka said to me, "You'd better come back soon; otherwise you will have no job waiting for you. Americans have tried to transplant many elements of their educational system on us, ignoring our culture entirely. You know, their educational system is not functioning here. Homerooms, classroom elections of officers, and instituting an American parliamentary system are all so strange to our children. PTAs are still foreign to us even though they have been in place here for several years. Parents and teachers are still confused with that. Anyway, you'd better come back here. The Second World War will officially end soon when our Prime Minister Yoshida ratifies the treaty in San Francisco. We must create a sound educational system that fits our culture here." I sensed the hint of presumption in his statement but I kept quiet.

Other teachers and PTA members gave me a farewell party at the school. It was at a time when going to America was quite a rare occurrence. The local newspaper, the *Chūnichi,* publicized my assignment to work at Sōkō-ji in San Francisco in the corner of the paper but someone saw it and announced it as if it were big news. I was indeed embarrassed about people's elaborate reactions and of being at the center of such a flurry. Several people made lengthy speeches regarding my upcoming career in San Francisco and wished me success there. Several women teachers and PTA mothers began sobbing with handkerchiefs in their hands. All in all, it was quite the *mise en scène* for a farewell party in those days. In fact, this unmerited party in my honor reflected the surrealism of my departure to a faraway land.

***

I left Nagoya on May 23, 1952 around nine o'clock in the morning. My entire family watched my departure. My uncle Ennosuke; aunts Hide, Tsuma and Sada; about eight cousins, including Muneö and his sister, Yoshiko; and Yoshiko's son, Hisao, strapped on the back of my Aunt Hide, all of whom were clad in nice outfits, came to see me off. Yamadai's Taka-sama and over a dozen temple members came to Nagoya's main railroad station with a big banner inscribed with my name and farewell words. Our group caught other passengers' eyes because it looked like a scene from a different time. Nin'yū Yamasaki came with my family. He looked as though he was bracing himself and did not speak much. Just before the train arrived, Taka-sama looked at me and said loudly, "On this occasion, Kazumitsu-kun, we are going to see you off. You are going to San Francisco as an overseas priest. We are very proud of this opportunity. We wish you well with all of our hearts." Then, he looked at everyone and said, "Let's cry out 'Banzai (long live!) Kazumitsu-kun' after me." He turned around, faced me again and cried out, "Kazumitsu-kun, banzai!" He raised both arms toward the sky. Everyone followed suit. "Banzai" was repeated three times, each with increasing crescendo. My eyes welled with tears and I could not see anyone anymore. I shook hands with Nin'yū. I touched my mother's shoulder as the train entered the station. It was a grand departure, and a grand beginning for my new life.

I found my seat on the train. My older sister, Minako, came along with me to Yokohama. I looked at everyone from the train window. There was only a minute and a half stop at Nagoya. When the train began moving, my family members walked alongside the train until they could no longer keep up the pace. It was an old fashioned, emotional parting. We had seen many soldiers off exactly in this way a few years back. I had left home for the two monasteries before, but this time I felt sadder. I especially empathized with my mother who, I was sure, was feeling a poignant sadness. Also, I regretted that I could not talk much with Nin'yū at the station. He waved his right hand slowly and gave me a muted smile. He had taught me, sometimes kindly and sometimes harshly, sometimes while sober, and sometimes while drunk, but I had learned a great deal from him. My father had chosen the right person to be my mentor. We had been close since I was twelve or thirteen years of age, in fact, all through my maturation period. Our relationship was that of a mentor and protégé. At times we were like teacher and student. But he had also been a close counselor who influenced the state of my life and its direction. He had lost all his children but one, and this time he was losing me. I cannot adequately express my innermost feelings about him.

***

At Yokohama, the ship was already anchored at the pier in the port. It was a cargo boat named S.S. President McKinley. The ship had about twelve passengers in six staterooms above the main deck. The passengers were allowed to embark in the afternoon of the day before its departure. My sister Minako and Taka-sama's daughter, Takako Katō, who was my same age, and my maternal grandfather's younger brother, Tomo-san, who was over sixty years of age, came to see me at the port. Tomo-san lived in Yokohama. All of them came up and looked at my stateroom. It looked new to them, I am sure. None of them had ever looked inside a large ship. A ship attendant came and introduced himself as the person assigned to take care of my cabin. He said he was from the Philippines but had citizenship in the United States. He served all my guests a dish of pink ice cream. First, Takako said, "My, this is strawberry ice cream! How delicious!" We scooped the strawberry ice cream and tasted it. None of us had ever tasted strawberry ice cream before. Up to that point in time, ice cream to us was only two colors, one being white with a faint taste of vanilla or sometimes the scent of lemon. Another was a reddish color flavored with *azuki* beans. Everyone seemed to like the ice cream. We all, of course, enjoyed the ambiance of the cozy stateroom. The bed was neatly made and placed beside the beige-colored steel wall.

The sound of our excitement buoyed up my spirit. Slowly though, I began feeling lonely. The next day I was going to leave my homeland for an unspecified length of time. Outside it was getting dark. The warm moist air of late May and a cloud of mist obscured the harbor. There was a vague halo around each light. A distant foghorn augmented my feelings of nostalgia, even before my departure. Despite the elaborate illumination surrounding us, the port was almost deserted in the early evening. I don't exactly remember the time but at around 8:30 p.m., everyone decided to go home. I walked with them to the entrance of the port. The departure of my ship was 10:00 a.m. the next day. Everyone promised to come back to see me off.

My stateroom was intended for two passengers but the other passenger did not show up that night. I spent the last night in Yokohama, or rather in Japan, alone in the room. The ship undulated slightly throughout the night. I could not sleep soundly because of all the sensations; sights, sounds, colors, smell, and the tactile images of my new experiences from the past few months continuously circulated in my mind. Some of my thoughts were sweet and tender but soon to be gone, perhaps, forever. I might never have the same experiences again in my life. In the stateroom I felt I was utterly alone, facing a totally unknown future. The kaleidoscopic changes of events occupied my mind without any interlude. For a while, I had no time to reflect on anything, let alone to recall Dōgen's teaching of "I am here, now." My thoughts then turned to Dōgen, who went to China when he was about my same age. I was astonished by this similarity. But Dōgen's journey was in the early thirteenth century. China was probably far more alien to him or to all Japanese people then. No one awaited him in China. This thought indeed encouraged me. I was indebted to Nin'yū for my deeper understanding of Dōgen, not only from the books he had lent me, but largely from our dialogues. Such was a common practice among those of us who practiced Zen Buddhism. I learned living Zen from him. I wondered whether Myōzen, a Rinzai monk and Dōgen's senior at Kennin-ji, who inspired Dōgen to go to China, was like Nin'yū to me? Dogen accompanied Myōzen to China and stayed at the same monastery until Myōzen's death there. How Dōgen must have felt in losing his close friend in the faraway land of China in the thirteenth century, I could not imagine. I was lucky, I thought, to have a close teacher like Nin'yū. Without his encouragement and guidance, I probably would not have practiced at the Kyūkoku-ji and Kakuō-zan monasteries or studied at the university, let alone have become the resident priest at Hōsen-ji in due course. And now, I was going to San Francisco as a result of his suggestion. My reluctance to making this big change in my life was overpowered by his encouragement.

I was profoundly absorbed in the memories I had with Nin'yū and each of my family members. I felt melancholic sitting alone in the empty metallic cabin. The beige colored inorganic metal wall reflected the lights from the harbor and brightened the room even though the room lights were turned off. I regretted again not having gone to Nin'yū and at the station to thank him for all he had done for me. Nin'yū had only raised his right hand and waved at me. I did the same to him. Then I thought it might have been a suggestion for me. What was he suggesting?

I recalled one of his episodes. After I became the priest of Hōsen-ji, Nin'yū came into the room one day. I was reading the *Shōbōgenzō* then. He looked at my room, saw the *Shōbōgenzō* on the desk and said, "You are reading that again. You are a slave to that, aren't you?" I picked up a stem of a chrysanthemum in a vase on the desk, held it before my eyes and looked at Nin'yū. I don't remember whether he looked at me or not, but he ignored my gesture and started walking toward the door. I said to him, "You haven't said anything about this." He looked at me and said, "You are testing me, aren't you? You are haughty. Condescension is a sign of stupidity, especially after reading a few pages of the *Shōbōgenzō* and thinking that you fully grasp it." Then, he began walking toward the door. But he stopped after a few steps, turned around and said, "All right. It's not an *udumbara* flower. So, what about it? What does that really mean?" He knew what my gesture signified; furthermore, he asked a question I had not expected. I had been imitating the famous story about the Buddha quoted in the *Shōbōgenzō*, from the chapter of *"The Udumbara Flower,"* as follows:

When the Buddha appeared before a large crowd of people on the Vulture Peak (*Gṛdhrakūta parvata*), he picked an *udumbara* flower and blinked his eyes once. Mahākāśyapa [one of his accomplished disciples], looked at the Buddha [holding an *udumbara* flower and blinking his eyes], and smiled broadly at him. Thereupon, the Buddha stated, "I have the essence of the True Dharma and the marvelous Mind of *Nirvāṇa*. I now give that to Mahākāśyapa.

Seven [past] buddhas and the buddhas thereafter all held the same flower respectively. This is the utmost form of holding the flower and from here on all [the buddhas] have held the same flower until now. This holding of the flower is evidence of upholding the True Dharma."

To Nin'yū's question I replied, "Did you ask me what the flower is?" Nin'yū affirmed, "Yes, what is it?" I answered, "It is the essence of the true dharma and also the marvelous jewel of *Nirvāṇa*." Nin'yū replied, "You are simply quoting from the passage. I am asking what is the *udumbara* flower, really? I was puzzled by his repetitious questions. I said, "You know the famous story of *udumbara*; the *udumbara* flower thus signifies the essence of the True Dharma and the marvelous Mind of *Nirvāṇa*." Nin'yū interrupted, "So, Mahākāśyapa understood and smiled." He continued, "Now, my question is what is the *udumbara*? Tell me, what is the essence of the true dharma that the Buddha saw in Mahākāśyapa?"

I did not understand what Nin'yū was asking. He noticed it, and said, "You are haughty. You are pretending to be the Buddha and you wanted me to act as Mahākāśyapa, didn't you? That's your half-baked understanding." His voice became louder as if he were angry with me. He said, "Look at the chrysanthemum! Does it look like the true dharma? You only showed me a dead flower."

I explained, "In '*Udumbara*', from the *Shōbōgenzō*, Dōgen said 'Holding the flower had existed before the Buddha's enlightenment, at the enlightenment, and [even] after his enlightenment. Holding the flower transcends the time of those people.' Dōgen further said, 'Those mountains, rivers, heaven and earth, the sun, the moon, wind, rain, and living beings each came holding the flower. Everything is holding the [*udumbara*] flower. Our birth and death, coming and going, are within the flower and the color of the flower. It is what we are learning now. That is the holding of the flower.' That is the flower—heaven and earth, life and death, all are flowers."

Nin'yū smiled and said, "You memorized that passage quite well, didn't you? But I am asking what do you see in this flower?" I said, "I don't know. You have said everything and I can add nothing." Nin'yū nonetheless continued, "Since you are an expert of the *Shōbōgenzō*, I would like to ask you; did you read the chapter of 'The Matter concerning [the Person] Beyond the Buddha'? I replied, "Yes, I read it some time ago." Nin'yū asked, "Tell me the gist of that?" I said, "It is too long and overly complicated to say it succinctly." "All right then," Nin'yū said, "Tell me the story in the section where Dongshan (Tung-shan, or Tozan in Japanese) was the protagonist." I said, "That is easy." Then I flipped the pages and recited as it was written:

The Venerable Master Dongshan told his students, 'You must know there was a man before the Buddha.' A monk asked, 'What sort of man was the man before the Buddha?'

Dogen then commented on this, 'We do not say he is not a buddha because he was before the Buddha's time. We don't say he is not a buddha because he was after the Buddha's time. We don't say he is not a buddha because he had surpassed the Buddha. It is not a buddha because he is earnestly reaching beyond the Buddha.'

Nin'yū said, "Very good indeed. You read it well. Now tell me what the flower in the chapter of the '*Udumbara*' truly is?" I was again confused by that question: "Well, this is difficult to explain with words. Besides, you asked me that question before." Without a pause, Nin'yū replied, "You are trying to escape from answering. We cannot stop here. We are only halfway to our meaningful dialogue, or *mondō*. All right, tell me more about the *Shōbōgenzō*, from the story of Dongshan."

Again, I recited the passage, "Dongshan … Of course, Master Hungxing of Mt. Yunju (Yün-chü) visited the master Dongshan. Dongshan asked him, 'Master, what is your name?' Master Yunju said, 'My name is Daoying (Tao-ying).' Master Dongshan asked him again, 'Tell me [again]. What is beyond that name?' Yungju said, 'If I say what is beyond, it would be not named Daoying.' Dongshan said [upon hearing this], 'I met you when I was at Mt. Yunju. Nothing has changed.' "

Nin'yū said, "Very good. There is one more story about Master Dongshan after that." I said. "Yes. That would be the encounter between Dongshan and Caoshan (Ts'ao-shan, Sōzan in Japanese)." Nin'yū said, "Tell me." I replied, "You know the story. You are testing me." Nin'yū said, "No, you are testing me. Remember?" I said, "Alright." Then I recited the following story: "The Master Caoshan visited Dongshan. Dongshan asked, 'What is your name?' Caoshan answered, 'Benji.' Dongshan further asked, 'Tell me beyond that.' Caoshan said, 'I will not say.' Dongshan asked, 'Why don't you say.' Caoshan then said, 'I won't name Benji.' This is all. I hope you will not ask me anymore."

Nin'yū said, "I will not ask you anymore. Actually, you have delivered your role very well. I will give you a grade of A for that. Ha-ha, ha-ha." Then, he looked at me seriously and said, "Do you know what Dōgen is really saying? He is saying 'your practice and *satori* (realization) are one—the two are inseparable. Therefore, Buddha is not a buddha. Buddha and not a buddha are one. When you are practicing, there is no notion of *satori*. *Satori* is itself the practice. You know, once you realize *satori*, *satori* becomes an object, that is, practice and *satori* are separated from one another. I am not using the logic of 'a whale is a mammal and a mammal is a whale.' I am talking about the absurdities of our common sense. If one stops at the point of reaching a buddha, then one is not beyond the Buddha. After all, the Buddha having the buddha form would not be a buddha. One practices and only practices the Buddha's Way; yet he could be separated from that practice if he realizes that he is practicing. Therefore, the practice is the Buddha, and beyond the Buddha. You know, it is like how the *miso* (soybean paste) that smells strongly of *miso* is not a good *miso*. I asked you at the beginning. 'What is the meaning of the *udumbara*?'"

Nin'yū took a deep breath and paused a moment. "I wonder what the essence of Buddhism is and the core of *nirvāṇa* while holding a flower? *Udumbara* is only a fig tree said to have blossomed once in three thousand years. But I don't think the *udumbara* is what the Buddha wanted to designate as the essence. So, it makes no difference between an *udumbara* or a chrysanthemum, or even a stone. My question is exactly that."

He continued, "The flower exists at this very moment but the flower carries the entire history of its species from the unknown beginning, from a seed to a big tree, again and again. It bears a dharma of cause and effect. The flower's causal chain includes the sun, the moon, wind, rain, day and night, spring, summer, mountains and rivers, oxygen, hydrogen, carbon dioxide and so forth—the whole lot. See, it exists in a chain of interdependency, just like us human beings. But still, the flower Mahākāśyapa saw in the Buddha's hand, he smiled, was a realization of the consecutive happenings of the flower. The flower changes every instant and so do we. You and I exist now, but you and I are, like the flower, coming from the beginning of our species, yet existing only at this instant. You and I came to this point of existence, depending, like the flower, on a whole lot of other existences. The Buddha and Mahākāśyapa understood that when their eyes caught eachother's."

He still continued like the master in the monastery giving a *honkō* (formal lecture) to his fellow monk students: "It was the dharma of 'impermanence,' or *anitiya*, that they had consented to. It was the dharma of 'no permanent self in an ever-changing world,' or *anātman,* that they had consented to. A glimpse of the flower signifies the essence of Buddhism. The flower is bright and beautiful at this moment, but it soon will wilt and no one can stop it. It demonstrates the dharma of 'impermanence.' We ignorant people lament when a flower withers. The *Dhamm-pada* (Pāli) says this." Then he recited, or rather sang, the passages from it. He moved his arms and legs and began dancing. He then tucked his kimono hem in the sash, lowered his hip and began stamping his thin bare feet on the *tatami* floor to the rhythm. For a while, Nin'yū enjoyed his quixotic realm and the two-thousand-year-old verses he sang echoed around the small Dharma Hall of Hōsen-ji:

All created are transitory (*anicca*).
When one realizes this by his wisdom (*paññaya*),
he does not heed [the world of] suffering (*dukkha*).
This is the Way (*maggo*) to purity (*visuddhiya*).

All created are suffering (*dukkha*),
When one realizes this by his wisdom (*paññaya*),
He does not heed [the world of] suffering (*dukkha*).
This is the Way (*maggo*) to purity (*visuddhiya*).

All existing are no-self (*anatta*),
When one realizes this by his wisdom (*paññaya*),
he does not heed [the world of] sorrow (*dukkha*).
This is the Way (*maggo*) to purity (*visuddhiya*).

He was wholeheartedly enjoying his newly-minted tune for the verses, along with his improvised bodily movements, which could hardly be called a dance. The whole scene was extramundane and a bit passé even then. Nin'yū's songs were often off key—with not a hint of a stellar performance.

I must admit that his singing and dancing had a unique character—just like his handwriting. Once, long ago, when I first saw his handwriting, I was surprised. At first glance it was like a clumsy childish scribble, yet those characters were charming in some way. Later I was surprised when I discovered the known Chinese calligrapher, Jin Dongxin, whose writing resembled that of Nin'yū. Nin'yū never mentioned that he studied the calligraphy of Jin Dongxin. He had a great depth of knowledge about Dōgen's works but never mentioned that he formally studied them. While dancing he said, "Kazumitsu-kun. The *udumbara* flower is the essence of Buddhism and the core of *nirvāṇa*. That's right—it signifies the whole teachings of Buddhism. You must also know at all times that *udumbara* is you. It's me, too. The chrysanthemum is you, you are the chrysanthemum; there is no difference. Do you understand that?" Nin'yū stopped dancing and smiled at me in a relaxed way as if he had just unburdened himself of a heavy load and said, "My share of this household chore is finished." He then left Hōsen-ji with the delightful last note, "Oh, what a wonderful day it is." During this *mondō* (question-and-answer period), I learned a great deal about Buddhism and its Zen interpretation. He never pretended his depth and breadth of understanding Buddhism. He was always humble about what he knew.

***

When I read the *Shōbōgenzō* alone, I was unable to interpret the content in his way. I had never looked at a flower that way either. In fact, when I read that section of the *Shōbōgenzō*, I only understood that I and the flower were subject and object, and understanding this, was adhering to the teaching of non-dichotomy or non-dualism. The flower had been a symbol of the buddha-dharma. Nin'yū had opened my eyes. It was not only "I," the subject, versus "others." For in the "objective" world, too, everything is one, undivided in the world of dharma. His interpretation was that not only the material world—but all of space and time—are one. Our mind is also one with them. Our minds are in them, and they are in our minds. I am the dharma and I am living in the midst of the dharma. I remembered, thereafter, feeling a close affinity and involvement with whatever objects I faced. How could I kill mosquitoes, flies, or any living beings? How could I break any trees or shrubs? It was not because I had made a vow of "no killing," but because I did not distinguish myself as such from the flora and fauna.

***

My vivid recollections of Nin'yū kept me awake while I was lying on the bed in the cabin. I thought I would never forget what he taught me. While I was wondering about all of those things, his image at Nagoya station came back to me. He had raised his right hand as if he were holding a stem of the *udumbara* flower. It might have been an *udumbara* he was showing me. Yes, he was telling me the essence of Buddhism with his gesture. He signaled to me not to forget it. Suddenly I again felt a deep sense of pathos and loneliness. How did Nin'yu feel about losing me? Nin'yu had been engulfed with tragedies. My departure was planned to be temporary. I wondered if that idea would still console him. I tried to shift my thinking to something else, but it was difficult.

I don't know how late I stayed awake in my bed in the cabin. I tried to put my mind on "*mu*" or "nothingness" and attempted to sleep. "*Mu*" is the state of "zero." It is an unthinkable state, "zero." Nin'yū taught me that when I practiced meditation I must put my mind at "zero," and not let the "*mu*" change to "one." Yes, *ex nihilo nihil fit,* or "nothing comes from nothing." I attempted to put my mind to just that. Adding or multiplying zero to numerous zeros, the result will still be zero. Zero is zero. Contrarily, "one" has the potential to develop into two, three or more. "Zero" has no quantum and cannot be substantiated in any form of quantity or quality. It is the way I had learned to meditate from Nin'yu, over and over. When I become zero, that state would be exactly the same as "I am the *udumbara*." Yes, *udumbara* is in fact "zero."

***

I decided to continue my journal writing even on uneventful days and nights on board. I was eager to write letters to Nin'yū when I got to San Francisco. I hoped he would write me back. I had been familiar with his unique handwriting for many years and seeing it again would give me immense comfort.

On board, alone in my cabin, my mind was at one again. Since I could not sleep, I let the one develop to two and three. My recollections continued. I recalled on one occasion when he saw me in my usual pastime, reading in my room. He sat by my desk and casually said, "Hmmm ... *kan-jitsugetsu* (sweet idling for days and months)." That expression was a known Chinese phrase close to the nuance of the Italian expression, "*dolce far niente.*" Then he said, "I might as well tell you a wake-up statement from the *Record of Things Heard,* or *Shōbōgenzō Zuimon-ki.*" He sat up straight and began:

In Sung Dynasty China, when Dōgen was reading the Records of Zen Masters, an experienced monk from Sichuan saw [him reading] and asked Dōgen, "What good comes from reading those records?" Dōgen answered, "I will learn how the ancients practiced." The monk said, "What will you do then?" Dōgen said, "I will teach people when I return to my home country." The monk said, "What will you do then?" Dōgen said, "I will save people." The monk further asked. "What then will you do? The most important thing is what will you do?" Dōgen was confused.

Dōgen recalled this episode later and said, "I was, in those days, reading the predecessors' records and studying how those people attained enlightenment. I thought those [readings] would be useful for me and for other people. But I realized after serious thought that they were useless for my practice and others. Only [earnest] sitting holds the ultimate importance.

(*Shōbōgenzō, Zuimon-ki* III, 7)

Nin'yū's good advice was usually in such a form. At that time, he suggested that I emphasize and practice sitting instead of just merely reading even Dōgen's *Shōbōgenzō*.

I was exhausted, and finally fell asleep after midnight. I woke up around five o'clock the next morning. I was awakened by the noise of the port of Yokohama which had begun at dawn. I was informed the day before that breakfast would be served at 7:30 a.m. in the dining room behind the pilot tower of the ship. I meditated on my bed for forty-five minutes to an hour. Sitting always brought me delightful serenity as well as a warm familiarity. I felt like myself. I walked the deck and looked around the harbor. The floor was shiny with dew. The scene was faintly familiar. Breakfast began on time. The captain, engineers and other officers of the ship all gathered at the table. First, we introduced ourselves, as this was the first time we had met. This was my first experience sitting at a table with foreigners, all of whom were Americans. With my poor level of English comprehension I could not understand most of what they were saying. Nonetheless, dining with the captain and other officers of the ship was harmonious and pleasant, although, for me, the experience was that of a totally unfamiliar terrain.

Around nine o'clock, the same group of well-wishers came back to the pier to see me off. They looked around the ship for a while and then sat in my room. A teenage American boy of Japanese descent, possibly high school age, came to the room and began unloading what he was carrying. He didn't greet us. My sister Minako whispered to me, "He must be your roommate." So I asked him in Japanese if he was, and he said "yes" in English. The cabin was filled with my guests so he left the room immediately.

My sister Minako, Takako, and Tomo-san prepared colored tapes and I held the end of everyone's tape until they broke off as the ship slowly left the pier. Perhaps it was a romantic scene, but with only a dozen passengers, it did not have the festivity of a grand farewell. My departure from Japan was not a grandiose affair as my sister had possibly expected by bringing those tapes. For me, however, it was the first experience of this sort and was thus a fond farewell. We left the pier at around 11:00 a.m. on May 24, 1952, about an hour behind schedule. At first, a tugboat pushed the large steamer backward. I stood on the starboard deck and waved while the ship slowly turned around and started to move forward. Then I moved to the port side deck and waved a white handkerchief until their figures were no longer visible.

***

When the ship moved out of the port of Yokohama, it began rolling with larger undulations. My young roommate, who told me that he was Japanese-American, made big gestures of annoyance and yelled that he was getting seasick. I was not aware of it immediately but he was with his mother, who was a second generation Japanese, or *nisei,* from the United States. His mother worked for the American Military Office in Japan and they were en route to their home in California. The young man was quite a nuisance. Most of the time, he ignored my requests to behave quietly. I had planned to read several books on this two-week journey but he intentionally interrupted my reading. He was an energetic teenage boy. On this boat, I became aware for the first time that my English language skills were nearly nil. I realized I was handicapped because my honest young roommate teased me unrepentantly on several occasions. I was angry at first, but it was true that I could not use the English language for even daily communication.

One morning before breakfast, I had been meditating on my bed for twenty minutes or so. His mother came into the room and shook

my shoulders, as if she were waking me. She said, "What are you doing? Why are you doing that? Don't do anything weird. People might
think you are crazy." I looked at her. I was not disturbed. But at that
moment I was puzzled about how she interpreted my meditation. Her
stern posture gave me the impression that I was *persona non grata* to
her. Several months ago, Reverend Tobase advised me to grow my
hair long and to wear Western clothes as a part of my preparation for
work in the United States. She did not know that I was a Zen monk.
Apparently my meditation and my ignorance of Americanism caused
her embarrassment. I had seen her earlier, and somehow expected
something like that might happen. I could not explain what I was
doing. Even though she and her son were Japanese descendants and
lived in Japan, they never spoke Japanese. I spoke to them a few times
in Japanese but the woman told me, in English, to speak English and
not to speak Japanese to her. Apparently, they were not interested in
Japanese culture at all. Or rather, they wanted to be a part of main-
stream American society. I stopped obvious forms of meditation in
the mornings but I tried to meditate while standing or sitting on the
chaise on the deck in the mornings and afternoons. I was hoping to
meditate and read as much as I could during this long ocean voyage.
My occasional meditations did not create further ado. I found that
it was difficult to meditate without an upright posture and without
a proper sitting place as Dōgen mentioned very fastidiously in his
Chapter on the "*Zazengi*," or "Significance of *zazen*, sitting practice":

> For sitting Zen, a quiet place is better. Make your sitting
> cushion thick. Do not let wind and mist come into the
> room. You must not let rain and dew come into the room.
> You must secure and protect the place [where you sit]. We
> learned that once the Buddha sat [on the ground under the
> Bodhi Tree and others sat] as if sitting on a great rock.

However, they piled grass thickly and sat on it. A sitting place must be well-lit, whether day or night and one must make the place warm in winter and cool in summer. ...

You must sit up straight. You must not lean left, right, front, or back. Your ears must be aligned with your shoulders. Your nose and navel must be in alignment. Your tongue must touch the palate. Breathing must be through your nostrils. Your lips and teeth must touch [each other]. Your eyes must be opened but neither too wide nor too narrow.

During this thirteen-day voyage from Yokohama to San Francisco, I discovered why the proper way to meditate was important. Meditation in a proper setting and in a proper way was essential, not only for Dōgen, but also for his teacher, Rujing (Ju-ching, Nyojō in Japanese). Rujing instructed Dōgen in the *Hōkyō-ki,* The Record of the Hōkyō Period:

One evening Rujing asked, "Dōgen, do you know the [proper] way of putting on footwear when seated on a chair [platform seat]?" Dogen made a formal bow and said, "How could I know?" Rujing compassionately answered, "The [proper] method of putting on footwear when doing zazen seated on a chair in the monks' hall is to cover your whole foot with the right sleeve [of your robe]. In this way you avoid being disrespectful [to the image of Mañjuśrī], the guardian Bodhisattva [of the monk hall]." Rujing continued, "When you are earnestly engaged in the practice of zazen, you should not eat rush oats, for it will cause you to become feverish." Rujing compassionately continued, "You should not do zazen in a windy place." Rujing continued,

"When you stand up and begin walking after having done zazen, you should definitely follow the method of proceeding a half step with each breath. That is to say, when you take a step [forward], you should not exceed half a foot in length. At the same time, you should always inhale and exhale once with each step."

Hereafter, Rujing carefully instructed Dōgen about what sort of clothes to wear and so forth. Dōgen followed Rujing, insofar as he was extraordinarily careful regarding the way of sitting. Long hair and long nails were prohibited. He even instructed him about how to urinate and excrete properly. As he said in the Chapter on "Cleansing," or Senjō, of the Shōbōgenzō: "A clean person is the person who cleans urine and feces and cuts the nails of his fingers and toes." When I was reading the Shōbōgenzō in my study at Hōsen-ji, I did not understand why Dōgen was so meticulous about forms and behavior in daily life. But on this voyage I began to understand the significance of proper sitting. Every step has to be properly done in order to practice the buddha-dharma properly. Zazen was not mere sitting. Through zazen practice, one must be the pivot of this entire universe. One must become a living nexus that penetrates the continuum of a primordial time to an unlimited future. In addition, one will also extend, in space, to unlimited horizons embracing all living and nonliving beings. In Zen, this state, the original nature, is called the state before your parents were born. It is the state in which no dichotomies exist.

In normal circumstances, I must sit firmly and solidly on the seat to be in that state. This voyage was an exception. I began paying no attention to my cabin-mate, and read my books for I had a welcome length of time in the monotonous transparency of ocean and sky. When he was out of the cabin, I meditated there.

Fortunately, his mother never came to my cabin again during the entire voyage and was no longer my concern. I recalled Dogen's Chinese journey. Dogen returned to Japan "empty-fisted" (brought nothing) after studying in China for more than four years. He had acquired something else, which was the core of Buddhism—realization of human's inmost axis of life, of "only sitting." On this voyage, I earnestly experienced the true value of the "only sitting." It was my whole-hearted homage to Dogen. Above all, sitting is the only activity that I knew onboard to bring me into the realm of peace, and doing so gave me undoubted serenity.

***

The ship finally arrived at the portal of San Francisco Bay. Our ship sailed calmly under the Golden Gate Bridge. On the portside of the boat were rolling hills with houses sprinkled along the hillside. I learned later that those were the towns of Sausalito, Belvedere and Tiburon. It was June 4, 1952. I stood on the deck and from there observed the wide vista of San Francisco, from sea level to hilltop. Streets were as straight as a checkerboard and houses lining both sides had bright pastel colors of blue, green and pink. I had never seen a scene like that in Japan. Those colorful houses were a strong contrast to the dark silhouetted cities of postwar Japan. Nearly seven years after the war, the damage of bombardment remained the dominant landscape there.

Before reaching the port of San Francisco, the ship stopped in the middle of the bay where Alcatraz Island was in full view. Immigration and custom officers came aboard. They checked my immigration status and asked a few questions regarding what I had brought with me. Then the ship slowly moved forward and turned around near the foot of the Bay Bridge into the pier. Until the ship was firmly anchored to the pier, we were on deck observing the procedure. It took a few hours. I saw Reverend Tobase's short and stocky figure in a brown robe over his western suit. He was with another middle-aged person in a gray suit and soft gray snap-brimmed hat. Both were standing side-by-side waiting for the ship to be tied up. Tobase, looking toward the ship, caught my eyes and waved at me with a grand gesture. The man next to him did not wave but was glancing constantly at me as though sizing up my qualities for my position at Sōkō-ji.

At last, in the early afternoon, we were permitted to disembark. I walked down the gangway to the platform of the pier. Tobase and his companion came to the lower end of the gangway and greeted me. Tobase introduced the man as Mr. Komiyama, the president of the board of directors at Sōkō-ji. I remembered his name from the documents he had signed. I greeted them courteously. I did not know what sort of position this was for a Zen temple. Japanese temples do not have boards or directors. Tobase, in Japan and in his letters, had never explained the organizational structure of his temple, so I thought the San Francisco temple had the same *danka* (supporters) system as in Japan.

Mr. Komiyama was in a gray double-breasted suit. He wore a matching gray hat in a slightly slanted fashion. I thought he was a *yakuza*. It was made in the USA and found out few days later that it was a fad in the U.S.. Mr. Komiyama talked to me with a Tokyo-style crisp diction and explained his role at the temple. We had to wait a few more hours until my luggage was unloaded onto the receiving area of the pier. I also had three or four big sacks of cargo I had brought at Reverend Tobase's request. In addition, there were large packages that had to be sent to Sōkō-ji later.

I loaded my personal belongings into Mr. Komiyama's new light green Buick. I thought the car was gigantic and luxurious. Mr.

Komiyama looked at me and said, "I like a big 'machine.' It's very comfortable to travel in and safer." He referred to his big new car as a "machine" in a slightly lofty manner. If it had been in Japan in those days, that car would be worth more than an ordinary man's whole wealth. As we traveled the streets of San Francisco, he explained that this was such-and-such and that was so-and-so, but nothing stayed in my mind. The place I remember from this first ride into San Francisco was the terminal for the Key System Transit Station at the Embarcadero. Back in Japan, Reverend Otsuka had told me the station was used to go to the University of California at Berkeley from San Francisco. As we drove, I realized that I was dead-tired even in the mid-afternoon. San Francisco was an entirely different world for me. Everything I saw was new—streets, houses, shops, offices, buses, streetcars, pedestrians, bystanders. Mr. Komiyama's kind remarks on selected landmarks were way beyond my comprehension.

We arrived at Sōkō-ji after a twenty-minute ride from the port. Sōkō-ji was a dark brown wooden building on a noticeably slanted street, facing Bush Street between Laguna and Octavia. I noticed that San Francisco had, besides its checkerboard street formation, an interesting architectural style. Residential houses were lined back-to-back without space between them. The area of Sōkō-ji was built higher than ground level. Houses had several steps in front, some without rail-supports. There were houses with interesting artificial façades facing the streets. Those facing Sōkō-ji were no exception.

The temple building, originally built as a Jewish Synagogue in 1895, had been named *Ohabai Shalome.* The building survived the infamous San Francisco earthquake in 1905. It was a grand old building both outside and inside. It had a broad façade, with the main entrance at the center and two small entrances on both sides. Both sides of the façade spires or towers had cone-shaped roofs. The large main hall had a colonnade of faint sunbeams filtering through the windows creating an ambience of ageless tranquility.

We went into Sōkō-ji from a side door on the right side of the main door. Immediately to the right, there were long steep newel steps leading to the second floor. The building was considered to be old even then in 1952—fifty-seven years old to be exact. The ceilings were very high. Newel posts supported the railing at the top and bottom of the stairs. There was also a six foot-long mid-landing area with matching newel posts at each corner. The interior of the building was painted reddish brown on the lower part of the walls and white plaster on the upper surface. The windows held beautiful stained glass bearing the Star of David insignia. Everything was impressively antiquated and it was a well-turned place of worship. I was told that the building was bought by Japanese immigrants in 1937 for Reverend Hosen Isobe, a Sōtō Zen priest, and converted to a Zen Buddhist temple.

Mr. Komiyama told me to carry my luggage into my temporary room at the back of the main hall. Sōkō-ji had a large hall for main activities on the ground floor. It seated approximately 500 people. There were two large rooms and a couple of small storage rooms. The air did not circulate in the area and it had a musty smell. The floor was also painted reddish brown. I saw holes here and there in this area of the building. At the right corner of the right-hand side room, there was an iron-framed bed with a discolored bare mattress on it. Mr. Komiyama lifted his chin to signify this was my room. I unloaded my belongings in one corner of the room. He said, "I'll ask Reverend Nazuka to give you some sheets and a pillow. We wrote you to bring your own bedding; did you bring it with you?" I said, "Yes, I brought my bedding, but it is still at the pier." Mr.

Komiyama nodded and said, "I'll tell Reverend Nazuka to lend you a few blankets until you get your own bedding."

Reverend Tobase came in with a female priest. Reverend Tobase introduced me to Reverend Nazuka who had just arrived from some business. Both priests looked around the room, Tobase said, "My, this is quite a place; I hope you can stand its condition for a while." He also said, "If you need anything, let us know. Nazuka Sensei left a bar of soap and a pair of towels in the kitchen." I followed them to the upstairs room, which Tobase used as his office. He passed his office and went to the kitchen. He said, "Let's have a cup of tea. Nazuka Sensei prepared the tea for us. She has boiled the water and it's ready to make tea." Tobase put hot water into a pot with tea leaves in the bottom. We sat and chatted for a while. Then Mr. Komiyama said, "It is dinnertime; let's go out to eat. How about going to 'China-meshi' (Chinese food) nearby?" Reverend Tobase said, "That's fine with me. How about you, Katō-kun?" I said, "That's fine." We went to a nearby Chinese restaurant on Sutter Street in Japantown, called Keirin-in. On the way, Reverend Nazuka informed me of the temple routines and my role there. We arrived at the restaurant in five minutes or so. The texture of Chinese rice and the scent of soy sauce were slightly different from those I was used to in Japan. Still it was close enough and I enjoyed my first formal meal with rice and soy sauce in the United States.

After dinner at Keirin-in, I expected to sit in Tobase's office, but he said we would talk things over in the morning; I should retire for the day. I found the pillow and sheets on the office sofa. Carrying my bedding, I fumbled in the darkness through the aisle of the main hall to get to my room. It took a little while to find the switch to turn the light on. I sat on the dusty mattress on the steel bed for a while and pondered what was going to happen from then on. This was the way my first day in San Francisco transpired. In spite of the very long day and many new experiences, I had a good night's sleep.

> Even if peach blossoms wanted
> to outlast summer,
> moon and wind won't wait.
> Were I to seek out men of the Han,
> not one would still be alive.
>
> Morning after morning
> flowers fade and fall.
> Year after year
> people move on, change.
>
> The place where dust now swirls
> was once a great ocean.
>
> – Han-shan

Chapter 14

REFLECTION

生といふは、たとえば、
人のふねにのれるときのごとし。
このふねは、
われ帆をつかひ、
われかぢをとれり、
われさををさすといへども、
ふねわれをのせて、
ふねのほかにわれなし。

われふねにのりて、
このふねをもふねならしむ。

この正当恁麼時を功夫参学すべし、
この正当恁麼時は、
舟の世界にあらざることなし。

天も水も岸もみな舟の時節となれり。

さらに舟にあらざる時節とお
なじからず。

Human life is
like a man sailing a boat.
Although I set sail,
steer my course and
pole the boat along,
the boat carries me
and I do not exist
apart from the boat.

By sailing the boat,
I make the boat what it is.

Study sincerely this very moment.
This moment is
not without the world of the boat.

Heaven, water, shore, and all
become the time of the boat.

For this reason, life is what

このゆへに、生はわが生ぜ
しむるなり、
われをば生のわれならしむるなり。

we have created. Such is the life
that is I,
the life that is exactly I.

— 道元

- Dōgen

(『正法眼蔵』「全機」)

(*Shōbōgenzō, (Zenki)* "Total
Function")

I learned the Sōkō-ji routine in a week or so. It was simple; Tobase
Sensei and I did a short, twenty to twenty-five minute-long *zazen*
and simplified chanting while Nazuka Sensei did most of the preparations for our breakfast. It was just like Hōsen-ji, insofar as no
members came and participated. The temple activities were much
quieter than I expected. On weekdays, after morning meditation
and chanting, we usually did not have much to do. Some days,
retired men and women dropped by and talked about local news
in the Japanese community. Tobase Sensei, Nazuka Sensei, Mr.
Komiyama and I visited members in San Mateo, San Jose, and
Monterey once a month. Without Mr. Komiyama's help, we could
not go to those places alone, for we did not know how to drive;
moreover, we did not know the areas well. On those trips I enjoyed
Mr. Komiyama's life-story from the time he came to the United
States, as well as his impressions of places such as the cannery in
Monterey where Japanese immigrants worked.

While I became accustomed to temple activities, my unfamil-
iarity with things in my new environment created a quiet anguish
every time I encountered situations even as small as buying toothpaste. Toothpaste was called *hamigaki-ko* or "tooth polishing pow-
der" in Japanese then. There was paste in tubes, too, but it was

too expensive for ordinary Japanese households to purchase. There was a kind man working at Jimmy's Drugstore, behind Sōkō-ji, at the corner of Sutter and Laguna streets, who patiently told me the names of items in American English. I carried a dictionary, but it was impossible to look up every little word. The differences in daily matters piqued my curiosity; even the shape and quality of kitchen knives and scrubbing brushes fascinated me. Although I made many mistakes during the long process, I gradually acquired the Japanese-American way of life.

Every time I faced difficulties learning about this new culture I pondered how Dōgen coped with those differences during his Chinese experience. It was, I imagine, much more difficult in the thirteenth century than in the early 1950's, even though he mastered Chinese characters before arriving in China.

***

Dōgen was born on the second day of the first month in 1200. If I take the liberty to convert to today's calendar it would be on January 19, 1200. When he arrived in China he was twenty-three years of age by today's standards. I was twenty-two years old when I left Japan-exactly one year younger than him. Dōgen went to Mt. Tientung monastery and joined more than 500 practitioners there in the fifth month of 1223. After meeting his teacher, Rujing (Nyojō in Japanese), Dogen had overcome those linguistic, cultural and monastic barriers and accomplished what he set out for. I know it was overly presumptuous on my part to compare my situation with that of Dōgen. My dilemmas would be far easier, yet my thoughts about Dōgen encouraged me enormously.

***

Five or six weeks after I arrived in San Francisco, one of the temple members told Tobase Sensei that he was going to take a two-week vacation to visit his family in Japan. Then he looked at me and asked Tobase whether I could fill in for him at work. He was working at the drugstore on Polk Street, which was not far from Sōkō-ji. His job was to clean the store before and after store hours and deliver medicines to various customers. He said the job was very easy. Tobase looked at me and said, "Ah, this is an ideal job for you. You will learn this vicinity while you deliver medicine. In so doing, you will also acquire English. It's a two-bird-one-stone solution." As you might guess, Tobase was all for it and I was too, but for a different reason. I needed to escape my boredom since I was idling in the temple most of the time. I needed a little adventure exploring San Francisco as well as receiving some income. The man said he would talk to his boss about it the next day. Around 9 o'clock in the morning the following day, he called and told me to come to the store anytime that day for an interview. I said to him that I would come to the store around 11 o'clock. It did not take that long to get there but I left extra time just in case I got lost in this still unfamiliar area. I put on the three-piece suit I had brought from Japan and went to the drugstore. I had not yet had a chance to ride a city bus or streetcar, so I decided to walk to the store looking at the city map Tobase had given me earlier. It was probably my first temple outing and I was a bit anxious since I had not even used a public telephone. I knew Sōkō-ji's telephone number but I had not yet called it. Furthermore, if I took the bus, I would not comprehend the conductor's street name announcements so my chances of missing the stop were high.

The drugstore proprietor was a man of about forty-five. When I greeted him, he smiled and stepped forward to shake my hand. I thought he was a very kind, friendly person, compared to my notion of the common attitudes of small business owners and employees. He then told me what I needed to do but most of his instructions were incomprehensible to me. Luckily, I was already informed about details of the job from the man I was replacing. My job was to dust the store, sweep the floor and deliver medicines to the customers' residences. He had probably heard about my English capability, for he gesticulated and talked slowly, explaining, "For this job you don't need to wear a suit and necktie. In fact it would be better if you wear a casual jacket and khaki pants." I understood him but it was still so soon after my arrival and I did not yet own a casual western outfit. That afternoon I went to a small clothing store in Japantown and bought a cotton jumper jacket and khaki pants. Although they were sold in Japantown, they were still made for taller people. The jumper sleeves were a bit too long but they had elastic bands at the openings for tucking up the sleeves. The khaki pants were too long, so I folded the cuffs over two or three times.

I went to work the following day walking as I had planned. The job was easy at first, but running up and down the steep hills of San Francisco at a hasty pace was taxing. I thought I had stamina and did not worry about it at first but soon learned that toiling up and down Nob Hill and the Marina district all day was quite arduous. I believe the proprietor told me to use a bus if needed, but I still preferred to walk since I knew nothing of the bus system or its routes.

A few clients gave me tips when I delivered their medicine but I did not know what to do with the tips so I simply returned them. Some customers were surprised by my refusal but tipping was not a Japanese custom and the man I replaced did not tell me about tips. One afternoon, about seven to ten days after I started to work, I delivered a bag of medicine to a middle-aged man on the fourth floor of an apartment complex. He was in his robe when he opened the door.

I asked, "Are you Mr. so-and-so?" The man said, "Yeah. Oh, you're a deliveryman from the drugstore. Okay, I'll bring the money." A minute later he came back and gave me the amount for the medicine. As I was about leave, possibly fifteen or twenty steps away from the door, he whistled and shouted "Hey!" at me, so I turned back toward him. Then, he threw something at me. It was totally unexpected and I did not catch it; instead, I shielded my head with my hands. It hit the back of my hand and fell to the ground. It was a quarter. I picked it up and threw it back without thinking. The coin fell just before his feet at the door. He began shouting at me but I did not understand what he was saying. I departed hastily, never stopping to look back. That evening, when I returned to the drugstore after delivering all of the items, the proprietor told me he did not need me anymore. I knew the reason; nonetheless, I felt very bad for the man I was substituting for. Moreover, I did not know how to explain and apologize for my actions. I later told Tobase what happened at the drugstore. He said, "Did he throw a coin at you? I wonder why he did that. Was he angry with you?" Then he said, "Don't worry about it anymore. What has happened has happened. It is useless to worry. I don't think he will lose his job on account of you."

***

This was the beginning of a series of events I encountered due largely to my ignorance about America's cultural and social customs. I grew up in a bygone cultural milieu. Western customs and cultures were still foreign to me. My new life in San Francisco was that of an abecedarian. I realized that I must learn this new culture step-by-step from alpha to omega. Disseminating Buddhism in this new country had to wait until I became more familiar with the English language and American customs.

I am almost certain that Dōgen experienced a much more pro-found culture shock than I did in the mid-twentieth century. He was well-educated and had a high level of literacy in Chinese, but there is no record of his conversational skill. Interestingly, he mentioned personal hygiene three times in his volumes of discourse. He stated that the mouth odors of Chinese monks were very unpleasant. When they spoke, even when separated by two or three feet, their mouth odor apparently overwhelmed him. Some of his experiences stemmed from cultural differences. Dōgen nonetheless integrated those differences into the fabric of Zen practice.

Dōgen recommended that his students use toothbrushes, so he provided instructions on how to make them. This toothbrush used wood or bamboo fiber, never animal bristles. It was not only lim-ited to oral hygiene; Dōgen was extremely particular about cleans-ing himself, even to the point of elevating it to a ritual. Our body was originally untainted and Dōgen's emphasis on cleanliness was to maintain a state of purity. Furthermore, when practitioners fol-low the exact steps of his ritualistic cleansing, they also cleanse their minds. Not only does one clean one's mind but also the en-tire buddha world. Therefore, for Dōgen, cleansing is integral to the practice of Zen. He incorporated many elements of Indian and Chinese culture into his way of practice.

Although my relocation was presumably easier than what Dōgen faced in thirteenth-century China, my initiation into American cul-ture still did not fare so well. Japan and its post-war culture might have still been "primitive," yet it was the product of a long evolu-tion. The popular mode of life prescribed by Americanization was *de rigueur* in postwar Japan. At that time, anything related to the old Japan was labeled as feudalistic even though some practices were wholly unrelated to feudalism. My upbringing in Zen culture justifiably abounded in its own unique tradition; however, it was still considered by many Japanese in the post-war period as old-fashioned and thus belonging to a designated class of "feudalism." I did not pay any attention to whatever people labeled Buddhism or Zen Buddhism. I knew it was a contradictory impulse; even as our societies change for the better, all of us crave the stability of tradition. Zen Buddhism embraces all of those contradictions and I was in the midst of it. It was just the fashion of post-war times and I ignored such expressions as a passing rumor. Rather, I was affected by Gyokusen's reasoning for me to come to the United States, which was *bukkyō-tōzen,* or disseminating Buddhism eastward.

The eastward movement of Buddhism, or *"bukkyō-tōzen,"* is an idiom meaning the disseminating direction for the course of Buddhism since Dōgen brought Sōtō Zen to Japan. Buddhism originated in India, moved eastward to China, and then further east to Japan. Dōgen originally used this term in reference to Bodhidharma, who brought *Ch'an* (Zen) Buddhism from India to China. When I consulted Gyokusen about coming to the U.S., Gyokusen used this term and hinted of this as his reasoning for approval. As I have mentioned, it is overly presumptuous of me to apply this word to my role in the United States. As far as I know, Dōgen used *bukkyō tōzen* twice in his *Shōbōgenzō.* One instance is in the chapter of "Wholehearted Practice of the Way," or *"Bendōwa,"* and the other is in the chapter of the "Continuous Practice," or *"Gyōji."* Let me quote from the former chapter:

Our country (Japan) is located east of the great ocean where layers of clouds and mists interrupt. However, around the time of Emperors Kinmei and Yōmei (532-572 and 585-587 C.E., respectively), Buddhist teachings from the Autumn (West) gradually moved eastward (*bukkyō tōzen*). I think it is fortunate for the people [of this country].

The following excerpt is from the latter chapter:

> Why after the period of Puzu during the Liang Dynasty (520-527), do some people go to India? It is an utmost foolish thing and it must be the result of their bad karma. Every step of those monks completes their ruin and departs from the true Dharma. Every step escapes from the home of the Buddha. What do those monks gain in India? They only suffer en route to mountains or the sea. They neither realize nor study Buddhism of the West (India). They do not realize Buddhism had moved East, or *bukkyō tōzen,* and instead simply wander around in India.

When Gyokusen used the term, he merely signified the eastward movement of Buddhism, but I related it to the above expression of Dōgen's. Bodhidharma brought *Ch'an* (Zen) from India to China, and Dōgen acquired it and brought it "empty-fisted" to Japan. Although Gyokusen used the term *bukkyō tōzen* to refer to the spread of Buddhism in the United States, it was not a term that was widely used in this context, even though the movement started more than a half-century before.

***

Buddhism was first introduced to the United States by a group of Buddhists in October of 1893 at the World Congress of Religions in Chicago. It was an event related to the four-hundredth year commemoration of Christopher Columbus's arrival to America. This event coincided with the common "Eastward Movement of Buddhism," or *bukkyō tōzen.* One of the delegates from Japan, a Rinzai Zen master, Shaku Sōen, introduced D. T. Suzuki shortly after the congress. D. T.

Suzuki's writings on Zen provided a firm Zen foundation in the United States and other English speaking countries. Oxford University Press had already published the series, *Sacred Books of the East,* which included various Buddhist texts such as *Saddharma-Pundarīka* or *The Lotus of the True Law*, which was translated by H. Kern (1884), and *The Questions Of King Miliinda,* which was translated from the Pali by T. W. Rhys Davids (1890). Besides these, there were other books already available in English; one example is *Buddhist Logic*—two volumes by F. Th. Stcherbatsky as parts of the *Bibliotheca Buddhica* series, published by Sciences of the U.S.S.R. in 1930. Later, Alan Watts studied Zen at the Buddhist Lodge in London while in his twenties. The Buddhist Lodge in London was headed by a noted Buddhist supporter, Travers Christmas Humphreys, who eventually introduced Watts to Suzuki. After the war, during the 1950s, Alan Watts popularized Zen Buddhism in America. However, by then several Japanese Buddhist schools, including Zen, were already in the United States. Those institutions served the needs of Chinese and Japanese immigrants in their Hawaiian enclaves and on the urban and rural West coast of the United States. In large part due to D. T. Suzuki and Alan Watts, Zen Buddhism fascinated many intellectuals and young people toward the end of the 1950s. Some who were not satisfied with studying Buddhism in only an academic context began engaging in the actual practice of Zen. At that time, Zen Buddhism included all activities and launched its first practice center in San Francisco's Sōkō-ji. Prior to this time the Los Angeles Zen Institute was founded and led by Rinzai Zen Master Joshū Sasaki.

***

As I began my new life in San Francisco, I sent Nin'yū Yamasaki many letters and he wrote me just as many in reply. To my amazement, he occasionally inserted correctly spelled English phrases into his letters, which he still remembered from his student days. Sometimes, after having had one too many drinks, he even recited phrases from the works of Shakespeare. One of his letters ended with the quotation, "All's well that ends well."

One day, about two months after I arrived, Tobase and I sat in his office, and he asked me, "How are you doing? Are you satisfied with what you are doing?" I hesitated a little but said, "No, Tobase Sensei. After breakfast, there is not much for me to do during the weekdays. I'm quite bored." It was true. The first several weeks I was busy learning daily chores and adjusting to a new routine but those novelties soon wore off. Tobase then said, "I understand. We must find some solution for that, shouldn't we? People work during weekdays and have no time to come to the temple, you know." Then after a short pause, he added, "I have a great idea. Why don't you get a 'schoolboy' job and also go to school?

'Schoolboy,' meaning you would be employed as a live-in helper, performing domestic chores while learning the language and customs of this new country. You will learn English that way. Remember, as we previously discussed, we need an English-speaking priest here. Not too long from now, I think, all members of this temple will only speak English. Acquiring the English language will be essential for this temple, and it's going to be a vital part of your work in the years to come. I will speak to the Board chairman, Mr. Komiyama, and other board members as well." I replied, "That is a good idea, but will I get any monetary assistance to attend school?" I was only getting room and board since we had made no remunerative arrangements; thus, I had no money for tuition or textbooks. Tobase said, "That poses a big question for you, doesn't it? That's why I said to get a schoolboy job. I've heard from someone that you can live in a wealthy home where you attend to housecleaning and other chores before and after school. Those positions are called 'schoolboy' for young men and 'schoolgirl' for young women. You will be paid thirty or even thirty-five American dollars a month. I think it is a wonderful system. You will learn how Americans live, how they think, and how they take care of things. Ah, what a splendid idea. A future Zen priest who will speak Zen and various Zen masters' anecdotes in English." The conversation ended with Tobase's optimistic tone.

A few weeks later, one of the temple members took me to a very nice house near the Presidio. Tobase was right; I received thirty dollars plus room and board in exchange for my work before and after school. My immediate goal then was to learn English; I decided to take the "schoolboy" job without hesitation. I also applied to attend the college during the fall semester of 1952, just three months after my arrival in San Francisco.

Reverend Tobase and I agreed that while I lived at the house where I worked as a schoolboy, I would still go to Sōkō-ji every weekend and on special occasions to assist him. In those days, six to ten children, ranging from the levels of kindergarten to high school, arrived on Sundays with their parents or grandparents. To accommodate the children, we decided to open a Zen Sunday School, although Buddhist temples in Japan rarely had such schools. Sunday School lessons were a copy of Christian churches. Sōkō-ji members recommended having Sunday school there. Sōkō-ji Sunday school consisted of brief sūtra chanting, followed by a simple sermon by Reverend Tobase. Some days, we added an abbreviated meditation period before chanting. Tobase could not speak English well, so I assisted him by translating his heavy Kumamoto dialect into my pidgin English, which conveyed his dharma talk with a humorous air. The children seemed to enjoy us. One Sunday School session at Sōkō-ji went like the following: "What shall we do today? Shall we talk about the Buddha?" Tobase always started like this: "We have a nice Buddha statue and you are so lucky to see him every Sunday, aren't you?" The children were puzzled and a minute of silence followed his question. Then, one child asked, "Why is the statue gold and shiny, Tobase Sensei?"

Tobase replied, "Well, first of all, the golden statue is easier for us to see than if it were a darker color, isn't that so?" Another child said, "Yes, and it looks very expensive. How much is it worth, Tobase Sensei?" Another said, "Yeah, it looks expensive. It must be very expensive. And it looks very important, too."

Tobase said, "Huh, you are very intelligent. Everyone is right. The statue looks very expensive and important. You know, one old sūtra said the Buddha had thirty-two special signs and one of them was that his skin was smooth, like the surface of gold. But is that all you see in this statue?" The children began talking about the statue in front of them and commented that he looked serious, wise, pensive, stern, smart, and so on.

Tobase listened to the children's various comments, and then said, "Well, someone said that the statue looks warm, someone else said that the statue looks stern, and someone said wise and serious. But there is only one statue there. Which part of the statue looks serious and which part of the statue looks stern? Why don't you look at it very carefully once more and tell me again what you see."

A few minutes later a child said, "Tobase Sensei, I said it looked serious before, but I see that he is not serious now. I said that because he is not smiling." Similarly, another also retracted his earlier comment. One child said that the eyes of the statue exuded warmness, and another said that the mouth expressed sternness.

On this specific occasion, Tobase's conclusion ended with "the statue has a head, face, eyes, ears, arms, body, legs, etcetera, so we see those just as they are. Descriptors such as serious, warm, stern, and so forth, are only one person's observation based on his or her conditioned manner of assessing the statue. Individual perceptions sometimes create problems, which invite such feelings as extreme detest or greed, and if fulfilled, make the person happy or the reverse. I see the statue has a head, two eyes and a mouth that are horizontal and a nose which is vertical." Tobase used this phrase, "horizontal eyes and a vertical nose," from Dōgen's *Eihei Kōroku,* or the *Extensive Record of Eihei Dōgen.*

Tobase then concluded, "It is important to see things as they are, such as eyes that are horizontal and noses that are vertical. Green mountains are green mountains and rivers, rivers; willow trees and flowers are just as they appear. Summer will be hot and winter cold. If there were no fuss and no nuisance, life would be very simple and easy." When Tobase talked with the children like that, it was refreshing and appropriate without a hint of contrivance.

Upon another occasion, Tobase told the following story to the children: "A long, long time ago, almost a thousand years ago in China, a Zen monk was traveling on a mountain road in cold winter weather. He saw a small run-down Buddhist temple in the evening dusk. So, he decided to stay there. Then a fierce storm blew in and made the inside of the temple unbearably cold. The monk found a wooden Buddha statue in the corner. He picked it up and placed it in the center of the hall. He prostrated to the statue and chanted a short sūtra in a shivering voice. Then, he chopped the statue and burned it for heat to save him from the frigid conditions. The monk muttered to himself, "What a wonderful Buddha statue."

Tobase concluded the talk by saying Buddhism is not a mere image worshipping religion but one of "becoming buddha" by acquiring the essence of its teachings with mind and body. Later, in the 1960s, I began reading a wider range of Zen texts, especially those of the Tang and Sung Dynasties. During this time, I came across a similar story in the chapter on Master Danxia Tianran (Tan-hsia T'ien-jan) in the *Wudenghuiyuan* (*Wu-têng Hui-yüan'*), or the *Compilation of the Five Works of Zen Transmissions*:

The Master Donxia encountered extremely cold weather at his temple, Huilin-si. He picked up a wooden Buddha statue and burned it down [to warm himself]. The head monk of the temple blamed him for that and said, "Why did you burn our wooden statue of the Buddha?" The Master brushed off an ember with his traveling cane and said, "I wanted to obtain the relics." The head monk said, "How could you find the relics from the wooden Buddha?" The Master said, "If there are no relics, then I will take an essence from this in burning it." The head monk was so shocked that his eyebrows and beard fell off.

I was always amazed at the breadth of Tobase's reading. Tobase's improvisation made it a more plausible story for children by saying almost the same thing as this *kōan,* but with a delightful, whimsical tone. Moreover, his animated presentation was charming.

***

I enjoyed every weekend and some special occasions at Sōkō-ji. Reverend Nazuka cooked Japanese food and invited those who came to services on Sundays. I learned a great deal about American life through conversations with those members who had been living in the United States since before the Second World War. However, my "schoolboy job" did not fare very well. I was fired at least six or seven times from the houses where I was hired. I was not familiar with operating many of those standard implements in American houses such as a vacuum cleaner, electric gadgets, a gas broiler and even an oven. I had never even seen the latter before and had no sense of cooking temperatures, either in Fahrenheit or in Celsius. My knowledge of heat in practical life at that time was limited to three simple terms: hot, warm or cold. Although, I did know that a temperature scale of Celsius registers the freezing point of water as zero degrees and the boiling point as a hundred degrees under normal atmospheric conditions.

On some occasions, I didn't understand what was being said or could not express what I wanted to say. I was definitely handicapped as a grown person whose communicative capacity had suddenly been reduced to ten or fifteen percent. It was a frustrating experience. There were many chores I had never experienced in Japan—such as waxing floors, polishing silverware, using a washing machine, and so on. Nonetheless, I was delighted and enjoyed learning how to use these household gadgets. On Saturdays, after I did heavier housework such as waxing floors, gardening, or washing windows, I went to Sōkō-ji, usually during the mid-afternoon. On Sundays and holidays I went to Sōkō-ji all day. Going to Sōkō-ji, then, was for me great consolation. I felt very relieved to see Tobase and Nazuka Sensei, who welcomed me. In those evenings, I watched Japanese films in the Sōkō-ji hall where Japanese-speaking people gathered, in part because it was the only Japanese theatre in San Francisco those days. Sōkō-ji, then, was to me almost my home. I noticed at that time that I was the envy of foreign students in similar situations, because I had Sōkō-ji to return to as if it were my home.

***

While I worked as a schoolboy, I went to college and took all of the classes offered in English for foreign students in two semesters. The classes were enjoyable and I liked meeting Italians, Iranians, Koreans and a few other foreigners. Each had different attitudes and habits in those classes. However, the desired level of fluency of my English had to wait for several more years, despite Reverend Tobase's optimism.

In the summer of 1953, during my first summer vacation from school, I asked Tobase Sensei for permission to work in the Sacramento Valley as a so-called farm hand. He said, as I expected, "That will be a good thing because lots of Japanese immigrants in the early days did that kind of work. You will learn how they survived in the new country. I will give you permission on the condition that you will come back every Sunday to help here." I agreed. My first summer work was picking fruit in orchards in the Sacramento Valley. Two of my college classmates joined me in this new venture. I was not expecting such harsh temperatures, which easily reached over 100 degrees Fahrenheit. The work was called "piece work," and we were paid according to the amount of fruit we picked.

It took a few days to learn how to pick the fruit and how to carry and place heavy wooden ladders in advantageous positions. We had to place the fruit firmly in flat wooden boxes and we were paid for each flat we filled. Each morning at a very early hour, we were transported on a truck from the front of our "hotel" to the orchard. We picked fruit all day long under the California sun. In the evening, I paid thirty-five cents to bathe at the back of a barbershop near the hotel. The hotel room was bare to speak kindly. It had only a rusty steel frame bed with a soiled blue striped mattress in the center and a simple wooden chair and desk painted in brown at the corner near the window. At the end of the hallway was a communal toilet. I had experienced communal toilets and baths before but I had never worked as a day laborer and been paid for piecework. Working in the hot sun reminded me of a passage from Dōgen's *Teachings for Tenzo* (a cooking monk) or the *Tenzo Kyōkun*:

> When I was in Tiantong, a *tenzo* at the monastery was named Yong. When I finished my lunch and was passing the east corridor to go to Caoranzhai [where his senior colleague, Myōzen was resting with an illness], I saw an old *tenzo* drying mushrooms in the courtyard in front of the Buddha Hall.

> He had a bamboo cane in his hand and no straw-hat on his head. The sun was strong and the ground was scorching. He was perspiring profusely but continuously dried the mushrooms. His back was bent over like a bow, his white eyebrows were furled, and it seemed as though he was having a difficult time.

> I went near the *tenzo* and asked his age. He replied, "Sixty-eight years old." I then asked, "Why don't you use helpers?" The *tenzo* said, "Others are not me." I said, "The old master is [so] diligent with dharma, but the day is hot and sultry. Why do you do this now?The old *tenzo* replied, "For what other time would I wait?"I refrained from asking [any more questions]. And when I was walking down the corridor I realized how important the *tenzo*'s role was.

I believe Dōgen interpreted the above quotation of *tenzo*'s role of drying mushrooms under the scorching sun-baked courtyard as the practice of Zen. When Dōgen asked the *tenzo* to use helpers, the *tenzo* said, "others are not me." Drying mushrooms is the *tenzo's* practice of Zen and no other person can practice Zen for him. When Dōgen asked the *tenzo* to do the work some other time, *tenzo* replied, "for what other time would I wait?" Again, the *tenzo* said that real time is only the present moment and there is no other time [to practice].

While I was picking fruit under the sweltering sun, I developed the habit of saying in Japanese, *tawakore wareniarazu,* meaning "others are not me," and *izurenotoki oka matan*, meaning, "for what other time would I wait?" I pondered these questions all summer long; what did the *tenzo*'s "others" mean? Did they signify "persons who are not present here and now"? Moreover, did "for what other time would I wait?" mean, "I am living in this moment and in no other time"? I inferred the following meanings: "I am what I am doing," and "reality is now and other conceptions of time are mere illusions." Whatever the old *tenzo* meant by these phrases, I repeated them. His valuable teaching helped me to survive arduous tasks all summer long. After only a week of picking fruit, one of my friends left the job. According to him, he could not endure working as a simple laborer. It was a "degrading experience" for a person with a college degree from Japan. His pride bothered him and he literally deserted his work. My other friend also left after a month or so, saying the job was too arduous and paid too little. He said that he had practically nothing left after paying the hotel, showers and meals. I also earned only a little; however, my income increased as my skill improved.

Every weekend, as promised, I returned to Sōkō-ji by Greyhound bus. My daily salary after paying living expenses and the weekly bus fare to the temple left me with only a few dollars. Still, I accumulated enough money over the weeks and I continued that job for over two months until Tobase said to me, "You look like a sturdy farmer. Your face is tan below the middle of your forehead, perhaps below your hat. Your hands are so rough, too." Then he added, "Don't you think you have had enough of that experience? Why don't you quit and come back?" Reverend Nazuka agreed with Tobase and nodded her head. I wholeheartedly agreed with them and a week or two later I stopped working in the valley. It was almost the end of that summer.

I returned to my "schoolboy" life. By that time, I had become an expert in the position and it gave the proprietor of the house a sense of ease. Naturally, our relationship became more congenial. There were no more special English courses for foreign students at the college and I was told to decide my major field of study. Since I already had a college degree and my main purpose of going to school was to attain a passing acquaintance with English, I decided to major in musicology. I thought it would be enjoyable and not require a high level of English competence. I learned English through reading music history as well as music theory.

The following summer, I worked six weeks as a helper for a Japanese landscape gardener, Mr. Kawabata, in San Lorenzo in the East Bay. Mr. Kawabata and his crew of two—comprised of a fellow named Al and me—went to Morgan Hill to pick up rocks, which we used to make rock gardens in the Bay Area. This year, it was a room and board arrangement in Mr. Kawabata's house. I went to Sōkō-ji every weekend as I did the past summer. He knew I was a Zen priest but he paid no attention to that. I was a twenty-three-year-old student. The locations where we worked were in East Bay residential areas—such as Berkeley, Oakland, Orinda and Lafayette. They were all hotter than San Francisco. The work was hard and my fingers became stiff for the first five or six days. Again, I repeated, "Others are not me" and "For what other time would I wait?" Al, a young man my age, over-heard me talking to myself and asked me the subject matter of my monologue. I explained it to him in my still limited English. I did not believe he understood it. It had been two years since I came to this country, yet my level of English fluency was not good enough to interpret Dōgen's experience in China to him. I sympathized with Tobase Sensei, whose expectations of my ability were disappointed.

Tobase Sensei's sentiment regarding my acquisition of English skills might have stemmed from his own communicative difficulties. Cultural differences still puzzled me from time to time. My first English instructor was Dr. Lois Wilson, who had just finished her doctorate from Stanford University. She was energetic and seemed fearless. One day, I was eating sweets in the college cafeteria. She came in and saw me eating. She sat next to me and asked what I was eating. I tried to explain and she asked if she might try the sweet. I hesitated because I had bitten the cake and had no other sweet to offer. She took my cake and helped herself to a bite. I was shocked at her manners but Dr. Wilson did not pay any attention and asked for another bite. I don't remember the occasion, but once she drove me in her old Studebaker over the Golden Gate Bridge. While driving, she asked me if the Japanese language has slang, jargon and swearwords. I said there are no swearwords in Japanese. She began laughing and teaching me swearwords one by one, of course with the pronunciations corrected.

Dr. Wilson was an enthusiastic professor who taught English energetically, yet at that time the teaching methodology for second language learning was not yet firmly established. English class names and content—such as conversation, grammar, and writing were not much different from the classes I took in Japan. American colleges and universities in the early 1950s were not prepared for a large influx of foreign students. International cities like San Francisco had, as far as I know, one or two adult schools that offered English courses for foreign students. The college I attended had four or five courses and learning levels were divided into beginning and intermediate levels.

Whenever I went to Sōkō-ji to help Reverend Tobase, he often asked, "How is your English? Can you speak English now?" In the beginning, he was only joking, but later he became serious for he had several non-Japanese speaking visitors at Sōkō-ji. Tobase and I had a difficult time communicating with them. One person who visited was an elderly man who smoked cigars profusely and talked incessantly in Tobase's small office. The cigar odor did not bother Tobase at all even though he was a nonsmoker. This man's frequent visits were usually on weekdays and I only met him on a few occasions. I remember him saying he was an emeritus professor from Columbia University. I did not understand why he was visiting Sōkō-ji so frequently when he could not even communicate with Tobase or anyone else there.

Another non-Japanese speaking person who came to the temple and seemed interested in Buddhism called himself "Reverend." He talked Tobase into letting him give a sermon on certain Sundays. He did give several sermons. I attended and heard his overly dramatic and long orations. The congregation was all Japanese *Issei,* or first generation Japanese immigrants, and almost no one understood him. Tobase asked me whether his sermon was any good, but my level of English was far from being able to give an adequate judgment. I was certain that Tobase had some apprehension about that man. Someone in the congregation told me that the so-called "Reverend" worked as an elevator operator at a high-class hotel in downtown San Francisco.

At about the same time, another much younger person came to Sōkō-ji. He too said he was a Buddhist priest. At one time, both

332

men alternately gave sermons on Sundays. I asked Tobase what sort of people they were, and he said they were ordained in some school of Buddhism but he was not certain which one. I asked him, "Does Mr. Komiyama know about them?" Tobase said, "Oh, yes. He has met them." I asked, "What does he think about those people giving sermons here?" Tobase said, "Mr. Komiyama was very courteous and treated them well." Then he continued, "Well, Katō-kun, don't worry about them. After all, no one understands their sermons anyway. Those men will get tired soon. I wish you could speak English well enough so that *nisei* would come to Sōkō-ji."

Tobase was right. The "Reverends" quit after several months. The younger Reverend stayed a little while longer but he, too, stopped coming to the temple. The emeritus professor also gave up, or found some other place to visit, and Tobase's office once again became cigar-odor free. Even so, he continued to ask about my English proficiency. Besides those visitors to Sōkō-ji, other curious people influenced by the "Zen Boom" began knocking at Sōkō-ji's door. The boom, led mainly by Alan Watts, Allen Ginsberg, Jack Kerouac, Kenneth Rexroth, and other writers and intellectuals, was in full swing. San Francisco's North Beach district became the West Coast center of the new "beat" generation. Perhaps, Tobase felt that he needed English even more now at Sōkō-ji. I began helping Tobase by interpreting his casual conversations with what English I had. My assistance was limited to the casual conversational level, and I never interpreted any of his public speeches for official occasions. It took two years, but Tobase finally realized that learning a second language was no easy task. He recommended that I pursue my schooling further, even after I received my second college degree. Naturally, I agreed since I found academic pursuits pleasant and befitting to my personality.

Sōkō-ji, unlike Tobase's initial introduction of it in Japan, was not a wealthy temple. Tobase's meager monthly salary was the maximum expenditure that the temple could afford. There was no way membership alone could support two full-time priests. The arrangement of my interim part-time priesthood without pay was appropriate, considering the circumstances. I was happy to have the opportunity to pursue my education.

***

I met Emi, my future wife, while I was studying English in college. Emi was studying voice in the Music Department. As explained briefly before, I thought music might be a good major for me since it is a performing art, unlike history or philosophy, which would require vast and accurate knowledge of the language. In the fall of 1953, in order to continue in the college, I declared music as my major. I did not know about the qualification test for all music majors; I had taken a few years of piano lessons in Japan, but was not advanced enough to major in piano. Nevertheless, I purchased two books on music theory. I still remember that the German composer and music theorist Paul Hindemith wrote one of the texts. It was very difficult, but I spent days and nights reading music theory during the late spring and the entire summer preparing for the test that fall semester. Luckily, I passed the test and became a student of musicology.

Emi and I began exchanging notes for some courses. I helped her in music theory, while she helped me by playing my compositions and arranged pieces on piano. The highlight of my music "career" was my "opus," a variation on a Japanese art song performed at a college event. There were a few other compositions performed at the concert that night. For the first and last time in my life, I conducted music in public. Emi and several friends of ours came to hear my composition. To my surprise, it was received quite well. The hall was packed and they seemed to applaud my piece of music quite sincerely. That event also marked the end of my musical pursuits. I knew my limit. I completed my second round of undergraduate coursework and music project in the spring of 1955. Then I had to leave the college because it offered no more courses that I could take, given my language proficiency. My English had improved some but I was not fluent.

***

Emi Fukuda was born in March, 1932. Emi had three brothers and two sisters. All the children in her family were born in the United States. Her oldest sister was Chikako, followed by her brother Hiroaki, sister Fumi, and brothers Tomiji and Masuó. The age span from the oldest to the youngest, Emi, was 12 years. At that time, Japan was experiencing the rise of military power. On September 18, 1931, Japan deployed military forces in Manchuria, which triggered the Manchurian Incident. The year Emi was born, a new country, Manchukuo, a puppet country of Japanese militarists, was founded in the northeast provinces of China. The last heir of the Qing dynasty, Boi (Po-yi) was placed as the head of the country. This was the beginning of a fifteen-year struggle with China. An American film, "The Last Emperor," depicted the life of Boi. International sentiment was on the side of China and antipathy toward Japanese in the United States grew stronger by the day. Later, when I was teaching at Chubu University, Boi's cousin was also teaching and he told me many stories regarding that turbulent and tragic era just being a member of the last Chinese imperial family.

Because of these mounting tensions related to the Manchurian Incident, Emi's father decided it was time to repatriate. The family returned to Japan in 1933 when Emi was only a year old. Soon after the company asked her father to relocate to Shanghai, China. Having a large family to support, he had no choice but to leave his family in Tokyo and move after a brief relocation. Two years later, when Emi was three, her mother, Teruko, contracted tuberculosis and was sent to a sanatorium in central Japan, near Lake Shirakaba. Even though Emi was only three, it was a traumatic event, and she vividly remembers her mother lying sick in bed. Her mother later came home after a long separation. Still her illness confined her to a room, which was off-limits to her children; they could only see her from a distance. Emi's grandparents came to live with the children and had the help of a live-in nurse. Her mother died in 1936 at the age of thirty-eight, before Emi reached the age of four. A few years later, a stepmother named Sada, a former all-girls high school teacher, came and helped raise the children. Sada had never had children of her own. Every time Emi faced difficult predicaments, she dreamt that her mother was beckoning to her. The same dream recurred until she became a mother herself.

Despite those upsetting circumstances, such as her father's work relocation and her mother's death, Emi's family was financially well-off. All of her brothers and sisters went to prestigious schools. Emi's first schooling was at a nursery school founded by the renowned Christian educator, Kagawa Toyohiko. Thereafter she went to a French Catholic school from elementary to high school, and she continued to a different order of a Catholic college in Tokyo.

I invited Emi to Sōkō-ji while we were studying music, where there was a piano used occasionally for Sunday school. I asked Tobase Sensei if it was alright for us to play the piano. His reply was, "Why of course, but don't break your fingers!" After hearing Emi play, Tobase once said, "I prefer Emi-san's piano to Wakō-kun's." Although I played rather roughly, Tobase, after granting permission for me to play piano, never complained about the cacophony I created in the room right next to his office. Both Tobase and Nazuka Sensei liked Emi and Emi's feelings were reciprocal. We used to have tea together in the kitchen, and Tobase, in his humorous Kumamoto dialect, and Nazuka, in her Niigata dialect, told us many stories of their lives. Nazuka Sensei was around fifty years of age and came from Niigata, an area facing the Japan Sea to the north and Siberia beyond that. She was mostly quiet and listened attentively, but occasionally she shared anecdotes about the Niigata area from her experience growing up there.

Speaking of dialects, I spoke with a Nagoya accent and used the expressions unique to Nagoya. Today, dialectical differences are disappearing due to the uniform mass media. Nonetheless, Emi was amazed at those differences in the Japanese language and I treasured those precious times we had together.

Emi and I were brought up in wholly different environments: she was raised in a westernized environment while I had a Zen upbringing. The differences included many factors, among them, Emi's upbringing surrounded by piano lessons, western cuisine, Christian schools, and the ambience of her house; whereas Tobase, Nazuka, and I grew up in Zen Buddhist temples. Emi was interested in all of us and each of our different backgrounds, which were poles apart. On several occasions, she said we were refreshingly different from the world she lived in. I also enjoyed the differences between Emi and I. Had our two years of friendship narrowed the gap? I am certain they did. We decided to marry. We consulted her elder brother Hiroaki and Reverend Tobase and Nazuka. I also wrote to my mother and Nin'yū Yamasaki asking their approval. All of them gave me their wholehearted support. Tobase added that the temple members would like to host a wedding reception at Sōkō-ji. In the early summer of 1955, Reverend Tobase married us in the hall next to his office at Sōkō-ji.

Chapter 15

DISSEMINATING ZEN

をほよそ西天東地に
仏法つたはるるといふは、

かならず坐仏のつたはるるなり。
それ要機なるによりてなり。

仏法つたはれざるには
坐禅つたはれず、
嫡嫡相承せるは
この坐禅の宗旨のみなり。

－ 道元

(『正法眼蔵』 「坐禅箴」)

Perhaps disseminating Buddhism
in Western heaven and Eastern
land means

the dissemination of sitting
Buddhism.
It is the utmost important clue.

If there is no buddha-dharma
then sitting practice is not transmitted.
Transmitting one by one is
this school of Zen (sitting practice).

- Dōgen

(*Shōbōgenzō, (Zazen-shin)* "Zazen
Needles")

My command of English was still far from my satisfaction level.
Occasionally someone praised my ability to communicate in
English but those comments must have been mere flattery. Dōgen
stated in his chapter "Manifestation of Reality," or "*Genjō Kōan*"

(from the *Shōbōgenzō*) thus, "If the body and mind of a person have not absorbed the dharma in full, he might think that he has already attained the state of dharma. Conversely, when dharma permeates the body and mind of a person, he might think he is still lacking somewhere." It sounds pretentious and presumptuous to compare the experience of *satori* with my English acquisition; however, I earnestly felt that my fluency level had not yet reached my goal. I thought that putting myself in a venue where I had to use English would help me improve.

After completing my musicology degree, I continued on to graduate school. This time I decided to study philosophy as I thought it might help to deepen my understanding of Buddhism. One day in late autumn, I met Alan Watts. It was 1955. A friend of mine took me to the place where Alan was Dean, above the Marina district of San Francisco, called the American Academy of Asian Studies. In addition to his prolific writings, Alan was busy with a lecture circuit and had regular radio programs. We talked about various Zen Buddhist topics and issues related to East and South Asia. After our initial meeting, I visited Alan often. The Academy was a beautiful Victorian mansion on Broadway, and his second floor office overlooked the bay, which was very pleasant.

After several casual meetings, Alan Watts offered me two jobs. One was to review Chinese Zen classics with him a few afternoons a week and the other was to teach Zen Buddhism at the Academy in the evenings. I was delighted with these opportunities. For me, the job was an unexpected and welcome chance to study Chinese Zen classics and polish up my Classic Chinese and Sanskrit. During Alan's tenure at the Academy, he invited many well-known scholars, artists, and practitioners of various Asian religions. D.T. Suzuki was among the speakers, and the opportunity to meet all of them exhilarated me. When Alan invited those guest speakers to dinners, he also invited me as a member of his hosting party. Alan also hosted many parties at his Mill Valley house, and on a few occasions, he invited people to outings at various meadows and fields in the Marin and Sonoma counties. Through these gatherings, I learned about many rare foods—European cheeses, cold cuts and so forth; many of them I had never even heard of before. At the beginning, I was a bit uncomfortable with those highly knowledgeable people but soon that feeling faded.

The Academy had a dining area below the ground level where I often had dinner with Alan. On one occasion, I talked about ancient Chinese table manners, and the expected way to treat invited dinner guests. In so doing, I quoted passages from the *Book of Rights*, or the *Liji* (Li-chi), which was one of the main Confucian texts compiled in the third century C. E.. Alan looked at me and said, "Gosh, I feel like a barbarian." I said to Alan, "I felt like an idiot coming to your party, not knowing the foods and how to eat them." He replied, "Katō-san, you are a rabbit with horns." I suppose the expression meant "impossible." Earlier that day, we went over a Zen text in which the expression "a rabbit with horns and turtle with hairs" appeared. I had translated the phrase as meaning impossible, fantastical or absolutely uncommon. It was one of Alan's adventurous moments. Alan often wanted to use expressions from Zen texts, but I didn't always know what he meant by them.

***

Alan Watts was born and raised in Kent, England. His mother taught children of repatriated overseas missionaries at her house. He told me that he grew up in a house decorated with Chinese and Japanese artifacts. This environment generated his interest in Zen Buddhism, Chinese philosophies and Indian religions. Alan began visiting Cambridge bookstores searching for information about Asian philosophies and religions. He also visited the Buddhist Lodge in London. There, Christmas Humphreys introduced him to D. T. Suzuki and Alan began to correspond with him. Alan talked about those days saying, "I had an absolute fascination with Chinese and Japanese secular paintings. Even as a child I had to find out about those strange elements, such as bamboo and long grass. There was something else I still recall about Buddhism: it is a religion without God, the religion of no-religion." His curiosity led him to explore more, and then his career took off with his 1936 publication of *The Spirit of Zen*. He was only twenty-one years of age at that time. He moved to the United States in 1938 and began writing extensively on Eastern philosophies and religions, including Taoism and many facets of Chinese and Japanese cultures. However, as far as I knew, he had never claimed himself as a Zen master or scholar; instead, he called himself an "intellectual entertainer." In that role, he did an excellent job. The Zen in "Zen boom" was impacted by Rinzai (Linji, or Lin-chi) Zen, which was explicated by D. T. Suzuki and Alan Watts. Sōtō Zen had not been properly introduced in the United States, yet most people in the "Zen Boom" did not distinguish between the two schools of Zen. This movement, however, gave me the chance to study Rinzai Zen and vast Zen archives.

Alan Watts and I sat together in his office at the Academy once or twice a week for nearly four hours, spending entire afternoons going over those texts line-by-line. For those meetings, I prepared for hours. Later, I published a book, *Lin-chi and the Record of his Sayings*, in Japan. It was the long-delayed culmination of my study meetings with Alan.

During this period, I met two famous artists from Japan, who were Alan's guests at the Academy. One visited for a short period, and the other was a resident artist of the Academy. The former was an accomplished calligrapher, Nankoku Hidai, who headed an avant-garde school of calligraphy in Yokohama. The resident artist, Sabro Hasegawa (he spelled his name this way), was also an avant-garde painter who used a variety of mediums, including traditional calligraphy ink and brushes. Both artists, after the Second World War, stood out in their fresh approach to new art forms and were the foremost in their fields. Sabro Hasegawa died just before Tobase left Sōkō-ji for Japan, and his funeral was officiated by Tobase and me. Alan Watts tirelessly helped Hasegawa's family during Hasegawa's illness and after his death.

The "Zen Boom" in San Francisco was at its height during this time and Alan Watts was the center of that movement. Through Alan, I met many active leaders of the movement, including Gary Snyder, Phil Whalen, Gia-Fu Feng, and Claude Dalenberg. Claude later adopted Buddhist precepts and changed his name to Ananda. Close to our residence on Portrero Hill in San Francisco, we met Laurence Ferlinghetti. I frequented Larry's City Lights Bookstore on the North Beach and met his associate, Shig, a Nisei man in his early thirties, every time I went there. I also met Mike McClure through our daughter, Kazumi, who was born in 1956. Mike had a daughter close in age to ours and we babysat for each other.

I enjoyed the "Zen Boom" quite heartily due to Alan Watts and his efforts to reinterpret D. T. Suzuki, Chinese Ch'an, and Japanese Zen. My work at the Academy of Asian Studies transpired between the spring of 1956 and continued until the summer of 1960. Alan resigned his position at the Academy at the end of 1959; he wanted to focus on writing radio lectures. I continued one semester after Alan resigned, but the Academy was just not the same without him.

***

The "Zen Boom" was a loud and trendy movement among those who identified themselves as members of the Beat Generation, or *beatniks*. "Beat Zen" followers flocked to the North Beach area for gatherings and I was unknowingly near its epicenter through my connection with Alan Watts. It seemed a little schizophrenic perhaps, as I was also close to Tobase at Sōkō-ji, the only traditional Zen temple in San Francisco at that time. It was probably perceived as "Square Zen" to some. Nonetheless, I enjoyed being an assistant priest there. Every weekend, Tobase and I sat alone in the spacious and serene hall on early weekend mornings while Nazuka was quietly preparing our "rice-gruel" breakfasts. We chanted and cleaned both inside and outside with no interruption, as if nothing else was ever going to happen. It was no different from my early days at Hōsen-ji. Sitting in pre-dawn darkness at Sōkō-ji was quiescent in comparison to the busy Zen Boom outside. I was living a secular life outside the temple. Performing my familiar daily Zen routine comforted me. Tobase's English was very limited but he had an aura of incorruptibility, and was revered even though he was surrounded by people who did not speak Japanese. My weekend assistance at Sōkō-ji continued until Reverend Tobase decided to return to Japan in November of 1958.

***

I learned years later that Tobase was born in 1896 and his tenure at Sōkō-ji lasted from 1951 to 1958; his age during that time interval was from fifty-five to sixty-three. Interestingly, Shunryū Suzuki Rōshi, a successor of Tobase at Sōkōji, also came to Sōkōji when he was fifty-five. His tenure ended with his death in 1971 at the age of sixty-seven. When reflecting on this fact, I admire their courage in coming to a new country with an entirely different language and unfamiliar customs in their mid-fifties. At that time in Japan, fifty-five was the normal retirement age for public employees as well as for workers in the private sector.

Reverend Tobase returned to Japan because he needed to assume the abbot's position at Kyushu Island's prestigious Daiji-ji Zen temple. I was alone for a while at Sōkō-ji after he left, since Reverend Shunryū Suzuki did not come to San Francisco until May of 1959. I met Reverend Tobase one more time in July, 1963, when I visited the Head Temple, Eihei-ji, where he was participating in a special service for the memorial of Dōgen's teacher Tiāntóng Rújìng (T'ien-t'ung Ju-ching), *Tendō Nyojō-ki*. We exchanged brief news with each other about how we were doing, and how the Sōkō-ji members were doing. That was the last time I ever saw him. He died several years later at his own temple in Kumamoto.

Reverend Shunryū Suzuki came to Sōkō-ji at the request of temple members. There was quite a contrast between Tobase and Suzuki. Tobase was audacious, dynamic, and solid, while Suzuki was a slightly built man with a childlike, gentle smile. He was warm, gentle, slow-paced, and totally unguarded. He remained considerate, tranquil and soft. Every time I thought about those two wonderful Zen priests, I recalled an anecdote from Volume 6 of Jinde Chuandeng-lu (Chiing-tê ch'uan-têng-lu):

When Chan (Zen) Master Zhicang was living at Xitang, in the West Hall [where a retired former abbot of other monasteries stays], a layperson approached him and asked, "Is there a heaven and is there a hell?"
The Master answered, "Yes, there is."
"Then, are there three treasures: Buddha, dharma and saṃgha?" asked the layperson.
The Master replied, "Yes, there are."

The layperson asked many questions, and the Master's answers were all "yes."

The layperson said, "Master, why are you answering all questions in that way. Did I do anything wrong?"

The Master asked, "Have you met any venerable masters before you came here?"

The layperson said, "Yes, I have met Master Jingshan before."

"What did Jingshan tell you?" asked Master.

The layperson said, "He answered 'No,' to every question I asked."

The Master replied, "Do you have a wife?"

The layperson said, "Yes, I have."

"Does Master Jingshan have a wife?" asked Master.

"No, he hasn't." said the layperson.

The Master said, "That is why Master Jingshan said, 'No,' to every question. That's it."

The layperson bowed to the Master and left.

I imagine this conversation puzzled the layperson. The essential state of things, which is *dharmatā* or dharma-nature, exists as a general principle of all things. All of existence appears as it is, but in each instant it changes. Therefore, in its essential state, existence is *śunyatā*, meaning nothingness or emptiness. In the anecdote—the yes or no replies of each master signify *dharma* and *dharmatā*. Whether considering the binaries of heaven and hell, or having a wife or not, both exist as *dharma*. But that which makes that *dharma* dharma is *dharmatā*, which in turn makes each *dharma* empty, or *śūnyatā*.

The philosophy of Immanuel Kant tries to think beyond the reality of such phenomena to noumenon, meaning an object independent of our mind. Other philosophers try to imagine the reality of heaven and hell and make it into an object of analysis, isolating "universals" and eliminating incidentals and particulars. Then, they can come up with an answer of sorts. Let me quote an interesting anecdote from Dōgen's *Shōbōgenzō*, in the chapter entitled "Manifestation of Reality," or "*Genjō Kōan*":

> Chan Master Baoche (Hōtetsu) of Mt. Mayu (Mayoku-san) was fanning himself. A monk came and asked the master, "The nature of wind is in ever continual motion and there is no place that wind cannot circulate. Why are you still fanning yourself, Master?"

> The master said, "Even though you know the nature of the wind, which is always in continual motion everywhere, you do not know the principle of the place where wind universally reaches."

> The monk asked, "What is the principle of the place where wind reaches universally?"

> The master did not reply but merely went on swinging the fan.

> The monk bowed to the master.

Dōgen stated wind as *dharma* and wind-nature as *dharmatā*. Dōgen postulates that everything exists, yet it exists in a temporary state, changing constantly with time. There would be no unchanging, permanent entity to grasp in *śūnyatā*; however, there is a principle that makes each *dharma* dharma. That ever-changing nature is the *dharma*-nature, or Buddha-nature (*buddhatā*). When one sees a certain thing, one is merely looking at its form, or *rūpa,* instead of its true Buddha-nature. Rinzai Zen uses the expression, "Seeing one's own nature is to become Buddha." Seeing one's own nature is not limited to a person but also the buddha-nature of all things, which has the potential to grasp ever-ceasing causal patterns. If one sees emptiness, utter contingency, or *śūnyatā*, one is seeing the whole universe and thus becomes Buddha.

Returning to the original point, Master Zhican, who said "yes" to all presently existing things, was confirming all *dharma* and Master Jingshan was referring to *śūnyatā*, "permanent" entities of that *dharma*. For some reason, possibly from their personality—Tobase and Suzuki reminded me of Masters Zhican and Jingshan, but not necessarily in that order. Both were very different yet similar. When Sōkō-ji played Japanese films on weekends for the community, I sat watching movies with Tobase. After his return to Japan, I once again sat watching the films with Suzuki from the balcony seats in the temple. During scenes involving someone's death or hardships, both Zen priests wiped away their tears. Fictional scenes affected both of those well-trained priests quite easily. Tobase, especially, had a quality of vulnerability that ran counter to his seemingly unshakeable constitution. When I reflect on both of them together, I always recall the two Chinese Chan Masters of the eighth century.

> I paid a leisurely visit
> to an eminent monk.
> Mist settled on
> range after range of mountains.
> The master compassionately
> pointed out the road home;
> The moon hung in the sky,
> a single globe of light.
>
> – Han-shan

I began teaching in the Philosophy Department at San Jose State College in the fall of 1959. In addition to teaching general Western philosophy courses, I had a chance to teach courses on Indian and Chinese philosophies in the fall and spring semesters. Quite remarkably, I was totally unknown to students, yet those courses filled to capacity. I liked teaching and felt it was a natural choice for me. Despite my enjoyment of it, teaching required long, arduous hours of preparation. I had to cut down my assistance at Sōkō-ji to shorter weekend hours so that I could satisfactorily devote my time to teaching. During my first college teaching assignment, I had no idea that my lifelong career had shifted from monastic to college teaching. I had a relatively secure tenure position as a member of the university faculty. Even so, my mind was precariously unsettled. I was born and grew up in a Zen temple, went through formal Zen monastic training at two monasteries, and came to the United States to serve as a priest. However, I could not support my family as a priest without additional income.

My teaching sailed through quite nicely. In my Indian philosophy class, I had approximately a dozen students from India. One of them invited me to his house and told me that Indian students wanted to know their philosophies from an academic perspective. I told him that I wanted to know their philosophies from a religious angle—such as how often they pray, how they pray at temples and with their families, and how they respect their deities. We found each other congenial and it was a good mutual learning experience.

In the late spring of 1960, I wrote to Gyokusen informing him of my college position. Gyokusen wrote to me that "It will be a good occupation," and that the occupations of professorship and priesthood can coexist harmoniously. Oshō denotes a teacher who both instructs practitioners and administers occasional confined practice sessions. He reminded me that a college professor is also a teacher who guides young adults to being good human beings, and

348

helps them prepare for their long journey through life. He included two Japanese medieval folkloric tales to reinforce his encouragement. Both stories were about oni: a nonhuman demon, fiend, or ogre from medieval times. It was unrealistic, but written in classic Japanese, it sounded medieval, mythical, and undistorted.

The first story, according to Gyokusen, was from the Collected Literature attributed to Ki-no Haseo (845-912 C.E.), or *Ki-no Haseo Monjū*. I have not read the book but he told me the synopsis as follows:

Ki-no Haseo, a noted intellectual and aristocrat, strolled along the streets of Kyoto. A man with an extraordinarily beautiful woman approached him and challenged him to gamble with dice. The man said if he lost he would present Haseo with the beautiful woman. He asked Haseo to bet on his wealth. Haseo found the idea amusing and accepted. After just one round, Haseo won the game. The man then asked Haseo to promise that he would not touch the woman for one-hundred days. Haseo agreed to keep his promise not to touch her for that period. He lived in his mansion with the woman. After enduring ninety-five days, he thought he had waited long enough, so he embraced her.

At that moment, the woman melted down to a puddle of water. This miracle utterly dumbfounded Haseo. The man who challenged the game happened to be an *oni* (demon), who appeared before Haseo and said that he was very disappointed with him. The *oni* said that he created the woman but she needed an apt model to follow for one-hundred days in order to become a complete woman. Thus, he chose Haseo, a known scholar and moralist, but Haseo had failed to be a good model. After speaking his mind, the *oni* left.

The second story Gyokusen mentioned in his letter was from the
Selected Collections, or Senjū-shō, attributed to a legendary Buddhist
poet, Saigyō. Saigyō (1118-1190 C. E.) was originally an elite samurai but at twenty-three years of age sought peace within himself and
left his samurai duty and household to become a Buddhist monk. I
don't know whether it was true or not but a story tells that he brushed
a boy off him when the boy was clinging to his kimono. He left
many outstanding poems backed with his Buddhist world-view.
Gyokusen's synopsis from the collection was as follows:

When Saigyō was engaged in Buddhist practice on Mt. Kōya,
he met a practitioner who had similar interests and they became close friends. However, this friend soon left Mt. Kōya
for Kyoto. Saigyō missed his friend. Then he recalled that
an *oni* collected abandoned human bones in desolate places
and assembled human beings from them. Saigyō decided to
construct a human being modeled after his dear friend. He
went to a desolate field and collected bones, which he then
assembled, using vines as he recited the secret charm. He
succeeded in creating a human figure, but his newly created
human figure had a dull complexion and no spirit. He wanted
to destroy it but could not do so because it was a human being. Finally, he abandoned it at a remote place on Mt. Kōya.

Later, Saigyō visited the man who knew the formula to make
humans but he was not there. He then consulted another man,
who told him every step to create a human. The man told Saigyō
that there was no fault in Saigyō's method. However, in order
to create a human being, the creator must undergo vigorous
training. Furthermore, one must assemble a figure with wholehearted devotion and dedication, not simply out of loneliness.

A teacher's task is exemplified by this story—not an easy job but one requiring whole-hearted devotion. The task is, according to him, to create actual human beings, just as Oshō did.

Gyokusen further noted that a worthy teacher has to devote him or herself wholeheartedly to professional activities. He then explained that Zen is a way of life, not a career choice. Zen not only co-exists with the teaching profession, but both endeavors mutually enrich and enliven the other. Therefore, Zen would enhance my teaching and vice versa. He added that I must remember my position as a dharma-heir of Dōgen at all times.

I enjoyed his thoughtful encouragement. I knew medieval Japan was full of *onis*, some angelic and some diabolic, and that they were well-suited to the dark societal underbelly of the Middle Ages, carrying important messages such as those tales related by Gyokusen.

***

In the fall of 1962 I had just started to teach at the University of California, Berkeley. Reirin Yamada Rōshi, the head Sōtō priest in the United States, came to San Francisco and visited my house. I was very surprised and humbled by his visit. He first explained his strong endorsement of my teaching career. Then, he asked whether I could find a teaching position in Los Angeles. Finally, he asked me to come to Los Angeles to assist him at the new Zen Institute he had opened in November of 1961 at Zenshu-ji. I would be a lecturer at the Institute. I was honored that he himself visited my house and invited me to come. On the other hand, I faced a serious problem finding a job in Los Angeles. I was not certain whether I could find a teaching position near the new institute.

Yamada Rōshi was a well-known Zen practitioner, as well as

an accomplished Zen scholar. He spent a good many years as a professor at Komazawa University, a Sōtō Zen supported university in Tokyo. I had read a few books and articles written by him, so I did not hesitate to move to Los Angeles, for it was a rare chance to study with this celebrated Zen scholar. In addition, I was very lucky to have found a teaching position at California State University, Los Angeles, which was then Los Angeles State College, about six or seven miles from the Institute. The opportunity to work with such an accomplished Zen Buddhist in the United States was a unique and lucky prospect for me and I was naturally excited. He was the head priest of the North American Sōtō Zen Temple and Zen centers from February of 1960, to October of 1964.

My assistance to him began in the fall of 1963 at his institute, where three monks and a nun were studying. One of the monks was Dainin Katagiri, who later assisted Shunryū Suzuki at Sōkō-ji and then at the San Francisco Zen Center. Katagiri then moved to Minnesota, where he opened the Minnesota Zen Center.

At the Zen Institute in Los Angeles, Yamada Rōshi gave a Thursday lecture series for the public on the *Shōbōgenzō*, which is the magnum opus of Dōgen. I assisted as an interpreter and translator. The time I spent with Yamada Rōshi was precious, but sadly lasted only fourteen months. After this period, Yamada Rōshi became the president of Komazawa University, and consequently ascended to become Head Priest of Eihei-ji, the Head Temple of Sōtō Zen in Japan, where he remained until his death in July of 1979.

After Yamada Rōshi's return to Japan, I remained in Los Angeles. My mind was no longer divided whether to devote myself as a Zen priest only or to devote myself to teaching and still remain Zen priest. I had decided that I would concentrate on my teaching, and that I would participate when they needed me at Zenshu-ji, located in Little Tokyo in Los Angeles. Zenshu-ji is the oldest Sōtō Zen temple in the United States, founded by Reverend Hōsen Isobe in July, 1922. The present location, 123 South Hewitt Street, was purchased in the early spring of 1923. Reverend Isobe made the initial payment of $500.00 from his own savings before he asked other people for temple donations. Reverend Isobe stayed at Zenshu-ji for ten years, moved to San Francisco and founded Sōkō-ji in 1933. He bought a synagogue and converted it to a Sōtō Zen temple in less than a year after he moved to San Francisco.

My teaching became my major undertaking, but I did so remembering the advice of Gyokusen and Zen Master Reirin Yamada. I knew that I must never forget my role as a dharma heir of Dōgen.

> I present these words
> to wise men.
> Once again, what are you thinking?
> The way is reached
> and you see your self-nature.
> Your self-nature
> is the *Tathāgata*.
> This naturalness,
> originally endowed,
> is perfect.
> Practicing for enlightenment
> will turn you towards error.
> By chasing the trivial,
> you lose the original,
> and instead
> guard foolishness.

> – Han-shan

Chapter 16

RAISING THE DHARMA-BANNER AT HŌSEN-JI

人のさとりをうる
水に月の宿るが如し。
月ぬれず水やぶれず
ひろくおほきなる

A person attaining *satori*
is like water reflecting the moon.
The moon neither gets wet
nor does the water fret on its surface.

ひかりにあれど、
尺寸の水にやどり、

Although moonlight is vast and large
it can dwell in an inch of water.

全月も弥天も
くさの露にもやどり、
一滴の水にもやどる。

Furthermore, the entire moon and sky
could abide in a drop of water on a
blade of grass.

− 道元

- Dōgen

(『正法眼蔵』「現成公案」)

(*Shōbōgenzō*, (*Genjō Kōan*) "Manifestation of Reality")

Over the years, Nin'yū and I continued our steady correspondence.
I sent him many letters and he wrote me just as many. In 1957, I
informed him that I had received my master's degree in philosophy.
Soon after, he suggested that I return to Japan and complete the

shinsan, which is literally translated as a ceremony of ascending the mountain (temple). By going through that ceremony, I would reach the rank of *dai-oshō* (great teacher), and become a formal abbot of Hōsen-ji. In order to reach that rank one must already be an *oshō* rank and then set up the dharma-banner by leading a *kessei ango* (a ninety-day confined practice); in other words, the *shinsan* ceremony symbolically stages one's leadership for that ninety-day practice as an abbot. Nine years earlier, before I became the abbot of Hōsen-ji, I reached the rank of *oshō* by visiting the two Head Temples after my inheritance of dharma-lineage. A *shinsan* ceremony would be my official confirmation of abbotship at *Ryū'un-zan* (Mt. Dragon-cloud). According to Nin'yū, Hōsen-ji's members, my mother, and my siblings were all eagerly waiting for that to be realized.

***

A Romanian theologian, Mircea Eliade, said that sacred buildings and mountains are projections of the whole universe. Buddhist cosmology considers Mt. Sumeru the center of the universe, surrounded by nine mountains and eight seas. On Mt. Sumeru, a scented tree reaches up towards the sky. The sun and moon also circle around this mountain. The scene was just as Mircea Eliade described; the "sacred mountain" represents temples, sacred cities, and even kings' palaces.

Concerning the word "dragon-cloud," on Hōsen-ji's mountain, *Ryū'un-zan,* there are many Zen temples that bear the word *ryū,* or dragon. The Buddha is sometimes referred to as a great dragon with neither blemish nor stain, which had brought clear and pure water to the world. In addition, *nāga,* the Sanskrit equivalent of *ryū,* means a snake or serpent, and is one of the eight guardians (*hachibushū*) who helped spread the Buddha's teachings. Dōgen used the word in the chapter entitled the "Dragon's Roar" or "*Ryūgin*" in the *Shōbōgenzō*:

A monk asked Master Ciji (Tsu-chi) of Mt. Touzi (T'ou-tzu) in Shuzhou, "Is there a dragon's roar around a withered tree?" The master said, "I would say there are roars around the skeleton."

[Dōgen commented on the story thus]:

The story of the withered tree and ashes of the dead are fundamentally non-Buddhist teachings. The withered tree of non-Buddhists and the withered tree of the Buddha-ancestors are far different. Non-Buddhists talk about withered trees but they do not know the withered tree. For them the withered tree is a dead tree, understanding that spring will never reach it. How could they hear the dragon's roar? The withered trees of the Buddha-patriarchs are the teaching of nature. The teaching of nature equals the withered tree. The withered tree will meet spring. The essential component is that trees can be described as withered. Mountain, sea, sky, and those trees are all withered trees. The trees that bloom are the dragon's roar around the withered trees.

Dōgen stated that to view the difference between withered or blooming trees is to conceive of them as a natural process of growth and decay, or the law of impermanence. The dragon's roar in the above is the wind whistling across the withered trees. The example indicates the extraordinary teaching and the true activities of life. Dōgen used this chapter to teach that the withered trees have dragon's roar and the one who hears it rightly understands the far reaches of the Buddha-dharma, or the state which is non-thinkable.

The Chinese "dragon" is a metamorphosed Indian *nāga*. According to the East Asian view, it is the king of living beings. The names of the eminent Buddhist philosophers, Nāgārjuna and Nāgasena, both contain the word. Famous temples in Japan, such as Ryōan-ji, feature the word dragon, in this case pronounced, *ryō*. Laypersons also use the word as Ryōma, Ryūzō, and so on, for the word dragon signifies superiority. Hōsen-ji's *Ryū'un-zan*, or Mt. Dragon-cloud, sounds mysterious if not profound. Hōsen-ji was initially built by Zen Master Gentō Sokuchū, the fiftieth abbot of Eihei-ji, and was named *Ryū'un-zan,* or Mt. Dragon-cloud, after that profound Buddhist word. I began to scrutinize the ceremony of ascending dragon-cloud mountain temple. I knew that going back to Hōsen-ji for the ceremony would be a big strain financially, beyond the temple's normal limits.

***

I wrote Nin'yū that I did not think it was a good idea to return to Hōsen-ji just for the *shinsan* ceremony and to attain a new rank. He said that he sincerely wanted me to reach that rank, for it should not be a burden but instead a merit. In his letters, he also said that Reverend Dōkō Ōtsuka, who gave me the leather ocean-liner trunk, had become the head-managing monk, *Kan'in* at Eihei-ji. Reverend Ōtsuka conveyed to Nin'yū that if I had the *shinsan* at Hōsen-ji, he would definitely come; furthermore, one of his sons would take the position of *shuso,* or the head-seat monk, at my *shinsan kessei* practice. I was indebted to Reverend Ōtsuka for his sincere encouragement for me to come to the United States. I received a letter from the Head Temple, Eihei-ji, not long after that.

It was from Reverend Ōtsuka, and contained the same sentiment as what Nin'yū had written me about his son's participation. In addition, Ōtsuka mentioned he was looking forward to seeing me on that occasion. When I received Reverend Ōtsuka's letter, the year 1957 was drawing to a close.

I consented to uphold the ceremony, despite my straitened circumstances. Nin'yū proposed to hold the *shinsan* ceremony the following summer. He told me that he would arrange everything for me before I returned. In earlier days, Sōtō monks were required to have the full *kessei ango,* or ninety-day practice, followed immediately after the *shinsan.* In later years, extenuating circumstances at many local temples permitted only an abbreviated ceremony without the accompanying ninety-day confined practice. I could not spend ninety days in Japan, as I had just started a Ph. D. program, and had to support my wife and our firstborn child. Hōsen-ji, in the wake of the war's destruction, was not equipped to provide live-in accommodations for many participating monks. However, the idea that I would be back for the ceremony apparently elated everyone at Hōsen-ji.

***

According to Sōtō Zen master Menzan's *Rules of the Monastery,* or *Sōdō Shingi* (1752), *shinsan* means officially taking over a temple's resident priest position. I had become the resident priest of Hōsen-ji when I completed its required courses, but I had not completed this ceremony designated by Menzan. To uphold this tradition, I felt compelled to return for this ceremony.

Kessei ango may have begun as a tradition in the Ch'an (Zen) school in China, influenced by Indian monasticism. The Ch'an practice had been widely exercised in the provinces of Jiangxi (or *Kōsei* in Japanese), and Hunan (or *Kōnan* in Japanese), during China's Tang Dynasty. Hence, this practice was also called *Jianghu-hui* (or *Gōko-é* in Japanese), taken from the first letters of the provinces. According to the Zen tradition, a temple's abbot must lead the *kessei ango* at least once in his lifetime. On this occasion, the resident priest is the principal person to raise the dharma banner, or *hōdō,* which indicates the temple event. This tradition supposedly began in Indian monks' abiding places rather spontaneously and the length of each practice was arbitrary. The Ch'an schools most likely transmitted the practice over a thousand years ago. *Shinsan ango* was also called, "establishing the dharma-banner [at the temple]," or *ken-hōdō.*

My mother also wrote me, explaining that she wanted to see me become an official priest of Hōsen-ji because all the preceding resident priests except Reverend Yagi, from whom I inherited the dharma-lineage, held their *shinsan* at Hōsen-ji. She explained that Nin'yū was very excited about this prospect and was already preparing the monastic roles for the ceremony, with the help of other community members. She also mentioned that Reverend Ōtsuka had visited Hōsen-ji and he, too, had expressed happiness that I would hold *shinsan* at which time his son would also become *shuso,* or the head-seat monk. Despite his busy schedule at Eihei-ji, Reverend Ōtsuka, told her he would come to participate in the ceremony.

Several days later, Nin'yū sent me a letter saying Reverend Mokudō Katō, who invited me to his room at Eihei-ji when I paid a reverence-visit there, had agreed to take on the role of official master. He would thus announce the event. Reverend Katō still resided at Eihei-ji, where he held an important position. I learned that Shinkō Nakamura became the new abbot of Iō-ji, the temple where I met Reverend Tobase of Sōkō-ji for the first time. Reverend

Shinkō Nakamura was a dharma-relative of Reverend Baidō Satō, the former abbot of Iō-ji. Since Iō-ji was a neighboring temple, Shinkō would doubtlessly come to participate in the ceremony. Shinkō Nakamura was several years older than I was when we attended the same middle school, but since he was the son of a Sōtō Zen priest, like me, I knew him well. The temple in which he grew up was on the Chita Peninsula facing the Pacific Ocean.

While I was a middle school student, I visited Shinko Nakamura's temple during many summer days and we collaborated in a few youthful mishaps. But now he had become an accomplished priest through nearly ten years of practice at Eihei-ji. Since I was so fond of him, I looked forward to seeing him at Hōsen-ji.

***

Thinking of Shinkō Nakamura reminds me of one summer in eighth grade, when I visited a classmate named Itakura. His home was a temple on the Chita Peninsula, near Shinkō's. The area had a good fishing port for local fish. During wintertime, the village harvested seaweed, or *nori,* and dried it in the chilling wind. Itakura's temple was built in a small wooded area in the midst of a vast vegetable field, which extended southward to the sea. The area was my favorite place to visit in the summer.

Itakura was not home, unfortunately. In those days, there was no way I could check beforehand since neither of us had telephones; furthermore, my decision to visit him was impromptu. I decided to swim in the ocean since I had come that far by train. While I was swimming, I heard someone call my name and looked around to find the source of the voice. It was Shinkō waving his arms at me. I swam to the shore. He said, "I just came from Itakura's temple and heard that you visited there." I said, "Yes, I did. But he wasn't there so I decided to take a dip in the sea." Shinkō said, "I thought so." He had broad shoulders, and was a tall, husky young man. At school, we had been in the same martial arts club. The Japanese military government forced all young boys and girls to take some form of martial arts while attending middle school. While talking to him, my ocean-drenched body dried off in the sun, so I put on my clothes to visit Itakura once more, hoping he had returned home.

On the way to Itakura's, we passed a watermelon field. Hundreds of watermelons lay on the ground, and the plant leaves were turning yellow and brown. Shinkō said, "Do you know how to detect a ripe watermelon?" I replied, "No, sir." He said, "In the field, you first find a plump melon that's a bit yellowish between the stripes, like this and like that." He pointed out a few watermelons, and continued, "The dark green ones are still too young. See? They are a bit small." I could not tell the difference. He then said, "I'll show you. I am going to pick the best one in this patch." He picked out a watermelon, cleared away the wilted vine and dirt and hit it with his fist. He broke it into two halves. Then he said, "Try it. That's the best in this whole patch." He buried his face in the watermelon. I followed suit. Bits of watermelon covered our faces. The melon was hot under the midsummer sun but very sweet. I had never had hot watermelon in my life, but it was good. We sat in the field and gorged ourselves.

Suddenly, we heard a loud voice behind us booming, "Hey, who is eating my watermelon? Hey who are you?" A farmer was coming toward us. Shinkō said, "Run, run away fast! Don't run to the sea!" I ran from there as fast as I could toward the pine grove; otherwise, with no obstructions, the farmer could have easily spotted us. Shinkō, too, was running toward the pine grove. Trees were quite numerous, in order to protect the village from strong winds or typhoons. The farmer again asked, "Who are you?" Then, Shinkō said, "Itakura." The farmer said, "Remember, I'll tell your parents about this." We reached the pine grove and found that the farmer was no longer chasing us. I asked him, "Why did you tell him your name was Itakura?" Shinkō replied, "There are at least twenty-five to thirty families named Itakura around here. He may be one of them. See, Wakō, that's *upāya,* meaning skill-in-means, or a wise device." We parted shortly after that. Shinkō's *upāya* stayed in my mind and strangely I had not remembered any remorse from this episode.

Several days later, I met Itakura at a Judo team gathering at the middle school. Japanese middle schools created several days during summer vacation for these events and it was one of those days. He said, "What did you do a few days ago? He scolded me for stealing a watermelon. I knew it was you." I said, "How did the farmer find out that it was you and not another Itakura?" He said, "You're a stupid fool. No other Itakura have boys my age. The farmer is much smarter than you." I was impressed with the farmer's cleverness, but asked Itakura, "What happened?" He said, "Nothing, but my parents knew that it was you and Shinkō who did that. Both you and Shinkō came to my house asking for me just about an hour before the happening. I was in Nagoya that day and came home around sunset." I said, "Hmm ... the farmer is smart, isn't he?" He said, "You know, my parents told me that I must not associate with watermelon thieves." I was a bit depressed to be a watermelon thief, but it was true and I regretted what I had done. Later in the month, I met Shinkō and told him what Itakura had said. Shinkō said, "Why do you worry now? That was a good lesson for you. You wouldn't do that again, would you? And worrying now changes nothing. I told you that was *upāya,* don't you remember? It was a good lesson for you." It was indeed a good lesson, whether *upāya* or not.

***

I heard from someone that after middle school, Shinkō Nakamura went to Eihei-ji for practice. I really wanted to see him at my *shinsan*, since I had not had a chance to see him after my school days. I knew he must have been an accomplished Zen monk by that time and I wanted to celebrate his accomplishment. Moreover, my *shinsan* ceremony would definitely be a felicitous and well-chosen occasion for both of us.

***

At about this time an unexpected incident happened at Sōkō-ji. Reverend Tobase and Reverend Nazuka both resigned from the temple. Nin'yū was preparing my *shinsan*, but I still had my duties at Sōkō-ji. I talked to the board members about my dilemma. Unlike my anxiety, I could simply solve the problem by shortening my stay in Japan. During the summer, Sōkō-ji observes an *obon* ceremony in mid-July, as is customary in American Japanese Buddhist temples. The date of my *shinsan* was set for August eighth. I decided to perform my *obon* duty at Sōkō-ji and would soon after leave for Japan.

I became an interim resident priest of Sōkō-ji. The year 1958 began and Nin'yū wrote in his first letter of the year that everything was set for my *shinsan*. The six monastic managing monks had been chosen: the *tsūsu* (managing monk), *kansu* (general managing monk), *fūsu* (assistant managing monk), *inō* (a monk overseeing the needs of all monks and creating a harmonious environment), *tenzo* and *shissui* (an annually appointed role responsible for *samu*, or cleaning and repairing activities). The first three managing roles overlap. The roles of *tsūsu* and *fūsu* arose since *kansu*, a manager of day-to-day practices, could not handle the entire monastic operation alone. The *kansu* role division into three managing offices happened in the Southern-Sung Dynasty (or Nansong), during which time Ch'an monasteries flourished. Today, the *kansu* (or *kan'in*) alone manages monasteries, but during formal occasions such as *shinsan,* monks still appoint *tsūsu* and *fūsu.*

***

While Nin'yū worked hard to prepare in Japan, we were living in Mill Valley. We were struggling financially and house-sitting for a friend to save the rent for several months. Their small house was adjacent to that of S.I. Hayakawa, a renowned semanticist who later became President of San Francisco State College and a U.S. Senator from California. Hayakawa was very kind to us for he knew that we were struggling to survive while I was researching for my dissertation. He later introduced me to San Francisco State College officials and they gave me a teaching position in the extension program. Emi worked at the Japanese consulate in San Francisco and commuted from Mill Valley, crossing the Golden Gate Bridge every day. I don't know how we managed all those factors at the time, and for me, going to Japan for the *shinsan* wouldn't be an easy task.

This was a big expenditure for both of us. It would place a heavy burden on Emi, having to work and care for a small child alone. There was no way my entire family could go under the circumstances, as much as I wished to introduce Emi and my daughter, Kazumi, to my mother and my family in Japan. The journey would have to be a solitary affair.

A few days after Sōkō-ji's *obon* service, in the latter part of July, I left for Japan. My air travel took much longer than the same trip would take today. The airplane had to stop at Honolulu, Hawaii, for refueling. There was no direct flight to Nagoya and I had to go via Haneda Airport near Tokyo; then I took the train to Nagoya. There was no fast bullet train as of yet. When I arrived at Nagoya station, my younger brother Kengo came aboard the train to greet me and help with my luggage. We took a taxi from Nagoya station to Hōsen-ji.

Everything en route to Hōsen-ji had changed in six years, including streets, shops and buildings. I saw small Japanese cars made by Toyota and Nissan driving on the streets. Six years seemed like a short time, and everything came back as if there had been no discontinuity. The smells, sounds, and scale of the Japanese city streets were all familiar. Yet, for my mother, family, and Nin'yū, six years had certainly been a long time to wait.

When we arrived at Hōsen-ji, everyone, including Nin'yū, was eager to see me. My mother didn't say a word, but she wiped away her tears. She looked older and tired, perhaps from all this commotion. Nin'yū held my hands tightly between his and said, "I have been waiting for this occasion. How great this is. How great, indeed." He had aged and grown thinner. He seemed to be lacking his usual vivaciousness. He repeated, "I thought this day would never come." I almost cried, feeling everyone's eager attitude. I believe it was Nin'yū who asked me about my life in the U.S. and Sōkō-ji. We talked about various topics, trying to narrow the gap we had.

After some time passed, Nin'yū said that after my Ph.D. was completed, he would like to propose to the Sōtō Administration Office to raise my rank from "second teacher" to "right teacher." I asked him about his rank, and he said he was at "second teacher," but he added that the ranking was not important for his particular position. I asked, "Why, then, do you want me to have the 'right teacher' rank, skipping the 'first teacher' rank?" He said, "It might be possible. I thought it would be convenient for you to have it." Then, after a pause, he continued, "Some people want you to wear a gold embroidered silk garment. However, you are right, for Dōgen only wore a black robe. A monk needs no rank. That is undoubtedly decadent. The title of right teacher is not important at all." That was, I thought, how Nin'yū used to speak, except with more vigor. The conversation did not continue that day.

I visited the houses of the members of the temple as they were going to help us financially and in other ways for my ceremony. I also visited neighboring temples to express my gratitude for their willingness to help on my behalf. I visited Kitamura-san at his temple. He had become the abbot of Byakugō-ji since the older abbot died during my stay in the U.S.. And, of course, I visited Taka-sama, my revered supporter, at his villa. He was happy to see me and I was equally happy to see him.

Kitamura-san visited me several days later. He wore a grayish western suit, necktie, shoes and a velour hat. I said to him, "You are decked out today. Where are you going?" He said, "If you are not doing anything, I want to take you to the city." I asked, "Where to?" He said, "No particular place, but we can go out to eat somewhere and talk." I replied, "I am not doing anything. I can go with you." I wanted to talk to him about many things, such as how the town, people, and temples had changed while I had been away. I put on my matching suit. The only difference was that my hair was long and his was shaved.

It was quite warm on that late July evening. The smell of supper preparations wafting through the moist air was ever so familiar and I enjoyed our outing. He asked me what I wanted to eat and I replied, "You know I'm still a monk. I eat anything. Anything you suggest will be all right. I have no preference; besides, I don't know any restaurant in town." He said, "Many people enjoy Genghis Khan Restaurant chains. Those are popular now. You know, meat is very expensive but Genghis Khan is relatively inexpensive and offers an ample amount. Everyone is hungry for meat. Let's try one of those, and you can tell people in America about your new experience."

We went to a Genghis Khan restaurant in the mid-city. Smoke and the odor of food permeated the entire restaurant. We took off our shoes, stepped onto the raised floor and sat at one of eight or nine tables. A server brought a *hibachi* (portable charcoal stove), over which she placed a strange-looking grill. Then, she brought out a platter of sliced meat and vegetables and a pot of sauce. I asked her, "Do we cook them on the grill? Do we dip them in the sauce before or after grilling them?" She instructed us to do the following: "First, you place your meat and vegetables on the grill. When they are cooked, you dip them in the sauce. This restaurant's sauce is very good. Lots of garlic and spices are in it." I had never knowingly eaten garlic before. My Zen monk diet forbade it, but I decided to try the garlic sauce. It sounded contradictory, saying that Zen monks eat anything offered, and here, to experience the forbidden food. I chalked it up to the fact that life is full of contradictions. The grill looked like a British soldier's shallow helmet during the Second World War except it had several grooves extending from top to bottom, and between the grooves were narrow openings. Kitamura-san and I finished one small serving of meat. It was not the ample amount we expected, nothing like the serving sizes of the United States. There was a young couple and two primary school aged children at the next table. The children were begging their parents to get more meat but the mother told them they had eaten enough. Japan's post-war reconstruction was almost over on the surface, yet when you looked carefully, the war's aftermath still affected daily life. Kitamura-san told me that the meat we ate was mutton. That was a new experience, too.

***

A few days before my *shinsan,* we held a rehearsal. The most knowledgeable participant in this ritual was Nin'yū and he instructed all of us about our respective roles. I was no exception, for I had to learn how to move my hands, feet and body at the right time. He also helped me compose appropriate statements, poems, and chanting sūtras. Moreover, Nin'yū gathered all of the necessary implements for this occasion. I was very grateful for his energetic help. He was more vivacious than the first day of my reunion with him.

The day quickly arrived. I put on the robe my father used to wear. In fact, all of my robes were his, except for one black robe, which I had worn for my *shuso* ceremony in my mid-teens. Under the circumstances, we could not afford to make a new robe even for this ceremony of "ascending the mountain."

My maternal uncle's house, which was just below the temple hill and right in front of the main entrance to the temple, became my place of retreat, or *angesho*. The *angesho* was the place where I was supposed to stop and take off my traveling outfit before ascending the mountain. If the temple had had a few smaller temples surrounding it, one of those temples would have been used as an *angesho*, but Hōsen-ji had no such temples. In front of my uncle's house, there was an announcement stating the following: "Place of Retreat for the Newly Appointed *Oshō*." My uncle Ennosuke was elated to undertake such an important role in this ceremony.

The time came, so I put on a crimson-colored robe and went to my uncle's house. There was a crowd of people who had come to see this festive event. Several monks, temple guests and temple representatives lined up in front of the entrance to my uncle's house in two columns and greeted me by prostrating and putting their palms together. I returned their bows and entered the *angesho,* where I had a cup of tea. We waited in the room for awhile until the exact starting time of the ceremony.

Apparently, Nin'yū had volunteered to be the *inō* for this occasion. He told a monk to strike the gong, which was a signal for all ceremony participants to take their positions. The monks began lining up in front of the *angesho* for the procession to Hōsen-ji. Reverend Dōkō Ōtsuka and his sons, Mokudō Katō, and Shinkō Nakamura came and waited at Hōsen-ji. There were two columns of monks, temple member representatives, dharma-relatives, and four banners describing the occasion.

> *Of all buddhas and tathāgatas, the most meritorious*
> *of religious practice.*
> *Of all felicitous occasions, this is the utmost event.*
> *All buddhas come and enter together here.*
> *Of all reasons, this place is the zenith of felicity.*

Following those banners, there was a lantern hung from a pole, which bore a carved dragon on top. After that lantern trailed another lantern, which I followed carrying a seven-foot staff. There was a large red umbrella sheltering me, which a monk carried behind me. Then my disciple, my brother Kengo, and my attendant, *jisha,* formed a queue and proceeded slowly toward the Hōsen-ji gate.

When I arrived in front of a temporary building that had been set up for the ceremony inside of Hōsen-ji I recited the appropriate dharma-phrases and burned incense. After that, I entered the *hondō,* which was a small but central ceremonial hall, and walked to the front of the main altar. I recited the dharma-phrase again and offered incense; then I put my sitting mat, or *zagu,* on the floor, and bowed three times. In this temporary building was placed the Medicine-guru or *Yakushi* as the main image at the center of the shrine. The medicine-guru was known in India as *Bhaiśajya-guru* who vowed to cure diseases, and for that reason, *Yakushi* became popular in China and in Japan. After I prostrated three times, I did the same before the guardian of the land and the hall of the founder. Then I went to the abbot's room, which in this temporary situation was next to the *hondō*. In the abbot room, or *hōjō,* a monk brought out the temple seals, which had been handed down to me from the founder, Zen Master Gentō Sokuchū. I received three large bronze seals and examined them as the official abbot. After this, I was led to the ornate ceremonial chair, or *kyokuroku.* Two columns of monks stood on each side of the room and watched me.

After this phase of the abbot ascension ceremony, it was time for me to officiate at a ceremony in the *hondō*. I celebrated this occasion by praying for the country's peace, and also peace for the world at large. I then recited the statement about opening the dharma-hall. Hōsen-ji called the dharma-hall a *hondō*. I also recited a statement about upholding Buddhist tenets for the world. This concluded the ceremony.

Every procedure had been carried out smoothly and without a single flaw. Everyone came and congratulated me after the ceremony. I was happy that I had decided to go through with it. The description on the banners once again entered my mind. Nin'yū came in to congratulate me and exclaimed, "Ah, I am absolutely satisfied with this. I didn't know whether I would live to see this or not, but I did. I am really happy." He looked very weary after the ceremony. I wanted to thank him for all he did for my *shinsan* so I said to him, "I don't know how to thank you for all of this, Matsubara-san (everyone including me called him by this name). You have done so much for me since my father's death. You have cared for this temple and for my family. Without you, I could never have reached the place I am at today. I am not only speaking about my monastic standing, but about all aspects of my life both here and in America."

Then, Nin'yū looked at me and said, "Well, do you remember that all existence is interdependent? We are here with a myriad of help not only from people, but from every animate and inanimate entity. Don't ever forget that. You and I are no exception. Besides, I promised your father that I'd take care of you. At the beginning of your path, you needed a guardian. Next, you needed guidance, so I did what I could do. But from now on, you don't need me anymore and I feel unburdened of a heavy responsibility. I am indeed relieved." He paused for a moment, and then concluded, "Well, it was a long day and if you will excuse me, I am going home to rest." I said, "Why, of course, you look a bit tired." He looked incredibly fatigued. Nin'yū left Hōsen-ji. I felt satisfied that our relationship had not changed. It was just like the good old days, except he had aged over the past six years.

Reverend Ōtsuka's son served as a *shuso* at my *shinsan*. He then returned to the University of Tokyo where he was a researcher in the field of nuclear physics. I did not know it at the time, but he had decided to remain a physicist at Tokyo University without further pursuit of becoming a fully-fledged priest in Sōtō Zen. Nuclear physics was the area in which he excelled. His older son became a priest and later took the abbotship of Reverend Ōtsuka's temple succeeding Reverend Ōtsuka.

***

Five days after my *shinsan*, *obon* season came. *Obon* for Sōtō Zen priests is a busy occasion. Since I was at Hōsen-ji, I decided to help with *obon* there and it was the second *obon* for me that year. Starting on the first of August, members begin coming to the temple to clear weeds and clean the tombstones in the cemetery behind the temples. It was a familiar scene during the month of August at that temple. August thirteenth, fourteenth, and fifteenth, my brother Kengo and I visited all Hōsen-ji members' houses. These dates were national holidays, during which time family members got together. Many of them asked me earlier to visit them when I would be back at Hōsen-ji. Some even asked me to stay without returning to California since I had now became an official abbot of the temple. I told them I hoped to come back after I finished courses at the university, and that I was learning a great deal about temple matters at Sōkō-ji.

I usually did not pay much attention to the weather, but mid-August in Nagoya that year was hot and sultry. At least I felt that way, since I had been living on the relatively cool and arid Californian coast. Visiting each house wearing a full set of kimono and robes, and chanting loudly at the shrine during those torrid summer days, especially in the afternoon, was indeed exhausting. I wondered why *obon* always occurred during the country's hottest season. When I was a student, it was convenient because it coincided with summer vacations; but for almost everyone else, *obon* was torture, especially in the Nagoya area, known for its hot and humid summer weather.

Every member's household has family shrines, which serve as a sanctuary for ancestral plaques. Priests' home visits are called *tanagyō,* or the "sūtra-chanting before the special *obon* altar for the ancestral spirits." Also, during the month of August, before and after the *tanagyō,* each of the temples nearby perform *bonsegaki*, or the "special food offering rite to hungry demons during *obon*," and neighboring temple priests have to help one another in performing *bonsegaki.* In the Sōtō school, the *segaki* ceremony was carefully detailed by Menzan Zuihhō in 1727. The essence of this rite was to practice giving, or *dāna,* to all sentient beings.

***

Nin'yū did not help with the *obon* that year because of his health. My brother said this was the first *obon* he had not helped with at Hōsen-ji. Furthermore, he did not assist any neighboring temple for its *bonsegaki.* I was so busy visiting members' houses until the *obon* season concluded that Nin'yū's condition had not even entered my mind. I visited Nin'yū after the *tanagyō.* He was sitting in a room in the old tenement where he resided along a narrow road. The back of it faced the Yamasaki River. He looked at me while he puffed tobacco and coughed a few times. I had brought a bottle of *sake* together with some food for him. He thanked me for that and said, "My wife is grocery-shopping at the moment and I am alone. So, excuse me for being a poor host. Kazumitsu-kun, I am sixty-eight years old now. I am forty years older than you, am I not? Most people retire at fifty-five or fifty-six. I deserve a peaceful rest during this *obon,* don't you think?" I replied, "Yes, of course. But are you all right?" He said, "Yes, I am all right." I said, "I am leaving for America soon. I promised the people of Sōkō-ji that I will come back after the *obon.*" Nin'yū said, "Yes, I know, you wrote me that. By the way, you have written me about your life there, but your letters were all about nice things. I have heard nothing about hardships there. When I talked to Tobase, he gave me a nicely painted picture of Sōkō-ji. That was not real, I know. I suppose the reality must be much different from what he said and what you wrote me. Tell me more about your life in San Francisco."

I told him some fragments of my life there, such as how I supported my wife and our child. I also told him about the school and Sōkō-ji. Listening to my account, he began to cry and wiped away tears a few times. I said, "Please don't cry, it is nothing to cry about." He said, "I knew you were going to go through some sort of hardships there. But I thought the outcome would still outweigh the hardships, and I knew you would survive no matter how challenging the conditions." Again, tears streamed down his cheeks.

I switched the topic to this year's *obon,* the members of Hōsen-ji, priests in the neighboring temples, and so forth. During this conversation, I casually slipped in the subject of generational changes. A few temples had changed abbots in the past few years. Nin'yū asked, "You visited the members' shrines and you noticed the generation gap of those temples, just in the past few weeks, didn't you? Hmm, impermanence emanates everywhere, doesn't it? There is always change. We exist amidst change and are never exempt from it. Besides the Buddha, a German philosopher named Schopenhauer theorized a natural law in which changes are omnipotent. Everyone knows that." I especially liked his philosophical talk this time. His keen observation of the *dharma* world and his realization of the Buddhist principle was exactly what Dōgen professed in the chapter on the "Manifestation of Reality" (or "True states of existence"), called "*Genjō Kōan.*" *Genjō* means all existence as they appear and *kōan* means that which makes *genjō genjō.* Nin'yū's use of "all things change" suggested just that.

I replied, "During the *tanagyō* and *segaki,* I was too busy to think about impermanence. I was simply going about my business." Nin'yū said, "That is all right, because you are living in impermanence. We are all nearsighted fools. When we chant, we think about how nicely we chant and how well we impress people without minding the meaning of the sūtras. Of course, most priests don't understand them anyway." I said to him, "You have not changed. Your manner of speaking is the same. You are exempt from the law of impermanence." Nin'yū laughed and said, "Ha, ha, ha…It's all right. You heard me say, 'we are all fools.' That includes you and me. On the lower plain, it is all right to be foolish and myopic, but on the higher plain we must grasp the true reality of existence. After all, that is the reason we visit the house of each member and perform *segaki* at temples. *Obon* is the time when people face generational changes and become aware of their own aging process. It is a time of veneration to all that exists. That is *kuyō.* We think of all sentient beings, like us, as products of nature. We offer our gifts to all living beings. Zen is a gift of life and it is to be given back to others. Priests chant sūtras whether they know their meanings or not, but they are fulfilling their duties. The essence of religion is to attain peace of mind. *Obon* is not for the dead, it is for the people who are very much alive. By the way, did you ever find Hemingway's saying that 'everything has a price tag in America'?" I replied, "It's not only America. It is the same everywhere, including Japan." Nin'yū laughed again, adding, "Of course, at *tanagyō,* every household gave you *ofuse,* the donation for chanting, appropriate to its own value system. Families pay a handsome price for *segaki,* don't they? That's their price for peace of mind. A price tag, ha, ha, ha…" Nin'yū laughed for a long time.

I said, "I'm very glad that you are really alright. I am so happy to see and hear your unchanging style of discourse." Nin'yū replied, "Don't be silly. Everything's changing. This is my short sojourn in this world. Do you recall what Dōgen said about true appearance? I am going to recite what he said, thus I'll quote from the *Shōbōgenzō*: 'All dharmas are true appearance, or *shohō jissō.* The appearance of Buddha and of the patriarchs is the uttermost true form. Therefore, the true forms lie within every dharma. The true form is what you see, as its nature, as its body, as its mind, as its world, as its clouds and rain, as its worry, happiness, excitement, calmness, as its cane and [the ceremonial] whisk, as its holding a flower and smiling, as its inheriting the dharma, as its study and practice, as its pine branches and bamboo sections.'"

He concluded this passage with the following statement: "So, I am what I appear to be: me. And remember there is an appearance of change at every instant. Everyone and everything cannot be excluded, Kazumitsu-kun. Don't worry about me. Mind whatever you are doing." I left his house feeling much better, particularly after hearing his usual way of speaking.

I had initially been reluctant to return to Japan for the ceremony, but after finishing with the formal ceremony, in addition to seeing Nin'yū, my mother, family members, the priests, temples, and townspeople, there were no time lags before my departure to the U.S.. On these summer nights, Mr. Ogasawara's frogs were no longer there to haunt me. Instead, I heard the sharp sound of crickets all through the night. I experienced a keen and realistic reminder of the distinct four seasons during the hot, muggy days and nights in Yobitsugi, which was a sharp contrast to the almost singular seasons of San Francisco. This summer, my *shinsan* ceremony, *obon* at Hōsen-ji, and visiting all those people was an unforgettably precious time in my life.

***

Soon after I visited Nin'yū, I began my farewell visits to relatives, temple members, and various temples. I found solace in doing that. It was as if I were still a member of the community. Of course, if I had neglected those duties, my rudeness would have embarrassed my family. Exchanging greetings and friendly chats with everyone was quite nice after all. Our conversations often centered on episodes from my childhood days.

The day before I was going to leave Hōsen-ji, on August 19 if

I remember correctly, I intended to visit Nin'yū once more at his house. Instead, he came to Hōsen-ji. It was still during the early part of the afternoon. When I saw him, I said, "Oh, I was going to visit you." He said, "Never mind. Since you are leaving tomorrow, I thought it would be nice to see you again here at Hōsen-ji. I don't know when we shall see each other next. This might be the last time. We don't know."

I replied, "Please don't say that. I'll be back in a few years, as soon as I finish things there. I'm sure you will be well till then." Nin'yū said, "Nonetheless, I wanted to see you." He sat down on a cushion on the *tatami*. He looked around the room before commenting, "This building is getting old, isn't it? After all, this was a former rental house. Fifteen to seventeen years have passed since then. We need to rebuild the temple soon. The next temple must be built according to tradition and it must be bigger than this." I said, "All the more reason for my return, so I must come back here mustn't I?" Nin'yū said, "Well, your brother Kengo is getting ready in a year or two to become a full-fledged priest. Everything is on course. Don't worry. Just do whatever you need to do. You had the *shinsan* and you are the official abbot here."

Suddenly, I sensed that everything was on its course without me. Of course, no one including me knew when I would return to the temple, and during my absence, the temple had to be kept up. A temple needs a resident in order to continue its existence. If I did not come back, I knew Kengo was the rightful candidate for priest residency at the temple.

Kengo, my official dharma heir, was twenty-four years of age at the time. He was preparing to complete the qualifications to become a priest. I thought he would make a good priest since he really liked the temple atmosphere. He enjoyed the chanting and rituals. All those years he had needed a teacher, I was in San

Francisco and could not help him. To my surprise, he had learned a great many of those sūtra chants and temple rituals on his own. I did not know what my mother meant when she said that she eagerly awaited my return. My brother's readiness to become the next abbot of Hōsen-ji gave me a sense of joy and relief, but in all honesty, I also felt a bit of sadness. I left Hōsen-ji for San Francisco the next day. This visit to Japan had lasted about four weeks and my schedule was so full that time passed all too swiftly. On the airplane back to San Francisco, I reflected on all that had happened at Hōsen-ji. Each memory played as vividly as the slow-turning frame of a kaleidoscope. I was certain that everyone enjoyed seeing me become an officially endorsed resident priest of Hōsen-ji. Why did Nin'yū say that everything was on its course and to just do what I needed to do, in front of my mother, and my brother, who would soon be a priest? I had mixed feelings. First, I regretted that I went there alone, not with Emi. Second, I felt a bit of sadness. At the same time, I was relieved from the responsibility to go back and become a priest of Hōsen-ji. I remembered my frustration when I first took the responsibility of the resident priest there.

***

A few days after I returned home to Mill Valley, I received a letter from Nin'yū. From the date, I discerned that the letter was written while I was still in Japan and before I last saw him at Hōsen-ji. He had written the following:

August 15, 1958
I don't know why, but these days I have become very inactive. I don't have any reason to change my destiny. I don't have any need for that either. Therefore, I don't go out much like I used

to. When I read, my eyes get tired quickly, so I limit that. My drinking, my constant companion, has lessened. I take only a small amount daily and I don't particularly enjoy it. It has become simply a habit.

Though not actively seeking, my state of mind reaches out to nirvāṇa and tranquility. I am taking good care of my old bones.

My family is faring better financially. Today, everyone decided to go to the beach and I am home alone, enjoying the radio and electric fan. The temperature is still 34 to 35 degrees Celsius and very hot, but I am enjoying the serene solitude.

If I don't write you, please think I am well. By the way, did Kitamura tell you that he is going to have his shinsan next year, commemorating the third memorial of the Zenchi Oshō, a previous abbot? Also, his temple is going to add a founder's hall and entrance to the existing building. He is getting more mature and much better. Furthermore, Iō-ji and Ōryū-ji changed abbots. I don't know whether your mother said so or not, but she is hoping for a big repair of the building and I think it is time to do that. Speaking of time, the world seems to be moving at a rapid pace. I will write to you about that in the near future.

Take good care of yourself and your family.

Nin'yū

About two weeks after receiving this letter, my brother wrote me that Nin'yū was hospitalized at the City Hospital in Nagoya. He did not know the nature of his illness. I wrote Nin'yū immediately. This time, together with my inquiry about his illness, I told him of my deep gratitude for all that he had done for me especially. His replies came three weeks after my inquiry.

October 29, 1958
You overestimate my help. Yes, you and I have had a long and close relationship. I, too, have enjoyed every minute of it. It was a good part of innen (meaning the cause-and-effect link, or pratītya-samutpāda) for us.

The results of all that I did were good fortunately, but when I took all of those chances, in the years after the war, I could not foresee the outcome. You were the one who saw it through.

Remember though that nothing stays in the same state—all will change. There is a saying, "virtue is not alone, there will always be company"—that is, the world is interdependent. Don't think about only your own salvation. Be kind to others. Think about others, and their salvation. That is the word of Dōgen.

No one will tell me, but I have cancer in my sinuses, a terminal illness for sure. I went through a big operation, which changed the shape of my face. My daughter, Masako, who works at the Matsuzaka-ya department store, fortunately has health insurance, and I happened to be her dependent so I am covered. I am resting in a single room, thanks to her savings. I feel that this is my last illness but in case I live longer, I will spend the rest of my life helping others in whatever way I can. I shall also practice Zen unremittingly to repay my gratitude to Buddha. The teachings of Buddha helped my wife and me immensely, so that we maintained relatively calm states of mind after the deaths of my children.

Do you know that over seventy people came to visit me

*here and, among them, seventeen were monks? I cried after
each of them left. I am, indeed, a lucky one. I will be very
glad to see you, if such a day ever comes.*

Nin'yū

Within ten days, I received another letter from him. It was a very
short letter:

November 8, 1958
*I was informed today that I must have another operation
tomorrow. In any case, our farewell is near. There won't be
a next time. Thank you for your patience during all these
years.*

*Looking back at my life—meeting with you and your
family, associating with you, helping you and being helped
by you—the last fourteen years were the golden years of
my life. I am thankful for that innen.*

*I am gratified by your thoughtfulness in all of your ac-
tions and I sincerely wish for your wellbeing.*

Nin'yū

On the next day, I received another letter from Nin'yū, dated the
same as the letter before. This was a letter in a formal envelope,
which gave me a strange feeling. It was his last poem, inscribed on
the thick rice paper. Customarily in Zen tradition, priests compose
a poem just before death, called *yuige,* left to their heir. In a few
seconds, my intolerable, ineffable pathos of this event overwhelmed
me so much that I could not feel or think anything. The letter read
as follows:

Yuige, the last poem:
On the road of confusion, on the path of enlightenment,
I wandered around the entire world.
Sixty-eight years,
Now, I am putting human karma to an end.

Formerly, Seventh abbot of Zentoku-ji,
and Thirteenth abbot of Kaigen-ji

November 8, 1958

Nin'yū Tokuon Oshō

On a separate sheet of paper, he wrote, "It may be a little hasty, but no one can escape from death. Goodbye." He had enclosed one small photograph of himself taken in Hōsen-ji's living room. On the back of the image, he wrote the following: "Taken at Hōsen-ji, in the spring of 1958."

This letter formally ended my long relationship with Nin'yū, but by enacting Nin'yū's *innen,* I knew our relationship would continue on forever. My karma with Nin'yū will persist within me throughout my life and thereafter.

I had received a similar formal letter on rice paper from him at my wedding ceremony in the summer of 1955. I have kept it in my "important file" case. When our daughter was born, Nin'yu authored her name, Kazumi, "Harmony is beauty." I brought out the letter and read it once again. I looked at both. I felt that one epoch of my life had passed. I earnestly lamented his passing. Emi, although she had never met Nin'yu, sympathized with my poignant sense of loss.

Especially during this time, these essential phrases in Mahāyāna Buddhism resonated within me:

諸行無常　All phenomenal things are impermanent.
諸法無我　All elements have no substance.
涅槃寂静　*Nirvāṇa* is quiescence.

三法印　　"Three Dharma Mudrās."

Quite spontaneously, Mahāyāna's phrase,"three dharma mudras" came to my mind when reflecting on his photograph.

Nin'yu Yamasaki after his release from military prison, located
in the northernmost island of Hokkaido. Photo taken in Nagoya.
He was 55 years of age and was a Zen Buddhist monk. For
that reason, his life was spared from the firing squad.

Nin'yū taught me the above phrases when my father was passing away. I knew Nin'yū would enjoy the quiescence. He had lost
all of his children but the last one, Masako. He had never had an
affluent life but enjoyed being plain and obscure. In my observation, he was satisfied with what he had and what he was, and never
wanted more. He had never been broken nor had he fallen. In fact,
I did not know he had formerly been abbot of two temples until I
read his last poem. He never had *shinsan* at either temple and remained in the rank of *oshō,* which was less than my rank. Yet, he
positively succeeded in living a rich life of *nirvāṇa* in our poor and
sordid world.

I did not inherit his dharma lineage but I inherited a lot from
him, more so than with any of my other Zen teachers or schoolteachers. He alone bestowed me with my level of life philosophy.
Nin'yū and I had suffered together during the Second World War
and thereafter. We dug up any usable objects from the burned site
of the old Hōsen-ji. Together we planted quick-growing vegetables
over that site and we shared them with others. Through our many
dialogues, he taught me sometimes quite ruthlessly and sometimes gently. I immersed myself in the reading of Dōgen and other
Eastern and Western authors, but he pulled me out of subjective
submersion and guided me to the right course. Our relationship was
truly that of mentor and protégé at a time when I needed guidance.
He was sans posthumous mythologizing, a true "buddha-bodhi"—
a teacher from whom one wishes to learn Buddhism.

Although time and space have separated us, his mark on my
life remains. His profound influence on me transcends an ephemeral bygone mourning period. He had now become my karma. I
knew then that his presence would permeate interdependently to
endless eons of time.

Chapter 17

A SOURCE OF THE STREAM

両武帝初見達磨之時	When Emperor Wu of Liang first met Bodhidharma,
即問「如何是聖諦第一義」	He asked, "What is the primary Truth [of Buddhism]?"
答曰「廓然無聖」	[Bodhiharma] answered, "In deep and broad Buddhism, there is no such thing."
進曰「対朕者誰」	The emperor further asked, "Who are you?"
又曰「不識」	Again [Bodhidharma] said, "I don't know."
使達磨不通方言	Upon this, he thought Bodhidharma did not know the dialect.
即何於是時便能爾耶	In any case, it did not go any further.
－ 道元	- Dōgen
(『正法眼蔵』「行事」下)	(*Shōbōgenzō, (Gyōji)* "Activities II")

On Friday, May 22, 1959, about nine months after my *shinsan* at Hōsen-ji, Reverend Shunryū Suzuki arrived in San Francisco. I was in the last phase of my graduate work. I thought my work at Sōkō-ji would lighten with his arrival and it did. Suzuki stayed at Sōkō-ji and literally spent the entire time in his office for he did not know the area or anyone in San Francisco. Shunryū Suzuki was a remarkably diligent priest. I remember several episodes which depict the many sides of Suzuki.

Shunryū Suzuki first surprised me when he arrived at the San Francisco airport, I believe it was around 9:30 in the morning. The members of Sōkō-ji and I prepared two or three big signs on which was written in bold Japanese letters, "Welcome Reverend Suzuki." At the airport several of us were holding our large signs, making sure we were visible as arriving passengers passed by. There were a couple dozen of us lined up, eagerly waiting to meet our new priest. A slightly built priest wearing a Sōtō Zen robe was among the crowd of passengers walking to exit the flight terminal. We thought he must be Reverend Suzuki, but he continued walking along with the crowd, looking straight ahead, paying no attention to our signs and Japanese faces as he passed by us.

We thought there must be one more Sōtō priest emerging from the exit. None appeared, so I ran after the priest and caught up with him. I asked, "Excuse me, are you Reverend Suzuki?" He looked at me and said, "Oh, you must be a person from Sōkō-ji. You are Katō-san, aren't you? Oh, how good of you to come here to see me." The Sōkō-ji members caught up with us. Suzuki was calm but everyone in our party was in a quandary, whispering and asking each other, "Is that Reverend Suzuki?" Suzuki realized that the group of people gathered there were there to greet him. He smiled and said, "Oh, what a big party. Are you all coming to see me here? My, I don't know what to say. Thank you. Thank you very much everybody." That is how we first met Reverend Shunryū Suzuki as he entered the United States.

I drove Reverend Suzuki from the airport to Sōkō-ji in my old Chevy. I wanted to use this time to become acquainted with him and provide him with pertinent information about Sōkō-ji. Along the way, I began telling him about the scenery and briefly mentioned the temple's routines. He simply listened to what I said without asking any questions. After awhile I stopped talking. He sat quietly observing the scenery from the front passenger seat. After a long period of silence he said, "This is a beautiful city, isn't it?"

***

Ordinarily a person who arrives in a new country is very curious about what he or she sees. He did not seem amazed by the scenery. Furthermore, when a person meets another for the first time, he usually talks to that person in order to get to know him, as well as to give a good impression to the other person. He did not do that. When we were near Sōkō-ji he said, "Katō-san, do you have a family?" I said, "Yes, we have a daughter." He said, "That's good. You look very happy. You are happy, aren't you?" I was a bit puzzled by his question and his statement. I said, "Yes, I am. I am very happy." Suzuki gently nodded a few times. A moment later he said, "You know, I don't know anything about Sōkō-ji, except for several letters informing me about it. I am certain I will need your help and care." I replied, "Of course, Reverend Suzuki, I am your assistant. You can ask me anything and please don't hesitate to do so." He said, "Thank you. I know nothing about the temple, members and its surroundings. You must tell me the proper things to do first. I won't know what to ask you." Then he scratched his head and continued, "I wonder whether or not you understand me." I understood him. I was once in the same situation. We arrived at Sōkō-ji safely around noon but did not schedule any formal gathering immediately, for he had just undergone a long and strenuous journey from Shizuoka, Japan. In the evening, the members invited Suzuki for dinner at the nearby Otafuku restaurant.

The day of Suzuki's arrival, my wife Emi and our daughter

Kazumi went to Sōkō-ji around seven o'clock in the morning to prepare a light lunch of hot noodles. Emi assumed it would suit him after the long flight. I introduced my family to Suzuki on that cold morning. He did not show any jetlag; instead, he looked refreshed. At first, as a Zen tradition, Suzuki began his initial arrival ceremony at the shrine. I assisted him. It involved prostration and a short chanting session. Then, we had lunch. Suzuki explained that he did not have an appetite for heavy food after a long flight but he graciously thanked my wife for preparing the meal. After lunch, we left Sōkō-ji to allow him to rest.

***

On Sunday, May 24, 1959, at ten o'clock in the morning, temple members arrived to meet the new priest. Some went to the airport or restaurant on the day he arrived, but this was his first formal assembly with the members. Suzuki was very gracious at all times and expressed his appreciation for their attendance. I introduced him to everyone. After a short period of chanting, it was time for him to give his first talk to the congregation, which he had not expected. He murmured, "Hmm, I am in a difficult situation, am I not?" It was "*Komatta-na*" in audible Japanese. He scratched his head as a gesture of hesitation. Apparently, I had forgotten to tell him that he had to give a dharma talk at just about all services, and this was no exception. He paused for two or three minutes, which felt like a long time for us. He then began the sermon by incorporating an old kōan into his first dharma-talk. He talked about Mañjuśrī from the *Blue Rock Record* or *Biyanlu*. The story was a timely choice, because it recounts the Buddha giving sermons to the crowd of *theras* (or elders), and the essence of this story is used in *shinsan* ceremonies.

The story goes as follows: One day before the Buddha gave the sermon, his attendant Mañjuśrī announced that it was a wonderful sermon, as though he had already given it. The underlying meaning was that the Buddha's presence was most important, not the sermon.

At Zen *shinsan* ceremonies, the abbot ascending to the seat replicates the Buddha's deportment. Suzuki had chosen his sermon in an impromptu fashion, echoing the way the Buddha behaved during his sermon in the Indian forests. Suzuki took this opportunity to utter another most appropriate and famous tale for his first talk.

The Bhagavat (meaning "world-honored one") stepped up to the dais. Thereupon Mañjuśrī struck the tree stump with a mallet and said, "The king of the dharma's teaching was thus. You must know it." Then the Bhagavat descended from the dais.

Did Mañjuśrī make a mistake by giving the closing remarks instead of an opening statement? Traditionally, the opening statement would address the audience with, "Superior people look at the utmost meaning [of the dharma]!" The presence of the Buddha alone was important and that in itself explained the utmost significance of the dharma. Indeed, the Dīgha-nikāya or the Long discourse III: 135 of the Pali Tripitaka (also the Three Branches of the Buddhist Tests in Pali), states:

From the time when the *Tathāgata* (the Buddha) became fully enlightened (the state of Supreme Enlightenment), to the time when he attained the final stage of the state of *nirvāṇa*, or *mahāparinirvāṇa*, where nothing was deficient—during that period of time, whatever he said and explained, was just that *(tathāgata)* and nothing else. Therefore, he is called *Tathāgata.*

Suzuki slowly and carefully explained that *tathāgata* in Mahāyāna Buddhism is the one who has arrived from thus and one who has followed the path and has completed all necessary practices to become a perfect human being. He added that *tathāgata* is one of the ten epithets of the Buddha; however, this term had become widely used in India to address respected individuals in general.

The topic was a little difficult and abstract for the temple members, but with Suzuki's careful delivery with long pauses between words, they warmly welcomed Suzuki's first lecture. Everyone seemed to understand the meaning of *tathāgata* in the Mahāyānistic sense of it. Using this timely topic of speech, his first dharma talk was a declaration to teach Buddhism as an official dharma successor. Suzuki's talk was not overly dramatic in its presentation—not brisk and not loud, but very warm. I thought of the impact of his ability to touch people and it reminded me of my *shinsan* at Hōsen-ji nine months earlier.

***

Even after Suzuki's arrival, Sōkō-ji remained a quiet place, especially on weekdays. Sōkō-ji did not reach outside its sequestered area. It reflected an ethos of homogeneity within the Japanese community, which was still present in the late 1950s, amongst the beatniks who were openly advocating nontraditional thought in the San Francisco area.

Reverend Shunryū Suzuki lived alone until his wife, Mitsu, and their son, Otohiro, joined him. I believe he was alone for over a year. During this time, I invited Suzuki to our modest apartment on Potrero Hill on a number of occasions. My wife and I cooked Zen-style vegetarian food and Japanese cuisine for special occasions, such as New Year's Eve and New Year's Day. On those days, I picked him up at Sōkō-ji in the late afternoon for dinner, or New Year's Day for breakfast. When we had dinner together, at his request, we ate quite early and soon after dinner, he always asked me to take him back to the temple. He often asked my wife and daughter to come along, so that we could all discuss common topics. I do not remember the exact time, but on two or three occasions, he said, "It is better to go back to Sōkō-ji early in case someone comes to visit the temple. I am sorry that I am a poor dinner guest, so why don't we talk and enjoy each other's company while driving back to Sōkō-ji?" The drive to Sōkō-ji was only twenty or twenty-five minutes. He was a good passenger and we all enjoyed those conversations, which made up for his hasty departures as a dinner guest. I thought that perhaps he was just timid and feared criticism.

I found out later that was not the case. On New Year's Day, 1960, we invited Shunryū Suzuki to our house for a New Year's Day breakfast. We prepared the traditional New Year's Day menu. As usual, he asked me to take him to Sōkō-ji as soon as we finished eating. I said to him, "This is New Year's Day. You can relax and enjoy the occasion. Everyone is probably enjoying themselves in the same way at home." He looked at me and said, "That's very good of you. I sincerely appreciate your hospitality, but I have to go back to Sōkō-ji. That is my job, you know. I will disappoint temple visitors if I am not there. Katō-san and Okusan (meaning "Mrs.", which was his way of addressing my wife), that is what I have to do."

At that moment, I suddenly realized that Sōkō-ji was his domain of practice. My face flushed with embarrassment. I was once critical of him for being timid but I was mistaken. I remembered Dōgen's words, "Others are not me. For what other time would I wait?" Zen priests learn in monasteries how to live, and how and when to clean; we clean for the sake of cleaning whether or not there is dust. Every moment is our practice of the Buddha's way. Behind Suzuki's gentle smile, I saw a Zen practitioner's determination.

***

My assistance to Suzuki continued and I enjoyed this role. Emi also assisted every Sunday to help with Sōkō-ji's Sunday school. Once she told me a touching story about Suzuki's thoughtfulness. It was during Suzuki's early days in San Francisco. Our daughter Kazumi, who was then four years old, asked her if it was all right to buy an apple for Suzuki Sensei. Emi told her that would be nice. So, Kazumi picked out one small but bright apple at the store. Emi asked, "Such a small one?" Kazumi replied, "But this is so beautiful." After returning home Kazumi carefully polished it many times, wrapped it nicely with soft, colorful tissue and placed it in a small box. The following Sunday, Kazumi carefully carried the box as if she were holding a treasure. Upon seeing Suzuki at the temple, Kazumi presented it to him. Suzuki held the box in both of his palms, raised it above his head and bowed. Then, he said, "Thank you. How very good of you to give me this. Is it all right to open it?" Kazumi nodded. He opened the box, took out the small apple and said, "Oh, what a beautiful apple. I haven't seen such a beautiful color of apple before." Then, he closed one eye and with the other eye looked at the apple. He said, "I see Kazumi-chan's beautiful heart in the apple." He called Kazumi "Kazumi-chan," an affectionate way of calling a small child. Kazumi had a big smile on her face. He then smiled at Kazumi and Emi and told them that it was really the greatest gift of the day.

Observing this scene, Emi was moved by the sincerity of his attitude. She told me that he expressed his genuine gratitude to a child. Emi liked Suzuki more than ever after this little episode. Likewise, all members seemed have a strong affinity for Suzuki without exception. His presence was a definite asset to Sōkō-ji.

***

After Shunryū Suzuki's arrival, he and I went through the temple's basic routines, just as Tobase and I had done upon my arrival to the United States. Emi taught half a dozen children at Sōkō-ji. Her education in piano and voice came in handy. In those days, Hakuyū Maezumi, a young monk (a year younger than me) originally assigned to Zenshu-ji in Los Angeles, lived in San Francisco and attended San Francisco State College for a short period. He often visited my house on Potrero Hill and we exchanged ideas regarding the significance of disseminating Zen in the West. The word Zen began appearing on papers and in journals, but real Zen was not even in its embryonic state, if at all, in San Francisco—the vanguard city of this movement.

***

One day, when we were sitting in Suzuki's office, a well-built Zen monk came in, wearing a monastic outfit. As he was entering, he introduced himself as Sōen Nakagawa. He was a well-known Rinzai Zen master at Ryūtaku-ji in Mishima, Shizuoka. I was surprised that he visited Sōkō-ji alone and without advance notice. Nakagawa went into the adjacent room and offered incense at the altar. Suzuki and I put on our robes and prostrated behind Nakagawa. Suzuki then said, "I am going to offer the Heart Sūtra, would you join us?" Nakagawa nodded. It was a tradition that when a Zen monk visits temples, the first thing to do is go to the shrine and prostrate. We chanted the sūtra together. Suzuki sat in the center, and Nakagawa sat on the first row of benches facing the shrine. I started the chant using the gong and then a wooden drum called *mokugyo*. We finished the simple rite. Then, Nakagawa picked up the book of sūtras on the table at the side of the altar. He saw the name of the book donor on the inside front cover. He suddenly shouted very loudly, "This is not Zen!" and threw the sūtra forcefully onto the floor. I saw him jump a foot or two into the air and stamp his feet down on the floor. I was shocked and could not move. I thought Nakagawa's exercise of Rinzai manner at a local Sotō temple was a bit out of place. Suzuki looked at Nakagawa, bowed lightly and moved forward, squatting to pick up the sūtra. Suzuki then said, "This sūtra is donated by Mr. and Mrs. Jōta Handa. This is a practice of our people and their way of kuyō (veneration). We treasure it." Suzuki gently dusted the sūtra, folded it and returned it to the altar and bowed sincerely with the touch of his conviction. Nakagawa did not say anything; instead he simply watched Suzuki. Suzuki turned around and said to Nakagawa, "It is an honor to have you here, Reverend. Let's have a cup of tea in my office." Suzuki then looked at me and said, "Katō Sensei, would you mind preparing the tea for us?" I went to the kitchen and prepared tea for them. When I brought the set of cups and the pot of tea to the office, they were talking rather cheerfully about Shizuoka. I realized that both men came from the same prefecture.

Nakagawa was tall and well-built, especially compared to Suzuki, and their manners were contrasting. I later learned that

Nakagawa had zazen groups in the United States and visited those places occasionally; but his visit to Sōkō-ji was unusual. He had apparently heard of Sōkō-ji and thus paid the visit. He tested Suzuki with the Rinzai style dharma combat; this, too, was very unusual. I thought Suzuki passed skillfully and definitely to Nakagawa's satisfaction. If that had been me, the dharma encounter would have ended with a shouting match or a bloody nose. When Ch'an was flourishing in China, there were countless dharma combats, which included shouting and slapping with sticks. Those encounters were part of the process of finding the true Ch'an, as it was difficult to express and teach what by nature defied linguistic expression. Later, in 1994, I published the book, *Lin-chi and the Record of his Sayings* (Nagoya University of Foreign Studies), a translation of *Rinzai Roku*, into English. I donated 2 or 3 copies to Hanazono University, a Rinzai Zen university.

***

One Saturday afternoon in August or September of 1959, I visited Sōkō-ji. Suzuki was sitting alone on a chair by the desk in his office. Reverend Tobase's nephew had dropped in casually and sat on the couch. He had come to San Francisco while Tobase was a resident priest at Sōkō-ji. After Tobase returned to Japan he stayed in San Francisco. He was about twenty-four or -five, and I did not know exactly what he was doing in San Francisco. He was a layperson who had graduated from a private university in Tokyo, with a degree unrelated to Sōtō Zen. I do not remember how the conversation began, but the young Tobase started to reprove people who worked for a small income, and stated that getting rich is of the utmost importance in life and that was what he cared about the most. He was not particularly arrogant, but adamantly stressed his opinion.

As soon as the young man finished that thought, Suzuki very swiftly jumped up on the couch and began slapping the young Tobase's head four or five times. It was so sudden that I was simply dumbfounded and froze. It was similar to the recorded activities of the Chinese Ch'an master Deshan (Tê-shan), except Deshan hit with a stick. The young Tobase guarded his head with his arms, and appeared confused beyond measure. Suzuki shouted, "*Baka*! (You fool!) Don't waste your time, wake up!" It was not too long after I had become acquainted with Suzuki. Even so, this behavior was unusual for Suzuki and I would not have ever imagined him in such a fury. After that, both men sat quietly for awhile. We resumed a normal conversation as though nothing had happened.

A month or so later, when I was in the office with Suzuki, I asked why he slapped the young Tobase. Suzuki smiled, scratched his head and said, "I overplayed a bit, didn't I? Tobase-kun came here a couple of weeks after that and asked me why I slapped him. I was hoping that he would come here for that. I told him that if he had held onto such a value system he would never be satisfied with life. Since he is a nephew of Tobase-san, I encouraged him to be a great human being (*dainin*). You know, in Zen Master Dōgen's 'Eightfold Realization of Great Human Beings,' the Dōgen stated that 'one must know that whatever one has is as much as he needs.' Thus, a great human being must have less desire and be satisfied with what one has and what one is. This idea may not be in vogue today, but I know that such an attitude would bring him less suffering, and bliss is to be found in that. After all, he is a nice young man and I like him. He thanked me for that." I felt like I had seen a new, gentler and more thoughtful side of Suzuki.

396

The last time I saw the young Tobase was the day of Suzuki's *shinsan* ceremony at Sōkō-ji. He was helping Sōkō-ji for that event. He smiled and waved his hand to me and I did the same. I did not know whether he would be coming to Sōkō-ji after Suzuki's *shinsan*. I did not ask Suzuki about him thereafter. I hope he learned what a great human being is.

***

On May 20, 1962, Shunryū Suzuki and the members of Sōkō-ji hosted Suzuki's *shinsan*, as the fourth abbot of the temple. This time I was the one who knew the temple and its members, and was expected to know the procedure to help Suzuki with his ascent to the mountain seat at Sōkō-ji. I reviewed the rules and procedures very carefully.

Suzuki invited Reirin Yamada Rōshi, then the head of the North American Sōtō Zen Dissemination Office in Los Angeles, and many others known to Sōkō-ji and Suzuki. Yamada Rōshi and others who resided in the Los Angeles area came to participate in this event. Yamada Rōshi took on the role of calling the assembly to order by sounding the wooden mallet, which was the traditional role of Mañjuśrī. A few temple members and I prepared a special cane for the abbot to hold. The temple did not possess certain items such as a large ceremonial umbrella, but we obtained one and carried it during the ceremonial procession through Japantown.

For this important ceremony, all of the Buddhist community including other schools of Japanese Buddhism in San Francisco and those from other areas gathered. It was a big event, and all of Japantown gathered for the celebration. Many children wore kimonos and followed the queue of two or three columns of priests. Representatives of the Sōtō Zen temple walked several blocks around Sōkō-ji. I was behind Yamada Rōshi in front of Suzuki, Hakuyū Maezumi, and Kōgi Sayama from Zenshū-ji in Los Angeles. Other priests followed, wearing their formal robes.

The procession ended in front of Sōkō-ji. Approximately two dozen congregants waited and greeted the crowd at the temple entrance when the parade matrix came through the temple entrance. This procession signified the arrival of the new abbot of Sōkō-ji and confirmed his abbotship. Then the main ceremony took place in the large main hall. The ceremony was the same as when I had my *shinsan* at Hōsen-ji in Japan. This time, Yamada Rōshi called the assembly together and confirmed Suzuki's official seating at Sōkō-ji. His *shinsan* ceremony went without flaw. Thus, Suzuki was officially made abbot of Sōkō-ji. This ceremony took place two days short of the date marking the three-year anniversary of his arrival to the United States.

Suzuki had already been very busy as the *zazen* practice group had increased and it demanded more of Suzuki's leadership. As mentioned before, *zazen* practice at Sōkō-ji began around six months after Suzuki came to Sōkō-ji and grew steadily thereafter. The Zen Center of San Francisco, which had officially launched at Sōkō-ji six months earlier (on October 25, 1961), grew to capacity. Furthermore, the group needed a live-in Zen practice location, which Sōkō-ji lacked, and the Zen Center eventually moved out of Sōkō-ji to a large house on Page Street, about a dozen blocks east of Sōkō-ji. San Francisco Zen Center's independence from Sōkō-ji happened in 1962. However, Suzuki remained at Sōkō-ji for several months more before he permanently moved to the center.

***

I believe it was just a few months after Shunryū Suzuki's *shin-san* at Sōkō-ji, when he was still living at Sōkō-ji, in 1962, when Suzuki asked me to accompany him to Stockton to see someone who was practicing Sōtō Zen. We left Sōkō-ji around ten o'clock in the morning. I drove my car which did not have air-conditioning. The temperature soared above one-hundred degrees and the air became arid as we drove inland from the Bay Area coast. Suzuki wore his usual attire: *juban* (kimono undergarments), a cotton kimono, and a black silk *kairyō-é* robe over his kimono. It was the lightest outfit that a Zen priest could wear. Still, three layers of a Japanese kimono ensemble in the unrelenting heat were torturous. I opened the car windows but hot air swirled in, which did not help lower our body temperatures. At one point, Suzuki said, "It is hot, isn't it? People who live around here must endure this temperature, mustn't they?" I thought that comment reflected Suzuki's personality, who in that relentless heat, still considered other people's suffering before his own. He was a Mahāyāna Buddhist to the core. He said no more about the heat.

Instead, he explained more about the person he was going to see. This person had been teaching Sōtō Zen in Stockton and Suzuki wanted to see him. When we arrived at his house, I was relieved to see he had an electric fan, but it did not do much to help lower the temperature. In his living room, there was a small shrine with a Buddha statue. In front of it he had placed an incense burner. Suzuki changed his informal robe to formal wear. I also put on my robe and stood behind Suzuki. Suzuki bowed at the shrine and asked me to start the chant. Our host seemed at a total loss and could not follow us in chanting. After the chant, Suzuki asked him some questions regarding his Sōtō Zen involvement. The person showed Suzuki a letter by the Head Zen Master, Rōsen Takashina, who encouraged his Zen practice. Curiously, the same Head Zen

Master encouraged Suzuki's *zazen* group, which became the San Francisco Zen Center, when he toured the United States the year before.

Suzuki then said, "Let's do *zazen* for a while." We sat for thirty or forty-five minutes in that scorching temperature. We did not talk much after that but Suzuki invited him to Sōkō-ji. We then drove back to San Francisco and the mid-afternoon temperature was even hotter than on the way. Suzuki simply said that the person we visited needed more practice. A few weeks later, Suzuki invited him to Sōkō-ji by telephone. When he came, we practiced *zazen* together, possibly for about an hour and a half, taking four or five minute intervals of *kinhin*, or walking *zazen*. We chanted two sūtras after *zazen*, but our visitor looked very uncomfortable. Later, Suzuki told me that after those two meetings, the man stopped being a Sōtō Zen priest. Suzuki said after that, "Zen has two thousand five hundred years of tradition, and acquiring just a fringe of it overnight is a bit too hasty. Don't you think so, Katō-san? He is not committing his body and mind to Zen, after all." In this event, Suzuki showed a different side of himself, compassionate but definitely stern as a monastic teacher, which I had not seen before. Dōgen said in the "True States of Existence," or "*Genjō Kōan*," that the ways in which the sea gives multiple benefits cannot be understood talking about each dharma, which gives countless benefits to other existing things. Each dharma has a myriad of assets which we cannot perceive. I profoundly respected Shunryū Suzuki's *buddhatā*, or buddha-nature.

***

I was very fortunate to have met and served Reverend Hodō

Tobase, and later, Reverend Shunryū Suzuki. I must also mention Reverend Nazuka, whose gentle and careful care helped me a great deal. Tobase was a newly arrived immigrant himself, but he guided me when I first arrived to the United States, in addition to handling Reverend Nazuka's day-to-day concerns. It was also very fortunate that I had experienced a variety of work while I was young, including occupations in drugstore delivery, farm work, and house-care. They were all rewarding experiences in their own ways; all tasks were a part of my Zen learning. When Suzuki arrived to this country, he was a newcomer, but he brought his mature Zen experience. Since he was richly endorsed and highly educated in Zen, he had all he needed to prosper in America. Americans needed a Zen teacher exactly like Suzuki, and in a short time after his arrival here he fulfilled this role.

Shunryū Suzuki *shinsan* procession in Japantown, San Francisco, 1962.
Zen Master Reinin Yamada, followed by K.W. Katō, and Hakuyu Maezumi.

Shunryū Suzuki *shinsan* procession in Japantown, San Francisco, 1962. second row, left to right: Kōgi Sayama, K.W. Katō, Zen Master Reinin Yamada, followed by Shunryū Suzuki.

Chapter 18

FUGAN-JI, THE SOURCE OF NOH

仏仏かならず仏仏に嗣法し、	Inheritance must be from a buddha to a buddha
祖祖かならず祖祖に嗣法する、	Inheritance must be from a patriarch to a patriarch
これ証契なり。これ単伝なり。	Master must match the acquisition. This is the single heredity.
− 道元	- Dōgen
(『正法眼蔵』，「嗣書」)	(*Shōbōgenzō*, (*Shisho*) "Inheriting Dharma")

I received a letter from my brother that Reverend Yagi had died in the late summer of 1961. As the only dharma heir of Reverend Yagi, I was first in line in Reverend Yagi's dharma consanguinity. However, when I heard the news by airmail, the funeral service had already passed since Japan does not have a custom to embalm the deceased person's body. Reverend Yagi was my father's dharma-cousin. He helped Hōsen-ji when we needed an abbot. Now, I had to help Fugan-ji in order to secure the temple's continuance. I assumed the position of abbot of Fugan-ji in Nara without hesitation, since I was the only dharma-heir of Reverend Yagi. Just a little more than three years after my *shinsan* at Hōsen-ji, I was destined to assume yet another abbot seat.

During my association with Reverend Yagi I learned very little about Fugan-ji. I visited Fugan-ji only once or twice during the years he was at Hōsen-ji, for I had no official business to visit there. Since I was now becoming the abbot of Fugan-ji, I needed to know more about the temple. Thus, I began looking through temple documents and was astonished by many findings of which I had not had the slightest idea of until that time. Reverend Yagi was not a talkative person; besides, he visited Hōsen-ji only whenever Hōsen-ji needed him. He found no need for mentioning details of his temple, Fugan-ji. Fugan-ji, I learned, is a historically important temple in both the Sōtō Zen tradition and also in Japan's performing arts history. It was founded in 1384, more than six hundred years ago and is the oldest Sōtō Zen temple in Nara. Fascinatingly, it played a major role in the development of Noh theatre.

***

I became the thirtieth abbot of Fugan-ji on November 20, 1961. I was pleased that my acceptance would keep the temple afloat instead of letting it sink into oblivion after six hundred years of existence.

Reverend Yagi's wife told me that two years before Reverend Yagi's death, on July 4, 1959, two gentlemen, one a devoted researcher of Noh Plays, Mr. Tsutomu Kōsai, and the other a professor at Hōsei University in Tokyo, Akira Omote, visited Fugan-ji. They had come to search the archives held at the temple. Most likely, Reverend Yagi, residing in this obscure temple, was astounded by their unexpected visit. Having had no members to support it, Fugan-ji was surviving on the income from the land it once owned before the end of the Second World War. Unfortunately, when the new Land Reform Law was enforced, absentee landlords had to give up their land to tenant farmers. The landlords had to transfer the rights of land ownership to the tenant farmers for a token remuneration. Fugan-ji was no exception and was stripped of most of its land other than a small plot that Reverend Yagi had used to grow vegetables for his family's use. Thereafter, Reverend Yagi helped his dharma-relatives in Osaka, Sango-ji, to earn some income. During the post-medieval warring period of the fifteenth and sixteenth centuries the area where Fugan-ji is located was subjected to repeated upheaval, resulting in Fugan-ji's descent to obscurity. In subsequent years, the official fiats over religious activities under the Edo regime from the seventeenth to nineteenth centuries further decimated this once radiant temple.

***

When Mr. Kōsai and Professor Omote visited Fugan-ji, they found documents stashed at the bottoms of many scattered chests. Apparently, some of those had been kept there since the late fourteenth century. The two gentlemen could not find the one document they were looking for on their first visit. Reverend Yagi did not believe their account of what they were seeking. During his long tenure at the temple, he did not view these documents as valuable archives. The two scholars continued to visit the temple many times thereafter. They painstakingly worked to find any documents which would reveal the connection between the temple and Zeami (1363-1443), one of the founders of the Noh Play. Assiduous research by Mr. Kōsai and Professor Omote fortuitously revealed Fugan-ji's past connection with Zeami. Mr. Kōsai found the documentation that confirmed the connection between Zeami and Fugan-ji. These documents were the ones the two gentlemen had been looking for during the past decades. They found the proof that Fugan-ji was the temple where Zeami, a co-founder of Noh theatre, studied and practiced Zen. His Zen experience at Fugan-ji culminated in his mastery of theatrical arts. The two scholars also revealed the early history of Sōtō Zen in connection with Fugan-ji.

***

Despite its very important place in the cultural development of Japan as the home of Noh theatre, I would like to dwell on the temple Fugan-ji's historical significance apart from its influence on the development of Noh theatre. Fugan-ji was founded in the year 1384 with a gift from Nakahara, the Lord of Tōchi (the former name of the present Shiki County in Nara, which is the area directly surrounding Fugan-ji). Fugan-ji is located in Yamato (the greater Nara area), which is the cradle of Japanese civilization. It was near the old capitals from the seventh to ninth centuries. In those early years, this area was a stronghold of Nara's Kōfuku-ji, the Head Temple of the Hossō School of Buddhism, which flourished from 710 C.E. on, especially in the Nara area. However, since the early thirteenth century, when an eminent Rinzai monk, Eisai, returned from China, Zen Buddhism in Kyoto and Kamakura (then the capital of Japan) became the new focal institution of Buddhism. In fact, the Kamakura Buddhist schools (Zen and Shinran's True Pure Land) became the most popular Buddhist schools in Japan, whereby Buddhism found deep cultural roots. The earliest Nara Buddhist schools were academic and pedantic to grasp the people's hearts. The esoteric Heian Buddhist schools emphasized praying for some specific purpose such as curing an illness or exorcism.

***

When Chikusō Chigon, the second abbot of Fugan-ji, invited Ryōdō Shingaku as a nominal abbot, there was no Sōtō Zen temple in the Nara area. It was at that time that Fugan-ji's activities began. A renowned Sōtō Zen monk, Ryōdō Shingaku, the sixth in Dōgen's lineage, was named founding monk at a new Zen temple at the foothold of Kōfuku-ji. When Fugan-ji was founded in 1384, it was 130 years after the demise of Dōgen, and only sixty-three years after Keizan founded Sōji-ji on the Noto Peninsula. Fugan-ji's founder, Ryōdō Shingaku, was in the second generation after Keizan. Sōji-ji was a dynamic hub of Sōtō activities in those days and so was Fugan-ji. As it was practiced at Sōji-ji, Fugan-ji in those early days selected an abbot for a three-year-term rotation called *rinban*. This system prevailed for 105 years. During the *rinban* system, thirty-one monks served as abbot for an average tenure of three years and four months. Fugan-ji served as the head monastery in the area for over four hundred years. Hundreds of monks studied and practiced there. Many of those monks later founded their own temples, which served as Fugan-ji's branch-temples in all parts of Japan. Today there are eleven original branch temples remaining, and from these further branching has taken place. Fugan-ji currently has over 230 tributary temples. Extrapolating from the numbers of those tributary temples, Fugan-ji was then a very important monastery of Sōtō Zen in the Nara province.

With those present-day scholars' painstaking discoveries, the connection between Zen Buddhism and the development of Noh Theatre was established. I was astounded to discover the amazing history of Fugan-ji, which fulfilled a vital role as a Sōtō Zen temple and contributed to the innovation of *mugennoh,* the Noh play of dream and fantasy. Zeami indeed grasped the Buddhist philosophy of "that which is made (all phenomena) is dream or fantasy".

***

The Noh play was one of the most important performing arts of medieval Japan, and remains so to this day. The plays include music, dance and dramatic elements in a full-length drama setting. A typical Noh play is performed by male actors who act their personified roles with singing, dancing and dialogues. A Noh play consists of a protagonist, called *shité.* Other elements include an antagonist, or *waki,* and musical accompanists, such as singers, a flutist, a small drummer, a middle drummer, and a large drummer. The chorus of singers narrates the story of the play with the accompaniment of the musicians. These theatrical elements were used in *sarugaku,* which were popular theatrical and musical entertainments since the Heian period, perhaps from around the early thirteenth century on to the time of Zeami. When Zeami and his father Kan'ami became the heads of Yūzaki guild, later called the *Kanze* School of Noh, the strata of patrons had widened, which included the *shōgun* and their high rank retainers. Then, Zeami began studying Zen Buddhism.

At this time, he created the arrangement of *mugennoh* in his innovative plays, which were backed by the Zen philosophy of *sūnyata,* or nothingness. If Zeami did not undertake this role creating the new layout of Noh scenarios, the Noh play was probably doomed to confinement as a simple *sarugaku* and would have possibly waned into a cameo or a line in a history book.

On the contrary, the Noh play reached its height in the late fourteenth century. It has maintained a continuing popularity to the present day. Noh companies tour not only in Japan, but also in the United States and Europe. The prototype of the Noh play, as I mentioned, began in the early thirteenth century as rustic country dancing or *sarugaku,* and was performed in unsophisticated country theatres, if not in open fields, in the Nara and Kyoto areas. This *sarugaku* began adding theatrical elements to its performances and thus evolved into dramatic performances. It was called *Sarugaku no Noh.* It was not until Zeami and his father, Kan'ami, began adding elements of elegance and sophistication that Noh plays became popular as a theatre artform.

The third *shōgun* of the Ashikaga Shogunate, named Ashikaga Yoshimitsu, patronized Zeami and his company. During that time, Zeami practiced and studied Zen with the Second Abbot of Fugan-ji, Chikusō Chigon, who was an actual founder of Fugan-ji. He called himself the Second Abbot, a gesture in respect to his master, Ryōdō Shingaku. The Second Abbot, Chikusō Chigon, was then a well-known Zen master who later became the abbot of Sōji-ji, the most active Sōtō Zen monastery of its time. Fugan-ji was also an active monastery for those who revered Ryōdō and Chikusō, its first two abbots. Ryōdō's birthplace was Yūzaki in Yamato, the same area where the Noh theatre of Kan'ami and Zeami was actively engaged. Zeami's father Kan'ami was the founder of Yūzaki-za, or the Yūzaki Guild of the Noh Play.

In the beginning, Fugan-ji did not serve as a local temple for laypeople. It was mostly a place of Zen monk practice. Over the years, Fugan-ji burned down twice. After the first fire, the temple rebuilt the monastery, as it owned a great deal of endowed land and had a rich and powerful supporter, Lord Tōdō of the Iga-Uëno province. But after the second fire, the temple had exhausted its resources in previously rebuilding the monastery, and Fugan-ji fell into obscurity without the strong support of lay people. The Tokugawa regime in the Edo period enforced the law requiring almost all subjects in Japan to belong to a Buddhist temple, for the sake of census-keeping. Households in neighboring areas already had their own temples. Since Fugan-ji did not serve laypeople, it could not accommodate the changes. Furthermore, almost immediately after the Second World War, following the American Occupation Force's advice, the Japanese government instituted a land reform system that affected the absentee-ownership of farmland. As a result, Fugan-ji had to give away almost all of the arable land it had owned and rented to tenant farmers.

Under the Second Abbot, Chikusō Chigon, Zeami was ordained at Fugan-ji in the year 1422, or as it was then called, the twenty-ninth year of the Ōei. Most likely his study of Zen began in the 1390s. According to the findings of both scholars, Kōsai and Omote, Zeami took the ceremony to receive Bodhisattva precepts. The receiving of Mahāyānan Bodhisattva precepts was exactly the same as my initial ordination at Hōsen-ji. Zeami had decided to become a Zen monk late in life, receiving his monastic name at the advanced age of sixty. According to the temple archives, Zeami's wife had died and was buried in the temple cemetery. Zeami, in memory of his wife, donated a piece of land to the temple. That too, was recorded in the Fugan-ji archives. The archives revealed that Zeami's dharma name was Shiō Zempō and his wife's was Juchin Zenni. I was fascinated to learn the radiant historical details of Fugan-ji from Mr. Kōsai's first book, *The New Study of Zeami,* or the *Zeami Shinkō,* which was published in 1962.

Although I became the abbot on paper, I was not able to visit Fugan-ji for quite some time because I was living in the United States. The temple was still the residence of Reverend Yagi's wife and her children. As I continued to study the temple my eagerness to visit it grew, so I visited Fugan-ji when I later visited Japan.

***

In the summer of 1982, I returned to Japan to attend an academic conference. While I was there I visited a specialized Noh bookstore, the Wan'ya Bookstore in Tokyo, while searching for some books on Zeami's plays and the aesthetics of Noh acting. In the bookstore I saw only one other person browsing the bookshelves. Soon, we began talking about documents regarding Noh plays. He was a man about my age or a few years younger but he had an amazing knowledge of the field of Noh. After exchanging a few words, I introduced myself as a professor in California and a Sōtō Zen priest. This initial meeting took both of us by surprise. He opened both of his eyes wide, and his mouth dropped open, to express astonishment about this remarkable and unexpected meeting. He in turn introduced himself as Professor Akira Omote of Hōsei University. I, too, was shocked to see him in such an unorthodox way. I had read the book, *New Study of Zeami*, or the *Zeami Shinkō* (1962), which Professor Omote had edited for Mr. Tsutomu Kōsai. Both gentlemen had researched the Noh play's relation to Fugan-ji; naturally, I wanted to meet them. In any case, I was shocked to meet the person to whom I owed a great deal regarding the history of Fugan-ji. Fate provided that we met by accident. What a course of destiny! In a tiny specialized Noh Play bookstore, in a city of eleven million people, I met a person to whom I wanted to express my gratitude for his study of the temple. Besides, I was in Tokyo for only three or four days. I told him that although I became the thirtieth abbot of Fugan-ji, I was presently living and teaching in California. He knew about me and he, too, was surprised to see me at the bookstore. He said that his knowledge of me was from Mrs. Yagi and that he was also hoping to meet me someday.

Professor Omote told me that Mr. Tsutomu Kōsai had died in 1979. He said that his research proved the relationship between Zeami and Fugan-ji. Mr. Kōsai's works culminated in the following three books: the *New Study of Zeami* or *Zeami Shinkō,* the *New Study of Zeami II* or *Zoku Zeami Shinkō,* and the *Study of Seishi* (Zeami's sobriquet) or *Seishi Sankyū.* I had only read the first book. I purchased the latter two books right then at Wan'ya Bookstore. Professor Omote and I spent a few hours at a coffee shop nearby and talked about the coincidence of our having had this chance meeting. In that first meeting, Professor Omote told me that there were several gentlemen who were studying Zeami and Fugan-ji, hoping to commemorate the six-hundredth year of Zeami's study at Fugan-ji. Among them were Hiroyuki Yamamoto and Hidëo Kanze of the Kanze School of Noh. Their plan was to build a memorial monument next to the temple gate, which was the only original building still standing, and also to present a commemorative Noh drama at the town hall. I sincerely agreed with their plans and promised to help by doing whatever I could. Professor Omote had done so much for Fugan-ji already, and he was now planning to erect a stone monument at the temple gate. I felt an immense sense of gratitude for his untiring work and dedication. During the course of our conversation I suggested using Dōgen's handwriting as a template for the monument inscription. This concluded our first informal meeting in preparation for the commemorative event.

***

After that initial meeting, he arranged for me to meet the headmaster of the Kanze School of Noh Plays while I was in Tokyo. I went with Omote to the headmaster's house the next day. It was a pleasant meeting. While we were discussing the monument, I once again suggested using Dōgen's handwritten letters, since Zeami had studied Dōgen's Zen. I informed Professor Omote of where to find the copy of Dōgen's handwriting. Within a short period of time, probably ten or eleven months after our initial meeting in Tokyo, we received more than enough donations from Hokkaido to Kyushu to build a nice, tall stone monument right next to the temple gate. Since we received more than we needed to build the monument, the group later decided to build another monument on Sado Island, where Zeami was exiled in his advanced years.

***

For the rest of 1982 and the early part of 1983, Omote and I corresponded via airmail a number of times. I was very fortunate that in the academic year of 1984-85 my request for a sabbatical leave from the university was granted. Also, during that year, I was invited to be in professor-in-residence at Chubu University in Kasugai, near Nagoya. All the plans fell into place. I could not desire a better arrangement, for I was able to attend the ceremony. In early June of 1984, Professor Omote and I met several times to prepare for the event at Fugan-ji. At one of those meetings, the late Mr. Kōsai's son came along with Professor Omote. He told us that someone acquainted with the Kōsai family would donate the stone for the monument, and that the Kanze School of Noh had also decided to participate by performing for the event. Everything went smoothly and tastefully.

I visited Fugan-ji several times more from Kasugai besides meeting with Professor Omote. He came all the way from Tokyo. I admired his sincere disposition and tenacity in planning and executing this project. He took entire responsibility for this task. Mr. Yoshio Maënishi, the proprietor of a Noh publisher and the Hinoki Shoten Bookstore in Kyoto, also assisted in this undertaking and promised to publish a small book for the event. The nucleus of people interested in Zeami and Fugan-ji who wished to build the commemorative monument, celebrating the sixth hundredth year of Zeami's study of Zen at Fugan-ji, was named the Association Celebrating the Zeami Monument at Fugan-ji, or *Fugan-ji Zeami-hi Kisei-kai*. Mr. Maënishi was elected to lead this project. Thanks to those people, every detail involving the building was faultlessly exercised.

***

The date for the unveiling of the monument was set for the eighth of August, 1984, at 2:00 p.m. This day was chosen to commemorate the day Zeami died, which was the eighth day of the eighth lunar month. Exactly six hundred years had passed since the temple had originally been founded in 1384. Fugan-ji existed before that time but it most likely belonged to the Hossō School. There were no recorded documents before the temple changed over to Sōtō Zen. My wife, Emi, and my three daughters, Kazumi, Eka, and Miho, joined me from Southern California to celebrate this event.

Before the unveiling ceremony at Fugan-ji, I officiated at the memorial for the founder, Ryōdō Shingaku, which was held in the main hall, or *hondō*. The abbot of the closest and most directly related temple to Fugan-ji, Keiden-ji, assisted me in the memorial rite. Included in this rite was a tribute to those who contributed their efforts to building the monument, but had passed away before this day.

Approximately six hundred people from all over Japan gathered in front of the temple. The stone monument was draped in white and tied with red and white cords, the symbol of happiness. Before the unveiling, several speeches were delivered commemorating the occasion. First was a congratulatory note by Mr. Jun'ichi Okuda, a historian of the area and the head of the post office, and the mayor of Tawaramoto, where Fugan-ji is located. Two young boys (grandsons of the supporters Tsutomu Kōsai and Hiroyuki Yamamoto) pulled the cords to unveil the monument. Afterward, there were a few more speeches, including those of Professor Omote and also my own, thanking the contributors to this cause. Lastly, everyone sang a song *Senshūraku,* or the Happiness for a Thousand Autumns, from a felicitous Noh play, *Takasago,* in unison. This chorus had a profound ending, for it signaled the ending of religious rites or other public performances for centuries in Japan. This happy event completed the first part of the celebration.

***

The day was extremely hot and muggy. The thermometer at the temple around two o'clock reached a record 36 degrees Celsius. Unfortunately, I still had to wear four layers of kimono robes and stand under the direct sun for about two hours. The Noh actors, who also wore several layers of formal kimono, must have been in agony. My wife later told me that she was very impressed with the Noh actors who sat with their spines straight in those outfits without moving or perspiring under the scorching sun for the duration of the event. Despite the weather, everyone rejoiced in this historic occasion.

The second part of this event took place in the large traditionally designed town hall, which was approximately fifty meters from

Fugan-ji. The hall accommodated approximately 300 people on the *tatami* floor. Fifty or sixty chairs were temporarily placed outside the hall. Still, over 200 people stood behind the chair section. In the late afternoon, the two sons of the master Hiroyuki Yamamoto and one other actor performed Noh dances. Lastly, Professor Akira Omote gave a lecture entitled, "Zeami and Fugan-ji." Visitors from Tokyo, Kyoto and Osaka had spent all afternoon and a good part of the evening participating in this event. My family members were all very impressed.

I wrote an article for the commemorative booklet, which complimented the event as a tribute to Zeami as well as to Fugan-ji. I introduced myself as the thirtieth abbot since the rotation-of-abbot system, *rinban,* had ended. I mentioned Fugan-ji's dazzling history as a Zen monastery where Zeami studied and practiced Zen. Fugan-ji then was closely related to Sōji-ji; Sōji-ji, as the hub of the then embryonic Sōtō Zen practice, energetically engaged in the expansion of its activities. Many of Fugan-ji's early abbots also served as *rinban* (rotation system) abbots of Sōji-ji. Thanks to the careful research of the Fugan-ji archives by late Mr. Tsutome Kōsai and Professor Akira Omote, Fugan-ji's relation to Zeami was brought to light.

According to their findings, Zeami studied under the tutelage of the Second Abbot of Fugan-ji, Chikusō Chigon. Chikusō, as documented in the *Record of [Sōtō] Abbots,* or the *Jūsan-ki,* had become the Twenty-second rotated-abbot of Sōji-ji on the first day of the eleventh month of 1409. Zeami had most likely met Chikusō while Chikusō resided at Fugan-ji as a rotated abbot, yet Chikusō was addressed as the Second Abbot of Fugan-ji throughout his life by the many people who admired him.

***

I mentioned Zeami's new style of Noh, *mugen-noh*, or the "Noh of Dream and Foam." Zen and Fugan-ji clearly influenced the *mugen-noh* of Zeami. The word *mugen*, meaning "dream and foam," was taken from the *Diamond Sūtra*. The sūtra has the following short verse at its very end:

> All that exists is
> like a dream, foam [*mugen*], or shadow,
> like dew or like lightening.
> One must see that.

The basic form of *mugen-noh* is as follows: at first, a traveler visits a known place where he meets a local who tells the traveler the folk tales of the area. Then, the traveler finds out that the local person happens to be the protagonist of one of the stories. The audience disregards the few hundred-year-long temporal gap. After a brief intermission, the person to whom the traveler had spoken to becomes the protagonist. Scenes depict life or death, love or hate, through singing and dancing. Each *mugen-noh* ends at daybreak and everything fades away to nil.

In my article, I stressed the Noh rendition of dualism, which is in essence emptiness. Dualities such as life and death, love and hate, are all illusory, so when daybreak comes, everything fades away like an evanescent dream or the dissipating foam on the surface of water. The world we live in is perpetually changing and thus unsubstantial, like dreams or foam. If we attach ourselves to any of those dharmas (things) in any form, we will eventually suffer in the end. Zeami rendered this thought on the dharma world, which was also depicted by Dōgen, who wrote that one ought not view things from space alone but also from temporal points. This spatio-temporal conceptualization is called Buddha-nature, or the very essence

of existence. All life is impermanent, continually changing, and interdependent; that explains the reality of our existence in time and
space. Dōgen's existence is based on each moment, within which
dualities such as life and death, love and hate, exist; yet, they have
no enduring substance or duration. Since both poles exist interdependently in a constantly shifting present, Dōgen dissolves the
dichotomized thinking to which people are so accustomed.

In the Chapter from the *Shōbōgenzō* entitled the "Mountains
and Waters Sūtra," or "*Sansui-kyō*," Dōgen wrote, "Green
Mountain always moves," and "an eastern mountain moves on water." In our common sense conception, mountains are stationary.
These statements are intended to break our attachment to the notion that mountains are immovable. The viewers of the mountains
themselves constantly change within the cycles of birth and death,
past and present, and into the future. People continually transform
themselves in each passing instant just like the mountains.

***

The highlight of the second part of the event was a Noh play.
Three Noh dancers performed the play named the "Well-side," or
"*Izutsu*," which is the most well-known *mugen-noh* by Zeami. The
following is a sample of the "*Izutsu*." In this scene near the desolate
ruins of Ariwara-dera Temple, lived Ariwara no Narihira and his
wife, a daughter of Ki no Aritsune. A monk passes by on a scenic
journey through the countryside. This antagonist introduces himself as a traveling monk, and then explains:

> *"I have traveled to Nara and I am now on the way to Hatsusé.
> I saw a temple and asked people about it. They said it was
> Ariwara-dera. I would like to look at the temple."*

Singers in the chorus chant in unison:

"Once upon a time, Narihira and his wife lived in this temple. The travelling monk wants to pray for and think about them. It was an autumn night."

The traveling monk then sees an attractive young woman offering water to the tomb in the dead of night. The young woman is a *shité*, or the play's protagonist. The woman sings, facing back toward the audience:

"Aka (meaning water, from argha in Sanskrit) for every morning break. I see the reflection of the moon on the water. Like this moon, my mind will rest in peace."

She turns around facing the front and continues:

"Autumn nights are so lonely. This is an old temple people rarely visit and I am hearing only the echoes of wind passing through the pine branches. Now, it is getting late and the moon in the west shines on the grass growing from the eaves of the building. I am yearning for the days long past which I thought I had forgotten, and I am living just for that nostalgia... I have been relying on the Buddha's guiding thread. Please lead me, bestow upon me your voice of dharma..."

The traveling monk interrupts:

"I have come to this temple to calm my mind and I see an attractive young woman, scooping up water and offering it with flowers to the tombs. I assume you are offering them to this tomb. What sort of woman are you?"

The young woman replies:

> *"I am a woman living in this area. But this temple was built for Ariwara no Narihira who was well-known. These are the ruins. I don't know much about Narihira but I wanted to offer water and flowers, wishing for his peaceful repose."*

The monk says:

> *"Yes, it is true that Narihira was a person who left his mark on the world. On the other hand, it was so long ago and long forgotten, except for here. You are a woman. Why are you praying for Narihira? You must have some other reason to come here."*

The chorus chants:

> *"Once long ago, the General Ariwara in his old age decided to live here where flowers blossom in spring and the moon is beautiful in autumn."*

After such persistent questioning, the woman finally reveals herself as Narihira's wife. She begins reciting her remembrances:

> *"In those days, he made a promise to the daughter of Ki-no Aritsune. Both were deeply in love. But one day he secretly visited an acquaintance [lover] in Takayasu. I thought of him traveling alone late at night with the strong winds on Mt. Tatsuta. I worried about him."*

The singers onstage now recite the following tale:

"Long ago in this part of the country, there were people living next to each other. There was a well and a child leaned on the side of the well and talked to her friend, mirroring her on the water at the bottom of the well. They expressed their mutual fondness. And they grew to a young age. A man, Narihira, sent a poem to the woman, the daughter of Ki no Aritsune":

We played at the well-side.
The well-side was tall then,
but now I grow taller,
and we do not meet.

The woman returns the poem to Narihira with the following addition:

My hair was parted when I played with you,
it grew longer, covering my shoulders.
But I do not think
of this hair being tied
to anyone but you.

The woman says:

"I am the woman of the well-side and the daughter of Ki-no Aritsune. At the well-side, we promised to be together for a long time and we lived in the shadow of the well-side for a long time."

The woman quietly retreats from the stage. The monk appears and says:

"The night at this Ariwara-dera is getting late. She is waiting for the dreams of the past to come back. She is sleeping alone on the floor blanketed in moss."

The woman reappears in time with the music, wearing the costume of Narihira, and says:

"Cherry blossoms are known for being short-lived. I waited for he who only comes home a few times a year. It was I who was waiting in misery. People started calling me 'woman who waits.'

But time has passed and I am now wearing Narihira's clothes... I am dancing as the man of the old days."
"I am ashamed but I profess to mimic Narihira, whom I loved. I shall dance as if I were him. My sleeves wave like snowfall. I am reviving olden times. The moon reflects on the water in the well as clearly as it did in those days. Where is the old moon? Since when did I begin to reminisce about the old spring? When was it?"

"The well-side, the well-side, you have grown taller, you must be old.
I know it is my body but [wearing your clothes] I long for our old love and I cannot see that this body is that of a woman. To me it is of a man, Narihira. Oh how beloved, and how longed-for! My deceased husband. He was colorful and fragrant,
so unlike a wilted flower... but, alas, the color is fading, only fragrance remains...the temple bell is ringing... the day is breaking... Now, it is only an old temple and wind passes

through the pine branches ... the banana leaves are torn.

My dream is also torn and blanching ... Alas, it is fading."

Thus, the story ends. Love and hate in *mugen-noh* are viewed as temporal, as well as the causes and conditions of suffering. Love and hate stem out of one's ignorance and is not substantive. In Zen, our ability to feel physically through our senses is in essence illusory. Phenomenal appearances differ in time and space. They are contingent on interdependent, causal relations, but when the causes level out so do the differences. For Narihira's wife, love and suffering for her husband were equally transient, and caused by her own karmic chain. Love, hate, life, death, suffering and pleasure—all are substantially *śūnyatā*. This includes not only human emotions but all physical and mental elements in this phenomenal world (*saṃskāra-dharma*). In fact, all sentient beings are only a temporary combination of psycho-physical aggregates; thus, they have no permanent self or substance.

*** *

To add a few words regarding the play, Zeami referred to the essence of impermanence, which explains that everything comes and goes in the stream of time, as *"yūgen."* The word depicts "beauty found in subtlety and profundity." It is like a cherry blossom that blossoms for only a few days in springtime. Its beauty is found in the fleeting state of a viewer's mind. *Yūgen* also reminds us that life is a momentary dream, delicate and frail, like foam on the surface of water.

Zeami brought forth human actions and reactions, in static yet kaleidoscopic scenes of the world. He expressed *yūgen* in his plays with warmth and compassion. It is most likely from Fugan-ji that Zeami acquired his Zen rendition of Bodhisattva virtues. For that, I am deeply indebted to Professor Akira Omote of Hōsei University, the late Mr. Tsutomu Kosai, and the late Mr. Hiroyuki Yamamoto, who initiated the ideas for the commemoration. I am also indebted to Mr. Yoshio Maënishi of the Hinoki Bookstore in Kyoto and to countless others who generously helped realize this event.

After the ceremony commemorating Zeami in August of 1984, I completed my residency at Chūbu University. I returned to California, and resumed my teaching. My tenure at Fugan-ji continued until the spring of 2008, since the Sōtō Zen Headquarters recently changed the rule that the abbot of Japanese Zen temples must register in Japan with a seal of abbots acknowledged by the local prefectural office. I could not register while living in the United States. My dharma-heir, Kengo, took over the abbotship of Fugan-ji. The policy change was timely, considering my age. I am grateful to have maintained Fugan-ji as a Sōtō Zen temple for over twenty years. I sincerely hope that Fugan-ji will remain a vital place for many centuries to come.

Chapter 19

IN CONCLUSION

仏法にあふたてまつること、	To have met the Buddha-dharma is difficult,
無量劫にかたし。	it is difficult in the measurable eon.
人身をうること、またかし。	Also to be human is difficult.
たとい人身をうくといへども、	Even if you were born as a human being,
三州の人身よし。	east, west, and northern people are good.
そのなかに南州の人身	Among them, [some] southern persons
すぐれたり。	are superior.
見仏聞法、出家得道、	The reason for that is they see buddhas, listen to dharma,
するゆへなり。	and then they become monks [and nuns].
－ 道元	- Dōgen
(『正法眼蔵』「八大人覚」)	(Shōbōgenzō, (Hachidainingaku) "Eight Great-men's Enlightenment")

My purpose for writing this memoir was not to chronicle the details of my life, but to write about Zen Buddhism, which I acquired empirically from many accomplished teachers with my whole being. I did not write it for self-glorification or so that I will not be forgotten. I am content with obscurity. Thus, I shall now conclude my personal narrative. It might be an abrupt end for some, but I have written everything that I initially intended to set down on paper.

In accordance with dharma-nature, all existence comes and goes. I am a dharma among a myriad of dharmas. I conceptualize dharma as *śūnyatā*—each existence is not singular, but an interdependent entity, void of enduring substance. That is *prajñāpāramitā*. The wisdom of *prajñāpāramitā* is not attained through *a priori*, logical scrutiny. It is an applied wisdom that must be practiced rather than theorized in one's daily life. To become one with *śūnyatā* has taken me a lifetime.

> *In fact, nothing exists,*
> *so there's no dust to wipe away.*
> *If you can understand this,*
> *there's no need to sit diligently.*
>
> *– Feng-kan*

I spent a great deal of time and effort in academia. I was not gifted with the English language, unlike my native-speaking colleagues. I do not deny that occasionally I felt frustrated and wondered whether or not my efforts were a Sisyphean task. However, I weathered those years and persevered through some bad patches. College teaching and Zen practice were synergistic, as Gyokusen had suggested. Without a doubt, my Zen foundation enriched my academic work. I received an institutional grant from the university for two years in the late 1970s. In 1984 I received the Meritorious Performance and Professional Promise Award and the Outstanding Professor Award the following year. During a sabbatical at Chubu University in Japan in 1994 I received a grant to publish a book from a prestigious "Science Research Grant" from the Japanese government's Ministry of Education, which culminated in the publication of *Bunka no Nagare Kara Miru Eigo (The English Language as Seen Through the Evolution of Culture),* (Tokyo, Sanshūsha, 1996).

My practice of Zen began when I was six or seven years old. My father, Gen'yū Katō, was a *tenzo*, or cooking monk, at the Shuzen-ji Monastery beginning around 1910 for about nine years. At the Shuzen-ji monastery, my father had acquainted his body and mind with the Dōgen tradition. He showed me that we are in the midst of dharma at every moment and we must be attentive to the time and space of our current actions. Images of my father performing various tasks, such as cleaning the temple building and grounds are still vivid in my mind. None of my friends' fathers did those chores, from what I remember. As a child I was unaware of the impact these images would have on me, and my realization of his way of life came many years after his death. My father's adherence to the way of Buddha did not lead to a life of renunciation or any negativism of any sort; rather, he lived a life of full participation. My father taught me the sūtras; I learned almost all that I know of Sōtō Zen sūtra chanting before his death in 1944. As far back as I remember, I was chanting sūtras in the *hondō* at Hōsen-ji, which became second nature. When I walked alone, or sat on benches waiting for trains at stations, I quietly chanted. The following is from Dōgen:

When you devote yourself to the study of the sūtras, they truly come forth. The sūtras are the entire universe—mountains, rivers, the earth, plants, and trees. They are the self and others, taking meals and wearing clothes, with [our] activities and mannerisms. Following each of them and studying them, you will see [that there are] an infinite number of sūtras that have never appeared before your eyes"

(*Shōbōgenzō*, (*Jishō Zanmai*), "The Samadhi of Self-Verification")

Indeed, sūtra chanting and *zazen* have given me instantaneous support and serene comfort in my life.

***

The word *zen* is originally from the Sanskrit transliteration of *dhyāna*, which literally means "meditation." The words *dhyāna, dhyā, dhyānika,* and *dhyāta* all relate to the act of thinking, meditating, or reflecting, and were used before Buddhist literature appeared, such as the *Ṛig-Veda, Brāhmaṇa* (a part of *Vedas*), and *Chāandogya Upanishads.* Zen monks and priests, however, practice quiet sitting, not *dhyāna* thinking or meditation. Their sitting practice is the opposite of thinking, which is to say, their practice of non-thinking maintains a mindful state without direct thought. Some practice for long periods of time, others for shorter periods, and some none at all. It is a Zen Buddhist's most important practice. Ideally, we practice all the time. However, we cannot sit all day and night and function in our real world. When I was a child, we practiced sitting thirty to forty-five minutes at least twenty-three mornings a month. My father's daily attitude showed me how our activities were an extension of *zazen*. Dōgen said that walking, living, sitting, and resting must be the same as *zazen*. We all have roles in the world. Full attention to whatever we are doing is *zazen*, or the Way of the Buddha. That was my first lesson of Zen, which I am grateful to have learned from my father.

Nin'yū Yamasaki entered my life when my father fell very ill and began helping with temple affairs. Nin'yū supported me during the most fragile and impressionable periods of my life, such as during the rapid psychosomatic changes of puberty. Our most difficult years together were close to the end of the war and for the several years in its aftermath. Those were the years the country was undergoing devastating changes. Japan, during that period, was aimless and the government seemed powerless to cope with the metamorphosis imposed on them on such a massive scale. It was a period when I did not know what to make of society or even my own future. Prostitutes clustered at major railway stations. Those who had no way to earn a living died of hunger. Some of my middle school classmates did not return to school after the war's end. Some had died of illness, hunger, or bomb-blasts. Some could not afford to come back to school and some had lost interest in finishing school. Nin'yū helped me through those years, including guiding me through all the necessary monastic requirements to become the abbot of Hōsen-ji. I consummated all those tasks before, during, and after the war with Nin'yū's thoughtful guidance and good sense of timing.

Nin'yū taught me how I should live among people while upholding Dōgen's spirituality. He taught me how to deal with sordid affairs and the inevitable entanglements I could expect to encounter in our contemporary social fabric. Nin'yū once criticized a local priest for not following Dōgen's monastic propriety. I was young and foolish, so I regrettably said to him that he, too, did not practice *zazen.* He then looked at me and said, "Are you worrying about me? I practice for ten minutes, twenty minutes or sixty minutes every morning before breakfast. Thereafter, my day follows *zazen* without breaking it for a moment. My walking, standing, sitting, and lying are nothing but Zen. That is my homage to Dōgen and to Zen. *Zazen* is my heart and without it I do not exist as I am." I was looking directly into his eyes while he was explaining this fact and felt his answer was absolutely genuine. I realized, then, that he lost all his children except the last one, mostly before they reached adulthood; *zazen*, most certainly, helped him to realize human lives are frail and inundated with sufferings. *Zazen* is neither remedial nor rectifies human sufferings, but his life of continual *zazen* made him live beyond his recurrent tragedies. He lived the life of *prajñā,* the knowledge of absolute nothingness, or *śūnyatā.* He lived in accord with the *Shushōgi,* or the "Significance of Practice and Satori," which is the sūtra we chant everyday as follows:

> Of utmost importance to Buddhists is the thorough understanding of the meaning of life and death.
> If the Buddha is within life and death, there is no life and death.
> Understanding life and death is in itself *nirvāṇa.*

I indeed had an outstanding teacher. While I did not inherit the dharma-lineage or any formal seal of learning from Nin'yū, in my reflection, he taught me real Zen.

***

In my late teens to early twenties, I plunged into Dōgen's works, especially the *Shōbōgenzō.* I was fascinated by Dōgen's views of this world, which I had not previously known. My initial reading was superficial, but Nin'yū educated me on how to grasp Dōgen's originality and immensity of erudition. I began placing Dōgen's works in chronological order beginning with his earliest work, *Hōkyōki*, which was written in 1226, up to his "Eight Awakenings of Great Human Beings" or *Hachi Dainingaku*, which was written in 1253, the last year of Dōgen's life. As he grew older his *satori* expressions expanded from the sphere of personal to universal experience. For him, the world was the Buddha's world. His awareness of *satori* and *samādhi* reached deeper and deeper and his perception of dharma and human nature, it seems, became more intimate over time. Dōgen was my life-long formal master, from whom I took and continue to take refuge in countless times. Dōgen lived eight hundred and fifty years ago. There are a myriad of differences, divergences, and complexities between his days and mine. Dōgen upheld the pure Zen practice of the Tang Dynasty, which he had learned from his teacher in China, Rujing. Rujing and Dōgen were critical of the secularized Sung Dynasty Zen that was practiced in those days. Dōgen's pure Zen form embraces Buddhism in its entirety, including Theravada's *Vinaya* practices, which were the early basis of monastic practices. He emphasized monastic propriety. In his words, "monastic propriety is the buddha-dharma." Unlike my experience, in his time practitioners lived apart from ordinary secular life. He devoted a large portion of his writings to monastic life and its decorum.

As mentioned in the opening of Chapter 5, the following is excerpted from the chapter entitled "Mind is Itself Buddha" (*Sokushin zebutsu*) from his *Shōbōgenzō*: "You must know clearly that the mind is mountains, rivers, and the great earth. It is the sun, moon, and stars." Is my mind a mountain? Is my mind the sun? I had never before encountered such thoughts until I read his works. Thereafter, I was drawn into Dōgen's world. I know Zen teaches that all existence is in and of the mind. A Chinese Chan master Mazu (or Ma-tsu) was known to teach his students with the following phrase:

A monk asked [Mazu], "Master, you teach that all existence is mind. What is it?" Mazu replied, "I make a crying child stop." The monk said, "When a child stops crying, then what?" The master said, "There is no mind. There is no buddha."

Does *zazen* help you reach Mazu's state of "no mind"? When I attempted to practice *zazen* in the midst of my busy schedule, I at first had a difficult time concentrating on my sitting practice. Physical pain in the early days of my practice did not pose much of a problem. But when I was pressured to meet a deadline of some sort, I perspired even sitting on cold winter mornings due to the imbalance of my body and mind. Sometimes, while I was supposed to sit still, I thought, "What am I doing?" or "Do I have time to do this?" or "I must do something else, instead." It is not a matter of priority. Busy schedules can always be adjusted to make time for *zazen*. I had to practice years to overcome these inner struggles to reach the "sitting for the sake of sitting" experience.

Dōgen carefully taught the way to do *zazen* in his *Fukan za-zen-gi* ("Universal Recommendation of *Zazen*"), his earliest treatise on *zazen*. The method and significance of *zazen* also appears in various chapters of the *Shōbōgenzō*. In his major work besides the *Shōbōgenzō*, the *Bendō-wa* ("Wholehearted Practice of the Way"), he writes:

The right transmission of this Buddhist school stresses that buddha-dharma passed on from person to person singularly is the best of the best [ways]. From the beginning of one's study, one needs not use incense-burning, prostration, reciting the names of buddhas, confession before the Buddha, or chanting sūtras. Just sit firmly and attain the state of casting off one's body and mind. Even if one spends only a short time in sitting practice, one's activities (or *karma*) of body, mouth and consciousness will be a cast of the buddha and one will be able to sit in *samādhi*. Thereby, the entire limitless world becomes the symbol of the buddha, and the infinite universe will become *satori*.

The above work was written in the year 1231, when Dōgen was thirty-one years of age, and only six years after he returned to Japan from Rujing's monastery in China. The above passage must be a reflection on his intense meditation experience under Rujing. Also, the state in which one meditates is expressed as "let one's karma of body, mouth, and consciousness be a cast of the Buddha." It is Dōgen's direct experience of *zazen—samādhi*, a state in which practitioners experience a deeper state of realization, one with time, space and the self.

In Dōgen's Zen, *zazen* is no different from *samādhi*. Dōgen devoted three chapters of his *Shōbōgenzō* on *samādhi*; *Kaiïn Zanmai* ("*Samādhi* of the Surface"), *Zanmai-ō Zanmai* ("King of *Samādhi*"), and *Jishō Zanmai* ("*Samādhi* of Self-Verification"). The first of the above dwells on his world-view but the latter two concentrate on *samādhi* itself. King of all *Samādhis* is *zazen*, according to Dōgen, as he stated in the Chapter entitled "King of *Samādhi*": "You must know that the full-cross-legged *zazen* is the king of *samādhis*. It is the enlightenment. All other *samādhis* are only the members of the family of the king of *Samādhis*. The full-cross-legged *zazen* is your true body and mind. It is that of the buddhas and dharma-ancestors." Dōgen's first experience of *samādhi* occurred when he was practicing at Tiendung Mountain under his master Rujing. He experienced the state in which "his body and mind [were] cast away." At first he was not certain of his experience and needed to confer with Rujing. It was when he had just turned twenty-seven years of age. After his return to Japan, he continued *zazen* and his experience of undistracted *samādhi* became a part of Dōgen's total personality. He used many existing examples to express his *samādhi* experience. One such example appears in or *Ikka Myōju* ("One Bright Pearl"):

> Xuansha (Hsüan-sha) was practicing under Xuefeng (Hsüe-fêng). One day, he wanted to see other masters, so he left for his journey. On the way to his visit, he stumbled on a rock. Pain penetrated his body and his foot began bleeding. At that moment, he awakened. After his awakening, he returned to Xuefeng instead of visiting other masters, and said, "It is no use bewildering other people."

Both his experience of and statement about satori do not make sense in an ordinary way. "Other people" is not "other people," but instead refers to the subject, himself. At that crucial moment, he realized the illusory nature of the self/other dichotomy. His awakening caused him to cast away body and mind. It is just as Linji (Lin-chi or Rinzai) describes the "true man of no rank." The *Record of Lin-chi's Sayings* states the following:

> The master ascended to the Hall and said, "In this lump of red flesh [our bodies], there is a true man of no rank. He always comes and goes through our sense-gates. Those who have not seen this, see! See!" At this time a monk came up and asked, "What is the true man of no rank?" The master came down from the chair, grabbed him and said, "You say it! You say it!" The monk hesitated. The master pushed him

away and said, "The true man of no rank, what a dried-up shit-wiping-stick." He returned to his room.

(from Kato, K.W., *Lin-chi and the Record of his Sayings*, Nagoya University of Foreign Studies, Nagoya, Japan, 1994, p.83 [2-7])

The "true man of no rank" is in the state Xuansha experienced when the pain penetrated him. "No use bewildering other people" means "I found it and I am going to live with it." Dōgen correlated Xuansha's experience with his own. His experience of *satori* further crystallized into a more subtle state over the years. In the chapter *Shoaku Makusa* ("Must Not Do Evil") of the *Shōbōgenzō*, he said: "To have this utmost enlightenment, one must listen to a good teacher or learn from sūtras, then you will hear, 'you must do no evil.' If you do not hear this, it is not the Buddha's true dharma."

Dōgen here extended his *satori* experience to committing no evil. The true dharma could be said in multiple concrete ways and this is one manifestation of it. "One must not do evil" is a true-to-form expression for Dōgen. It is not an ethical commandment. The act of committing evil or not are *karmic* positions, and *karma* cannot be avoided as long as one lives. There is no temporality of *karma*. *Karma* has no mark in time. In this view, there is neither evil nor good.

Dōgen stated that *satori* experience must be extended into ordinary daily activities, even the simple acts of washing one's face or drinking a cup of tea. Our daily life must be *satori* and *samādhi;* by extension, every second of our life must be *satori* and *samādhi*, meaning the state of *zazen*. So, if our daily activities are *satori* and *samādhi*, we need not search vainly for buddha. Every moment of our life, if we are in a state of *satori* and *samādhi*, would be a certainty, without a speck of doubt, for there would be no illusions and dichotomies; instead we would be fully awake and engaged in the present.

***

I think of Dōgen's reality in the context of today's world. Dōgen's notion of dharma suggests to us that a harmonious way to coexist with the people around us is to equate ourselves to them. Dōgen wrote of his concern for his practitioners' well-being. He was extremely careful about personal hygiene, devoting two chapters on this topic in the *Shōbōgenzō*. First and foremost, he wrote that practitioners must maintain homeostasis, the physiological process of maintaining equilibrium. His desire for cleanliness is in accord with our natural inclination toward equilibrium, addressing biological as well as aesthetic matters. Zen practitioners are thereby able to sustain greater equilibrium with nature. We are all part of this dharma-world, including our ecological system.

Nothing remains unchanged. People's ethics change right along with natural changes. The Victorian moral code became obsolete as libidinous behaviors became en vogue. Old genteel classes have lost their social standings to new, rich, and powerful arrivistes who have become the foci of the masses. The churning of social hierarchies continues as it has many times over. Judeo-Christian ethics, it seems, have lost their grip on previously espoused ethical tenets. Humankind's unabashed and tenacious appetite for the consumption of material possessions has shifted the social fabric over time. What will come next in our history is yet to be known. Changes stir up uncertainty and anxiety within most of us. That is *samsāra*. We

436

need to be liberated from this cycle. In the Mahāyānan sense, we all need to become buddhas.

An unenlightened dichotomy in our way of thinking prevents this experience of emptiness. We collect things and discard them on a whim. Everything transforms from useful material into useless waste. This process embodies *saṃsāra.* We eat food, drink water and breathe air—without them we could not exist. We are linked to those things, and all of those actions are executed in "time." The notions of gain and loss are also linked to "time," and if we think our life exists in this moment alone, and only pay attention to the present, gain and loss no longer appear to hold such vital importance.

After prostrating many times before Rujing, Dōgen said [to Rujing]: "I happened to hear the poem you composed about the wind-bell. The first line stated, 'the whole body [of the bell] is like a mouth hanging in emptiness.' The third line stated, 'it speaks universally of *prajñā* for the sake of others.' Should the emptiness spoken here be regarded as that definite entity known as 'empty space?' Ignorant people may refer to the latter. Recently, students who have not yet clarified the Buddha-dharma equate blue sky with emptiness. Truly, they are to be pitied." Rujing compassionately replied:

What I spoke of as emptiness refers to *prajñā.* It is not [the same as] that definite entity known as empty space. Emptiness is neither separate [from phenomena] nor identical [to it]. Therefore, it is neither the common sense view of voidness nor is it a one-sided affirmation of the reality [of the void]. The abbots of various Zen temples have not yet understood [the true nature of] the phenomenal world, much less the void.

Having *prajñā,* one can know that there is no self-existing sub-stance in each dharma, which makes up the phenomenal world. Dōgen's Zen is neither the pursuit of a state of ultimate truth nor some sort of remedy, but simply the state of being connected to reality. Since I had observed and practiced Dōgen's Zen from my early days, I realized that Dōgen's Zen is centralized in its practice of *shikantaza,* "just sitting." Our varied practices (or daily activi-ties) are like petals of a flower with sitting practice as its pistil.

Dōgen said that all buddhas and tathāgatas have correctly trans-mitted the true and supreme enlightenment (or *anuttara-samyak-saṃbodhi*) from one to another. As it is passed on impeccably from buddha to buddha, the "*samādhi* of self-utilization" (*jijyuyū-zanmai*) is its criterion. Each person has originally a dharma-na-ture, but it will not emerge if one does not practice. Awakening is the realization of one's dharma-nature, thereby one also realizes dharma in nature. The right way is to correctly meditate. This is the right path to *samādhi* but one must not seek it. *Zazen* in this case is the *zazen* within the work of the Buddha (from the *Wholehearted Practice of the Way*, or the *Bendōwa*).

***

During my thirty-four years of teaching in American universities my life and its milieu have been ever changing. Over the three de-cades that I taught I observed many social and intellectual shifts on American university campuses. Cultural changes were likely related to the rapid world population increase. In the year 1950, according to a United Nations survey, the world population was ap-proximately 2.52 billion and in 2006, it reached 6.54 billion, more than a two-fold increase. All of that growth had taken place in a short span of a little over fifty years. Living over eight decades, I wonder whether this earth can sustain its population. Can we pass onto future generations the earth we inherited from our predecessors without insurmountable damage?

We are all part of this universe; therefore, we must respect each and every dharma that coexists with us even though we are incapable of knowing all of the attributes of each of them. Dōgen said in the "True states of existence," or "*Genjō Kōan*," thus:

> Use one's whole body and mind to know all things,
> and use one's whole mind to hear sounds of all things,
> in order for one to attempt to understand them.
> However, it is neither a mirror reflecting forms nor is it the
> reflection of water on them. When one side is realized,
> the other side is in darkness." He further stated, "Suppose you
> board a ship and go far into the ocean where you cannot
> see any land or mountains—the ocean looks round when you
> look around. You cannot see any other thing. However, the
> ocean is not simply round or square. We cannot possibly
> know the countless attributes of the ocean."

We must use our natural resources extremely carefully, with due respect. Reverence for life in Zen means reverence for all *dharma* (Sanskrit: statute, law; that which is established firmly. Here, every existence is *dharma*). As Dōgen instructed, save the pail of water that was used to clean the rice. It is economical, but more profoundly, as Dōgen said effusively, we must show respect for all *dharma* on this earth.

Dōgen learned frugality from his Chinese teacher. Their frugality was not just for their own purposes, but also to nurture the earth wherein they subsisted. Mere exploitation of the earth is *hiṃsā,* meaning violence, which comes out of ignorance. Nonviolence, or *ahiṃsā*, is the first precept of Mahāyāna Buddhism, literally meaning "no killing" or "no slaughtering." The negative prefix, *a,* followed by *hiṃsā*, meaning hurt, injury or acts of violence, concerns both body and mind. Nonviolence in Buddhism is not limited to living beings and extends to all animate and inanimate existence. We must try to sensibly understand nature's processes, as our lives are in the midst of it. Living with *dharma* is not unique to the human experience alone; it is universal.

Our lives must be in tune with our surroundings. That necessitates being in rhythm and harmony with all earthly existence. We are embraced and nurtured by this earth. Each of us maintains equilibrium with our environment. We, as dharma kin, family, and peers, strive to survive in this intertwined world of *saṃsāra*. *Nirvāṇa* is the thorough acquisition of dharma, or complete equilibrium with existence. Attainment of that state will keep us free from *saṃsāra*. *Nirvāṇa* will be a dynamic and positive state assuring us of our humanity.

***

A brighter side of my life occurred in 1959 when Shunryū Suzuki came to Sōkō-ji Temple in San Francisco, which became the earliest Sōtō Zen practice venue outside of post-war Japan. I brought several students from the American Academy of Asian Studies to Sōkō-ji. In fact, I introduced Claude Ananda Dalenberg to both Tobase and Suzuki. I also brought many other young people interested in Zen practice to Sōkōji, such as Della Goertz, Jean Ross, Betty Warren, and Phil Whalen. Bob Hayes and Roger Malek joined the *zazen* group at Sōkōji. Bill and Laura Kwon and Richard Baker also attended and sat with Suzuki.

I remember one day in 1962, while I was teaching at the University of California at Berkeley, Suzuki's student, Richard

Baker, came to my house on Potrero Hill and asked me whether he should continue his academic studies at Berkeley or just pursue Zen. I don't remember exactly how I answered that question but I most likely recommended that he finish his degree. After all, teaching had become my major life undertaking. As I taught at universities both in the United States and Japan, I continued to chant the sūtras and studied them just as Dōgen taught his students:

> The sūtras are the *Tathāgata's* whole body. To revere the sūtras is to worship *Tathāgata,* and to meet the sūtras is to greet *Tathāgata.* The sūtra volumes are *Tathāgata's* bones; therefore, the bones are sūtras. If you don't know that bones are *Tathāgata* yet, [then] you are not yet on the Buddha's Way. The true form of every dharma is the sūtras. Humans, heaven, oceans, the empty sky, this world, and that world are all true forms. They are [also] sūtras, *[Tathāgata's]* bones

> (*Shōbōgenzō,* (*Nyorai Zenshin*), "*Tathāgata's* Entire Body")

***

In our society, we make judgments on a daily basis. Such decisions could affect one's whole life. When you make a choice to do this or that, you are choosing to do so at your own risk. That is a form of struggle, or "*kattō.*" Its direct meaning in Japanese is "tangled in vines." "*Kattō*" is the name of a chapter from Dōgen's *Shōbōgenzō.* Dogen used the word as the very source of the Dharma (or Buddha's teaching) that disciples inherit from masters, or the vein of Dharma. *Kattō* may be intertwined with vines of all sorts but Dōgen reinterpreted this to mean that we are all intertwined, and the whole is inherited from our masters. The struggle of "*kattō*" in ordinary usage suggests that when one makes a decision based on one's desires, he or she falls into a paradoxical dilemma. Modern capitalistic society encourages the freedom to choose what one desires. Human beings are expected to use their minds and bodies to socially elevate themselves. But the human desires echoed by the social ethos for elevation generates further desires and cravings. This cycle incubates and accelerates never-ending desires unless one realizes that such a rat race is in fact futile. In our society we are often conditioned to chase goal after goal, responding to stimuli much like Pavlov's bells.

One day, in the early spring of 1979, I received a special delivery letter from the president of the university where I was teaching. It was a letter stating that I had been promoted to the rank of full professor a year earlier than the norm. I was elated by this unexpected promotion. A day or so later, however, I became zombie-like and spiritless. It was a peculiar state of aimlessness and loss. I had always thought of myself as first and foremost a Zen practitioner. But unknowingly, my mind had been conditioned by the hierarchical treadmill of academia to strive for a higher rank. I worked according to the life Baizhang stated: "A day of no work is a day of no eating." I was concentrating on my work and not worrying about what I thought were petty concerns. Unintentionally, I had become immersed in the process of academic ethos. When I reached the goal of that hierarchical system, I lost the passion I had for my work. I became conditioned like a robot in an assembly line. After a few days of serious scrutiny I realized that my effort to accomplish that goal stemmed from a subliminal desire to master the system. If and when I reached a goal, I would most likely find another goal that would set me off pursuing until it was attained. Our desires are endless and as long as we do not become aware of them, they will continue arising from our ignorance, or *avidyā*. Our desires drive us to run around in the circle of *saṃsāra*. Did I want a life of chasing goals only? Would it be all right if I were satisfied with who I am and what I have?

How, then, do you curb your desires? First of all, desires come from the senses: what you see, hear, smell, and so on. Your desires arise from illusory perceptions or thoughts of what exists in the world. Your enduring desires may be to stay young and healthy, to avoid death, or to amass perceived necessities for your sound survival. When you gain or achieve something, you satisfy your desire for awhile. When the loss occurs, you suffer a feeling of denial or betrayal. Is it not rational to think that the maximum gain and minimum loss would lead one to an ideal state of existence? Does gain guarantee happiness and does loss create certain misery?

What if one constantly fails to meet one's goals? Does he or she continually perceive themselves as mediocre or a failure? If one struggles to achieve his or her goal, yet cannot reach it, will that person be deprived of humanity? It is quite possible to become depressed thinking of one's unworthiness. Every now and then, I meet a person who regrets what he or she has just done and says, "I shouldn't have done that," or "I should have done that instead of this," or "Oh, I meant to do that, not this." Constant regret leads to a sorrowful life. Some people drive themselves to uncontrollable rage when they face an impediment to achieving a goal. Wouldn't it be a pitiful life if one were constantly trying to reach goals that were created by and for themselves? People are unknowingly wasting time by chasing dreams and foams, evanescing bubbles of air. Objectively speaking, that seems absurd. If you mind each step or each moment of your life, you will be fulfilling your life and that in itself is the most worthy goal.

All schools of Zen Buddhism teach practitioners not to set goals

such as attaining *satori* or *nirvāṇa*. If you do, you become a slave
to your goals and will find yourself forever living "on the way" to
goals. Our daily lives and awakened state must be one. Linji (Lin-
chi, Rinzai) said, "If you love what is sacred, realize sacred is just a
word, 'sacred.' Those ordinary students see Mañjuśrī in the heart of
Mt. Wutai. They are already falling into error. There is no Mañjuśrī
in the heart of Mt. Wutai." Linji further instructed:

> Followers of the Way, if you wish to have a viewpoint which is
> in accord with the Dharma, it is only that you not be beguiled
> by others.
> Whether you meet them within or without, kill them right away!
> When you meet the Buddha, kill him. When you meet a patri-
> arch, kill him.
> When you meet an *arhat*, kill him. When you meet parents, kill
> them.
> When you meet relatives, kill them. Thus you will begin to at-
> tain liberation.
> You will be unattached and thus able to pass in and out to be-
> come free.

> (*Lin-chi and the Record of His Sayings,* Kazumitsu Wakō
> Kato, Nagoya University of Foreign Studies, 1994, p.104)

Linji is telling us to cut off all goals, dependencies and attachments
in order to attain freedom and find our true selves. The meaning behind these words is the same as Nin'yū once wrote on the wooden
board on our outing to the pond. I was still in my early adolescence
and did not fully grasp the meaning of his writing: "Sword that
kills—the sword that gives life." Nin'yū probably meant "to kill
Buddha is to become a buddha."

Our ordinary life is constrained by connecting the past and the future. Often we have to make decisions in view of this; that is, we must reconcile our past with the anticipated future, or some space other than the place where we are in the present. I was able to make such decisions. Fortunately, my Zen practice has helped me not to entrap myself too deeply in that process. As Dōgen writes of detachment:

> Bodhidharma tells students, "The time has come [for me to depart from this world], if you have anything to say, say it now." A monk named Daofu said, "My statement is that I do not attach to letters, and I do not detach from letters. Yet everything works out fine." The patriarch [Bodhidharma] said, "You have received my skin [my approval]."

In the above quotation, from the chapter of *Kattō*, "Intertwining vines," letters still signify all existing things, including our thoughts and imagination. Yet all schools of Zen were founded on the firm stance that Zen "does not depend on words and letters." After all, everything written is *śunyatā* (or nothingness); goals, names, words and letters are all expressions of *śunyatā*. Sūtras, too, are in the language of *śunyatā*.

***

We must accept the world as it is because all dharma are in their respective places. So just do whatever you are doing, then, you will be the master of your place. Linji said, "In each place, if you become the master of that place, then all places become the true realm. It is simply that you must not accept everything spoken by everyone who comes along, for your single doubting thought is the point at which evil demons enter the mind … You can put a stop to thoughts and not seek their resolution outwardly." Even though the present world is far from perfect, nor ever will be perfect, you can still live without any hindrance. Hindrances are obstructions between subject and object. Reality is when a person (the subject) and the world (the object) become one without obstruction and that is *prajñā,* or wisdom. D.T. Suzuki called it "intuitive knowledge." Indeed, it is the world in which a subject and an object become one before differentiating between the two. It is the experience of absolute nothingness.

Our environment is, as everyone knows, constantly changing, as are we. To cope with the changes one needs to flow with time, and live each moment diligently. At each moment, we experience things directly. To illustrate this principle, I will quote from Dōgen's interpretation of the *Heart Sūtra,* or the *Prajñāpāramitā Hṛdaya Sūtra:*

> When Avalokiteśvara (Kwanyin) profoundly practiced the *prajñāpāramitā* (meaning "enlightened state" or "wisdom-completed"), he experienced with his entire body that the five *skandhāḥ* (form, perception, reflection, action and knowledge) are all empty. Emptiness is form, perception, reflection, action, and knowledge. There are five *prajñā* and seeing through them is itself *prajñā.*

The *skandhāḥ* are known as the "five aggregates." Form is *rūpa* in Sanskrit, a generic term for all forms of matter. The five *skandhāḥ* designate a human in succinct terms; form is a body and the rest is the totality of one's mind and mental functioning, which are all empty.

Everything is void of everlasting substance; thus it is called *śūnyatā.* Our actions of walking, standing, sitting, and lying down are no exception. All forms and all goals are no exception.

When Dōgen heard his master Rujing's poem while he was practicing under Rujing, it gave him a lasting impression. The poem and the episode of it are as follows:

> *The whole body [of the bell] is like a mouth hanging in emptiness. Not asking north, south, east or west, or the direction of the wind, it universally speaks of prajñā for the sake of others—Di-ding-dong, di-ding-dong.*

***

Over the years, I have tried to follow in Dōgen's footsteps by paying attention to neither my dharma nor my potential to become a buddha. I attempted to simply pay close attention to each instant of my action, trying to be one with what I was doing. I am mindful of every movement in my daily life: how I study, research, or teach, and how I sit, stand or walk. It was the tradition that Dōgen founded when he taught his students. That tradition has not changed since the time of Dōgen. Zen monasteries post a sign at the entrance, which inscribes the phrase, "Watch your step!" It means that all practitioners must pay attention to each movement of their minds and bodies. We all have *buddhatā,* or dharma-nature—that is the potentiality to realize a buddha within. The chapter entitled *Juki,* "Prediction", of the *Shōbōgenzō* tells us: "Don't foolishly think that the dharma you possess should be known or seen. It is not so. The dharma that you know is not necessarily what you possess. You can neither see nor know your possessions." It may sound contradictory but it is said that the content of the Buddha's enlightenment is thorough realization of *dharmatā*. It is like the season of spring, which, in temperate zones, creates the spring-like weather and blooming flowers; but spring itself cannot be seen. Our own real nature is *dharmatā*; although it is not seen, it makes us human. Since *dharmatā* is common to all phenomenal existence, animate or inanimate, we have common characteristics to all humans, and other flora and fauna of the world. Hence, in Mahāyāna Buddhism, we are all related to each other. Thinking of this, I enjoy every second of my life living with a myriad of dharma.

***

"Peace of mind" comes when you become *zazen* itself and maintain life in that state, *samādhi*, wherein you have nothing to seek or shake off. Dōgen's word for that would be the state of peaceful and joyful existence, or *"anraku no hōmon"*. I try to extend that to all of my actions, as Nin'yū once said to me that he practiced *zazen* twenty or thirty minutes to an hour, and thereafter he extended that state of *zazen* all day, without cessation. I decide to live each moment in full, and think of time as never being ahead of or behind me. My perception of the world seems different at every instant. It may well be that I am awakened by each moment's novelty and vivacity. Every time I listen to silence, taste the coldness in winter, smell the earth and grass after a rain, or touch *akāśa* (empty sky), I experience each second of time and space together. Each now is my karma, my birth and death, suffering and *nirvāṇa,* my whole life, my renaissance, and my perpetual repetition of reincarnation. This practice of mine continues.

I must keep practicing, for practice is *karma* and *karma* is my life. Practice and awakening are one, with no beginning and no ending; thus, I have no need to seek awakening outside of my own

life. Awakening and *saṃsāra*, birth and death, this life and recur-
ring reincarnations, and all dichotomies are in this thusness. I am
happy to be surrounded by all *dharmas* and the *dharmatā,* which
made them what they are. In retrospect, I sincerely feel fortunate to
be a Zen Buddhist. I have met many Zen practitioners from whom
I acquired living Zen. I learned valuable lessons from each of them
by witnessing their positive self-utilization of *samādhi*. Most of all,
I revered Dōgen's teachings of Zen, which made my life what it is
and that life has made me what I am.

***

Our lives are imminently filled with congenital predicaments stem-
ming out of impermanence, especially when someone close to us
dies. Poignancy and grief are very much a part of our lives and we
have to accept it.

Once, quite a few years ago, I believe it was in the early 1980s,
I was in a Tokyo Hotel at night watching NHK (Japan's public
broadcasting station). Immediately after the news, NHK aired
a program called "Eihei-ji" (the main monastery of Soto Zen).
During this program, Mokudō Katō Rōshi and Shinko Nakamura
Rōshi appeared and talked about Dōgen's Zen and life at Eihei-ji.
I was moved just watching them since I knew them while I was
growing up in Nagoya. Mokudō Katō Rōshi died on September 3,
1979. Two years later his disciples and friends published a book of
his sayings entitled the *Record of the Sky Flower,* or *Kūge-goroku.*

In the early 1970s, I traveled from Los Angeles to Japan and
visited Hōsen-ji. Shinkō Nakamura came to see me there. It was a
hot summer night. He disrobed the upper portion of his kimono and
told me to do the same. I did. He said, "This is where there is neither hot nor cold, isn't that true? Now we can have a heart-to-heart

449

without worrying about the weather or our appearance." We sat around half-naked late into the night talking about many subjects. Shinkō Nakamura Rōshi died during the summer of 1999.

The *rōshi* I am much indebted to is Reverend Dōkō Ōtsuka. Reverend Ōtsuka was the *rōshi* who gave me his treasured ocean-liner leather trunk when I came to the United States. He was a highly educated monk from Tokyo University. He was elected to be principal of one of three Sōtō Zen high schools when he was still young. Reverend Ōtsuka's posture was always impressively upright as he was practicing *zazen*. I became acquainted with him when I went to his temple in Yagoto, Bucchi-in, to help during the month of *obon*. He became Eihei-ji's managing monk, or *kan'in,* and later became the abbot of Hōkyō-ji, which Dōgen's disciple from China, Jakuën, or Jiyuan in Chinese, founded near Eihei-ji in 1261.

I believe it was in the summer of 1968 when I was in Nagoya with my family that Reverend Dōkō Ōtsuka invited all of us to an upscale western restaurant near his temple in Nagoya. He chose a western restaurant since he assumed that my children had begun to miss western cuisine, having been in Japan for so long. I was a bit worried about this, as the restaurant was incredibly expensive, especially for five of us. Moreover, the place really did not fit his Zen lifestyle. When I mentioned my concern to Reverend Otsuka, he smiled and said to everyone in the room in English, while making fanning gestures toward my children: "One day, Magu, a Chinese Zen master, was fanning himself. A monk came and said to him, 'The nature of wind is always circulating and omnipresent. Why do you fan yourself?' The master answered, 'You only know the nature of the wind as circulating, you don't yet know the truth of its universal presence.' Do you understand this?" He looked at my wife and children and exclaimed, "This may be a bit difficult for you, perhaps. Anyway, the story continues. The master did not answer and simply went on fanning himself. The monk looked at him and bowed."

Reverend Ōtsuka smiled at my children and repeated, "I just eased your father's worry. I know it was too difficult for you but someday when you are a little bit older your father will tell you about this story." I explained to Reverend Ōtsuka, "That was a nice answer given my concern. Thank you. I will tell that story." He interrupted me by saying, "Zen monks eat everything that is offered to them." He opened his mouth wide and gestured as if he were eating; my children giggled. I had heard the same expression once from Nin'yū Yamasaki many years ago.

Before we bade farewell to Reverend Ōtsuka, he gave me a paper box of about one cubic foot and said, "Don't open it now. Open it later, after you go back to Hōsen-ji. Please take it to America. I'd like to share it with you." That was the last time I ever saw Reverend Dōkō Ōtsuka. The box contained a statue of Dōgen, sitting on the meditation hall chair. On the back of the chair, Reverend Ōtsuka wrote, "Summer confined practice, 1963." It was also a memento of when he led that practice at Eihei-ji five years ago as the head managing monk, or *kan'in*, there. Kindly, he gave it to me. Sixteen years earlier, he had given me his leather case, from his youthful American journey. When I returned home from our trip I placed this small statue of Dōgen on the bookshelf in my living room and it has been there ever since that summer of 1968. It always gives me comfort, composure, and reminds me of Ōtsuka Roshi's warm encouragement. He died on February 21, 1976. Reverend Mokudō Katō officiated at his funeral.

That summer was the first time my wife and three children met my mother. Kazumi, my oldest daughter, was twelve; second oldest daughter, Eka, was five years old; and youngest, Miho, had her second birthday in Japan. My mother and my family took a trip to

Kyoto and the Kii peninsula. We didn't know it then, but my mother had cancer of the liver and died later that year, on December 19, 1968. At least my mother had a chance to see her son one last time and meet her son's wife and children.

When my mother married my father, he was the first married priest at Hōsen-ji. No woman had ever lived at Hōsen-ji before. Though my mother never explicitly said so, it was undoubtedly difficult to enter a domain that had been dwelled in by only male monks for nearly 200 years. She became a widow in 1944 with four children, from the ages of nine to fifteen. While people living around Hōsen-ji struggled at the end of the war and for several years thereafter, my mother shared vegetables she harvested from her little farm on the burnt site. She also let some of the neighbors use portions of the land so that they could plant vegetables. She never scolded me loudly; instead, she made me sit up straight and talked over with me whatever she thought I needed to hear. Needless to say, she was eagerly waiting for me to become the abbot of Hōsen-ji. Before that happened, I decided to come to the United States and she generously gave her endorsement. It must have been hard for her to consent to let me come here, as I was the oldest son and much needed at Hōsen-ji. I do not know when my mother took the bodhisattva (or Mahāyānan) precepts, but she certainly lived by them.

***

I went back to Nagoya when I heard that my mother was terminally ill and that the end of her life was near. I saw her and talked to her briefly the day I arrived there. The next day she lost consciousness and the day after that she died. Several hundred people came to her funeral. On the plane ride back to California, I was deeply saddened by her death, which I did not experience fully during the commotion of the funeral. I quietly recited the Sōtō sūtra, the *Shushōgi,* "The Meaning of Practice and Verification."

Indeed, loss of life is, for survivors, a most difficult reality to accept, but one must remember that it is the natural sequence of life and there is no way to avoid it. It is *saṃsāra. Saṃsāra* literally means "flowing." That which flows like a river flows into the sea, evaporates in time, rises to the sky, and transforms into a cloud. Then, it falls again into the river. Thus, perpetual recurrence, without end, of our birth and death is called *saṃsāra.* Ancient Indians thought our lives moved cyclically from one life to another until its release. Zen, however, does not accept this *saṃsāra* theory, instead, everything occurs in one instant only and that is now.

Each death of a family member or friend affects me, since individual existence is firmly bound to the interdependence of everyone. Dōgen also experienced personal loss when two of his practitioners, Égi Jōza and Sōkai Shuso, died in the winter of 1242. According to the *Eihei Kōroku, "The Extensive Record of Zen Master Dōgen,"* these deaths occurred at Kōshō-ji in Uji, south of Kyoto. Dōgen offered his respects to both Égi and Sōkai. Égi, I suppose, according to his monastic rank of *jōza,* was a novice monk and thus still young. Sōkai, who held the rank of *shuso,* was twenty-seven years of age. Dōgen offered two dedications. One in particular was a mournful message to Sōkai. It moved many monks and especially Gikai, a disciple of Dōgen. There was no way we can know who Sōkai was, or the circumstances of his death, but his death moved Dōgen and many of the monks who practiced with him. From the *Extensive Record of Zen Master Dōgen*: The master [Dōgen] said, 'At twenty-seven years of age, before he repaid his old indebtedness, he was taken like an arrow [flying] to the empty sky and then to *naraka* (meaning the realm of Yama-rāja, the king of death).' The master continued, 'Last night Sōkai withered and fell.' The practitioners all wept." Coping with the deaths of those we care about is always difficult, and so it was even for Dōgen and his fellow practitioners. He repeatedly described death as the natural course for all those in existence and we must accept it as such. In his chapter on "Life and death," or "*Shōji*," from the *Shōbōgenzō*, he wrote:

> To think life morphs into death is wrong. Life is a position in time with a before and an after. Therefore, in Buddhism it is thought that life equals no-life. Death is a position in time with a before and an after. Death is [therefore] no-death. When you say, "death," death is the word itself and nothing else. For this reason, when you are alive, you are alive. When you die, you are dead. You must not wish for either life or death.

(from Akiyama, Hanji, Dōgen Zenji to Gyō, (Zen Master Dōgen and The Practice), Tokyo, 1940, p.269-270)

There is a similar passage from the chapter *Genjō Kōan*, "Manifestation of Reality":

> Firewood becomes ashes but ashes never again become firewood. You must not take the view that firewood comes first and ashes afterward. You should understand that firewood dwells in its own position as firewood, with a distinct before and after. Yet before and after are wholly disparate. Ash remains in its own position as ashes, with a before and an after. Human life is just like firewood, which becomes

ashes but never again returns to firewood. After a person dies, he or she never comes to life again. For this reason, we do not say that life becomes death; this is the Way of the Buddha. Thus, life is called no-life. Death does not become life. This is the Way of the Buddha's wheel of Dharma, called no-death. Life is a position in time, and death is also a position in time. By way of illustration, it is like spring and winter. One does not think winter becomes spring or that spring becomes summer.

In our common view, we all know that firewood burns and becomes ashes. Dōgen thus said, "We must not think firewood comes before ashes." We must not view things only in the context of their place in the chain of cause-and-effect. Firewood has its own original form and so do ashes, and they each are part of a chain of before and after. Yet when viewed in isolation of their before and after, firewood is only firewood and ashes are only ashes. The sūtra, *Sandōkai*, "Harmony of Difference and Equality," states: "All the objects of the senses transpose and do not transpose. Transposing, they are linked together; not transposing, each keeps its place." Transposition, I understand, is common to human nature. When notions of before and after [or cause and effect] are cut off, time intervals vanish. We have this one instant. Life becomes only life, and death only death. A person's death will never become life again.

As a Sōtō Zen student, I recited the following phrases from the *Shushōgi,* "Meaning of Practice and Verification": "The most important issue of all for Buddhists is thorough clarification of the meaning of birth and death. If the Buddha is within life and death, there is no life and death. Simply understand that both life and death are in themselves *nirvāṇa*; there is no life and death to be hated nor *nirvāṇa* to be desired." Upon my mother's death, I

455

repeated the above phrases many times, wishing for her blissful repose. If one's karma follows causal patterns, my mother shall be in *nirvāṇa*. My wife Emi empathized with my loss after I returned to California.

We only live on this earth for an allotted period of time, like mango fruit—as Nāgasena told King Milinda (Menandros) in the *Question of King Milinda,* the *Milindapañha* (*The Questions of King Milinda*, Translated from *The Pali* by T. W. Rhys Davids, Dover Publications, New York, 1890 (Part I), 1894 (Part II)). Some mango stay on the tree until full and ripened, but some fall by wind, rain, insects, and so on—a short or long life being a part of the curious course of nature. In fact, our deaths allow others to live on this earth. That is *dharma*.

***

A quote from the chapter entitled "Sky-flower" or "*Kūge*" from Dōgen's *Shōbōgenzō* is:

"People with obstructed views are called '*eigen.*' Those who have '*eigen*' assume that they are seeing flowers in the pure and empty sky. For this reason, they confusedly see things that [in fact] do not exist in the three worlds and the six-paths. If the obstructed views are corrected, these flowers in the sky will not be seen." The goals we set for the future are like "sky-flowers."

Dōgen thus stated:

If you acquire the True-Dharma Eyes (the enlightened buddha's eyes), you will see things clearly and without any flaw. That is the true nature of enlightenment. It was transmitted until now without interference. This is called '*eigen kūge*' (sky-flowers in the eyes of an obstructed view). Bodhi, *nirvāṇa*, dharma-body and self-nature comprise the petals of 'sky-flower.'

Sky-flower is often used as an illusion in Buddhist texts, something that does not exist in reality. An example would be Chandrakirti's *Prasannapāda,* which is a commentary on Nāgārjuna's following notion:

That which exists has its own self-nature because we acknowledge its main causes and conditions. That which does not exist—a sky flower, for instance, has neither causes nor conditions.

Nāgārjuna used this term as an example of a thing that does not exist. Dōgen, on the contrary, is equating the "sky-flower" to *śūnyatā* (emptiness or nothingness). The following excerpt is from the chapter, "Sky-flower":

The Buddha Śākyamuni said, "A person with the eyes of obstructed views sees the flower in the sky. But if the person's obstructed views are removed, the flower in the sky ceases. There were no scholars who could understand this up to now. If one does not know *śūnyatā,* he does not know sky-flower. If one does not know sky-flower, he does not know, see, or meet a person with the eyes of obstructed views. If one meets the person of obstructed views, then he will know a sky-flower. After seeing the sky-flower, one must see both flower and sky cease to exist."

Dōgen affirmed that the "sky-flower" is *śūnyatā*. *Śūnyatā* is not negating real existence; rather, it holds that all existence and constituent elements that make up existence are dependent upon causation. Since causal factors are changing at every instant, it follows that there can be neither static nor ever-lasting existence. *Śūnyatā* denies the possibility of any form of static phenomenal existence, and states that all phenomenal existence is relative, temporal, and interdependent. Dōgen thus affirmed that "the world of buddhas and dharmas embraces the sky-flower" and that the sky-flower is *śūnyatā*. The "sky-flower" might be an illusion for many but for Dōgen it is "the flower that manifests the true world"—the world as seen when one attains the state of *prajñā*. It is the same flower as the one Buddha held when Mahākāśyapa looked upon it and smiled.

***

Now, looking back on my life, I can reflect on how wonderful it has been, but it has also definitely been inundated with burdensome facets of *saṃsāra*. I lived through Japan's militarist regime during and after the Second World War. When that regime fell at the armistice, I experienced the chaotic shortage of food to the level of famine. The shortage of clothing led to patches all over garments to the point where the original fabric was almost undetectable. There was a shortage of living space, so we lived in a cave for a while. I also witnessed money's loss of value; it became worthless in a short period of time due to an extreme inflation rate. Still, since my life has been endowed with Zen Buddhism from childhood, it would be worth repeating. I lived in monasteries where we practiced Dōgen's guidelines for life. I had the fortunate opportunity to read what Dōgen had instructed practitioners.

Attendees of my monthly English lecture series at Zenshuji Soto Zen
Temple, Los Angeles. First row, from left to right: Emi Kato, Marie
Takahashi, K.W. Kato, Yuhoko Wadhwa. Second row, from left to right:
Pasquale Galante, Sunil Vernekar, Loretta Livingston, Muriel Sasaki,
Penelope Morris, Curtis Steinback, Reverend Shumyo Kojima.

Attendees of my monthly Japanese lecture series at Zenshuji Soto Zen Temple,
Los Angeles. Front row, from left to right: Reverend Shumyo Kojima, K.W.
Kato, Mitsuko Namiki, Emi Kato. Second row, from left to right: Atsuko
Kubota, Teruko Uekuma, Jane Hideko Henderson,
Ted Uekuma, Sanae Walters.

459

Those who were not able to gather for our group photo:

Deb Simone

Rabbi Michael Perelmuter

Ralph Brown, Jr.

John Flores

My life, especially my time as an educator, was a succession of winding and unwinding. But my unwinding occurred at a faster rate, and in most cases, was instantaneous. I suppose even serious matters normally did not linger on for too many hours or days. If I let problems go, and did not cling to them, they dissipated almost instantaneously. Sadness, disappointment and anger sometimes lingered on within me but never for too long. It is *karma*, the theory of cause-and-effect, or *hetu-pratyaya*. The cause inevitably invites effect directly, indirectly internally, or externally. However, when the cause is removed, the effect disappears simultaneously since this law is based on before and after. Cause-and-effect necessarily involves time. Those who exist in this world are governed by the law of causation. Again, I quote from Dōgen's *Shōbōgenzō*:

> The law of cause-and-effect is clear and nothing is hidden. Those who act with base behavior will fall and those who do good deeds will rise without a trace of mistakes. If cause-and-effect ceases to exist, there will be no one to become a buddha. If the Dharma-ancestor [Bodhidharma] did not travel from India [to China], you would neither hear buddhas nor see buddhas ("Believing on Causal Law Deeply" or "*Jinshin Inga*").

In cause-and-effect theory, every action is a cause, which will have a definite effect. When someone strikes a gong, the gong sounds loud at the beginning and gradually wanes. Impermanence is consistent with the law of cause-and-effect.

> Look at the flower
> inside the petals.
> How long, do you think,
> will its beauty last?
> Today it dreads
> being picked by someone,
> tomorrow morning it will wait
> for someone to sweep it away.
> What a pity!
> The feeling of loveliness
> after many years
> turns to old age.

This world
resembles the flower.
How long can you keep
your crimson cheeks?

– Han-shan

***

Dōgen established the tradition of paying attention to every second in life. As in *zazen*, we must be attentive to every action of our life—whether walking, sitting or lying down. That tradition has not changed since the time of Dōgen in the Sōtō Zen monasteries. I try to watch every step of my actions but when that becomes lax, I repeat the important words posted at the entrance of Zen monasteries to realign myself on the right path:

無常迅速 Impermanence is swift!
脚下照顧 Watch your step!

For this work, I am indebted to Ōkubo, Dōshū, *Dōgen Zenji Zenshū I & II, Shikuma Shobō, 1969*. I also used Iwanami Shoten's *Nippon Shiso Taikei* as a resource.

May this merit extend universally to all, so that we together with all beings realize the Buddha Way.

K.W.K.

ABOUT THE AUTHOR

Kazumitsu Wako Kato came to the United States to serve as an assistant priest at the Sokoji Soto Zen Temple in 1952. Dr. Kato is Professor Emeritus of California State University Los Angeles and Professor Emeritus of Nagoya University of Foreign Studies in Japan. He taught Western Philosophy, Eastern Philosophy, Comparative Civilizations—East and West, Buddhism, and Japanese Civilization at the university level in California and Japan from 1959 to 1999, receiving the California State University Los Angeles Meritorious Performance and Professional Promise Award in 1984 and Outstanding Professor Award in 1985. In 1994 he received a Science Research Grant from the Japanese government's Ministry of Education. Other published works include: *Poesia Zen* (K.W. Kato Chinese to English translations of Han-Shan's poems translated into Spanish) by Francisco Caudet Roca (Endimion, Madrid, Spain, 1969); *Lin-chi Rinzai: The Record of his Sayings* (Nagoya University of Foreign Studies Press, Nagoya, Japan, 1994); *Bunka no Nagare Kara Miru Eigo (The English Language Viewed From the Flow of Cultural Evolution)* (Sanshu-sha, Tokyo, Japan, 1996); *English Etymology: From A to Z* (Maruzen Library, Tokyo, Japan, 1998). Dr. Kato resides in Pasadena with his wife Emi, where they enjoy frequent visits from their children and grandchildren.